Marilyn Monroe

ALSO BY CHARLES CASILLO

Outlaw: The Lives and Careers of John Rechy
Boys, Lost & Found
The Fame Game
The Marilyn Diaries

Marilyn Monroe

The Private Life of a Public Icon

CHARLES CASILLO

St. Martin's Press ⚏ New York

Library of Congress Cataloging-in-Publication Data

Names: Casillo, Charles, author.
Title: Marilyn Monroe : the private life of a public icon / Charles Casillo.
Description: First edition. | New York: St. Martin's Press, August 2018. |
    Includes index.
Identifiers: LCCN 2018004352 | ISBN 9781250096869 (hardcover) |
    ISBN 9781250096883 (ebook)
Subjects: LCSH: Monroe, Marilyn, 1926–1962. | Motion picture actors and
    actresses—United States—Biography.
Classification: LCC PN2287.M69 C39 2018 | DDC 791.4302/8/092 [B]—dc23
LC record available at https://lccn.loc.gov/2018004352

First Edition: August 2018

10 9 8 7 6 5 4 3 2 1

For Kelvin

CONTENTS

PART 3: CLOSE TO CAMELOT

PROLOGUE

She was the most famous woman in the world. Millions of people would have been thrilled to have her phone number, have lunch with her, talk to her, kiss her. Yet she felt alone.

She was alone.

Nestled in her bed in Los Angeles, fighting the effects of the drugs in her bloodstream, Marilyn Monroe made numerous phone calls. At one point she called her longtime friend Henry Rosenfeld, a fashion mogul, in New York. They talked about her upcoming trip to the East Coast. She was trying to make plans, to create a future she could look forward to. Then the dark feelings took over again.

Marilyn's delicate frame of mind—her crushing loneliness, her fear of fading and losing her beauty, power, and ability to be loved—made her more fragile and needy than ever. She likely made a few more calls—exactly to whom is not known. There was no one to whom she could really talk honestly because the person she felt they wanted was a dazzling creation based on being spectacular and sexual, and she feared that person was disappearing.

She probably tried the White House at least once.*

Early the next morning, Sunday, August 5, the FBI showed up at the telephone company in Santa Monica to confiscate Marilyn's phone records

---

* The author Anthony Summers stated in his book *Goddess* and subsequent television interviews that a scrap of paper with a White House phone number was later found within her bedclothes.

for that night. A telephone company executive told the publisher of the Santa Monica *Evening Outlook,* Dean Funk, that he knew the FBI had been in the general telephone offices and had taken the record of her calls that night. They have never surfaced.

After talking to Rosenfeld, Marilyn started to go under. The "womby-tomby" feeling she liked began to take over.

At about eight that evening Peter Lawford called her, suggesting that she come to his dinner party.

Marilyn's voice was very slurred, her tone downbeat. "Peter, you're really a wonderful guy, and Pat is wonderful," she murmured.* "And Jack and Bobby are just great. I want to tell you how much . . ."

---

* Pat Kennedy Lawford, the actor's wife, and sister of John and Robert Kennedy.

PART 1

A BROKEN GIRL

ONE

MAMA

Perhaps her darkness began the very moment she was conceived, back in the days when illegitimacy was viewed as being born damaged and undesirable. "I am alone," she wrote mournfully. "I am always alone no matter what." Marilyn Monroe would never know her father, and throughout her lifetime her erratic mother would remain a disturbing, enigmatic figure.

Gladys Pearl Monroe—who would become the mother of Marilyn Monroe—did not have a stable or happy life. She was born in 1902 to Otis and Della Monroe. Della was a tempestuous woman, considered a beauty in her day, with a round face, dark curly hair, and almond-shaped eyes. Otis was ten years her senior, a dreamy man with reddish hair and a deep scar on his cheek, which he acquired in a fall. Otis had an artistic nature and dreamed of going to Paris to study painting. His actual career, however, was much less creative. He was a house painter who eventually landed a job at the Pacific Electric Railway painting trolley cars in Los Angeles. Their son, Marion Otis Elmer, was born in 1905.

The family was constantly uprooted; they had no lasting friends and few possessions. They moved a dozen times in six years, living in rented houses or furnished rooms. Otis had always been unpredictable; he would go on drinking binges and disappear for days. When a furious Della would demand to know where he had been, he would mumble vaguely, "I don't remember."

Della wasn't sure if his behavior was a result of drinking or deteriorating mental health. He suffered from terrible migraines and blackouts, and by 1908 he started showing signs of serious mental illness. His symptoms, along with his headaches and memory loss, were extreme mood swings and violent fits. He was committed to Southern California State Hospital, where he died nine months later, in July, at the age of forty-three. The cause of death was given as general paresis—the doctors diagnosed his swift decline as nonsexually transmitted syphilis.

Della bluntly told her children that Otis "went nuts and then went to God." Always quick to judge, she did have a strong attachment to religion; at the time she would take Gladys and Marion to a nearby Protestant church to "pray for the wealth of their own spirit." But she was often tempted by things of the flesh, with the flesh frequently winning out.

At thirty-three Della was a young widow, more interested in her own love life than in the lives of her two children. "Mama liked men," Gladys observed. In 1912, after breaking engagements with several different suitors, Della married twenty-nine-year-old Lyle Graves, who had been a coworker of Otis's. The marriage lasted a mere eight months.

By the time she was forty-four, Della's once-striking looks were beginning to coarsen, and she was eager to find a new man. At a New Year's Eve dance, she met and became enamored of a distinguished-looking widower, Charles Grainger—an oil driller. After a whirlwind romance she desperately wanted to move in with him. Grainger, however, had reservations about taking on a woman with children.

Della had already farmed out eleven-year-old Marion to live with relatives in San Diego. Gladys would also be in the way of the new romance. At the time Della and her teenage daughter were living in a rented room in a hotel in Venice, California. The owner of the hotel was Jack Baker (called Jasper), who also ran a concession stand on the nearby beach. Della eagerly encouraged a relationship between twenty-six-year-old Jasper and her fourteen-year-old daughter so she could begin a life with Grainger.

Gladys was a petite and lovely girl, with delicate features and long, wavy chestnut hair that in good light had a reddish hue. She was barely five feet tall but of regal bearing, and her figure was well proportioned and rounded.

In 1917, ten days before her fifteenth birthday, Gladys married Jasper. She was legally able to marry him because Della declared on the marriage license that her daughter was eighteen. Seven months after they married, Jasper and Gladys's son, Robert Kermit (nicknamed Jack), was born. Two years later the couple had a daughter they named Berniece.

The marriage, however, was not a happy one. Jasper was a drinker and had a volatile temper. He felt that his child bride was more interested in going out and having a good time than in being a wife and mother. Gladys was erratic and hard to know. As a result there are varying accounts of what she was really like. She could be vague and distant or angry and full of fire. Sometimes she was effervescent and outgoing and flirtatious with other men. Her moods were constantly shifting.

When they traveled to Kentucky to visit his family, Gladys went off on a hike with Jasper's younger brother. Already fed up with his wife's dubious fidelity, when they returned, Jasper beat her with a horse bridle.

Back in Los Angeles, Gladys filed for divorce citing "extreme cruelty by abusing [and] calling her vile names and using profane language at and in her presence, by striking and kicking." Though such charges were not unusual in divorce papers of the day, Jasper countered by accusing his wife of lewd and lascivious conduct. The court sided with Gladys and awarded her custody of the children, but her victory was short lived.

Thinking her an unfit mother, Jasper ignored the court order, gathered up Jack and Berniece, and took them back to live with him permanently in Kentucky. Gladys followed Jasper and the children to Kentucky to be near them, hoping she could eventually persuade Jasper to let them live with her. She worked for a while as a housekeeper and a babysitter, but after a few months she grew weary of the work.

The hopelessness of her situation set in—a single mother at twenty-one—troubled by drastic mood swings followed by periods of debilitating depression. It was uncertain how she'd take care of herself, let alone a five- and a two-year-old. At first she wasn't concerned about how she would provide for the children. Her first order of business was to take physical possession. But eventually she was forced back to reality by practical questions. How could she work all day and leave the children without supervision? Would it be possible for her to earn enough to support them? She decided the best thing to do was return to Los Angeles. Partly because she felt the children would have a better life there, partly because she felt restless and unfulfilled.

On her return to Los Angeles, Gladys found work in a movie studio, Consolidated Film Industries, as a film negative cutter. There she met a high-spirited woman named Grace McKee, who would have a huge impact on her life. Twice divorced, Grace represented the more flamboyant side of Gladys's personality—without fear of repercussions. Grace was a vivacious, fun-loving woman who patterned her life on the movies she saw regularly and the movie magazines she read religiously. Her unadorned appearance was plain; she was short and plump with puffy cheeks and thin lips, but she livened up her appearance with flashy clothes and makeup. She often changed her hair color, sometimes to platinum blonde, a bold color in the era.

Seven years older than Gladys, Grace McKee had moved to Los Angeles in the previous decade in hopes of becoming an actress. Silent film stars, like Mary Pickford and Theda Bara, were just beginning to become the major female celebrities of the day. Grace was like thousands of other girls who flocked to Hollywood to get aboard the new trend.

By 1923 Grace's dreams of becoming a star had not materialized, but she was working in the industry in a film lab, and within a few months of meeting she and Gladys formed a sisterly bond and moved into an apartment together in East Hollywood. Described as a woman of "loose morals," Grace swept Gladys into a seductive fantasy lifestyle based on the movie stars she avidly read about.

Together the two became what was known as "modern women." The flapper era was coming into full bloom—women were bobbing their hair, wearing heavy makeup, smoking, dancing, and drinking. They raised the hemline of their skirts above the knees for the first time.

Grace persuaded Gladys to dye her brown-auburn hair a fiery red—like the exciting rising star Clara Bow, who would become Hollywood's very first "It Girl." Bow's fun-loving, promiscuous on-screen reputation was becoming the rage. Grace and Gladys followed suit and tried to model their own behavior on that of screen sirens like her. Sometimes when

Gladys felt herself falling into a depression, as she often did, she could put on lipstick and go out—carrying herself like a lady—to have some drinks and find a man to spend some time with who might momentarily relieve her melancholy.

At other times Gladys found herself looking for the stability of a man to take care of her. In 1924 such a man presented himself. Martin Edward Mortensen was a meter reader for the Southern California Gas Company. Mortensen was passably attractive, smitten with Gladys, and exceedingly dull. Grace begged her friend not to get involved with him; Mortensen personified the type of life—the moralistic societal norms—they were rebelling against.

Gladys, however, never really seemed to know who she was or what she wanted. She remained a dichotomy. At times she followed the formal religious beliefs of the Christian Science Church—and her reserved, ladylike demeanor would take the forefront. But when she wasn't in the mood for her religion, she'd return to a manic phase, a wild party girl with flaming hair and painted lips who chased after men.

A devout Lutheran, Mortensen was more attracted to Gladys's religious side than to her flamboyant exterior. She decided to play it safe, however, and married him on October 11, 1924. But Grace's intuition had been right: Gladys found life with her new husband insufferably boring, and seven months later the honeymoon was over. She fled the marital bed to move back in with Grace.

Mortensen did make some attempts to win her back, but Gladys would have none of it. For the time being she felt more wedded to her wild life with Grace. Mortensen filed for divorce stating that Gladys had "deserted" him.

By late 1925, the twenty-four-year-old Gladys was in trouble again. Separated from her husband (she had no idea where he was, nor did she care), she discovered she was pregnant by a man with whom she had suddenly fallen passionately in love.

The man was Charles Stanley Gifford, her supervisor at work. He was robust, confident, and ambitious—everything the pallid Mortenson was not—and seemed to be the man she had been waiting for. Unfortunately Gifford, dashing and newly divorced, was not interested in becoming serious. After having two children with his first wife, he was just getting a taste of freedom again, and with his dapper suits, dark wavy hair, and thin mustache, he considered himself a real ladies' man. Gifford liked to brag about his female conquests—of whom he considered Gladys as just the latest.

She told Gifford she was pregnant on New Year's Eve, hoping that the sentimentality and goodwill of the occasion would make him feel warmly toward her—perhaps even propose. But Gifford had no such intentions. He offered her money (which she refused) and informed her that she was lucky still to be legally married to Edward Mortensen: At least the baby could take his name.

Norma Jeane Mortenson—who would one day be the most famous woman of her generation—was born on June 1, 1926, in the charity ward of Los Angeles County Hospital. In filling out the birth certificate, Gladys listed her first two children as "dead." Under the father's occupation, for unknown reasons, she wrote "baker." Baker was her first husband's last name. For years to come the child would be known as Norma Jeane Baker—even on most of her school records.

In addition to that error, either because of nerves or because she didn't know the exact spelling of her husband's last name—Gladys wrote "Mortenson" rather than the correct "Mortensen" as the father's surname.* Even her name was a mistake. The man named as the father on Norma Jeane's birth certificate didn't exist.

Unsure of how to proceed in life, Gladys took Norma Jeane home to live with her and Grace, hoping things would work out. But in the first days it became clear that she was not well at all. She moped around the apartment and fell into a deep depression, neglecting to care for her new daughter. When Norma Jeane was a few days old, Gladys had a delusional episode in which she imagined that Grace was trying to poison the infant. In confusion she grabbed a knife and attempted to stab her friend.

---

* Most likely she was confused about the spelling. In 1929 she heard of a man named Martin Mortenson dying in a motorcycle accident in Ohio, which led her to believe that her ex-husband was dead. At one point a young Norma Jeane was told that her "father" had died in an automobile accident.

Grace managed to wrestle the knife away from her, but it was clear that the excitable atmosphere was no place for an infant.

Gladys's mother, Della, had recently returned from Borneo in Southeast Asia, where she had journeyed in an attempt to track down—and reignite the passion of—her lover Charles Grainger, who had traveled there on business, leaving her behind. The couple never married and had been living together on and off for seven years. But the trip had not gone as planned, and Della returned dejected, just in time to meet her new granddaughter. Noting Gladys's emotionally fragile condition, and aware of her own instability, Della tried to find a living arrangement that could be beneficial to all concerned.

As it happened, Della was living across the street from a couple, Wayne and Ida Bolender, who took foster children into their home, and she suggested that they become Norma Jeane's primary caregivers. Presented with the choice, Gladys decided on the life involving less pressure, less responsibility. After leaving her first two children to be raised by their father, Gladys already felt like a failure as a mother—the emotional pressure she was feeling gave no indication she could do better this time.

Only twenty-four, she missed the free-spirited existence she had been living with Grace before she became pregnant; she was still hoping for a chance at a new beginning, something that might satisfy her. It wasn't too late. Grace made her feel that—in the land of dreams of Hollywood—between the two of them there was nothing they couldn't accomplish.

Gladys felt her daughter would be safe with the Bolenders and agreed to send Norma Jeane to live with them. For now she could return to spending her days in darkness, cutting film, wearing white gloves to protect the negative, and her nights continuing her search for something that would fulfill her, with an ever-changing cast of strangers.

TWO

Wayne and Ida Bolender seemed like the perfect solution to the problem of Norma Jeane. The Bolenders had no children of their own and took in foster children to supplement their income—the state paid twenty-five dollars a month for each child they housed. They lived across the street from Gladys's mother on a two-acre farm in Hawthorne, Los Angeles, and would be happy to take in the infant. When she was twelve days old Norma Jeane was sent to live with her first foster family.

A devoutly religious couple (some would later call them fanatics), the Bolenders managed to remain financially comfortable throughout the years prior to and after the Great Depression—Wayne kept a steady job as a letter carrier, and he had a small printing press on which he would print religious pamphlets to distribute in his spare time. They always had a number of foster children living with them. Gladys, who continued to work, paid for Norma Jeane's keep out of her own pocket for the next seven years.

Ida was a severe-looking woman with a long face, prominent nose, and coal-black haphazardly cropped hair. The Bolenders were members of the Unified Pentecostal Church. Della Monroe was also a member of this church, and they had Norma Jeane baptized at the church by Aimee Semple McPherson, the flamboyant and popular evangelist.

These early years were confusing for Norma Jeane. She was surrounded by children—her foster brothers and sisters—but often these kids came and went. Norma Jeane became particularly close to a boy named Lester, who was born only a couple of months after her. Lester and Norma Jeane resembled each other, shared a bedroom, and became so inseparable that they were referred to as "the twins." Ida often dressed them in matching outfits.

The Bolenders adopted Lester and later said they seriously considered adopting Norma Jeane as well, but for one reason or another they never did.*

When Norma Jeane was one, Della Monroe had a mental snap and broke into the Bolender house looking for her granddaughter. Ranting and hallucinating, she elbowed through the glass of the front door. Muttering about sin and family, she found Norma Jeane slumbering in her bed and began to smother the child by pressing a pillow onto her face. In a fit of religious zeal, she was trying to destroy her daughter's "sin." Ida rushed in and saved Norma Jeane. The police were called, and a screeching, babbling Della was hauled out.

Della was taken to Norwalk State Hospital, where she was plagued by hallucinations and delirium. She died at the hospital a month later. The death certificate lists the cause of death as myocarditis, which is an inflammation of the heart muscle, with "Manic Depressive Psychosis" being a contributing factor.

"We treated her as our own child," Ida Bolender said in 1966, "because we loved her." By the standards of the era, her years with the Bolenders were not a time of extreme abuse toward Norma Jeane. But the little girl did not feel secure or at ease. Unfortunately for her, the Bolenders were the wrong kind of caretakers for the inquisitive, sensitive, imaginative child, who would ask questions like "Who is God?" "Where does He live?" And "How many people are there in the world?" In conjunction with their

---

* It has been suggested that Gladys would not allow it, which may be the case. She wanted to believe that she might reach a place in her life where she would be stable enough to take custody. Nonetheless the Bolenders never adopted any of their foster children other than Lester: If they adopted a child, they would no longer be paid for his or her upkeep.

love, they were strict disciplinarians: Rules. Regulations. Schedules. Judgments.

They raised her in a way they considered correct. There is no evidence that they were intentionally cruel to Norma Jeane. She was well dressed (Ida often made the children's clothes) and well fed (most of the food came from their farm). But to her they were "terribly strict. They didn't mean any harm—it was their religion," Marilyn said. "They brought me up harshly and corrected me in a way they never should have: with a leather strap."

The Bolenders were certainly stern, but they were believed to be decent people. They felt they were doing what was best for Norma Jeane. "I was hard on her for her own good," Ida would reason. Still, although she may have needed their guardianship, she didn't feel their affection.

Ida and Wayne Bolender have been described as being Pentecostals, Baptists, or Catholics. No one denies that they were extremely religious. Norma Jeane loved to playact, and her first desire was to be an actress when she grew up. Ida, however, was strongly against it, sternly admonishing the child that her ambition was sinful. Norma Jeane was not permitted to go to the movies. Ida vehemently warned the child, "If the world came to an end with you sitting in the movies, do you know what would happen? You'd burn along with all the bad people. We're churchgoers, not moviegoers."

Ida also denounced the sin of vanity. She railed against women who took time over their appearance or who seemed to be boastful about their looks. To Ida an abundance of pride was the devil's work.

With her stringent way of viewing all behavior through her religion, Aunt Ida complicated Norma Jeane's feelings of what was right and wrong. Things that felt natural to her blurred with the idea of being sinful, ashamed, and wrong. For example, Ida apparently caught Norma Jeane involved in childhood sex play, either involving touching herself or perhaps exploring with her foster brother Lester. To Aunt Ida this was an abomination, interest in the human body was sinful.* Without explanation, Norma Jeane was made to be "afraid and ashamed" of her genitals.

---

* As an adult Marilyn developed a passionate interest in the human body. She intently

In response to the guilt she was forced to feel, Norma Jeane developed an overpowering fantasy while attending church. She "wanted desperately to stand up naked for God and everyone else to see." She recalled: "I had to clench my teeth and sit on my hands to keep myself from undressing. Sometimes I had to pray hard and beg God to stop me from taking my clothes off."

Feeling that there was nothing wrong in her behavior, in her dreams she was naked. Norma Jeane envisioned herself entering the church "wearing a hoop-skirt with nothing under it. The people would be lying on their backs in the church aisle, and I would step over them and they would look up at me." The impulse to appear naked in her dreams had no sense of sin about it. Imagining people looking at her made Norma Jeane feel less lonely.

Norma Jeane never felt as if she belonged, and she was uncertain if she was loved. She was a very bright, intuitive little girl. She had a strong sense of people, places, and things. She understood the structure of a family, and learned early on that she really wasn't part of one. When she was very young she would call every woman she'd see "Mama." "There's a mama!" she would exclaim. When she saw a man she'd say, "There's a daddy."

One morning when Norma Jeane was three, while Ida was giving her a bath, Norma Jeane called her "Mama."

"I'm not your mother!" Ida said. "The woman who comes here with the red hair—she's your mother. Don't call me 'mother' anymore. Call me Aunt Ida."

Norma Jeane was stung and confused—but the one she was really concerned about was Ida's husband, Wayne. This was the man she thought was her father. Norma Jeane spent her life obsessed with a father figure. "But he's my daddy," the child said, panicking, pointing to Wayne Bolender.

"No," Ida replied. "You call him Uncle Wayne."

---

studied anatomy—reading books about how the body was put together and worked, and hanging anatomical illustrations on the walls of various apartments, particularly those by the sixteenth-century physician Andreas Vesalius.

It was a moment she would always remember. It hurt her profoundly. Why didn't she belong? Why didn't she live with her mother? Why couldn't she have a daddy?*

Something in her broke. At a very early age she had a sense of being different, of belonging to no one. For Norma Jeane this was a defining moment—very damaging to her sensitive heart, to her fragile sensibilities.

Learning that the woman with the red hair was her mother came as quite a shock. She knew of the woman, but she wasn't aware that she was her mother. Gladys did try to visit Norma Jeane at the Bolenders' on some weekends, but her appearances there were sporadic. Anyway, the little girl did not relish these visits. She recognized her mother as "a pretty woman who never smiled." The first time Norma Jeane said, "Hello, Mama," Gladys stared at her daughter. Even after she knew she was her mother, the woman with the red hair remained elusive and a little scary to Norma Jeane. There was something strange about her: Silent. Tense. Detached.

Gladys, like her mother, Della, was a weird mixture of modesty and religion with hedonistic passions. During the times she led a promiscuous life, Gladys always had the consequences of sin in the back of her mind. Gladys and Della chased men, got married, divorced, abandoned children, went on the hunt for a new man, and then went to church on Sunday.

On some occasions her mother would have Norma Jeane stay over at her place for the evening. By this time Gladys was living alone in a small apartment. Marilyn would remember hiding in Gladys's closet, frightened of her mother. She tried to be as quiet as possible, to disappear, to vanish within the wardrobe. She remembered that at night, when she was reading a book, her mother would complain, "Norma, must you turn those pages so loudly?" Even the sound of a page turning frazzled and unnerved her.

For Norma Jeane there was never a feeling of stability or permanence. Everyone and everything was not what it seemed; what was familiar and safe was actually strange and transitory and could be taken away from her at any moment. These feelings were reinforced again and again.

---

* Norma Jeane could never bring herself to call her foster father "Uncle" and continued to call him "Daddy."

Shortly before she was seven, a small black-and-white dog followed Wayne Bolender home from work. Norma Jeane loved animals, and the Bolenders allowed her to keep the rambunctious mutt, which she named Tippy. Foster siblings remembered Norma Jeane playing with the dog for many happy hours.

One day Norma Jeane returned from school and found Tippy's bloody corpse next to a garden hoe. A neighbor, infuriated by the dog's incessant barking, had cut the dog in half. This was another devastating event. Ultrasensitive from her earliest years, Norma Jeane could not bear to see anything die. (When Marilyn Monroe was thirty-five years old, she was contracted to act in *Something's Got to Give*, a comedy about a woman who is reunited with her family—including the family dog—after an absence of five years. Marilyn requested that the dog in the script be named Tippy. By then a Method actress, she knew that saying the name of her beloved childhood pet would stir up intense emotions that would enhance her performance.)

The loss of Tippy was so overwhelming to Norma Jeane that the Bolenders grew alarmed at the extent of her grief. At a loss what else to do, they called Gladys. Visiting the farm to console Norma Jeane over the death of her pet brought out maternal feelings in Gladys. Observing the living situation, she no longer felt comfortable with the strict, confining way the Bolenders were raising her daughter. She recognized that Norma Jeane was being stifled. She saw the girl's sullenness, her uncertainty, her inability to really connect with others. Norma Jeane, she felt, needed to be exposed to the real world. She announced to the Bolenders her intentions to take back her daughter, and although they didn't approve, they were powerless to do anything about it. Norma Jeane would have to go.

The idea of leaving the only home she had known to be with this puzzling red-haired woman was terrifying to Norma Jeane. The day in late June 1933, when Gladys arrived to pick up Norma Jeane and collect her things, the child was found cowering in a closet.

THREE

BE A GOOD GIRL

Gladys took Norma Jeane to live with her in her small apartment near the Hollywood Bowl, not far from Consolidated Film Industries. Very soon, however, she began doubting her ability to care for a child. Reality set in. Gladys quickly realized that she had rushed into her decision. The apartment was too small. She was working full-time. Mother and daughter were virtual strangers.

One day Gladys showed Norma Jeane a gold-framed photograph of Charles Stanley Gifford, explaining, "This is your father." Norma Jeane was enthralled by the handsome man staring from the photo with piercing eyes and a thin mustache, rakishly wearing a fedora and a trench coat with the collar turned up. He was a mystery, a fantasy. To Norma Jeane her mother was weird and distant. It was the man in the photo to whom she related. She could project onto him everything she needed at the time. It was her father who might swoop in at any moment, recognize her sadness and confusion, and rescue her. Norma Jeane would spend a lifetime looking for this man in others, wanting to know him, loving him, passionately wanting him to love her back.*

---

* As an adult, still wanting to be rescued by a father, she would attempt to re-create him in the men in her life. At a Manhattan party Marilyn confessed that she longed "to put on a black wig, pick up her father in a bar, and make love to him. Afterward she would ask, 'How do you feel now to have a daughter that you've made love to?'"

Gladys became aware that she wasn't acting like a mother toward Norma Jean. Coworkers who mostly knew Gladys to be fun loving—always ready with a joke—began to notice that each day under the pressure of caring for her daughter, she was becoming more sullen and depressed.

Gladys turned to her friend Grace McKee for advice. Grace still had tremendous influence in all of Gladys's decision making and was well aware of her fragile, unbalanced phases. Grace was a practical, take-charge person. She did everything in her power to keep Gladys functioning. Grace convinced Gladys that living with Norma Jeane was possible—it was the tiny apartment that was the problem.

Gladys agreed. If only she had a house, then she could begin to make it a home. But while Gladys concentrated on finding a suitable place, Norma Jeane would have to live elsewhere. Grace suggested the child live with a theatrical couple from England, the Atkinsons, who were now in Hollywood. Both Grace and Gladys were friends with "the English couple," and so the decision was made that Norma Jeane could board with them.

George and Maude Atkinson and their daughter, Nellie, all worked on the fringes of the movie business but kept busy making a living in extra work and bit parts. Living with the Atkinsons introduced Norma Jeane to an entire new world. The couple smoked, drank, and liked to laugh, play cards, and have a good time. They gave Norma Jeane a grass skirt and taught her how to dance the hula, to juggle oranges, and to throw knives. She found them "happy, jolly, and carefree." It was confusing for Norma Jeane because she had been taught by the Bolenders that this kind of behavior was sinful. With her first foster family she hadn't even been allowed to sing and dance.

What puzzled her more is that the Atkinsons were kind to her. She liked them. Ideas of what was sinful and what was fun, what was good and what was bad, who was nice and who was evil, were all being jumbled in Norma Jeane's head. She found herself praying for them before going to bed.

Against tremendous odds, Gladys managed to put a down payment on a house at 6812 Arbol Drive, near the Hollywood Bowl. It was not a modest house—it had six rooms, including four bedrooms, a large living room with a fireplace, and a back porch. She used all of her savings and, in a tremendous display of determination, secured a loan from the New Deal Home Owners Loan Corporation. The purchase was an astonishing accomplishment for a single working woman in 1933.

In a manic phase of encouragement, Gladys bought furniture at auction—attempting to make the house the cozy domicile she had envisioned. Especially meaningful to her was a baby grand piano that had been owned by the actor Fredric March.*

Gladys invited the Atkinsons to board with them. Gladys and Norma Jeane would have two rooms, the Atkinsons would take the other two bedrooms, and the rest of the space would be shared.

Unfortunately the pressure of taking responsibility for her daughter, buying a new home, and making a complete life change was too much for Gladys's already tenuous state of mind. The cracks in her stability started to show almost immediately.

If the stress of all these life changes weren't enough pressure on Gladys, two events crashed through any hopes she had for a peaceful life. In August she received word that her son, Jack, her firstborn child, had died of a kidney infection at the age of fifteen. This brought to the forefront her earlier failure as a mother.

The second bit of news came in a phone call from a cousin who informed her that her maternal grandfather, Tilford Marion Hogan, had gone mad and hanged himself at the age of eighty-two in Linn County, Missouri. Her mother and father had mental problems; now she learned that her grandfather had suffered the same fate. She was self-aware enough to know that she herself had always been unstable. The recent drastic changes she had made to her life had left her shaky and unsure. After three months of living in the house, Gladys fell apart.

Like her mother, Gladys started having hallucinations. She would lie on the sofa in the living room kicking and screaming that someone was coming down the stairs to murder her.

Norma Jeane witnessed her mother's final break with reality. She was

---

*   Years later Marilyn would track down this piano. She bought it, had it painted white, and kept it in her New York apartment.

having breakfast with the Atkinsons in the kitchen when Gladys threw herself down the staircase—seemingly to try to inflict the maximum amount of damage on herself, with frightening bangs and thuds as she hit each step.

Atkinson went to investigate. "Is it my mother?" Norma Jeane asked. "Yes," he said. "But you can't see her. Just stay in the kitchen like a good little girl. She's all right. Noting serious." But Norma Jeane saw her mother on her feet, screaming and laughing. An ambulance was called, and two men wrestled with her screaming, out-of-control mother. Finally they subdued Gladys and took her away. She was taken to Los Angeles County General Hospital and later transferred to Norwalk Mental Hospital.

Gladys's doctors diagnosed her as a paranoid schizophrenic. The chief medical officer's report states: "Her illnesses have been characterized by (1) preoccupation with religion at times, and (2) at other times deep depression and agitation. This appears to be a chronic state."

Grace decided to let Norma Jeane continue living with the Atkinsons until definite decisions could be made regarding the newly purchased house. Because they were busy at the movie studio all day, in the early mornings the Atkinsons dropped her off on Hollywood Boulevard, where two movie theaters—Grauman's Chinese and the Egyptian—became her day care. From morning to night in the summer Norma Jeane sat in the front row, watching the feature again and again. Her own world was gloomy and grim—here she found laughter, adventure, music, and love.

It was a solitary world, one that existed alone in darkness, but her imagination opened and expanded with regular visits to the movies—which now were not considered sinful but a glorious, magical part of life.

A year after Gladys was committed, Grace had the court declare her an "insane incompetent," and became her legal guardian. This also meant that she would make the decisions on what would happen to Norma Jeane. In the fall of 1934, with Grace now in control of Gladys's estate, the Arbol Drive house was put up for sale. She auctioned off the furniture to cover expenses. The Atkinsons moved to a new house. Norma Jeane was not their legal responsibility, and they did not take her to live with them. It was once again necessary to find her a place to live.

Although there is no doubt that Grace McKee loved and cared about Norma Jeane in her way, her own life and happiness as a divorced single woman still came first. Approaching forty, she was a working woman and was still fascinated by the world of movie stars and acting. Although she would eventually petition the courts to become Norma Jeane's legal guardian, she didn't want the full-time responsibility of a seven-year-old. It was much easier to be a part-time mother and a sort of agent-in-waiting, until the time Norma Jeane was old enough to become a girlfriend who could really help Grace fulfill her Hollywood dreams.

Recently Grace had become obsessed with the sensational twenty-two-year-old screen goddess Jean Harlow. Known as the "Platinum Blonde" and the "Blonde Bombshell," Harlow was the biggest female star in the world. Although her private life was chaotic and troubled, she represented the sparkling life of beauty and fame that Grace had dreamed of. Grace was too old to become Jean Harlow—but Norma Jeane wasn't.

"Don't worry, Norma Jeane," Grace would say to her. "You're going to be a beautiful girl when you get big. You're going to be a movie star. Oh, I feel it in my bones."

In 1933 Harlow had starred opposite Clark Gable in the steamy melodrama *Red Dust*. It was probably Grace who took Norma Jeane to see Harlow films, and the actress became the child's favorite star, too. Norma Jeane also began to fantasize that the handsome and charismatic Clark Gable was her father—he resembled the man in the photograph.

Norma Jeane realized that Grace's feelings were based more on who she would become rather than who she was. But it was attention, which she was starved for, and it represented a kind of love.

Meanwhile Grace shuffled her ward here and there, always looking for someone who might adopt her, take her in, or keep her for a while until some other arrangements could be made. Because of this the timeline in this period of Norma Jean's life is chaotic and muddled.

Grace first placed Norma Jeane with her sister and brother-in-law, Enid and Sam Knebelkamp. The couple cared for Norma Jeane for a period of time at the end of 1934.

After the child's brief stay with the Knebelkamps, Grace placed her in the home of Harvey and Elsie Giffen, a well-to-do couple who came to love the child. Their daughter was a good school friend of Norma Jeane's, and her time there was happy. They wanted to adopt Norma Jeane, but they had plans to move to New Orleans, and neither Gladys nor Grace wanted her living so far away.

When the Giffens moved, Grace approached Reginald Carroll and his wife to adopt Norma Jeane. Carroll had been Gladys's friend and coworker, and he and his family lived in Los Angeles. This family was also willing to adopt Norma Jeane, but Grace said that Gladys would not allow it. According to her, Gladys still had hopes of getting well and raising Norma Jeane on her own.

Just how many foster families* Norma Jeane stayed with is confusing because, as she later explained, she stayed in some homes only briefly. "It was quite a few," she said. (Marilyn's final count was ten, including an orphanage.)

It was somewhere in this disorganized, murky period that she was sexually abused for the first time. In her autobiography Marilyn revealed that she was living in a boardinghouse at the time. The wealthiest resident of the house was an elderly Englishman she called "Mr. Kimmel." One evening this man called Norma Jeane into his room and locked the door. "Now you can't get out," he told her, as if beginning a game.

He put his arms around her. She kicked and fought, but he was stronger. She couldn't break away. All the time he was abusing her he kept whispering, "Be a good girl. Be a good girl." It has never been disclosed what exactly Mr. Kimmel did to Norma Jeane. Sometimes it has been labeled "rape," other times "fondling."

When he finally released her, Norma Jeane ran out to tell what had happened to the woman who, at the time, she was calling "aunt."**

"I want to tell you something about Mr. Kimmel," she said. "He . . . he . . ."

Before she could get it out, the woman slapped her across the face.

"Don't you say anything against Mr. Kimmel," she snapped. "He's a

---

* Many of the homes she was placed in were chosen by Grace and were known to her or were even Grace's family members.
** Norma Jeane called most of her foster guardians "aunt" and "uncle."

fine man! He's my star boarder!" At that moment the man came out of his room and gave Norma Jeane a nickel, advising her to go buy some ice cream. She threw the coin back at him.

The following week Norma Jeane was at a religious revival meeting with the people she was staying with. There she witnessed Mr. Kimmel "praying loudly and devoutly for God to forgive the sins of others."

Years after the incident, when Marilyn Monroe was the biggest star in Hollywood, she told the story to her ghostwriter, Ben Hecht—one of the foremost journalists and screenwriters of his day—when they were working on her autobiography in 1953. She is often credited with being one of the first major celebrities to speak publicly about sexual abuse.

When talking of childhood trauma, Marilyn admittedly changed names and locations so that the story couldn't be traced. "I don't want to hurt people or hurt myself sometimes. We all want to protect ourselves," she explained. But because she altered some details of the incident, some journalists dismiss it, concluding that it never happened. They also cast doubt on Marilyn's sexual abuse because of her tendency to be a fantasist, prone to exaggerating her hardships in order to create sympathetic publicity in the early stages of her career.

There is no tangible evidence that Marilyn Monroe was sexually abused as a child (of course that is true in many cases of childhood sexual abuse). Most of the evidence is in what can be pieced together from what she said publicly and privately. For example, she told an early mentor, Lucille Ryman Carroll, that she was raped when she was eight years old and that "she wasn't a virgin" when she married.

During this period Norma Jeane was moved around a great deal. As a little girl without parental figures, often unsupervised, living with an ever-changing cast of characters, it seems likely that she would have been targeted and that something happened to her—rape or fondling or even an inappropriate kiss—that ravaged her religion-based upbringing.*

Privately Marilyn told her doctors and close friends that she was sex-

---

* During the breakdown of relations with her business partner, Milton Greene, after the agonies of *The Prince and the Showgirl*, she summoned a lawyer to her hotel suite in New York. The attorney was stunned when Marilyn, gulping straight vermouth, began relating her rape at the hands of a grown man when she was a child. Somehow she

ually abused by others—not just the elderly English boarder. She revealed to her poet friend, Norman Rosten, and foster sister, Bebe Goddard, that she was assaulted by her older cousin when she was sent to live with an aunt for a period of time. She also confessed to Lucille Ryman Carroll that at the age of eleven she was regularly brought "behind the barn" for sex with one of her foster parents.*

Yet perhaps the most persuasive proof of Marilyn's childhood sexual abuse is in her fractured psyche, her divided adult self. We know that she began to stutter after the first attack, and she struggled with stuttering throughout her lifetime. Much of her adult behavior has the characteristics of someone who has been sexually abused in childhood: Shame. Low self-esteem. Depression. Nightmares. Substance abuse. Suicidal thoughts.**

Marilyn herself admittedly added to the mysteries of her childhood. "I've never told all about my life. No one would believe it all could have happened," she said. "They'd say I was talking for publicity. It was pretty terrible."

Whatever happened to Norma Jeane, time and success did not blunt her pain.

When the last few placements did not work out—and she was running out of options—Grace at last took Norma Jeane to live with her. But in this crucial time period, something came along that once again changed Grace's priorities. In the spring of 1935 Grace met Erwin "Doc" Goddard, a handsome southern man, ten years her junior. The six feet five inches tall Doc literally swept Grace off her feet. She finally had her Hollywood ending.

Doc was a fun-loving, heavy-drinking man who lived feverishly in the

---

seemed to be connecting the physical violation to what she—via Arthur Miller—saw as a violation of her finances.

* It has been reported that Marilyn alleged this to get sympathy from Lucille Ryman Carroll and her husband, John Carroll, although Lucille believed it to be true.

** For the rest of her life Marilyn would battle with low self-esteem. All through adulthood she was unable to sustain relationships. She was neurotically mistrustful of people and had an extreme fear of abandonment. She felt that people were always using her and yet she allowed them to—constantly reenacting the role of a victim. Marilyn was also described as "frigid" by at least one of her doctors, and she had difficulty achieving orgasm.

moment. The affair was immediate and intense. Grace married Doc in Las Vegas on August 10, 1935. The couple moved into a modest home in Van Nuys. Grace brought Norma Jeane to live with them, but it only lasted for a month.

If there had been any chance at all of Norma Jeane permanently living with the newly married couple, it was destroyed when Doc (whom she was instructed to call "Daddy") entered the nine-year-old's room one night and kissed and fondled her. Rather than take a closer look at her new husband's character, Grace decided that Norma Jeane had to go. With no foster families immediately available, Grace made the decision to put Norma Jeane in an orphanage.

Without a doubt one of the most defining moments in the life of Marilyn Monroe was when she was committed to the Children's Aid Society Orphanage in September 1935. It affirmed all her worst fears: She belonged to no one. For Norma Jeane, whose main desire was to fit in and be loved, this was the worst possible place. It was a place of shame.

Marilyn would never forget that day. Grace methodically packed up her few belongings in a box: underwear, a dress, a coat, shoes and socks. Of course she realized that she was being sent away again—she was familiar with the process by now.

Grace put the box in the car; Norma Jeane sat on the passenger side. After a very short drive, Grace pulled up in front of the building. "This is where you will live," she told the girl. "I'll come and see you as often as I can. They'll take good care of you here—better than I can at home."

They stepped out of the car. Norma Jeane looked at the building and saw the sign: "Orphanage." Then realization seized her and she began screaming, "No! No! I'm not an orphan!" She didn't belong in this place. Somewhere her mother was alive. "I'm not an orphan!" she screamed again. A panicked Grace tried to pull her in by the arm. Norma Jeane planted her feet hard on the sidewalk and made herself so rigid that the staff had to come out and carry her in, still screaming.

Norma Jeane couldn't get over the fact that she'd been placed in an orphanage. She never got over it. While there, she learned to cover her real feelings very well. By the age of nine, she had already discovered that survival meant adapting quickly. When placed in a difficult situation she had to make do to survive. Hide inner turmoil. Do what was expected. Present a contented front.

The days were regimented and went by in an orderly, joyless fashion. Norma Jeane did one thing after the other as they were scheduled. She made her bed, ate her meals, played sports, and participated in the orphanage activities. She was polite, quiet, well-behaved. She was tall for her age and considered skinny and awkward. Sometimes she was called "Norma Jeane, the human bean." Her stutter was more pronounced now, so she spoke very little.

Her hatred of the orphanage festered. It was a harrowing, horrible experience aggravated by a suppressed hostility toward Grace. "When I came to the orphanage it seemed no one wanted me," she said. "Not even my mother's best friend." The psychological horror for her was worse than hard labor or physical torture.

After she was a star, the biographer Maurice Zolotow visited the orphanage, seeking an answer as to why the child had been forced to wash so many dishes. He encountered a Mrs. Ingram, who was still working there. "I really don't know why Miss Monroe tells these terrible stories about us." Mrs. Ingram sighed. "We don't have to give the children any work assignments, we have a staff of twenty-one here. . . . We do give the children small jobs and pay them for it. We do this deliberately to give the child a feeling of being useful. Now, this story of Marilyn's, that we made her wash dishes three times a day, is just plain silly."

Marilyn felt the emotional pain of the orphanage so deeply that she had a tendency to magnify the degradation she had been forced to endure there. Her mind transformed the psychological torment into physical drudgery.

This use of hyperbole made Marilyn seem a canny publicity machine who made up stories to create sympathy from her adoring public. After she became a star, various reporters went out to investigate the awful conditions she had endured at the orphanage. What they found were professional people in a well-run facility who cared for the children.

Yet Marilyn never revised anything she said about the orphanage. Instead she made sure that the worst version of her life was the official one.

We will never know for sure how much of it happened as she recalled it. Was it her aching sense of being abandoned—to foster parents, to an orphanage, by Grace—that she saw as the real abuse? To her it was all the same.

Marilyn's second husband, the playwright Arthur Miller, observed that Marilyn could "walk into a crowded room and spot anyone there who had lost parents as a child or had spent time in orphanages. There is a 'Do you like me?' in an orphan's eyes, an appeal out of a bottomless loneliness that no parented person can really know."

By the beginning of 1936 the staff was worried about her. Norma Jeane was anxious, withdrawn, stuttering. The matron wrote in her file: "If she is not treated with much reassurance and patience at such times, she appears frightened. I recommend her to be put with a good family." The administrator conveyed this to Grace, and it seems she was shamed into action.

That February, Grace petitioned the Los Angeles Superior Court to become Norma Jeane's legal guardian. Her petition was granted a month later, which meant she started getting government checks for Norma Jeane's care, although the child remained in the orphanage until June 1937.

Grace took eleven-year-old Norma Jeane to live with her and Doc once again. Why she would risk Norma Jeane living with Doc again if there had been an incident of abuse with her husband in the past is puzzling, but Grace didn't have many options. As the girl's legal guardian she was collecting a stipend from the state—from a legal standpoint it was up to her to keep a roof over Norma Jeane's head. From her own point of view this living arrangement was only very temporary anyway; she was already on the lookout for a new place she could deposit the child

She found a home within Norma Jeane's own family—Norma Jeane's aunt Olive, who had been married to Gladys's brother, Marion. Gladys, of course, was still in a mental institution, and it is likely that Marion also had a psychotic breakdown: In 1929 he left for work, telling his wife that he would be home in time for dinner. He was never seen again.

Olive took Norma Jeane in not out of a sense of family or even obligation but because they needed the money the state paid for her care.

Grace agreed to give them half of the state's stipend. Norma Jeane was not happy in this household either, and she would tell many miserable tales of her brief time spent there—without identifying the family. It was there that she was sexually assaulted by her cousin Jack, and it became necessary for Grace to move her yet again.

In those years Norma Jeane had a strong bond with Grace—and that bond would continue into her young adulthood. Not having many affectionate experiences to compare it to, she relied on her connection to Grace. She wasn't much of a mother figure, but she was all the girl had.

When Marilyn became a celebrity, after a while she stopped mentioning Grace in interviews. By then she felt anger and resentment toward her. Marilyn felt tremendously betrayed by this woman who had showed her kindness but at the same time kept her at a distance so that she never had to take full responsibility.

Grace never got to revel in Marilyn's success—the dream they shared that Norma Jeane would one day be a huge star like Jean Harlow. In September 1953, when *Gentlemen Prefer Blondes* was playing in packed movie theaters, Grace killed herself at the age of fifty-nine, her body ravaged by cancer and addicted to alcohol and drugs. Like Marilyn, the cause of her death was ruled to be an overdose of barbiturates.

But it was because of Grace McKee-Goddard that in 1937, Norma Jeane got the one lucky break of her young life. Grace took her to live with her own aunt, Ana Lower, who lived in the nearby Los Angeles suburb of Sawtelle.

FOUR

THE WORLD BECAME FRIENDLY

"Aunt Ana" was a fifty-eight-year-old white-haired woman who had been divorced for many years and had no children of her own. She did have a modest income from renting bungalows and cottages she had bought with her former husband. The state was still paying thirty dollars a month for Norma Jeane Baker's care—but that isn't why Ana took her in. The gentle, grandmotherly Ana and the preteen Norma Jeane adored each other.

Up until the last years of her life—even when talking about the horrors she had experienced in foster care—Marilyn was always to single out her time with Aunt Ana as the exception. "I did enjoy that period," she'd say. "I loved her very dearly."

Aunt Ana was a Christian Scientist, and although Norma Jeane's mother and grandmother also practiced this religion, this was the first time she would be around it for an extended period of time. Christian Science's basic principle is that all healings—as they occurred in the Bible—can be claimed for ourselves and our friends and families. Because of its belief that sickness is an illusion and can be healed by prayer alone, the church had its own "healers" and did not believe in medical intervention. Ana Lower was a healer in the church—an official practitioner.

Norma Jeane began menstruating in the fall of 1938. It was the beginning of another lifelong struggle for her. She experienced abnormally painful, irregular periods (later she would be diagnosed with endometriosis). As a Christian Scientist, Norma Jeane was not permitted to use any kind of medication that might relieve the pain—even aspirin was forbidden. Prayer was the only medication allowed. She would writhe on the floor in agony or curl up in a fetal position while Aunt Ana did her best to comfort her by holding her in her arms and praying.

When Norma Jeane turned twelve an additional physical change occurred. The skinny awkward girl, "Norma Jeane, the human bean," became beautiful. She developed breasts and hips and an amazing physical presence; for the first time she felt visible.

Being beautiful meant attention and power and maybe even love. Her dream of being so beautiful that people would turn to look at her when she passed by had come true. In private Norma Jeane started to think that her beauty might be a ticket out of boredom, drudgery, and despair. She was becoming aware of her female power—and she reveled in it. Suddenly she started showing up at school wearing lipstick and tight sweatshirts.

Up until then she felt "outside of the world," she would explain. "Now the boys started paying attention. Even the girls took notice because they thought 'Hmmm, she's to be dealt with.' I had this long walk to school—two and a half miles. . . . It was just sheer pleasure! Every fellow honked his horn. And workers driving to work were waving, you know? And I'd wave back. I thought, 'Gee, what happened?' The world became friendly. It opened up to me."

Gladys was in touch with Grace from time to time. She was now a patient at Agnews State Hospital and had written to her friend asking her to inform Norma Jeane that she had a half brother, Robert, who had died, and a half sister named Berniece, who was now nineteen and who had recently married a man named Paris Miracle. The half sisters—each totally surprised to discover the existence of the other—began to correspond.

A fellow student at Emerson Junior High, Bette Sue Dugger (later Westcott) became good friends with Norma Jeane. "I never knew Marilyn Monroe," Bette Dugger would say more than seventy-five years later. "I only knew Norma Jeane Baker. She was a very pretty, very sweet girl who lived with her aunt. In later years, when I'd see articles about her, I was always very surprised to read about the sad parts of her childhood. It wasn't something she wanted us to know about."

What was important to Norma Jeane was fitting in. She was already compartmentalizing parts of her personality. "She never once talked about wanting to be an actress," Bette remarked. The two girls were schoolmates until Bette's parents moved to another district.

"We lost touch after that, which I regret," Bette said. "I just feel that if we had stayed in touch it might have made a difference. She would have known she'd always have a safe place to come to, out of the limelight. Because I never knew the sex symbol. Maybe sometimes she felt like she wanted to be 'Norma Jeane' again. But by then she didn't have anyone who would have recognized that sweet girl."*

By the end of 1941 Aunt Ana, who suffered from a heart condition, felt she could no longer take care of the teenage Norma Jeane. With nowhere else to turn, Grace McKee-Goddard once again took Norma Jeane to live with her. Although she was still living with her husband, Doc, she felt that the danger of him going after Norma Jeane again was minimal—his two daughters from a previous marriage, Nona (who went on to have a minor career in movies as Jody Lawrance) and Eleanor, were living with them. Norma Jeane would share a room with Eleanor "Bebe" Goddard, who was the same age. Both girls were attending Emerson and became close for a while.

When Norma Jeane was fifteen, Doc Goddard got a job offer in West Virginia. Grace and Doc decided that he should take it. Even though Norma Jeane had been living with them, Grace felt that it would be too much of an expense to take Norma Jeane along to start over in West

---

* In 1960 Bette was married to Ken Westcott, who was working as a prop master for Desilu Productions. One day Marilyn was scheduled to come to the studio to pick up Eli Wallach, who had been a guest on a show. "He asked me if I'd like to meet Marilyn," Westcott recalled. "I told her my wife was Bette Duggar, her junior high school friend. She immediately lit up. She became very excited and asked me for Bette's phone number. She said she would call—but she never did." What the Westcotts didn't know was that at that time Marilyn was getting ready to make *The Misfits* and heading into the last two chaotic years of her life.

Virginia. Los Angeles foster care would stop paying for her keep if Grace moved Norma Jeane out of state.

Once again it was left up to Grace to find living arrangements for the girl. Ever resourceful, this time Grace came up with a different kind of scheme. Norma Jeane was maturing, she was lovely—why not marry the teenager off? Grace didn't have to search far to find a suitable contender for a marriage: She literally looked to the boy next door. Grace's next-door neighbor, Ethel Dougherty, had a handsome twenty-year-old son named Jim who Grace thought would make an ideal husband for Norma Jeane. Handsome, blue-eyed, and popular, Jim Dougherty was a former Van Nuys High School football captain and class president, currently working the night shift at Lockheed Aircraft.

Grace hastily arranged for them to have a date to a Christmas Eve dance. There was indeed a spark between the two. Before long Grace approached Ethel suggesting that perhaps her son would consider marrying young Norma Jeane. A sympathetic Ethel asked her son.

"My God, she's just a baby," he replied.

"Think about it," his mother urged. "It will keep her from going back to the orphanage." Jim took Norma Jeane on a few more dates and decided that, yes, he would like to marry her. She told her schoolmates at Van Nuys High that she would not be returning to school after she completed tenth grade.

After their wedding the young couple moved into a one-room bungalow. Norma Jeane tried hard to be a good wife. "At that time she needed to feel secure and she needed to feel loved," Dougherty said. "She wanted to feel like she belonged to somebody. That was very important to her."

For a while Norma Jeane seemed content in the marriage, with the notion that she was safe at last. As a married woman she was now considered an adult—no one could move her or place her with strangers. But as it had been throughout her life, she was living in a situation she had been placed in and had no control over, and, as always, she did her best to make it work.

Norma Jeane was an expert at fantasizing and playacting. With Jim she never really felt like a wife; she was a little girl playing housewife. "The only family she had at that time were her dolls," Dougherty observed. "She had rag dolls. And porcelain dolls. All kinds of dolls. I'd find them on the bed because that's where she kept them. They'd be there when she needed them."

In her new role as a wife, Norma Jeane longed for her father. There was never any doubt in her mind that Charles Stanley Gifford, the man in the photograph her mother had always kept and showed her, the man who looked like Clark Gable, was her father. She got his number and built up the courage to call him. Gifford abruptly hung up on her. "She was real sad," Dougherty remembered. He had to sit with her and comfort her for a while.

Dougherty maintained that they were both content in the marriage. Norma Jeane was an "immaculate housekeeper" and a "good cook." What is more likely is that she was simply going through the motions of what was expected of her. She was used to presenting a robotic facade of the girl that people needed her to be. As a wife she cooked, she kept house, she made love.

She tried to love him and at times she felt she did—Jim was all she had. Yet Dougherty occasionally sensed that there were some signs that Norma Jeane was not the happy newlywed she tried to project. "She was two different people, really," he revealed. "She was a Gemini. I could see Norma Jeane some days. Some days I didn't recognize the girl. Who was she? She'd be deep in thought or something. But she'd always come back and be Norma Jeane again."

After a year of marriage, with the war in full swing, Jim enlisted in the merchant marines. He was sent to Catalina Island for training, and for a while Norma Jeane joined him there. He was shipped out to the Pacific in the spring of 1944 and would be gone for long periods of time. With her husband away, seventeen-year-old Norma Jeane went to live with Jim's mother. Her mother-in-law was working at Radio Plane, an aircraft plant, and she was able to get Norma Jeane a job there folding and inspecting parachutes.

One day that fall—and it was one of the most fateful days in the life of Marilyn Monroe—while she was working, an army photographer named David Conover came to take publicity pictures of attractive young women working in the American factories—to boost the soldiers' morale.

On an assembly line, Conover came across Norma Jeane. He asked her to pose and snapped. He was stunned. Something happened between Norman Jeane and the lens. Conover was the first person to discover what many, many others would soon learn: The camera loved Norma Jeane.

Excited by her potential, Conover asked Norma Jeane to pose for him again. Norma Jeane wrote to her foster sister, Bebe Goddard, that Conover advised "I should buy all new clothes to go into the modeling profession. . . . He said he had a lot of contacts that he wanted me to look into."

Conover continued photographing Norma Jeane, building up a professional portfolio for her. And he was true to his word. When he felt she was ready he introduced her to the modeling agent Emmeline Snively.

At the Blue Book Modeling Agency, Emmeline Snively assessed the nineteen-year-old hopeful, but she didn't get a sense of sexuality. Instead she found Norma Jeane to be "a clean, shining, pleasant, expressive-faced little girl. We said, 'the girl-next-door type.' She looked at the board of cover girls and said, 'Oh, those girls are so pretty.' But I thought what a wonderful little doll she would be on a cover someday."

Snively talked Norma Jeane into straightening and bleaching her hair, assuring her a blonde would get more jobs. "She started out with less than any girl I ever knew," Snively said, "but she worked the hardest . . . she wanted to learn, wanted to be somebody, more than anybody I ever saw before in my life." Some of the emptiness that her husband had sensed in her was being filled as professionals became interested in her beauty as a commodity.

In her excitement Norma Jeane wrote to Dougherty to inquire how he felt about her modeling. "I told her if she was enjoying herself it didn't bother me much." But Dougherty was soon to find out "it cost more to be a model than she made. She took all the money we had in savings and bought clothes with it. It was alright. I didn't mind. She enjoyed doing it and . . . it just grew after that." Dougherty thought it was fine. It was just something for her to do until he got home.

———

One of the first people to whom Snively sent Norma Jeane was the photographer Laszlo Willinger. "I made some tests with her," Willinger recalled. "From that time on I used her for years. . . . She was a very good model. I had her on, easily, a hundred magazine covers. Her face and figure were well known long before she became Marilyn Monroe."

Some seventy years later Willinger's assistant during that time, Christian Larson, remembered: "I did her body makeup—that could be a legacy in itself. She did cheesecake and lots of semi nudes. She was very comfortable with her body, no hang-ups at all about displaying herself around the studio completely naked. One time when she was booked for a shoot she called and said she couldn't make it because she discovered that she was allergic to penicillin and developed a rash. Laszlo didn't believe her. So I went over and picked her up. She came out of the dressing room and did a charming little striptease for us. Sure enough she was covered with little red welts. She said, 'See? I told you so!' I'll always remember the cute way she said it."

Norma Jeane was appearing on magazine covers both locally and internationally. Dougherty, still traveling in the merchant marines, recalled, "I was in Buenos Aires and here was a magazine with her picture on the cover. I told the guys 'this is my wife.' They said, 'Sure. Sure it is.'" They didn't believe young Dougherty was married to the incredible cover girl.

Dougherty was beginning to get concerned. When they had an opportunity to talk he would tell her, "When I get out of the service and come home, this stops. We're going to have a family."

Norma Jeane always replied, "Yes, that's true. That's true." But she was starting to feel differently.

In 1946 her appearance on five magazines in one month led to an interview with 20th Century-Fox casting agent Ben Lyon. He was knocked out by Norma Jeane. "The most beautiful girl you've ever seen in your life," he gushed. He wanted to give her a screen test right away, but he needed permission from the studio head, Darryl F. Zanuck. Rather than risk being refused, Lyon came up with a plan to test her on the set of a Betty Grable movie, *Mother Wore Tights*, currently shooting on the lot. His

scheme was to sneak Norma Jeane onto the set when it wasn't filming, using cameras from that production to test her.

To ensure the success of the test he brought in Leon Shamroy, one of
their top cinematographers, and Alan "Whitey" Snyder to do her makeup.
Whitey would become a close friend, and after she became a star, he would
do her makeup for all her movies and important events of her life.*

For Norma Jeane's first performance on film she was directed to walk
across the set, sit down, light a cigarette, and put it out. Then she walked
upstage, looked out a window, and exited off-camera.

The film was developed and ready to be viewed a few hours later. The
screen test lasted for only a few minutes, but Shamroy was amazed. "I got
a cold chill . . ." he said later. "She got sex on a piece of film like Jean
Harlow. . . . Every frame of that test radiated sex."

Lyon slipped the test into the daily rushes that Darryl Zanuck would
be viewing. After it screened Zanuck took a puff of his cigar and said,
"That's a damn fine test." As a result Norma Jeane Dougherty was offered her first movie contract. The terms were that she would be paid
seventy-five dollars a week for six months. Then she would be reviewed,
and if the studio decided to extend her contract for a year, her salary
would rise to one hundred dollars per week.

In 1946 Grace McKee-Goddard and her husband, Doc, moved back
to Los Angeles. Now that Norma Jeane was twenty, Grace no longer had to
look after her or worry about her living situation. Grace was of course
thrilled with Norma Jeane's bright-looking future—but in her marriage
with Doc, Grace had started drinking heavily and the ravages of alcohol-
ism were taking a toll.

In August 1946 Grace accompanied Norma Jeane to the Fox studio
to sign the contract with her since, being under the legal age of twenty-
one, she still needed a guardian's signature. The moment was bittersweet.
Norma Jeane was a promising young actress—being compared to their

---

* She would specify that on the occasion of her death, no one was to "touch" her face
  other than Whitey Snyder. With her wicked sense of humor she once gifted him with a
  money clip engraved, "Whitey dear—While I'm still warm—Marilyn." (The talented
  Snyder did indeed make up Marilyn's corpse, being the makeup artist who truly was
  there for her in the beginning and at the end.)

long-ago idol Jean Harlow. A shining new life seemed to be waiting for her after the signing of the contract. For Grace, already rapidly on the decline, it was like signing something away, something she had once held very dear, giving up the title to a dream she had helped create.

But Norma Jeane was not yet completely ready to start down a new road toward stardom. Lyon explained that they needed to change her name. Norma Jeane Dougherty, he said, didn't sound like a star, and her contract with Fox gave them the right to rename her.

"You're a 'Marilyn'!" he exclaimed finally. According to him, she responded, "That's a lovely name." Now the new "Marilyn" was concerned about keeping something that was connected to her previous self. "I wanted my mother's maiden name, 'Monroe,' because I felt that rightfully was my name," she explained. "I couldn't take my father's name very well. I wanted at least something that was related."

"In everything she did, she wanted to be perfect," her foster sister Bebe Goddard remembered. Now that Marilyn's career was taking off, the young starlet knew she could no longer be a factory worker or a housewife. Her husband was looking forward to coming home and having children.

Still in the service, Dougherty was on the Yangtze River in China when the mail came on board his ship. Dougherty received a letter from an attorney stating Norma Jeane's intention of divorcing him. When he arrived back in Los Angeles he went to see his wife. She presented him with divorce papers. Dougherty spent the whole day with her trying to change her mind. But she had already made her decision: She was going to start over as Marilyn Monroe.

Also around this time of transformation, her mother was let out of Agnews State Hospital. She lived for a while with an aunt in Portland, Oregon. She sent her daughter pleading letters, until Marilyn saved enough money to send her so she could come back to Los Angeles. Marilyn rented two rooms in Aunt Ana's apartment so that, at last, mother and daughter could attempt living together. Gladys, however, was by no means the "mother" or confidante that Marilyn had always hoped for. She remained strange and remote—obviously mentally ill. She insisted on wearing a nurse's uniform and had become obsessed with Christian Science, reading compulsively from *Science and Health*.

Also during this period, Marilyn's half sister, Berniece, from Gladys's first marriage, to Jack Baker, visited Los Angeles with her husband, Paris, and their daughter, Mona Rae. At last Marilyn had a chance to meet her half sister. For a while they were all living in apartments under Aunt Ana's roof. Marilyn tried to persuade Berniece to move to Los Angeles with her young family, but Paris didn't want a life there.

Gladys also decided that she didn't want to live with Marilyn. After a brief stay she felt she had to make it on her own, and with vague plans in her vague head, she traveled back to Oregon. Gladys would remain a shadow, a phantom figure for the remainder of Marilyn's life.

With her provisional family spreading out and making their way in the world, Marilyn began living alone for the first time in her life. It was scary, but it was also a relief. She had to answer to no one and could concentrate on creating Marilyn Monroe.

Although she worked tirelessly at improving herself, Fox didn't utilize the young beauty except for some extra work. She can be glimpsed fleetingly as she passes by and says hello in *Scudda Hoo! Scudda Hay!* a comedy about a pair of prize mules. She also had a bit part as a waitress in *Dangerous Years* (1947).

Based on this very limited work, the studio dropped her. Yet her agent, Harry Lipton, recalled that Marilyn soon recovered from the shock and became diplomatic. "After all it's a case of supply and demand," she said. Marilyn already was beginning to understand the movie industry. There were dozens of pretty young girls in supply on a studio lot. It was up to her to single herself out.

FIVE

After her contract with 20th Century-Fox was dropped, Marilyn fell into a shadowy, drifting period. She led a vagabond existence, living hand to mouth. Sometimes she had some money from modeling gigs, and other times there were long stretches in between jobs. Many days she could only afford one meal.

Her biggest enemy was loneliness. Marilyn had always been alone; it was all she knew. But now she was old enough to understand that it wasn't the only emotion, the only condition. She saw people around her with friends and family, and she longed for some kind of connection. "I looked at the streets with lonely eyes," she said.

Marilyn had nobody, really, to depend on, living in between two lives: her Norma Jeane, waif, child-bride days, which included Jim Dougherty, Grace Goddard, and Aunt Ana (all of whom were rapidly slipping farther and farther away from her day-to-day life), and her starlet years, which were just beginning. Without roots, she moved very quickly and easily from place to place. "I had no family. I mean I had no place to go just to have a roof over my head," she would say.

Los Angeles could be a lonesome, sordid town for a young girl without family and connections. Marilyn started to learn to use what she had to get by. Survival kicked in. To survive Marilyn could be a chameleon. The biggest talent she had—all the more potent combined with her beauty—was the ability to become what people wanted her to be. It wasn't something she did in a calculating way; for Marilyn it was instinctual.

The whole town seemed to be an engine fueled by sex. Marilyn was learning about the seedy underbelly of Los Angeles always hiding under respectable facades. The Blue Book Modeling Agency, for example, managed by the very proper and soft-spoken Emmeline Snively, also doubled as an escort service. During the war some of the models went out with different men two or three nights a week. Emmeline would later point out that Marilyn never did.

More and more Marilyn was discovering that everything helpful, everything related to money, everything that assisted in advancement, everything that represented protection—had an infrastructure of sex.

Very soon Marilyn began getting attention the only way she knew how, by wearing tight clothing, often without panties. Sometimes she would wear a bra under tight sweaters, as was common with glamour girls of the day, because it showed off the figure.

Marilyn's hair cascaded past her shoulders—now the color was a very soft, dark blonde or honey colored with hues of amber. Her skin was creamy, pale, almost translucent, which she contrasted with glossy red lipstick. She often wore white. She had a perfect body, and she flaunted it the way some might flaunt a stellar education, or family connections, or great wealth. It was her calling card.

A friend recalled lending her eighty dollars, which Marilyn used to buy twenty-five bras she would sometimes stuff with tissue and wear under tight sweaters so her breasts would stick out even further. "This is what everyone looks at," Marilyn explained. "So this will be great. When I walk down Hollywood Boulevard everyone will look at me."

"Honey, you don't want them to do that."

"Oh yes I do," Marilyn replied. "I want everyone to love me."

This was indicative of Marilyn's personality at this time, dressing provocatively and giving off sexual signals, combined with an innocent "who me?" quality that worked.

It wasn't an act. There were complexities underneath her provocative exterior. She grew up feeling that she could be uprooted at any moment. Affection was temporary because she didn't belong to anyone. She often told people she was an orphan, because she felt like one. Marilyn's vulnerability startled people because she looked cheap, but when they took the time to talk to her they found that she was sensitive and good. And her desire to learn, to improve, to be great, was very real.

Later she would refer to the "wolves" back in those lonely, drifting days. She would admit that they were always after her, trying to get her to go to bed. In the 1950s, during the height of her career, Marilyn maintained that she always refused these wolves. Many people who knew her claimed differently.

The actress Susan Strasberg, daughter of the legendary acting coach Lee Strasberg, said that Marilyn once confided that during her lean years she had made ends meet by working "in the world's oldest profession." Of course she may have exaggerated her experiences for effect. Marilyn was always an exceptionally private person, with parts of her life that she would never reveal to anyone. There are incidents, experiences in the life of Marilyn Monroe, that will never be fully known.

Marilyn was not immoral. She was a young woman who was brought up without a moral compass, having no guidance or lasting female role models, or *any* role models for that matter. What she knew was what she had learned out in the world, on the streets of Hollywood, and she used that knowledge for her own survival. Her sexuality was what they valued. Her sexuality was all she thought she had to offer—so sometimes she gave it. How could it be wrong if it gave such pleasure?

There was an innocence incorporated with Marilyn's sexuality which makes it difficult to judge. She grew like a wildflower, never knowing she had anything to contribute until someone found something beautiful in her. Her innocent attitude regarding sex—something she successfully conveyed on screen—made her a trailblazer. Innocence and humor mixed with sex would become character traits of Marilyn's movie star personality.

In August 1947, still with no steady source of income, Marilyn attracted the attention of an established Hollywood couple, John Carroll and Lucille Ryman Carroll.

The head of talent at MGM studios, Lucille was already well placed in Hollywood—one of the few women who had power in the movie industry. Her husband was the actor John Carroll, whose resemblance to

Clark Gable was so striking that his career was relegated to second-string status. In August, Carroll was playing in the Cheviot Hills Golf Tournament with male stars like Henry Fonda, John Wayne, and Tyrone Power. To add sex appeal to the event, nubile starlets were assigned a star for whom they would caddy. Marilyn was paired with Carroll.

Lucille watched bemused on the sidelines. Marilyn was wearing a pair of very revealing shorts and a tight sweater. "She thought the only thing she had were her breasts," Lucille commented. "She felt 'This is my only chance at stardom.'" The Carrolls found Marilyn to be a fascinating creature under the seductive but tawdry-looking exterior. The contrast of her lack of social skills with her exquisite face and body had a quirky adorability, like a kitten's. In fact Lucille would call her "a stray little kitten." John said to his wife, "We must help this little girl."

What the Carrolls expected from Marilyn isn't totally clear. Both Lucille and John Carroll would always claim that their interest in her was strictly in her well-being and career potential. But there is something strange, almost with a whiff of impropriety, in their preoccupation with Marilyn.

The previous year the couple had a beautiful eighteen-year-old runaway, Lila Leeds, living with them. Miss Leeds, known as a "bad girl" struggling starlet, missed an important test Lucille had set up for her at MGM because she had gotten high the previous evening. (In 1948 Leeds would make headlines when she was arrested with Robert Mitchum for possession of marijuana.) Later, the Carrolls were the subject of an article in the gossip magazine *Confidential* alleging that the couple often threw all-nude parties.

In 1947 Marilyn seems to have surpassed Lila Leeds's place in their affection and devotion. Certainly the couple, who were twenty years older than Marilyn, were captivated by her. Lucille would refer to her as "a cute little trick." And even though she stated that Marilyn was "constantly" trying to seduce her husband, Lucille gave her many of her expensive evening gowns as well as cash gifts for cosmetics and other living expenses.

Shortly after the Carrolls met her, they took Marilyn into their home. For more than six months Marilyn lived in the couple's apartment in West

Hollywood—the El Palacio Apartments on Fountain Avenue—and on weekends at their sprawling horse ranch in the Valley.

In December 1947 John Carroll drew up and signed an informal contract with Marilyn under which he would pay her one hundred dollars a week, agreeing to "use my best efforts to guide and counsel you to the end that your professional career will be furthered and enhanced."

As weeks turned to months, the Carrolls continued to pay Marilyn one hundred dollars a week, but she was becoming a problem. She bombarded them with phone calls during the workday. Marilyn would call Lucille at the office on her private line asking about trivial things like what color lipstick to wear or how she should do her hair. Or she might call with an imaginary crisis, like the time she claimed a Peeping Tom was watching her through the bathroom window.

Ultimately Lucille talked to her husband, and decided to continue with Marilyn's salary but move her into the Studio Club, a residential facility in Hollywood for aspiring actresses. The rent was fifty dollars a month, and Lucille paid six months in advance.

In the days of the Hollywood casting couch, there weren't many avenues for an unknown actress to take toward movie stardom. In the male-dominated world of the 1940s and 1950s, if a woman wanted opportunities in the film industry, giving sexual favors was something that was expected of her.

Like many starlets of the era, Marilyn discovered the Hollywood party circuit. These were weekend parties that single executives in the movie industry held in their mansions, making use of the abundance of very beautiful, very young women who were trying to break into the business. Known as "party girls," they were viewed by the executives as a kind of salacious smorgasbord.

Marilyn went to these gatherings looking for contacts, but what she sought from these men was—if not love—recognition and respect. And while she did come into contact with some top players in the industry, many didn't take the time to get to know Marilyn. As far as they were concerned, she was just another sexy blonde with a nice body. Often these men were vulgar, degrading, and could also turn violent.

Marilyn would remember being held down in a room by two men while another tried to rape her. Orson Welles recalled being at a party where Marilyn was surrounded by men and one reached out and tore off her top, revealing her breasts. Marilyn, Welles said, laughed with the others at this indignity. Laughter hid her fury.

When Marilyn was a star she loathed the powerful men who ran the studio system, and she did everything in her power to defy them—and they hated her because she knew what they were. "Hollywood is a place where they'll pay you a thousand dollars for a kiss and fifty cents for your soul," she wrote contemptuously.

In 1948 Pat DiCicco, a sometime Hollywood agent and movie producer, invited Marilyn to one of Joseph Schenck's infamous poker parties at his Holmby Hills home. Because she had been briefly under contract with his studio, Marilyn knew that Joe Schenck was the sixty-nine-year-old chairman of 20th Century-Fox and one of the richest and most powerful men in the film industry.

Schenck was dazzled by this new girl, who was so unlike other starlets who worked his parties. He was fascinated by the way she would cover up her shyness with exhibitionism, her wit with silence. Feeling socially awkward, Marilyn might retreat into an inscrutable haze, heavy-lidded and sensual—something she would do for the rest of her life.

Soon she became a regular at Schenck's parties, silently standing behind his chair as he played cards. After she was a star, Schenck would deny he ever had an affair with her. Marilyn, however, would candidly talk to her friend Amy Greene (wife of the photographer Milton Greene) about "servicing" him. Schenck would call her, and she would go over and "do what she had to do. Sometimes it took hours," Marilyn confided. "I was relieved when he fell asleep."

Adrift in a sea of self-assured lechers and users, Marilyn craved protection. Often she would stay in the guesthouse on the property of Schenck's Italian Renaissance mansion. But she kept her place at the Studio Club—a way for her to maintain her self-respect. Marilyn might allow people to take from her, but they would never own her. "I was never kept," she said proudly later in her career. She held on to her soul.

———

Still, Marilyn brought enormous pleasure to Schenck's life, and he cared very much for her. He called his friend Harry Cohn, who headed the competing studio, Columbia Pictures, and asked if, as a special favor, he would try Marilyn out with a six month contract. "I'm indebted to her," he said. Cohn agreed, and Marilyn was signed to a Columbia contract in March 1948. As a favor to the powerful Joe Schenck, they cast her in a low-budget movie to be called *Ladies of the Chorus*. She was on her way.

Being part of the new studio, Marilyn was assigned to take acting lessons with Natasha Lytess, who was Columbia's head drama coach. The two women would form an intense teacher-student relationship, fraught with complexities, that would last for the next seven years.

What probably had an immense influence on how the relationship between Marilyn and Natasha progressed was the sad news in the same time period that her beloved Aunt Ana died—a great blow to Marilyn. She had been one of the few people who had shown her love and kindness as a child. Aunt Ana was also one of the last remaining threads that connected Norma Jeane to Marilyn. It was scary to let this part of her identity go.

On the day of their first meeting, Natasha appraised her new student and was singularly unimpressed. Marilyn was wearing a clingy, red knit dress cut too low in front with heels so high she could hardly walk. A trollop's outfit, Natasha thought.

Marilyn shrank under Natasha's condescending gaze. Columbia's head acting coach was a volatile thirty-seven-year-old woman but looked older; bone thin, with a mop of graying hair, intense dark eyes, and a prematurely lined face. Her superior demeanor and thick German accent made Marilyn feel that everything about herself was wrong, while all of Natasha's opinions must be astute and important.

Natasha's first critique of Marilyn was, "I can't hear you, my dear. When you speak, your mouth closes up. You will have to work on diction. Diction, diction, diction—this right now is most important for you." She made Marilyn read the same scene again, instructing, "Open your mouth wider, even more—that is good. That is better. Louder. Louder."*

"I will do whatever you tell me," Marilyn replied

Natasha's scorn soon turned into fascination. It's possible that Natasha became close to Marilyn—long after her duties for the low-budget *Ladies of the Chorus* were finished—because she saw potential in her. What was more likely the cause of Natasha's fierce devotion to Marilyn was a strong sexual attraction, the typical mixture of lust and disdain she routinely aroused. "She moved [in a sensual way] so that all the men in the studio whistled at her," Natasha observed. "But her face was childish with disheveled hair . . . it was an extraordinary thing to see. . . . It was just as if she were two different persons."

Ladies of the Chorus was Marilyn's biggest break so far, and she clung to Natasha during the making of the film. "She feared everything," Natasha said. And Marilyn's fear and vulnerability made her seducible. Natasha seems to have taken advantage of Marilyn's uncertainty, luring her into a dedicated teacher-pupil relationship with the promise of turning her into a real actress. She presented herself as a mother figure, a champion, and a protector—things Marilyn found irresistible. In Marilyn the older coach saw a beautiful young woman who was an artistic blank—a mound of clay with no sense of self, no ego, that Natasha could shape into everything she herself wanted to be.

Natasha put a lot of pressure on Marilyn sexually. Marilyn understood that her body was what people desired most. She offered it easily to people whom she appreciated. It was a way for her to say "Thank you." It was a way to say "Help me." Because Natasha was working hard to help her, Marilyn likely felt compelled to give herself sexually a few times in the beginning, a very casual experimentation that would later turn into fury.

For the next seven years Natasha would become a key part of Marilyn's life. Natasha coached her through twenty films, and after 1951 Marilyn refused to perform in a scene unless Natasha was on the set.

---

* It is Natasha Lytess who was responsible for Marilyn's distinctive articulation and sometimes artificial, exaggerated lip movements, which, early in her career, helped make her such a singular movie personality.

But she was also able to draw a line. In many ways Marilyn became submissive to Natasha (as she would with other teachers), but she still held on to a piece of her own free will, which prohibited Natasha from having total control. Natasha said, "I took her in my arms one day and said, 'I want to love you.'" Marilyn looked at her. "Don't love me, Natasha," she implored. "Teach me."

In *Ladies of the Chorus*, Marilyn would be performing two numbers, "Anyone Can See I Love You," a routine love song, and "Every Baby Needs a Da-Da-Daddy." To help polish her singing, the studio introduced her to the vocal coach Fred Karger. At thirty-two Karger was talented, athletic, and as handsome as a movie star.

Marilyn had a fine singing voice—warm and sensual, although it was too soft—and Fred was encouraged by her fantastic ambition. He tirelessly went over the songs with her. As they got to know each other, Marilyn discovered that Fred was recently divorced and had custody of his six-year-old daughter, Terry. At the time, Karger was living in a big house with his mother, Anne, and his sister, Mary—along with her two young children. Naturally Marilyn was in awe of his extended-family life. She would remain close to Karger's mother and sister for the rest of her life.*

Marilyn always greatly appreciated anyone who tried to help her, but she developed a huge crush on Karger—which quickly developed into love. Before him, Marilyn had never felt sexual desire for anyone, nor had she reached orgasm—not even during her teenage marriage. "Sex is baffling when it doesn't happen," she admitted. "I used to wake up in the morning when I was married and wonder if the whole world was crazy, whooping about sex all the time."

Karger introduced Marilyn to a world in which love and sex existed hand in hand, a relationship of mutual give-and-take pleasure. Unfortunately Karger took more than he was willing to give. As Marilyn did with the entire world, she tried to make herself more beautiful in an attempt to make Karger want her. The world fell for it; Karger did not.

Still hurting from his divorce, Karger harbored an underlayer of an-

---

* The two of them were among the few people invited to Marilyn's funeral.

ger toward women. Marilyn's insecurity made her a perfect scapegoat for him to unleash his hostility on. Suddenly he'd insult her intellect, the way she dressed, or her naïveté.

"I've been thinking maybe we should get married," he said. "But it's impossible. I have to think of my daughter." He explained that if something happened to him it wouldn't be right for his child to "be brought up by a woman like you. I mean, it's not that you're not capable of being a mother, but, it's, well, it wouldn't be fair to her."

Marilyn gasped. She immediately understood what he meant by "a woman like you." A woman good enough to laugh with, have dinner with, sleep with—but certainly not someone who was intelligent enough, or had the moral compass, to be a mother to his daughter. "You couldn't possibly love me if that's what you think of me," Marilyn whispered. She painfully started to distance herself from Karger, to give him the freedom he seemed to want.

That Christmas she bought him a gold watch that cost five hundred dollars. Natasha Lytess said scornfully that Marilyn gave expensive gifts because she couldn't give of herself. But that wasn't true. She had given herself completely to Karger. As usual Marilyn was broke and had to pay for it in installments. On it she had only the date inscribed: 12–25–48. She explained that someday he would love someone else. If Marilyn's name were inscribed on the present, he would no longer be able to wear it. It took Marilyn two years to finish paying for that watch.

For all the conflicting backstage drama and passions surrounding the production of *Ladies of the Chorus*, the resulting film was a bloodless trifle, notable today only because it gives us the first extended on-screen look at Marilyn Monroe.

The clichéd musical is a sort of rags-to-riches fairytale with a burlesque backdrop. Adele Jergens and Marilyn play mother and daughter burlesque dancers, Mae and Peggy Martin. When Peggy becomes the show's headliner, she meets a society millionaire who wants to marry her.

Marilyn's performance is for the most part natural and relaxed, with only a few wooden moments where her inexperience shows. It is also interesting to see Marilyn before she had slight cosmetic alterations on her face. Her appearance is somewhere between Norma Jeane and Marilyn Monroe (closer to Norma Jeane), with very few hints of her legendary screen characteristics—the hooded eyes, the whispery voice, the open smile are nowhere to be observed. Although she's playing a "burlesque queen," there is nothing overtly sexy about her performance. The Monroe glow is certainly in evidence, if at a somewhat lower wattage.

Nevertheless, a big disappointment was waiting for Marilyn when, in spite of her appealing work in *Ladies of the Chorus*, she was let go. Studio executive Harry Cohn had the power to dismiss her—and he did so. After viewing the movie he invited Marilyn to his office. Following some perfunctory praise for her performance, he invited Marilyn to accompany him on a trip to Catalina on his yacht. Marilyn had been around the business long enough to know what the invitation implied. The problem was, Marilyn did not sleep with men simply because they could advance her. She rejected him in the most agreeable way. "Of course I'd love to take a trip with you on your yacht, Mr. Cohn," she cooed. The executive smiled. Then Marilyn added, "And I so look forward to meeting your lovely wife."

Cohn was livid. How dare this tart be a wiseass with him? Dispensing with trite pleasantries, he told Marilyn he'd give her one last chance: She could have sex with him right there. Once again she refused. Cohn was enraged and dismissed Marilyn from his office.

Later Marilyn would say, "I was determined, no one was going to use me or my body—even if he could help my career. I've never gone out with a man I didn't want to." Shortly afterward, she received word that her contract was not being renewed.

A small consolation came when, on the film's release, Marilyn received her first review in the *Motion Picture Herald*: "One of the bright spots is Miss Monroe's singing. She is pretty, and with her pleasing voice and style, she shows promise." Regardless of the encouragement, Marilyn was once again unemployed, broke, and without any prospects. Her only choice was to go back onto the party circuit, where the studio executives continued to regard her and most of the other party girls as objects to be used and enjoyed, like a fine Scotch or a good cigar.

SIX

RISING

On New Year's Eve 1948, Marilyn was invited to yet another party, at the home of movie producer Sam Spiegel. It promised to be the kind of party that by now Marilyn was growing weary of—filled with mogul types skulking through the crowd, rattling the ice in their drinks, leering and flirting, on the hunt for a girl they could slip a business card to, or better yet, take to one of the vacant bedrooms.

It was there that Johnny Hyde spotted Marilyn. The incandescent sight of her blinded him to anyone else in the room. Marilyn was the most extraordinary thing he'd ever seen. Hyde was the vice president at The William Morris Agency, the top talent agency in the world.

At fifty-three Johnny was thirty-one years older than Marilyn. Small, wiry, with a tough, distinguished face that looked as if it had been carefully drawn by a talented caricaturist, Hyde was barely five feet tall, with thinning hair. But he was always elegantly dressed in impeccable suits, and he exuded an attractive air of power and confidence.

Hyde was a tempestuous man currently in his third marriage. Through his occupation Hyde met hundreds of desirable women, many eager to have a sexual relationship with him. "It was said around the office that he signed more actresses with his dick than most guys did with a fountain pen," writer Frank Rose noted. One actress he signed (and bedded) said that his dick was as tiny as the rest of him.

Although known as a womanizer, Hyde actually had a serious heart condition (he suffered from a defective valve). With his health failing, he was restless, eager for one last shot to grab the brass ring that had eluded him. It seemed that all his life he had been searching for something and at last, with Marilyn, he had found it. He had plans to go to Palm Springs for a brief vacation before starting the New Year, and he invited Marilyn to join him. It was in Palm Springs that their affair started.

There was nothing covert about their relationship. Within weeks of their meeting it was understood that Marilyn was Johnny Hyde's new girl. Hyde adored her, and he wanted everyone in town to know it. In time he left his wife and four sons to devote himself exclusively to Marilyn.

Used to Hollywood infidelities, Hyde's wife, Mozelle, had the ability to look the other way when it came to Hyde's flings. But she sensed that his obsession with Marilyn was different: "I tried to take it for a long time," she said of this affair, "but in the end it was impossible."

Hyde rented a house for them to live in on Palm Drive in Beverly Hills, which he had partially remodeled so that it looked like her favorite restaurant, Romanoff's. True to form, Marilyn didn't live with him full-time, keeping her independence by taking a modest room at a nearby hotel. She continued to study with Natasha Lytess, who once again disapproved of Marilyn being involved romantically with a man.

It wasn't the typical scenario of a powerful older man taking a much younger beauty as his mistress. Hyde had great belief in Marilyn as a performer, even surpassing Natasha's devotion. When she told him that she hoped someday to be a great actress, he was the first person not to snicker.

"He was the first man I ever met who didn't think I was a dumb blonde," Marilyn recalled. "He knew I couldn't talk very well, but he understood I was frightened of people. He loved me, I think, and I loved him." Realizing that one of her biggest drawbacks was her lack of confidence, Hyde brought her to the prominent plastic surgeon Dr. Michael Gurdin.

Gurdin and Hyde agreed that Marilyn had some flatness in her chin, which when filmed in close-ups could cause a problem. This was corrected by a cartilage implant, the procedure performed by going in through her mouth so it wouldn't leave a scar. The alterations were minor, but in an

industry where every physical flaw is magnified, it made a big difference
to a performer who would be photographed as much as Marilyn, and
who would become a standard of female perfection.

By now Hyde realized he was dying. He constantly begged Marilyn
to marry him. Marilyn gently refused, explaining that, although she loved
him, she wasn't "in love" with him. All she could do was offer Hyde her
body. He was dumbfounded. His life was filled with meaningless fucks—
he prided himself on the number of his conquests. The more Marilyn said
no to marriage, the more he wanted her. It became his unyielding obsession. He revealed to her that he wasn't going to live long; if she was his
widow she would be a very wealthy woman. Still Marilyn refused. Ultimately Hyde decided he wanted to be with her on any terms.

Early in 1949, while Hyde was attempting to get Marilyn cast in a good
role in a memorable movie, she auditioned for a part in the latest (and last)
Marx Brothers' comedy, *Love Happy*. It was not the kind of picture Hyde
had in mind—an unfunny, forgettable movie about stolen diamonds, with
Groucho Marx playing a private detective.

Marilyn was sent to the set, where she met the producer, Lester Cowan,
who introduced her to Groucho and Harpo Marx. "Can you walk?"
Groucho asked her. She nodded. He made it clear that he wanted a woman
who, when she walked by, could cause the pipe a man was smoking to
whistle and shoot off tufts of smoke.

Marilyn walked across the soundstage for him. *Bam!* "You have the
prettiest ass in the business," Groucho whispered to her. "I'm sure he meant
it in the nicest way," Marilyn would later explain. Harpo honked his horn
and whistled.

Marilyn's thirty-eight-second appearance in the movie is quite literally a walk-on. She sashays into Groucho's office in a strapless evening
gown, telling the investigator that she needs help because "Some men are
following me." There is some ogling, leering, and double-takes, and he vol-
unteers to take her down to the bus station. "Boy, did I want to fuck her,"
Groucho said much later. "She was the most beautiful girl I ever saw in
my life."

———

While Johnny Hyde was in Europe for the wedding of his client Rita Hayworth to Prince Aly Khan, Marilyn found herself in financial trouble again. She was looking for modeling work to pay some bills. As luck would have it, the photographer Tom Kelley called with a job. Marilyn knew Kelley; she had posed for some beer advertisements in the past. This time he was looking for a model to pose nude for a calendar.

After thinking it over for a few days she called Kelley and told him she would like to pose.* She did ask that the photographer's wife be present. "But none of your helpers, please," she added. Then, after further consideration, she asked Kelley if they could shoot it at night. The photographer agreed to all of Marilyn's requests.

On May 27, 1949, a few days before her twenty-third birthday, Marilyn showed up at Kelley's studio. As promised, his wife, Natalie, was there to help set up the shoot. Natalie draped plush red velvet over a backdrop. The photo session lasted for two hours. In some shots Marilyn is posed kneeling in front of the velvet-covered backdrop with her hands behind her head. One of those shots would be called "Golden Dreams." Then the backdrop was tilted back so Marilyn could lie down on her side and seductively stretch out her body while twisting slightly so that her pubic area was not visible. "She had the greatest figure I think I've ever seen in my life," Kelley commented.

After she became successful, Marilyn spoke of the nude photo shoot many times, never with the slightest hint of regret. "He sort of stretched me out on this red velvet," she explained. "I was little embarrassed. There I am with my bare tochas out. It was a little drafty. He was very nice. He kept going 'Ahhh, my God!' I said, 'Well maybe it's not too bad.' Red velvet! When I was a kid I used to dream of red velvet. But anyway I never thought I'd end up nude on red velvet."

In another sense it was getting back at Aunt Ida, who had taught Norma Jeane that displaying the human form was wrong. Here she was glorifying it.

———

* Actually Marilyn had already posed topless and seminude quite a few times for photographers like Laszlo Willinger and Earl Moran—perhaps she felt too close to movie stardom to risk a career-killing scandal by doing so now.

————

Meanwhile Hyde was still attempting to secure a script for her that had a "star part." When he read the screenplay for John Huston's film noir titled *The Asphalt Jungle*, to be made for MGM, Hyde immediately thought of Marilyn for the very small but important part of the gangster's mistress, Angela Phinlay.

The character was that of a naive, young, somewhat greedy girl, lost in a world of crime and corruption, dependent on a much older man, getting by on her angelic looks and bewildered demeanor. Instinctively Hyde knew this was exactly the right kind of role for Marilyn. Hyde asked Huston to see Marilyn as a professional courtesy.

Huston didn't know that Hyde had already given Marilyn the entire script and that she had been rehearsing it for days with Natasha. In the scene she would be performing, Angela was supposed to be lounging on a couch. Noticing that there was nothing to lie down on, Marilyn asked Huston if she could perform reclining on the floor. Since Huston wasn't really interested in her, he couldn't have cared less how she played the scene. But after she finished the performance, according to him, he couldn't imagine anyone else in the role. Marilyn, however, felt differently about her reading.

"Oh that was just awful, Mr. Huston!" she cried. "May I please do it again?"

Huston allowed Marilyn to begin again, but it was unnecessary. He had already decided to give her the part.

During shooting, the word around town was that Johnny Hyde's mistress was very good indeed. As a baby-faced bimbo, Marilyn's performance in *The Asphalt Jungle* was a standout because of the layer of kittenish vulnerability she brought to it. Even with her limited screen time, she was featured in the movie trailers and posters.

Although most of the audience went to the preview expecting a gritty crime drama, on exiting they commented on appraisal cards: "Hot blonde" or: "Let's see more of the blonde."

The reviews for *The Asphalt Jungle* were excellent, and it went on to be nominated for four Academy Awards. *Photoplay* declared, "There's a beautiful blonde, too, name of Marilyn Monroe, who plays [Louis] Calhern's girlfriend, and makes the most of her footage."

It was as if all of Hyde's belief in Marilyn had been justified.

However, soon after the movie's triumphant release came yet another disappointment: Marilyn was not offered a contract with MGM. Astonishingly, the head of the studio, Dore Schary, told Hyde that Marilyn "wasn't photogenic" and that she didn't have "the sort of looks that make a movie star."

What was it about Marilyn that made so many in the industry not only dismiss her but downright dislike her? (Years later Darryl Zanuck admitted he hated her.) Most likely it was the morality of the day, the double standard of male and female sexuality.

Hollywood is a small town; the columnist James Bacon called it "a four letter town" and Marilyn was known to come from an impoverished background. On the party circuit she was observed with a mixture of lust and disgust. Where it was possible to look at Marilyn and see beauty, talent, and a genuine desire to improve, instead they saw her lack of proper upbringing. She didn't speak properly. She didn't dress properly. She didn't behave properly. Her clothes had been cheap—in style and in price—so to them she had been cheap. To their amusement and scorn, she often didn't wear undergarments.

In spite of Hollywood's rejection of her, Hyde's belief in Marilyn remained unshakeable. Knowing that roles like Angela in movies as good as *The Asphalt Jungle* don't come around every day, Hyde decided it was better for Marilyn to continue taking small parts in mediocre films. It would give her experience on movie sets and help build her confidence, while keeping her face (no matter how briefly) in front of movie audiences.

In *Right Cross*, a boxing film, she's glimpsed fleetingly in one scene in which Dick Powell tries to pick her up. In *Hometown Story* she has an insignificant part as a receptionist in a newspaper office, where Natasha Lytess's overemphasis on Marilyn's diction in her training is already becoming apparent. If her career kept going down this path, all the good attention she had received in *The Asphalt Jungle* would soon be forgotten. Time was running out, not only for Marilyn, but also for Johnny Hyde.

Over at Fox, Joe Mankiewicz was casting a first-rate project entitled *All About Eve*. This was a backstage story about an aging Broadway actress, Margo Channing, to be played by superstar Bette Davis, and the young fan, Eve (Anne Baxter), who befriends her with a hard-luck story, and then betrays her by using all of Margo's show-business friends as pawns to climb the ladder of success. The only characters Eve doesn't manage to fool are an acerbic theater critic, Addison DeWitt (George Sanders), and his protégée, the lovely but no-talent Miss Casswell.

Well aware that most Hollywood executives perceived Marilyn exactly the way Miss Casswell was written—the gorgeous plaything of an important man—Hyde implored Mankiewicz to cast her in the role. Like Angela in *The Asphalt Jungle*, Miss Casswell was a small part with a few standout scenes which would allow Marilyn to shine.

Mankiewicz cast her. "It was suggested that the character would do whatever she had to do to get ahead, and I sensed that in Marilyn there was a certain amount of cunning as well as innocence," Mankiewicz observed. "On one hand, she was vulnerable. But, on the other, calculating. She knew what she was doing, that one."

Marilyn was nervous about being able to hold her own in scenes that included the great Bette Davis. Ironically Davis—whose marriage with costar Gary Merrill (a man a decade younger than her) was breaking up, assumed that a young woman who looked like Marilyn had it easy. "I felt a certain envy for what I assumed was Marilyn's more-than-obvious popularity," she said later. "Here was a girl who did not know what it was like to be lonely. Then I noticed how shy she was, and I think now that she was as lonely as I was. Lonelier. It was something I felt, a deep well of loneliness she was trying to fill."

The actress Celeste Holm, who played Margo Channing's unassuming best friend, had a low opinion of Marilyn on the set. "I never thought of Marilyn as being an actress. . . . I thought she was quite sweet and terribly dumb and my natural reaction was: Whose girl is that?"

It was only costar Gregory Ratoff in the role of a Broadway producer who truly recognized Marilyn's charisma. "That girl is going to be a big star," he said in his heavy Russian accent.

"Why?" Holm sniffed. "Because she keeps us waiting for an hour?"

"No. She has a quality," he replied.

The quality is in evidence from the moment she makes her entrance on the arm of George Sanders, playing the influential theater critic. It's a party scene, and Marilyn is luminous in a Helen Rose strapless ball gown. "I can see your career rise in the east like the sun," Sanders purrs admiringly when she successfully flirts with an influential producer.

Once again word leaked out that Marilyn was doing a superb job in a major movie, and Hyde was able to negotiate a new contract for Marilyn with 20th Century-Fox, ironically the first studio to sign her three years earlier, only to drop her because Darryl Zanuck felt she had no future.

The contract offered her more money than the previous one she had signed; this one was for $500 a week for the first year, giving the studio the right to renew. If she was optioned for the second year her salary would be raised to $750 weekly, $1,250 for the third year, $1,500 for the fourth, $2,000 for the sixth, and if she was still making films for Fox in 1957, she would receive $3,500 for that last year of the contract.

The film was released in November and was a box-office success. It was nominated for a record fourteen Academy Awards. Having seen her in *The Asphalt Jungle* and *All About Eve*, Hyde knew that all of his intuitive faith in Marilyn had been correct. One of the greatest accomplishments of his life was discovering Marilyn. One of his greatest tragedies was that he wouldn't live to see her become a star.

Sometime that December, almost two years after he met her, Hyde talked to his lawyer about changing his will so that Marilyn would inherit a third of his estate. The will had yet to be drawn up by December 16, when Hyde went to Palm Springs for a short vacation before the holidays— while Marilyn was Christmas shopping in Tijuana with Natasha. The following day he suffered a massive heart attack and was rushed back to Los Angeles. Marilyn hurried to Cedars of Lebanon Hospital to be with him, only to discover that his family didn't want her there.

To them she was simply a mistress, typical of the type, a gold digger, a homewrecker. Finally they could exercise power over her. She had no legal rights to Hyde, and they refused to let her into his room, even though as she lingered nearby in the hallway she could hear him calling for her. The following day Hyde died.

With the loss of Hyde, Marilyn went wild with grief. He was the only person in her life who loved her unconditionally and proved it every day.

What would she do without him? She had been forbidden by his family to attend the services at Forest Lawn Memorial Cemetery, but that didn't stop her. Dressed in black with a dark veil over her face, Marilyn sat in the back with Natasha. Hyde's son Jimmy described the scene at the cemetery to biographer Fred Lawrence Guiles. "All I can recall clearly is Marilyn screaming my father's name over and over again. It shook everyone."

SEVEN

Marilyn's reputation for being a Hollywood whore—which stuck with her among the studio men throughout her life—was solidified by her affair with Johnny Hyde and his untimely death. Shortly afterward, his family ordered Marilyn out of the Palm Drive House. She probably could have fought them, but she didn't. She left many of her belongings behind and moved back in with Natasha.

The death of Johnny Hyde put a mystique around his young mistress—unknown by the public but notorious in the industry. The men from the party circuit—who had not showed any particular special interest in Marilyn a few months before—were suddenly red-hot for her. The fact that a man as powerful and respected as Hyde was so passionate about Marilyn Monroe gave her a level of intrigue.

What was it about this blonde that set her apart from the many other beauties Hyde came in contact with during his long career? Why was she different from the magnificent specimens in the business who had crossed paths with Hyde? Suddenly executives in the movie business had to know. Marilyn was more afraid and more vulnerable than ever before. She became a dab of honey in the center of a circle of horny bees.

One of the men who came sniffing around her was the prestigious and powerful director Elia Kazan. He was in Los Angeles with the acclaimed playwright Arthur Miller, trying to get Miller's screenplay *The Hook* produced.

Kazan, who was notorious for his lust for lovely young women, had heard about the late Johnny Hyde's delicious young mistress and wanted to find out for himself what all the fuss was about. A friend of his, the movie director Harmon Jones, was working with Marilyn on her latest small part in *As Young as You Feel*, another insignificant film Fox had cast her in. This gave Kazan a chance to visit the set and see Johnny's girl for himself. He took Arthur Miller along with him.

When Marilyn appeared on the set, Kazan and Miller watched her film the scene. It was a nightclub scene, where Marilyn walked across the floor in a black dress, grabbing the attention of an older man.

After the scene Kazan asked Marilyn out to dinner: "I wouldn't say a word. Just be with you and then take you home." Although Marilyn refused, he was appealing to her biggest vulnerability—the fear of being alone. He was presenting himself as her greatest desire—a father. When he invited her out again a little later, Marilyn accepted.

Before saying good-bye to Marilyn, Kazan introduced her to Arthur Miller. When they shook hands, Miller would say, "the shock of her body's motion sped through me, a sensation at odds with her sadness." It could have been the feeling of destiny that was giving Miller such a jolt—both their lives would be altered drastically because of this brief meeting.

But it was Kazan whom Marilyn started dating. If he was expecting a fling with a sexy piece, Kazan was astonished to find much more—which he only felt comfortable enough to admit privately in a letter attempting to explain Marilyn to his wife: "You couldn't help being touched. She was talented, funny, vulnerable, helpless, in awful pain, with no hope, and some worth and not a liar, not vicious, not catty, and with a history of orphanism that was killing to hear. She was like all Charlie Chaplin's heroines in one."

It wasn't long before Kazan achieved what every man in Hollywood had been trying to do. He was having an affair with Marilyn—taking Johnny Hyde's place in bed. At this time Marilyn, of course, needed a protector. Someone who was respected in show business. It was only an illusion that Kazan would really protect her—but for now that illusion was enough.

A few nights later Arthur Miller encountered Marilyn again, this time at the home of Charles Feldman, a Hollywood lawyer, agent, and producer who was part of the party-circuit set that passed girls around like hors d'oeuvres on a serving tray. Kazan decided not to attend the party because he had made a date with yet another woman. (He was in the land of beauties, three thousand miles away from his wife on business, and he was going to take full advantage of it.)

At the party Miller regarded Marilyn differently than the others. True, he lusted after Marilyn, but he also felt her humanity. Since most of the women at the party were more conservatively dressed, Marilyn stood out, wearing a skintight gown that—in contrast with her girlish face and innocent demeanor—seemed outlandish and vulgar.

Unlike Elia Kazan, Arthur Miller was not a great seducer. He was awkward and uncomfortable with women. But something about Marilyn made him open up. Miller sat quietly with Marilyn and told her about his life and, his frustrations, the marital dissatisfactions he was going through with his wife, Mary.

Miller had been brought up in a traditional Jewish family in Brooklyn, New York. At the age of twenty-five Miller married Mary Slattery, a woman he considered sensible but stubborn. They had two children, a boy and a girl. His life was "all conflict and tension, thwarted desires, stymied impulses, bewildering but unexpressed conflicts." He felt he was wasting his life. Elia Kazan summed up his exasperation, "He had sex on his mind constantly. He was starved for sexual release."

From a young age Miller was ambitious with his writing. In 1949, at the age of thirty-three, he wrote his breakout work, *Death of a Salesman*. Considered a masterpiece at the time, it was a tremendous hit and won him a Tony Award, the New York Drama Critics Award, and the Pulitzer Prize. Some friends noticed that with success he had become pompous and preachy, but Marilyn was turned on and took it as intelligence.

Marilyn kicked off her shoes and curled her legs under her, listening to him intently. Instead of making a pass, Miller grabbed one of her toes and held it gently. The esteemed playwright might as well have been holding her heart.

Moved by her sensitivity and eager to flatter her, Miller suggested she go back East and study acting, that she would be wonderful in the theater.

Marilyn was overwhelmed that someone could envision her on Broadway. "People who were around, and heard him, laughed," she said.

"But he said, 'No. I'm very sincere.'"

Even though Marilyn was sleeping with Kazan at the time, Miller was indeed lusting after her. In *After the Fall*, his autobiographical play about his relationship with Marilyn, Miller confessed, "The first honor was that I hadn't tried to go to bed with her! She took it for a tribute to her 'value,' and I was only afraid! God, the hypocrisy!"

While Marilyn was overwhelmed that he admired her mind, Miller was flattered that she'd be available for sex. Their initial attraction was based on the fact that they were each other's fantasy come to life.

Kazan would remain in Los Angeles for a while. Miller flew back to New York a few days earlier than planned, fleeing from his feelings for Marilyn. Marilyn and Kazan saw him off at the airport. Miller, although frustrated, was in a monogamous relationship with his wife. But he was now tortured by his desire for Marilyn. "Flying homeward, her scent still on my hands, I knew my innocence was technical merely, and the fact blackened my heart. But along with it came the certainty that I could, after all, lose myself in sensuality."

Invigorated by Miller's interest, Marilyn set out to improve her mind, to feel worthy and gain the respect of the intellectuals she was starting to come into contact with. "Oh, I started going to UCLA," she explained later. "I had never finished high school. I took a course in Background in Literature. Arthur sent me a list of books I should read and I started to read to find out such things as the history of this country."

Miller wrote to Marilyn from New York, "Bewitch them with this image they ask for, but I hope and almost pray you won't be hurt in this game, nor ever change."

Marilyn wrote back to Miller declaring that she needed someone to respect. "Most people can admire their fathers. But I never had one."

In his reply, Miller didn't encourage her to look up to him; instead he suggested she admire Abraham Lincoln, recommending that she read Lincoln's biography by Carl Sandburg. Though overwrought with guilt over his passion, he did not discourage her from keeping open the line of communication between them.

After Johnny Hyde's death, without anyone looking out for her career, Darryl F. Zanuck cast Marilyn in a string of very small parts in forgettable movies. For example, in *We're Not Married* she's plays Joyce, a pawn to make an almost-divorced Macdonald Carey's wife (Claudette Colbert) jealous. In *Love Nest* Marilyn is a WAC who moves into her married army buddy's new apartment building. Most likely she would have finished off the entire seven-year contract in roles like these, and a lesser personality than Marilyn would have been overlooked in these forgettable roles. Instead people walked out of the movie theaters remembering "that blonde."

But, after a suggestion made by her journalist friend Sidney Skolsky, another studio, RKO, became very interested in Marilyn's potential, and asked to borrow her for their production of *Clash by Night*—a dramatic film about working-class people in a fish-canning town. Although not a success on Broadway, *Clash by Night* was written by the well-respected playwright Clifford Odets.

RKO was giving the screen adaptation a first-rate production, casting Paul Douglas and Robert Ryan in the leading roles, along with Barbara Stanwyck as Mae, a fallen woman who marries for stability but has an affair with a man she finds more exciting. The great filmmaker Fritz Lang was set to direct. Marilyn had the supporting role of Peggy—the girlfriend of Mae's macho brother, Joe. Peggy is an earthy, high-spirited young woman who tries to assert her independence in a town where men slap their women around.

Marilyn's Peggy is part tough cookie and part vulnerable little girl—but remarkably lusty and uninhibited. She swills beer, eats with gusto, and licks her fingers. In this small part Marilyn is juicy without the usual glamour trappings. Her hair is short and curly, and she's costumed in baggy blue jeans, a plain two-piece bathing suit, and drab dresses.

Even at this early stage in her career, Marilyn was already getting the reputation for being extremely difficult to work with. She was late every time she was called for a scene. Cast and crew members would remember the torment she went through before facing the cameras, vomiting before each call, her sensitive skin breaking out in red blotches.

Barbara Stanwyck remembered Marilyn as being awkward: "She

couldn't get out of her own way. She wasn't disciplined, and she was often late, but she didn't do it viciously, and there was a sort of magic about her which we all recognized at once."

On the set, however, Stanwyck was more annoyed by Marilyn than taken by her magic. The actress Jane Russell recalled: "I was riding with the director Nick Ray on the RKO lot when we passed a girl wearing very 'stressed' blue jeans and a man's shirt tied under her bosom and showing quite a lot of midriff. Nick stopped the car and said, 'I'd like you to meet this kid. . . . She's having a tough time on her picture with the lady star (Stanwyck), who is being very sarcastic to her.'" As she walked alongside, he called, "Marilyn, I want you two to meet. Jane, this is Marilyn Monroe." Stanwyck found Marilyn's unprofessionalism annoying, along with Natasha's meddling. She was probably even more peeved at the media's attention to the new blonde star.

When reporters visited the set, they would pass over the seasoned professionals, announcing: "We wanna talk to the girl with the big tits." Marilyn resented it to a degree too, but it was expected of her, so she continued to give it.

In spite of the friction on the set, critics were surprised by Marilyn's intelligent performance. Alton Cook wrote in the New York *World-Telegram*: "This girl has a refreshing exuberance, an abundance of girlish high spirits. She is a forceful actress too. . . . Her role here is not very big but she makes it dominant." It was becoming more and more difficult for Zanuck and the executives at Fox to ignore the fact that Marilyn was capturing the attention of the media and the public.

Emboldened by her growing popularity, Marilyn once again decided to try to meet her father. She knew that he had bought a dairy farm in Hemet, near Palm Springs, and for moral support, she asked Natasha Lytess to drive up with her.

Marilyn brought along the latest magazine with her on the cover. During the long drive Marilyn and Natasha discussed her "father issues." As they approached the farm, Marilyn got nervous and decided to call Gifford first.

Marilyn and Natasha pulled over to a pay phone and she shakily called the man she knew to be her father. When she had him on the line she introduced herself, Gladys's daughter, *his* daughter, adding that she was "Marilyn Monroe now. . . ."

Gifford cut her off sharply: "Look, I'm married and I have a family. I don't have anything to say to you. Call my lawyer." Once again he hung up. Marilyn was devastated. Part of the reason for becoming a movie star was so that people would accept her. Now here was someone she wanted recognition from most, treating her as a nuisance. "It did her no good," Natasha said. "It broke her heart."

Marilyn's career was about to explode, and the tremors were being felt all over Hollywood. It wasn't easy for Zanuck to admit he had been so wrong about her—but the bottom line for Fox was money. If Marilyn Monroe films were going to bring the studio profits, they were going to use her. Zanuck started looking around for a film for Marilyn to follow up her serious part in *Clash by Night*. He decided on a very dramatic role in *Don't Bother to Knock*, with a screenplay written by Daniel Taradash, based on the novel *Mischief*, by Charlotte Armstrong.

In *Don't Bother to Knock*, Marilyn plays the part of Nell, a disturbed young woman recently released from a mental hospital, who gets a job babysitting for a wealthy couple who are staying at an upscale New York City hotel.

After Nell is spotted in the window from across the courtyard by Jed (Richard Widmark), an airline pilot who has just been dumped by his girlfriend, he shows up at her room with a bottle of rye. After some flirting, Jed becomes aware of Nell's strange, disconnected behavior, and it becomes apparent that this damaged girl is the last person who should be caring for a child. As she retreats further and further into a psychotic fantasy world, Nell begins to believe that Jed is her fiancé who died in a plane crash over the Pacific.

From the beginning the director, Roy Ward Baker, didn't want Marilyn for the part, feeling "she looked too beautiful and it was impossible to make her *un*beautiful for the beginning. . . . The story never would have happened to a girl who looked like Marilyn Monroe whether she was nuts or not."

Although Zanuck was trusting Marilyn with a lead, the production surrounding the movie would be modest. *Don't Bother to Knock* was to be shot inexpensively in black-and-white; all the action takes place in the interiors of the hotel; and the production had a working schedule of twenty-eight days. This meant that Baker would have to shoot quickly. Marilyn wouldn't be able to indulge her already maddening habit of asking for many takes as she explored the character in front of the camera—with Lytess coaching from the sidelines. As a result, much of what we see in *Don't Bother to Knock* is Marilyn's performance in the first take—demonstrating that, at least at the time, she could work somewhat professionally without endless retakes.

But there was still the unusual practice of having a drama coach on the set. Marilyn wanted, needed, someone there to tell her she was performing up to par. The industry was still ambivalent about her as an actress. Natasha was solid, and Marilyn fed off of her strength.

In spite of Baker's original misgivings, Marilyn's performance is mostly instinctively convincing. She makes Nell's outer layer shy and reserved as she tentatively ventures out in public, reacting with her uncle, the parents of the young girl she's to babysit, and the child herself. Although still relatively inexperienced (and not yet acquainted with the Method style of acting she would learn at the Actors Studio), Marilyn would intuitively use the dark memories of her mother, the fears of insanity, and the basic sense of aloneness and abandonment to make the character of Nell real for her.

In the last seven minutes of the film, Marilyn does some of the best dramatic acting of her career. Her youthful face is blank with confusion. The vulnerability, the childlike wonderment and the wounded spirit, that would become a part of her screen persona, usually wrapped in sexuality, is used to convey madness.

The staff at the hotel realizes that Nell is unhinged. Security is called. Trying to escape, she steps out of the elevator into the lobby, blinking in confusion. Her dress is torn, her face scratched. When cornered, Nell holds a razor blade she has stolen from the lobby's convenience store. She brings the blade to her face. With her bewildered expression and crumpled, defeated body, Nell/Marilyn conveys what it feels like to be lost and completely alone in the world.

With her final moments in the movie, escorted off to yet another institution, she conveys all the fragility and desperation of Blanche DuBois in *A Streetcar Named Desire*. One almost expects Nell to exclaim that she has always depended on the kindness of strangers.

The movie was a modest moneymaker for Fox, but reviews were mixed, leaning toward negative. Some saw Marilyn's potential, but most were perplexed at seeing the glamour girl play serious. Archer Winsten of the New York *Post* was facetious but balanced: "They've thrown Marilyn Monroe into the deep dramatic waters, sink or swim, and while she doesn't really do either, you might say that she floats. With that figure, what else can she do?"

On the set of *Don't Bother to Knock*, Baker witnessed firsthand a new phenomenon that was just beginning around Marilyn but would continue for the rest of her life. Baker said he "never knew anyone who came along when Marilyn was present who didn't want to touch her—the continuity girl, the cameraman, the gaffer. It was extraordinary."

After she completed her leading role in *Don't Bother to Knock*, the studio decided that the most important thing was to just keep Marilyn working, to continue churning out films with her in them and see what happened. No matter how big or small her role, as long as they put her on the poster they could be assured that people would turn up.

We're Not Married was a series of vignettes about five couples who suddenly find that their marriage licenses are not valid. Marilyn's segment of the film lasts less than nine minutes. They put her in *O. Henry's Full House* as a streetwalker, and she had a few lines with Charles Laughton.

She was used to somewhat better advantage when she was cast in *Monkey Business*, even though it was another supporting role. Cary Grant and Ginger Rogers would be playing the leads. Grant is a chemist who, along with some help from laboratory monkeys, concocts a youth serum he and his wife accidentally ingest. Marilyn was cast as a voluptuous secretary— whose physical attributes far surpass her office skills—to whom Grant turns his attention when his mind reverts to that of a twenty-year-old.

EIGHT

The baseball legend Joe DiMaggio was flipping through a newspaper when he came across a publicity photo of Marilyn—posed swinging a bat at home plate during a practice game with the Chicago White Sox, wearing a pair of very white shorts.

But perhaps because it combined his two greatest passions—baseball and a beautiful woman—DiMaggio could not get the photo out of his head. At his urging, his friends made a series of phone calls until they tracked down someone who knew Marilyn: the press agent David March, who was good friends with her. March promised to give Marilyn a call and try to set up an introduction.

When March called he got right to the point. "I have someone I want you to meet, Marilyn. He's a nice guy."

"Are there really any nice guys left?" she asked solemnly.

"This guy is," March replied. "It's Joe DiMaggio."

"Who's he?" Marilyn asked.

After considering it for a moment she added, "He plays sports, doesn't he? Baseball or football or something." Expecting someone flashy and cocksure, Marilyn was reluctant to go out with a famous athlete—even if he was retired.

March told Marilyn she had nothing to lose. She wasn't going out much, and having dinner with new people might help her out of her funk. Finally she agreed. To make it less awkward, March promised to make it a double date. He would bring his girlfriend, a young actress named

Peggy Raba. He set the meeting place at an Italian restaurant, the Villa Nova, on Sunset Boulevard.

Exhausted from her demanding work schedule—and likely from lack of sleep—Marilyn arrived at the Villa Nova almost two hours late. But when she slid into the booth, she was pleasantly surprised. She had imagined a brash loudmouth, but she found DiMaggio to be quiet and dignified, wearing a conservative dark suit. It was a busy night; the patrons of the restaurant were excited to be in the presence of *his* celebrity. Men kept approaching the table: DiMaggio was a baseball legend, and they threw their personalities around, trying to impress him. Marilyn was amused—usually it was she whom men were wooing.

DiMaggio didn't pose or preen. His modest demeanor and his total confidence in his accomplishments appealed to her. The other men in the room seemed vapid next to DiMaggio's silent intensity. Marilyn sensed other qualities in him too.

The sportswriter Jimmy Cannon, a close friend of DiMaggio, once described him as "the shyest public man I ever met," adding, "I doubt if anyone fully understands his lonely character." Marilyn instantly related. In spite of the fact that these were two popular and successful people, they recognized the aloneness in each other.

Unexpectedly she was drawn to DiMaggio. She was fascinated by the flecks of gray in his dark, shiny, carefully combed hair, the silver strands seeming to accessorize his gray suit. What intrigued her most about the retired ballplayer was his silence. Yet his reserve made her unsure of his feelings toward her. Normally men came on to her by bragging or being overly attentive—she understood how to handle that. DiMaggio wasn't giving off any obvious signals at all. He hardly looked at her, and she wondered why.

The truth was that he was simply shy and intimidated by her. DiMaggio was already crazy about Marilyn and afraid to show it, but "you could almost feel him going to pieces," David March recalled.

After coffee Marilyn—still not completely sure of DiMaggio's feelings for her—stood up to leave. He surprised her by offering to walk her to the car. When they reached her car he confessed he didn't have a ride home. Would Marilyn mind driving him to the Knickerbocker Hotel? Marilyn's hopes soared. During the ride he said, "I don't feel like turning in just yet. Would you mind driving around for a while?"

Marilyn had been very tired when the evening started off, but she was energized now. She was happy to drive around the streets of Hollywood. By now Marilyn knew that DiMaggio was a baseball legend, but she knew nothing about sports. At thirty-seven, he was retired and making a living doing sports commentary on television. He also owned a seaside restaurant in San Francisco called the Yankee Clipper. He was divorced from Dorothy Arnold. Their five-year marriage had produced a son, Joe Jr., who was now twelve.

And they talked a little, revealing just a tiny bit of themselves, and by the end of the evening they both realized that they very much wanted to know more. Marilyn would say that "scores of men had told me I was beautiful," but when Joe DiMaggio complimented her it "was the first time my heart had jumped to hear it."

She needed someone in her corner, and Joe, who loved her almost at once, was on her side. He made that abundantly clear from the very beginning. He let her know that he only wanted what was best for her. Strong, silent, smart, DiMaggio was just the kind of man she needed.

In 1952 a nude photograph of an alluring blond woman kneeling with one arm up, concealing half her face, was appearing on calendars that hung in barbershops, auto-mechanic garages, and men's lockers all over the country. Simultaneously Marilyn Monroe was becoming the most recognizable blonde of the era. For the first time men began paying as much attention to the face on the calendars as they did to her splendid body. It looked like her. "Could it be?" they asked one another.

In the morality of the early 1950s, nudity was equated with pornography. The fact that a young, nationally known woman had posed naked was scandalous enough to destroy a career. It was getting to the point where 20th Century-Fox was going to have to confront the problem. There were many frantic meetings behind closed doors at Fox. There were consultations with lawyers and the best publicity men. The consensus among all was that Marilyn should deny that she was the beautiful blonde on the calendar.

But Marilyn—with her uncanny sense of self and an understanding of the public's perception of her—had other ideas. Even with all the attention being paid her, she wasn't quite a star. This could do it. Since her fame was built on sexuality, she felt that with the right backstory, her public would stay with her: Marilyn would tell the truth.

She had been scheduled for an interview with the journalist Aline Mosby the following week. During the interview Marilyn told Mosby in a confidential whisper: "A few years ago when I had no money for food or rent, a photographer I knew asked me to pose nude for an art calendar. His wife was there, they were both so nice, and I earned fifty dollars that I needed very bad. . . . They want me to deny it's me. But I can't lie. What should I do?"

On March 13, 1952, Aline Mosby broke the story in the Los Angeles *Herald Examiner*. The headline read: "Marilyn Monroe Admits She's Nude Blonde of Calendar."

It was shocking to the public that they could see a movie star's naked body. Within days this was a major news story all over the world. The thing that titillated the public the most was that Marilyn refused to say that she regretted posing. Instead she joked about it.

When a reporter asked her what she had on, Marilyn shrugged and said, "The radio."

The nude calendar story only played into the public's paradoxical view of Marilyn Monroe. She was a bad girl who was really a good girl—it was the world that made her bad. Marilyn understood both sides of her appeal, and knew how to exploit them. Part of the public wanted it to be acceptable to admire provocative and sexual personalities—but society told them it was wrong. Marilyn's innocence made it acceptable.

That April, *LIFE* put her on the cover with the very true headline: "The Talk of Hollywood." It was clear that the public was insatiable for new information about Marilyn Monroe, and reporters started seriously digging into her past for a new angle. It was inevitable that the journalist Erskine Johnson would uncover that Marilyn was not the orphan girl she had claimed to be since the beginning of her publicity. Erskine had discovered that Gladys Monroe Baker was alive.

Once again Marilyn was summoned to the Fox executive offices to explain herself. This time she truly would have preferred the story to re-main unknown. But she had no choice. Her mother *was* alive.* Again she had to face the media to explain herself.

When explaining to the press that her mother was alive, Marilyn went for the simple truth: "My mother spent many years at the hospital," she said. "Through Los Angeles County, my guardian placed me in several foster families, and I spent more than a year at the Los Angeles Orphan-age. I haven't known my mother intimately, and since I'm an adult, and able to help her, I have contacted her. Now I help her, and I want to keep helping her as long as she needs me."

20th Century-Fox's selection of *Niagara* for Marilyn's next movie showed her new status in Hollywood, which was to emerge full-blown in 1953. *Niagara* is in every way a star vehicle. A film noir about an adulterous woman, Rose Loomis, played by Marilyn, plotting with her lover to kill her husband (Joseph Cotten) as they vacation in a resort near Niagara Falls. Staying at the same resort is a young honeymooning couple who be-come embroiled in the sinister plot.

Marilyn had been potent enough in black-and-white. In *Niagara* she exploded onto the screen in magnificent Technicolor. At one point in the film Rose requests the DJ to play her favorite song, "Kiss." In a remark-able, lingering close-up Marilyn sings along with the record, her sultry voice the perfect complement to her seductive image on the screen. It is here that the indelible Monroe legend was born.

Although she was very popular before *Niagara* was made, its release was the starting point of the image of Marilyn Monroe that is woven into the fabric of America—the tousled blond hair, the porcelain skin, the glossy red lips, the heavy-lidded eyes, the beauty mark above her lip.

The world's intense fascination with her was now out of even her

---

* After they tried, unsuccessfully and very briefly, to live together in 1948, Marilyn's mother took off. In Boise she married a man named John Stewart Eely. Marilyn felt ambivalent about her mother's marriage. She was happy that she was well enough to have met a man and set up a household with him. She wanted her mother to be happy—but it seemed odd that she was never well enough to give herself to Norma Jeane. She was still just the lady with the red hair.

control, and it frightened her. Joseph Cotten observed, "When we filmed on location at Niagara Falls, great crowds gathered to see her. She couldn't cope, retreated into her shell."

Niagara is a tawdry, entertaining thriller. Most reviews of the day, however, focused on Marilyn's physicality. *Variety* wrote: "The camera lingers on Monroe's sensuous lips, roves over her slip-clad figure and accurately etches the outlines of her derrière as she weaves down a street to a rendezvous with her lover." Yet Pauline Kael later saw the darkness underneath that Marilyn might bring to other roles: "The only movie that explores the mean, unsavory potential of Marilyn Monroe's cuddly, infantile perversity."

But that would be the last time Marilyn would ever be given the opportunity to play a lustful character whose sexual appetite was her guiding force. Her next character—the world's most gorgeous dumb blonde—would be so potent, so beloved, that it would erase any notion in Hollywood that Marilyn Monroe could or should ever play anything else.

PART 2

THE PREFERRED BLONDE

PART 2

NINE

Marilyn Monroe was born to play Lorelei Lee in *Gentlemen Prefer Blondes*.

Once in a great while the stars align in Hollywood, and there is a perfect marriage between an actor and a role. Marilyn had one of the greatest breaks in her career when she was cast in the role of the diamond-loving Lorelei Lee in *Gentlemen Prefer Blondes*. It was the perfect role for the perfect actress in the first perfect time and place. No one could have played the role of Lorelei Lee better than Marilyn Monroe in 1952.

Gentlemen Prefer Blondes is a madcap musical comedy about a gold-digging blonde who is engaged to the millionaire she loves but gets into trouble on a transatlantic cruise to France with her girlfriend Dorothy (played by Jane Russell). During the cruise hijinks ensue, and trouble brews when Lorelei persuades an aging millionaire, Piggy, to give her his wife's diamond tiara—which the latter promptly reports as stolen.

The journalist Denis Ferrara has joked that Jane Russell was the best leading man that Marilyn Monroe ever had. Cast as Dorothy, Russell is the wisecracking, tough-as-nails-on-the-outside-but-compassionate-and-protective-on-the-inside gal pal. The media was anticipating a feud between the two bombshells. In his column Earl Wilson predicted it would be "the Battle of the Bulges." Russell would be getting top billing and was being paid $150,000 for the picture.

Fox held Marilyn to the contract she signed before her remarkably rapid rise, and her salary remained at $1,500 a week. Russell did witness the antagonism Marilyn felt toward the Fox big boys, who continued to treat her as if she were a struggling starlet. But the conflict wasn't about money. Marilyn was incensed that the studio still hadn't given her a private dressing room.

Fox kept telling her she wasn't a "star"; it was their way of keeping her in line. In spite of all the fan mail, publicity, and adoration, she was still a contract player. "I was always being talked down to," she said. Yet, when she was driving a friend to the airport, she saw her name up in lights on a marquee advertising *As Young as You Feel*. Dazed with disbelief, Marilyn pulled over to the side of the road and stared at the marquee. "So that's what it looks like," she said, marveling.

It emboldened her to go to the head office and ask for a dressing room. "What makes you think you're a star?" they retorted dismissively. "Then I got angry," she told journalist Richard Meryman in a tipsy interview.* "I said, 'Well whatever I am, I *am* the blonde—and it is *Gentlemen Prefer Blondes*.'" Marilyn didn't think they'd give her a dressing room "but they did."

The anticipated feud between Marilyn and Jane Russell never happened. "She was like my little sister," Russell said. Marilyn understood that *Gentlemen Prefer Blondes* was her moment to seal the deal once and for all. It was the opportunity to become—for all time—the blonde *everyone* prefers. "I never saw anybody work harder in my life," Russell observed. "Sometimes she was so engrossed she'd forget to eat lunch." Russell would bring her a hamburger. At the end of a long day of shooting, Marilyn would go back to Natasha's to continue working on the script for several more hours.

Marilyn had never danced professionally, and she paid particular attention to the dance numbers. The much-admired dancer Jack Cole had been assigned to choreograph the musical sequences. Cole was known to be very demanding and tough with his dancers.

According to Jane Russell, he would work with the two leading ladies for hours. After many run-throughs Russell would flee the rehearsal in ex-

---

* After the interview for *Life*, Meryman noted that Marilyn became more candid after she started drinking champagne.

haustion while Marilyn begged Cole to continue going over the dances late into the night.

Marilyn was especially anxious about how her big number in the movie, "Diamonds Are a Girl's Best Friend," would be staged. She needn't have worried. Cole had complete understanding of Marilyn's persona, and masterfully choreographed movements that perfectly suited her character. Understanding that she was not a trained dancer, he taught her to sometimes make her gestures subtle and precise.

Rather than teach her dance steps where she would need to be fast on her feet, much of Cole's choreography has to do with her manipulating her expressive torso, arms, hands, and fingers—even her facial expressions. He gave her small physical movements made gigantic by her powerful magnetism. She clutches her gloved hands to her chest, shrugs, winks, and points her fingers in either direction like a pistol. Sometimes she simply works her luscious bare shoulders.

For "Diamonds Are a Girl's Best Friend," the costume designer Travilla designed Marilyn an elegant, shocking pink satin strapless evening gown with an oversize bow in back, which he accessorized with matching opera gloves and lots of jewelry, keeping in line with the theme of the song.

With all the talent that worked on it, nurturing and enhancing Marilyn's inimitable magic, "Diamonds Are a Girl's Best Friend" became the focal point of the movie. The number would become a classic in movie musical history and forever associated with Marilyn Monroe.

Audiences were gaga over the movie and enthralled with Marilyn. She absolutely glows. Her inner light is so radiant that it's difficult to believe anything dark ever happened to her—you don't want to believe it, yet you know there's darkness there. Audiences wanted to love Marilyn and protect her.

And the critics seemed well aware that Monroe was something special and was going to be around for a while: "And there's Marilyn Monroe! Zounds, boys, what a personality this one is!" wrote the *Los Angeles Examiner*. "Send up a happy flare. At last, she's beautifully gowned, coiffed, and a wonderful crazy humor flashes from those sleepy eyes of hers."

After *Blondes* Marilyn Monroe was no longer a popular movie actress who captured the hearts of her generation. She became an eternal iconic image, a beloved symbol: She was of this earth but also out in the strato-sphere, her name inscribed in the annals of history. Marilyn became well aware of her place in popular culture as "*The* blonde." It caused her, in turns, extreme delight or deep anxiety. She was now a star. She had dreamed it. She had worked hard for it. Now she intended to keep it.

Marilyn's next film was the kind of lightweight romp the studio was now sure audiences wanted to see her in: *How to Marry a Millionaire*, written by Nunnally Johnson and directed by the Oscar-nominated director Jean Negulesco.

Encouraged by the pairing of Marilyn with sex symbol Jane Russell, the studio cast Marilyn opposite two movie queens from the previous de-cade, Betty Grable and Lauren Bacall. It was to be the first comedy the studio was filming in CinemaScope, a new wide-screen process that showed a huge, panoramic view of the movie being projected.

The plot revolves around three Manhattan models on the hunt for a wealthy husband. Both Monroe and Grable are "dumb blondes." It's Ba-call, as the smart and sassy brunette, who hatches the scheme for them to pool their resources so they can live in an expensive Manhattan apart-ment long enough for at least one of them to snare a millionaire—preferably rich enough to take care of them all.

"We had a great time on *How to Marry a Millionaire*," Lauren Bacall said. "Marilyn was just sweet. . . . She was late a lot. But she wasn't late to make a statement, she was late because she was frightened and because she was insecure. And she had, you know, quite a lousy childhood, I think."

Bacall described how Marilyn's insecurity manifested on the *Millionaire* set. "During our scenes she'd look at my forehead instead of my eyes; at the end of a take, look to her coach, standing behind Jean Negulesco, for approval. If the headshake was no, she'd insist on another take. A scene often went to fifteen or more takes, which meant I'd have to be good in all of them as no one knew which one would be used. Not easy—often irri-tating. And yet I couldn't dislike Marilyn. She had no meanness in her—no bitchery. She just had to concentrate on herself and the people who were there only for her."

Sometimes the growing pressures and demands would get to Marilyn, and she would confide in Bacall. "She was going with Joe DiMaggio at the time," Bacall remembered. "She would come into my dressing room and say, 'Oh, I really just want to be with Joe eating spaghetti in San Francisco.'" Of course it was more complicated than that. Marilyn continued to be torn but—at this time—her desire to be a great actress was greater than her desire to be safe.

Marilyn would credit this movie with broadening her female audience. Her character, Pola, is very nearsighted and refuses to wear glasses in public for fear that men won't find her attractive. The gorgeous Pola becomes all the more adorable because she'd rather bump into waiters and walk into walls than be seen wearing glasses. This display of insecurity added a touch of vulnerability to her knockout looks. Women of the day had their own self-doubts about their appearances, and they were touched by the fact that Marilyn Monroe—considered the most desirable woman in the world—also showed uncertainty about the way she looked.

When *How to Marry a Millionaire* was released, it was another blockbuster. The New York *Herald Tribune* said: "Her stint as a deadpan comedienne is as nifty as her looks. Playing a near-sighted charmer who won't wear her glasses when men are around, she bumps into the furniture and reads books upside down with a limpid guile that nearly melts the screen."

It was extraordinarily difficult for Marilyn to transition from being "a nobody" into being an integral part of the consciousness of the world. Her name was synonymous with beauty and sex—that's what they loved about her. Because Marilyn wanted to be loved more than anything else, she tried to live up to what was expected. She was simultaneously gratified and terrified of the image that surrounded her: How could she ever live up to everyone's expectations?

Murray Garrett, who had started photographing Marilyn at events as early as 1950 and became close to her, observed: "If she went to a premiere it's because that's what Fox wanted. They didn't seem to care that she was a human being who could have a terrible headache or be nauseous. That was something I saw quite often with her. She would get physically ill from her nerves. And often I'd ask, 'Hey are you okay?' And she had a marvelous answer to that. It was: 'Sorta.'"

Garrett got a glimpse of the quandary she found herself in when he witnessed her first taste of great fame during her appearances in 1953. "She was not the same every time," he noted. "She understood that she was sexy, but she couldn't understand why she was so disrespected by the members of the press—they were not treating her like the special person that she was. For example, they would scream out for to her to stick out her rear or to bend over forward so we could see her bust come bulging out of the dress she was wearing. Those were things that she didn't want to do anymore. She had started it a few years before to get attention. Now that she made it she resented having to do it all the time. She was not someone who was pleased with what went on in Hollywood. She didn't like the rules that were set up in becoming a star, and then the things they required you to do if you managed to make it."

All at once intense adoration would become frightening. She said, "If they love you that much without knowing you, they can also hate you." Garrett said: "The mob would start getting out of control. She would say to me, 'Could you get me out of here?' And I'd say, 'Marilyn, I don't think that's something I should be doing for you. If you need to get out of here, walk into the mob, get into a car, and leave. There are plenty of limos out there. If you feel that it's out of hand and you're being pushed around you should say, 'Hey I've had enough tonight and I'm leaving.' Then the part of her that was enjoying it would take over and she'd start posing again. A little while later, when I got near her, she'd say. 'Oh my God, I've got to get the heck out of here.' And an hour later she would say, 'Oh, my God, get me away from this.' It was just amazing. Here she was the biggest thing that anyone had ever seen in Hollywood, and no one really understood it. Including herself."

At breakneck speed 1953 went on to be a pivotal turning point for Marilyn. On June 26 Marilyn, along with her costar Jane Russell, was escorted to a block of wet cement in front of the Grauman's Chinese Theatre. In front of throngs of photographers and onlookers, together they would immortalize their own prints among those of the industry greats.

Marilyn was already in preparation for her next picture, a formulaic Western to be called *River of No Return*. In the movie she would play Kay, a down-on-her-luck "tramp" with a good heart, who works as a saloon singer during the gold rush in 1875 Canada. When Kay's crooked fiancé abandons her with a macho widower and his young son, Kay must travel across Indian-infested territory with them, often taking to the treacherous river on a wooden raft as they fight off Indians and other dangerous enemies.

Marilyn had no interest in appearing in a Western and thoroughly disliked the script, but the studio appeased her by hiring the popular, handsome hunk Robert Mitchum for her leading man (as the rugged widower) and the respected director Otto Preminger, who was responsible for classic films like *Laura* and *Forever Amber*.

In late June 1953 the cast and crew departed for Canada, where they would be shooting all the outdoor location shots—the movie was to be filmed in wide-screen CinemaScope to take advantage of many stunning backdrops for the outdoor drama.

Along with Natasha Lytess, Joe DiMaggio decided to accompany Marilyn to the location. He told her it was to keep her company, look out for her, and give her moral support. But another reason was to keep an eye on any sexual heat that might develop between his beautiful girlfriend and the notorious ladies' man Mitchum—especially since they had a few steamy scenes together.

Soon the filming became tumultuous and antagonistic. Preminger grew agitated by the presence of Marilyn's coach, Natasha Lytess, on the set and her meddling in Marilyn's acting. He vehemently disagreed with the control Natasha was exercising over Marilyn's characterization— with some justification. The overexaggerated lip movements and articulation that Natasha emphasized in her performances had worked perfectly for the first part of her career, when she was playing cartoonlike dumb blondes. But as a gutsy frontierswoman, she sounded bizarrely out of place.

River of No Return has the distinction of exhibiting Marilyn Monroe's worst performance: Working from a mediocre script, with a hostile director and an incompetent coach, Marilyn seems lost as to how to play the down-on-her-luck Kay. At times she appears to be attempting a hard-boiled, husky-voiced saloon singer, and in others she slips into Lorelei

Lee's baby voice. The result is a performance that comes across as awkward and petulant.

Yet this contrived Western is not without some merit. The outdoor location scenery is spectacularly beautiful, and Marilyn Monroe is even more so. At twenty-seven, Marilyn's physical appearance was as magnificent as it would ever be. And Marilyn and Mitchum manage to generate some on-screen chemistry, particular as he rubs her legs to warm her up after being soaked with freezing water.

While Marilyn was back at the studio shooting additional footage for *River of No Return,* Milton Greene arrived in Los Angeles from New York to photograph her for *Look* magazine. Greene was the hot photographer of the moment—considered a superstar in the field. But the person he most wanted to meet was Marilyn, and he asked her press agent to arrange it. Marilyn looked at Greene's portfolio—stunning portraits of Hollywood personalities that were both glamorous and revealing—and agreed to a meeting. When Marilyn first laid eyes on Greene the first thing that struck her was his boyish good looks.

"You're just a boy!" she exclaimed.

Greene didn't miss a beat. "You're just a girl!" the thirty-one-year-old photographer shot back. They clicked instantly.

Like Marilyn, Greene had been a stutterer as a child, and he was also awkward and shy. In contrast to his robust and outgoing brothers, Greene was scrawny and anemic-looking, but burning with ambition to improve and make a name for himself.

As an adult he rapidly rose through the ranks to become a superstar among fashion and celebrity photographers. With his success he learned to cover his anxiety with a calm and relaxed demeanor, "even when you knew everything was screaming inside," a friend said. Like Marilyn, Greene would go through phases when he would attempt to quiet his internal turmoil with alcohol and pills.

Feeling unappreciated and lost in the assembly-line type of production of the studio system, Marilyn once again needed to feel recognized and singled out. Greene fit the bill. He saw something in her no one else had since Johnny Hyde—he saw her potential to go further.

A photo session was set for 10:00 a.m. at the offices of *Look* magazine. Greene brought the clothes and all the props he wanted to use. Marilyn arrived on time, her makeup already done. Greene shot her in a bulky sweater, smoking and strumming on a mandoline, and naked under a black, floor-length sweater-robe she teasingly opened to allow an inviting flash of creamy flesh. There was a remarkable give-and-take between photographer and model, and their chemistry emanates from the photos.

Always on the lookout for someone who could help her and be on her team, Marilyn was able to focus on the person who was in front of her to lean on for courage and direction. For the moment it was Milton Greene. She zeroed in on the possibilities of what they might accomplish together.

In spite of the multifaceted attraction they were developing for each other, Greene had recently become engaged to the dark, elegant, and self-assured Cuban-born Amy Franco, who had been a model and then a fashion buyer for Lord & Taylor.

Marilyn was in the midst of a deepening relationship with DiMaggio. Yet they felt an affinity for each other that was apparent to everyone who encountered them. Although she originally considered Marilyn a tacky sexpot, even Amy acknowledged their bond: "You have to understand that Milton and Marilyn spoke their own language," she said. "I'm not talking sex. . . . I'm just talking about the connection between two human beings."

Greene left Hollywood and went home to New York, but their bond was too strong to end there. When the pictures came out in *Look* he received a dozen roses from Marilyn. An excited call followed: "You made me look interesting!" she declared.

In October, Greene returned to Los Angeles with his new bride. Marilyn met Amy at a party given by Gene Kelly, who liked to entertain at his house on Rodeo Drive, informal get-togethers where the guests would play charades.

Milton and Marilyn continued to reveal more of themselves over long dinners. All the while Greene continued to take extraordinary photos of Marilyn. She told him about her past struggles to make it in Hollywood and what she had to go through to achieve her current level of success. She was proud of her accomplishments, but she was afraid—afraid that if she kept playing the same type of characters over and over the public would grow tired of her.

She was resentful that the studio treated her like a commodity and refused to listen to her ambitions to play different kinds of characters. Above all else she was passionate, and Greene got caught up in her passions. She needed someone on her side who understood and connected with her image of how she saw herself—a serious artist. Greene saw it.

"I'll help you," he told her.

TEN

DISSATISFACTIONS

Without even notifying Marilyn, the studio announced to the press that her movie following *River of No Return* would be a musical comedy titled *The Girl in the Pink Tights*. Her leading man would be Frank Sinatra.

Until then Marilyn had accepted all the roles the studio offered her and worked exceedingly hard on each film set. Marilyn would get top billing in the *The Girl in Pink Tights*, but Sinatra would be paid $5,000 a week, while Marilyn would continue to get $1,250, holding her to the terms of her 1951 contract.

Although Marilyn knew her worth to the studio, she kept repeating that she didn't care about the money. She wanted Zanuck and the other Fox executives to appreciate her. She demanded that they allow her to see the script before preproduction. The studio refused. Meanwhile DiMaggio would remind her of the importance of money—money meant respect. DiMaggio still disapproved of her career; he would have preferred her to get out of show business altogether and let him take care of her. But he loved Marilyn, and so he couldn't help but get involved in conferring with her lawyer and her agent. Most of all he wanted to marry her.

Natasha Lytess, on the other hand, sided with the studio. She wanted Marilyn to make *The Girl in Pink Tights* and encouraged her to do so. Not that she thought it would be a good movie—she couldn't know one way or another about that; no one had seen the script. Natasha was worried about what would happen to *her* salary if Marilyn didn't work.

Completely financially dependent on Marilyn, Natasha asked her for five thousand dollars for a down payment on a house. Marilyn didn't give her that, but she sold a fur stole that Johnny Hyde had given her so that she could give Natasha one thousand dollars. On the inside some anger toward Natasha started to build.

Following Joe DiMaggio's advice, Marilyn responded to the studio's demands with silence. She simply stopped attending meetings, answering the phone, or responding to telegrams from Fox regarding *The Girl in Pink Tights*. Marilyn and DiMaggio spent most days holed up in her Doheny Drive apartment, ignoring the phone and not answering the door.

Marilyn's behavior baffled and confounded the studio. There were thousands of Hollywood starlets dreaming of being exactly where she was. "Why doesn't she just content herself with being blond, beautiful, and bewitching? Think of all the girls who would be happy just being Marilyn Monroe," stated a coworker at Fox. They were offended by her artistic aspirations. They made fun of her and laughed at her for trying to take herself seriously. They thought she was absurd.

After three months she had still given Fox no indication that she would be doing *Pink Tights*. Outraged, they threatened to replace her with a pretty young starlet named Sheree North. In an attempt to intimidate Marilyn into doing what she was told, Fox set out to demonstrate how unspectacular and disposable she really was.

They intended to create another Marilyn Monroe, threatening that all it would take was a starlet with a nice figure and a pretty face, blond hair dye, and some revealing costumes. It didn't work.

Finally, desperate to get Marilyn in front of the cameras, Zanuck sent her a copy of the script. *The Girl in Pink Tights* would have Marilyn playing a primary-school teacher who becomes a burlesque queen in order to put her boyfriend through medical school. Mortified, she announced that she "blushed to the toes" at the thought of herself playing "a rear-wiggling school teacher doing bumps and grinds in the great name of medicine."

She dashed off a polite but curt answer to Zanuck informing him she had read the script: "I am exceedingly sorry. But I do not like it." Zanuck was beside himself with fury. On January 4 he suspended Marilyn without pay.

Uncertain of her future at the studio, Marilyn was secure in DiMaggio's love for her. He was due to leave for Japan in late January. It was baseball season there, and he was scheduled to coach Japanese players. DiMaggio wanted Marilyn to be with him on the trip. He had been asking her to marry him for a long time, and now she said yes.

They both agreed to a quiet wedding. Their names had appeared in the press enough; a simple ceremony at San Francisco City Hall sounded best. Marilyn had, however, promised Fox's head of publicity, Harry Brand, that if she ever married she would let him know. True to her word, she informed Brand that she would be marrying DiMaggio. When Joe and Marilyn arrived at the judge's chambers on January 14 they found the hall jammed with at least five hundred reporters, photographers, and fans.

The couple exchanged rings. Joe slipped a platinum eternity band set with thirty-five baguette-cut diamonds onto Marilyn's finger. After the three-minute ceremony they posed for some pictures and answered a few questions from the reporters. "Marriage is my main career from now on," Marilyn said, caught up in the moment's excitement and romance.

After a quiet honeymoon in a secluded mountain lodge in Idyllwild near Palm Springs, they reentered the world as man and wife. Although they deeply loved each other, the differences in their expectations of married life would become more apparent with each passing day. He would resolve that he would accept her career—and then he'd explode in fits of rage and jealousy. When she confronted him, he'd turn his anger inward and become silent.

To fulfill DiMaggio's obligation to go to Japan and train Japanese baseball players, Marilyn and DiMaggio left from San Francisco and headed for their first stop in Hawaii. Marilyn was used to enthusiastic crowds— as was DiMaggio—but the mob that waited for them at the Hawaiian airport was unruly and assertive in a way that neither of them had ever experienced. They grabbed at Marilyn and kept reaching for her hair, pulling it out by the roots. This kind of physical aggression was something new to Marilyn, and she was really afraid. Shaken and manhandled, she said she wanted to go back home—but she was assured that in Japan the people would be more subdued.

But when the famous couple landed at Haneda International Airport in Tokyo, the fans were just as fanatical. When the plane landed, Marilyn was astonished to see hundreds of policemen trying to hold back ten thousand frantic movie buffs screaming, *"mon-chan! mon-chan!"* which means "sweet little girl." Marilyn was too terrified to get off the plane. They opened the door and let the other passengers out while Marilyn secretly crawled through the baggage hatchway to a waiting limousine. When they arrived at the Imperial Hotel, the staff closed the lobby doors and stood guard, but crazed fans hurled themselves at the doors, shattering the glass.

The next day, to satisfy the legion of fans, the DiMaggios gave a press conference. For the first time Joe would experience just how much Marilyn's fame eclipsed his own. He was used to being the center of attention— he was a sports legend, an American hero. But it was Marilyn everyone wanted to see and hear about.

While DiMaggio was training the Japanese baseball players, Marilyn received an invitation from the head of the U.S. Far East Command, Gen. John E. Hull, to entertain the troops in Korea. Marilyn, who gave the soldiers a great deal of credit for her success—she was their favorite pinup girl—wanted to go.

Naturally Joe was against it. Their first argument as a married couple followed. DiMaggio had married her to whisk her away from show business, which he loathed, so she would be out of the spotlight and could devote her attention to him. Now he was starting to realize that no matter what, Marilyn would always belong to the public.

Since Joe would be busy anyway, Marilyn decided to go to Korea to entertain the thousands of U.S. troops stationed there. "It's your honeymoon," DiMaggio said sullenly. It was an early indication that their marriage was doomed.

On February 16 she flew to Seoul, where she was greeted by a blast of frigid air. The temperatures were below zero, and Marilyn hadn't brought casual, warm clothes. The army outfitted her with army boots, khaki pants, and a sheepskin-lined leather jacket.

When Marilyn agreed to entertain the troops, the army assigned the twenty-one-year-old pianist Al Guastafeste, who was called "Gus," to do the musical arrangements for Marilyn and conduct the rehearsals with the other members of the band.

"We went down to Osaka army hospital to meet her," Guastafeste recalled. "I can see her today as if it were yesterday. She was wearing tan corduroy pants, a black long-sleeve sweater. Very little makeup. But her eyes were so blue and clear. She was sparkling."

Guastafeste discovered that Marilyn approached this performance with the same perfectionism that she did with any movie assignment. "She would ask me, 'Gus, can you hear my lyrics? Are they clear? Are my movements correct? Am I in time with the music?' Every time we stopped going over something, she always had another reason to go over it again." Guastafeste kept reassuring her that he would be there for her.

Marilyn's costume was a skintight beaded dress with spaghetti straps, which left much of her skin exposed. "This was February; it was freezing," Guastafeste continued. "I told Marilyn, 'Wear your fur coat. You're going to catch a cold!' She said, 'Oh no! This is how they want to see me.' That's why I admired her so much. All she was concerned about was entertaining the troops and making them happy."

Marilyn would make her entrance to cheers, whistles, and popping flashbulbs. "She had all kinds of movements in her songs, which of course aroused them in more ways than one," Guastafeste said. One journalist quipped: "She sang a little. But nobody minded that."

In Korea the show traveled from location to location in ten helicopters. The temperature was usually zero degrees Fahrenheit in the frozen Korean terrain. Guastafeste goes on: "But she had to sleep the same way we slept—in tents. In freezing weather. We had sleeping bags on top of a cot." She took icy cold showers, washing as quickly as possible. For food she went on the chow line with everybody else.

Guastafeste remembered: "Over there in Korea—during those times—the soldiers were throwing away the food they didn't finish, you had all the little kids hanging around taking the food out of the garbage pails. Of course when Marilyn saw this, she told the kids, 'Here, take this.' Then we all did that."

Marilyn always made time to shake a soldier's hand, and while she was there she patiently posed for thousands of pictures—always beaming, always flashing her famous openmouthed smile—it was reported that so many pictures were snapped of Marilyn that Korea ran out of film.

In four days Marilyn completed nine shows (and quite a few brief appearances) for more than one hundred thousand soldiers. Guastafeste sat next to Marilyn en route back to Japan. He asked her what she wanted to do with her life. Marilyn replied, "I want to be a dramatic actress."

By the time she returned to Japan and was reunited with DiMaggio, Marilyn was suffering from pneumonia. Still she was elated. "Joe," she exclaimed, "you never heard such cheering!"

"Yes I have," he replied, reminding her of his illustrious baseball career. "Don't let it go to your head. Just miss the ball once. You'll see they can boo as loud as they can cheer."

When DiMaggio and Marilyn returned to San Francisco, she was still recovering from pneumonia. While she convalesced in DiMaggio's house, he was called away to New York on business. Marilyn had never been loved the way DiMaggio loved her, and that meant a lot to her. She hated to lose anyone, and even though she was starting to feel delicate cracks in the marriage, she still clung to the idea that they could work it out. She needed to believe in some kind of permanence.

Always tugging at her was the part of Marilyn that wanted to be a good wife and mother, and when Joe returned, she did her best to live a domestic life, living quietly in his two-story house. She made it a point to become a loving friend to Joe's twelve-year-old son, Joe Jr., and she visited him at his boarding school. She would remain close to him until the day she died.

But after a few months she grew bored and dissatisfied. During the day DiMaggio wanted to watch television most of the time. At night he would work at his restaurant. Marilyn would sometimes sit in the back reading, in between greeting his customers. Before long she was once again itching to work.

DiMaggio still had hopes of changing Marilyn, but he felt the best thing to do was be supportive until he could ease her into a more traditional married life. For the time being he moved to Los Angeles with her, and rented a house on N. Palm Drive in Beverly Hills, while she resumed her career. She signed with Famous Artists Agency, where Charlie Feldman was a top agent. (In fact he had been handling her career—without pay—for a long time.)

Feldman finally convinced Fox that *Pink Tights* was not a suitable project for Marilyn. The studio threw up its hands; after all the headlines and fuss made about the picture, Fox quietly dropped any plans for making the movie at all. Apparently Zanuck felt that, without Marilyn, the screenplay wasn't good enough to be carried by any other actress.*

---

*   In March 1954 a Broadway show entitled *The Girl in Pink Tights* opened on Broadway. It has often been reported that this was the Broadway show that Marilyn's aborted film was based on. However, by the time the eponymous play premiered, Fox's musical had already been shelved. The two scripts had nothing to do with each other. It is unknown whether the highly publicized, unmade Monroe vehicle influenced the title of the Broadway play in an attempt to make audiences connect the two separate vehicles: By now everything and anything associated with Marilyn Monroe was newsworthy and sure to pique the public's interest.

ELEVEN

Marilyn Monroe was unlike any movie star Hollywood had ever dealt with—and if 20th Century-Fox wanted her in their movies, they were going to have to give a little. Her tough stance didn't make them respect her, or even like her any more than they had before, but they had to acknowledge her phenomenal appeal—and to them that translated into dollars.

Fox approved a new contract for her to go into effect the coming August, and they would give her a one-hundred-thousand-dollar bonus if she agreed to costar in a musical extravaganza called *There's No Business Like Show Business*. In spite of it being a big splashy musical, Marilyn was not thrilled with the project. The script used a threadbare plot as an excuse to string together a bunch of spectacular Irving Berlin musical numbers.

But for her next film, Charlie Feldman had managed to persuade Darryl Zanuck to buy the film rights to *The Seven Year Itch*, a Broadway smash that offered her a deftly written comic role—and she would be directed by Billy Wilder, one of the best in the business. Although hers would be another dumb-blonde character, *The Seven Year Itch* would offer her quality comedy. Feldman himself would produce. With the promise of that superior project, Marilyn agreed to sing and wiggle her way through *There's No Business Like Show Business*.

The plot, if it can be called that, follows the rise from obscurity to fame of a show-business family known as "the Five Donahues." The matriarch of the family would be played by the big, brassy, belting theater star Ethel Merman; the patriarch would be the veteran song-and-dance man Dan

Dailey. Donald O'Connor, Mitzi Gaynor, and Ray Anthony were cast as their adult children. They would provide the razzle-dazzle showmanship for Irving Berlin's classic songs. Fox cast Marilyn to add the sex appeal.

Although she could appear happy at times on the set, at home Marilyn was having difficulties with DiMaggio. Their brief marriage was in trouble. DiMaggio continued spending days watching television, chain-smoking, and waiting for Marilyn to come home from the studio. Marilyn, exhausted from a grueling day of work, would arrive late, only to have a long argument with DiMaggio. Some would say that, in his anger and obsessive passion for Marilyn, DiMaggio would become physically abusive. Upset and riled from an evening arguing with DiMaggio, Marilyn would need pills in order to get to sleep.

Marilyn would show up at the studio groggy and half doped from the previous night's sedatives. "When I come to work in the morning, my hair looks as if Joe has combed it with a baseball bat," she joked.

Marilyn collapsed three times on the set, causing the movie to be shut down each time. "She's been overworked and is ill a lot," the publicity department announced. The public had no idea of her growing dependency on sleeping pills. Instead it was reported that she had the flu, which lingered. She really was run down and sick. On each occasion she was ordered home to rest by the studio doctor. Each time the press would speculate that Marilyn was pregnant.

Freed from the stilted dialogue and let loose to interpret Irving Berlin's wonderful lyrics, Marilyn actually does her best work in the movie's musical numbers. Hearing her perform "After You Get What You Want You Don't Want it," Irving Berlin gushed, "Marilyn's interpretation gives it a sexiness I didn't know it had." Berlin also went "dizzy with delight" when he heard her rendition of "Lazy." Earl Wilson reported: "When Marilyn sings, you can't take your eyes off her voice."

In *There's No Business Like Show Business*, Marilyn completely transforms another, much-better-known song with her sensual interpretation. When the movie was released, her performance of the "Heat Wave" number would become the most-talked-about scene of the film. Marilyn's costume—a Carmen Miranda–like headdress, bra top, and flared skirt slit up the middle—is part of the seduction: "Hot and humid nights can be expected," she promises.

Released in time for the Christmas holidays, *There's No Business Like Show Business* was the kind of flashy but mindless musical entertainment that audiences of the day ate up, and they came in respectable numbers to feast on this lavish spectacle.

When it came to Marilyn, the focus was on her sexuality. The *New York Times* dismissed her performance, scolding that the "wriggling and squirming" in her musical numbers were "embarrassing to behold." *Variety* did advise that "Miss Monroe's treatment of her vocals must be seen to be appreciated."

Immediately after completing *There's No Business Like Show Business*, Marilyn started filming her next movie—which was considered a quality production with a substantially higher level of sophistication. After seven years of monogamy the sexual spark begins to go out of a marriage, leaving one (or both) partners to start desiring some action outside the relationship. That is the intriguing premise of George Axelrod's farce *The Seven Year Itch*.

Marilyn was excited to be working with a director for whom she had a lot of admiration, Billy Wilder, responsible for such classics as *Sunset Blvd.* and *Sabrina*. George Axelrod, a master of the witty double entendre, was adapting his Broadway play for the screen.

The plot of *The Seven Year Itch* revolves around a man, Richard Sherman (Tom Ewell), who is left alone in Manhattan while his wife and young son have gone to the country for the summer. After seven years of marriage, Sherman's head is filled with heated sexual fantasies that have him pacing nervously around his apartment and talking to himself. On his first night alone a delectable "Girl," played by Marilyn, rings his doorbell to let her into the building because she has forgotten her key. The beautiful blonde has sublet the apartment upstairs for the summer. Marilyn is not given a name in the movie because she is everyman's fantasy figure—a "living doll" with a voluptuous body and a baby face who keeps her panties in the icebox in an effort to stay cool during the scorching summer.

Wilder was intrigued by the idea of directing Monroe, who, as far as he was concerned, embodied irresistible contrasting qualities that always seemed to be compellingly at odds with one another. "She had a kind of elegant vulgarity about her. That, I think, was very important," he observed.

Marilyn left for location work in New York on September 8, 1954. Her presence in Manhattan dominated the newspapers for her entire stay—usually with the kind of coverage that announced her arrival: "Marilyn Wiggles In."

During her stay Marilyn was seen around town socializing with Milton and Amy Greene. It was as if she were a rare exotic bird and the press were avid watchers waiting for any sighting of her. It was reported that, while at El Morocco, Marilyn ordered a glass of milk before leaving for her hotel. The reporter also noted that "on the sidewalk outside the club she removed her shoes," going on to say she still was not wearing stockings, considered quite unseemly in the day.

The Greenes seemed protective of her. In the previous months Marilyn had secretly kept in touch with Milton. During several meetings with Greene, she talked intensely, compulsively, about the possibility of breaking away from the studio and forming her own company so she could pick and choose her own properties, directors, and costars. It was a radical plan for a twenty-eight-year-old female star—but there had never been a star quite like Marilyn Monroe. Greene had his lawyer look over her Fox contract to see if there was any loophole to get her out of it.

It would have been easy to film the brief outdoor scenes on a soundstage at the Fox lot. But both the studio and Billy Wilder saw millions of dollars in free publicity by bringing Marilyn to Manhattan and having her perform a couple of scenes in front of the press and the public. Describing it as "A Marilyn Invasion," Earl Wilson reported that "Miss Monroe's widely seen physique will be glimpsed right out in the public streets."

The columnist Walter Winchell called DiMaggio and told him he should come to town and watch Marilyn film the upcoming segment. DiMaggio argued that he had no interest in filmmaking, but Winchell convinced him that something extraordinary would be taking place. Joe changed his mind and decided to join Marilyn in Manhattan, just in time to catch the filming of one of the most iconic scenes in cinema history.

Although he couldn't know it at the time, it would be the last straw in their marriage.

The publicity bonanza was scheduled to be filmed at 1:00 a.m. on September 14 in front of the Trans-Lux Theater on Lexington and Fifty-second Street. Wilder chose to shoot the scene in the middle of the night because the city streets would be less hectic, but still a police barricade held back thousands of onlookers. In the segment, "the Girl" and Sherman are coming out of the movie theater after seeing *The Creature from the Black Lagoon*.

Marilyn is wearing a white halter dress with a pleated skirt that is now one of the most recognizable costumes in Hollywood history. As they stand on a subway grating, a train passes underneath, causing the Girl's skirt to fly up, revealing her panties. "Isn't it delicious?" she squeals.

The special-effects man, Paul Wurtzel, had been positioned under the sidewalk grating along with a giant fan, and on cue he would turn on the machine, causing a blast of air to sweep up the pleats of her dress. Marilyn's exhibitionist side took over, and she thoroughly enjoyed doing take after take as the gusts of cool air blew her skirt up, sometimes above her knees, sometimes to the waist, and at times over her head. Her panties were exposed. The cameras rolling, the photographers clicking, the crowd cheering, "Higher! Higher!" she turned this way and that, smiling and posing.

DiMaggio stood watching the exhibition with Winchell. Wilder looked over at him: DiMaggio's face, rigid with tension, had gone white. "He had the look of death," Wilder observed. "What the hell is going on here?" DiMaggio rasped. He turned away and headed back to the hotel.

When Marilyn returned from the location, exhausted, in the early morning, they argued terribly. Guests in neighboring rooms could hear them shouting at each other through the walls. The following day Marilyn had bruises on her arms that had to be covered with makeup—caused by DiMaggio either roughing her up or grabbing her tightly with passion and despair.

They continued to be seen together for a few remaining nights in Manhattan—although rumors of their inevitable breakup were already circulating. They were photographed with tense smiles at the Stork Club, having drinks with Milton and Amy Greene. Amy noticed the bruises on

Marilyn's arms. But when a journalist got a moment with Marilyn alone and asked her if there was trouble in her marriage, she filtered reality: "Everything's fine with us. A person's life is more important than any career."

In reality she was starting to find out that DiMaggio didn't fit into her future plans. They loved each other deeply, but she was discovering that wasn't enough. A woman like Marilyn needed to be stimulated and excited. She was interested in everything and always yearning to learn about new things. DiMaggio was content sitting in front of the television watching sports; he liked Marilyn being there. It wasn't necessary to make every day an exploration, an event. But Marilyn was burning with unrealized potential. She had to find some way to develop and release it.

Naturally Marilyn became closer to Milton Greene, who had always recognized her as an exceptional human being and singular talent—at the moment, that was oxygen to her. With her marriage unraveling, Marilyn needed a champion more than anything else.

Greene himself wanted to expand his creativity by branching out into the movie world. In his vision he saw himself forming a company with Marilyn. In late 1954 it seemed that anything was possible for her.

Back in Los Angeles, Marilyn began talking to Joe about a divorce— although she was wounded by it. She informed him that they would no longer share a bedroom in the house. DiMaggio kept thinking that she wouldn't go through with it, and, in her fear of being alone and unloved, she continued to give mixed signals, sleeping with him the night that she filed for divorce, and even on the night the divorce was actually granted. It was a way for Marilyn to assure herself that his love would remain solid—and through the years she'd turn to him again and again. Through triumphs and tragedies, affairs, movies, and even another marriage, she never let DiMaggio go completely—and he continued to hold on to her.

On October 6, on the arm of celebrity lawyer Jerry Geisler, a very tearful Marilyn announced to a mob of reporters that she was filing for divorce. Geisler would handle Marilyn in what she planned to be a very quick, friendly, and uncontested divorce from DiMaggio.

DiMaggio was in fact devastated. His obsession with Marilyn exploded publicly and embarrassingly weeks after she filed for divorce on November 5, 1954. As his confusion, passion, and anger muddled, he was determined to prove that Marilyn was having an affair with her vocal coach from Fox, Hal Schaefer.

If DiMaggio had caught Marilyn in an adulterous situation he could have used the evidence to stop the divorce proceedings. Years later Schaefer admitted to a relationship: "Being in love with me was not permanent in any fashion with Marilyn. It was very difficult for her to hold on to anything. Because of her childhood she was standing on sand all the time. She didn't have any foundation."

DiMaggio was convinced that they were using the apartment of Marilyn's friend Sheila Stewart for trysts. While he was having dinner with Frank Sinatra, the two cooked up a harebrained scheme. The plan was to break into the apartment where they believed the couple were staying and catch them in the act of making love.

The two powerful celebrities had two detectives, Barney Ruditsky and Phil Irwin (and possibly a few other hired men), meet them at the apartment—to knock down the door. It sounded like an explosion. What turned this crime of passion into "theater of the absurd" was that the four men smashed into the wrong apartment, that of a fifty-year-old neighbor, Florence Kotz, who was fast asleep in her bed and later described it as a "night of terror."

Embarrassing as it was all around, it only cemented further Marilyn's reputation as a woman who could drive men mad. Two powerhouses, Frank Sinatra and Joe DiMaggio, had been embroiled in an escapade provoked by a preoccupation with her romantic activities. "The wrong door raid," as it came to be known, only fanned the flames of the public's burning fascination with the love life of Marilyn Monroe.

Marilyn continued making plans to form an independent film production company with Milton Greene. She took off, leaving a series of forgettable scripts originally intended for her. "I'm leaving Hollywood and coming to New York," Marilyn declared. "I feel I can be more myself there. After all, if I can't be myself, what's the good of being anything at all?"

TWELVE

Wearing a brunette wig and traveling under the name Zelda Zonk, on December 23, 1954, Marilyn flew back to New York with the express intention of reinventing herself. For the time being she would be staying with Milton and Amy Greene.

Milton Greene's home in Connecticut had a barn he had converted to a studio for himself. Greene fixed it up for Marilyn to stay in. It was a perfect place for her to find temporary refuge. Since it was separate from the main house, she had the security of a nearby family who she felt cared for her and were trying to help her—sometimes she babysat for Greene's one-year-old son, Joshua (she would play with him for hours)—and yet she had the privacy, the alone time she needed. She walked in the woods for hours every day. It was the first time she had ever lived in an organized home, and Marilyn found herself fascinated by the ordered way Amy Greene ran the house: The beds were made, meals were prepared, the dishes were done. "They're the only real family I've ever known," she gushed.*

But Marilyn was not so immersed in her life in Connecticut that she was not thinking about her career. One night Tennessee Williams came over and announced to Marilyn, "I'm finishing a new play called *Cat on a Hot Tin Roof,* and I want you to play Maggie." The play was a lusty southern drama, and Marilyn loved the idea of playing the sexually frustrated

---

* Susan Strasberg noted that Marilyn was always attaching herself to families.

Maggie, who is constantly trying to seduce her impotent (latent homosexual) husband so that they can produce an heir and get a big share of his dying father's inheritance. For several weeks she talked of nothing else. Knowing her inability to get anywhere on time, in addition to her extreme nervousness in public, Milton talked her out of live theater. "I don't think you could do this, kiddo," he said. "You're a movie star."

Greene had his lawyers, Frank Delaney, Irving Stein, and Lloyd Wright, go over Marilyn's old contract with Fox. (These lawyers would only be paid sporadically. Marilyn was again broke—and was expected to remain so until Marilyn Monroe Productions was official and was actually bringing in a profit.) The legal team felt there were enough loopholes to get Marilyn out of it. There was another contract with Fox that Charles Feldman had drawn up but Marilyn had never signed. "You can't have two contracts at the same time, both invalid," Greene declared.

On January 7, 1955, Marilyn and Milton officially launched Marilyn Monroe Productions at a press cocktail party, held in the Upper East Side apartment of the lawyer Frank Delaney. Eighty handpicked journalists and celebrity friends attended, along with wealthy businessmen whom Greene hoped might become investors.

Being the main asset of the company that bore her name, the "new" Marilyn, in white satin, looked every inch the movie star that defined the old Monroe. Marilyn was the president of Marilyn Monroe Productions, owning 51 percent of the shares of her own company. The remaining shares belonged to Milton Greene, who would act as vice president. "It feels wonderful being incorporated!" Marilyn exclaimed.

Fox—hearing of Marilyn's new production company—was in a dither. They released a statement saying that she was still very much under contract with them. They claimed ownership of Marilyn and took responsibility for her success.

Marilyn did not want to cut ties with Fox completely. In her mind her company and an agreement with Fox could coexist. She tried to clarify her intentions: "I've never said I won't make pictures for 20th Century-Fox. I think *The Seven Year Itch* is the best picture I ever made. I love working with Billy Wilder, and I learned a lot from him. I need somebody to help me, and he gave me great help."

For the time being Marilyn moved into the Gladstone Hotel on Manhattan's East Side, and began to take some acting classes with Constance Collier, the seventy-seven-year-old English stage and screen actress who had also coached Audrey Hepburn and Vivien Leigh.* She would return to the Greene's house on weekends. But her ambition was to study with Lee Strasberg at the Actors Studio, and she was already making plans to become part of the classes there.

At the urging of Elia Kazan, Marilyn joined the Actors Studio, where she would learn the Method, a technique developed by Strasberg based on the teachings of Russian theater innovator Konstantin Stanislavsky. Founded in 1947 by Kazan, Robert Lewis, and Cheryl Crawford, it was a place where professional and aspiring actors could study the art of acting. It was now run by Strasberg.

The basic philosophy of Method acting is "sense memory," meaning that actors should call up a memory from their own life experience to recreate the same emotional state as the character they are playing. Strasberg encouraged actors to be introspective. He would ask: "What would motivate me, the actor, to behave the way the character does?" This was the serious approach to acting that Marilyn had been craving. All along she had had the feeling that there were better ways for her to dredge up deeper-felt performances, to become a more nuanced actress—by incorporating emotions from her personal history into her characterizations, now she felt she had found them.

The Actors Studio was a nonprofit organization that was supported by contributions and benefits. It was a prestigious establishment. Actors who belonged to the studio at one time or another were Paul Newman, Joanne Woodward, James Dean, and Marilyn's friend Shelley Winters, among many others.

---

* Truman Capote talks about attending Collier's funeral with Marilyn in April 1955 in his book *Music for Chameleons*.

It was stars like these that gave the studio its prestige. Imagine what a name like Marilyn Monroe could do by being associated with the Actors Studio—the nation's greatest celebrity giving up everything to come and study with Lee Strasberg! He wanted her as a student, to help her accomplish her dreams, but he also had one eye on the amount of publicity and money her name would bring to the school.

Since this style of acting relied on understanding past experiences and behavior, psychoanalysis was recommended. That is not to suggest that Marilyn started psychoanalysis for the sole reason of improving her acting—being analyzed was all the rage at the time—but it certainly was one of the motivating factors. Therapy, she thought, would unlock her mind and slowly free her of the torments of her past.

On the recommendation of Milton Greene, she started seeing Dr. Margaret Hohenberg—who had been his analyst for several years—five times a week.

Going into deep therapy did indeed open up a terrifying can of worms in Marilyn. With Hohenberg she explored her lack of self-esteem, her obsessive need for the approval of others, her fear of being used and abandoned, and her inability to have lasting relationships. The hurt, isolation, sexual abuse, abandonment, and humiliation were brought to the surface and would become a defining factor in her work, relationships, and life: It would eat away at what little confidence and self-worth she had, and ultimately destroy her.

From this point on, both Lee Strasberg and his wife, Paula—a plump, dramatic, anxious woman who had once been an actress and believed in the Method—would play very important roles in Marilyn's life. When Strasberg first met Marilyn, he was struck by this already extraordinarily popular movie star's burning desire to be a serious actress. He was taken by her intelligence, charisma, and questioning mind.

Marilyn had almost no confidence in herself, so she found people to have it for her. With her substantial beauty and special qualities, it wasn't difficult to find friends, photographers, agents, and lovers who gave varying degrees of encouragement. When one of them did something that she perceived as a slight or an insult, she left them and found someone else to foster her belief in her worth.

Almost immediately Strasberg began devoting himself to Marilyn. And she, always on the lookout for a mentor who instilled faith, looked to Strasberg as a father-figure Svengali. Studying with Strasberg *would* improve her acting, but it also slowly destroyed any kind of work ethic she had.

All that mattered now was giving the most perfectly nuanced and real performance possible—to hell with schedules, direction, or even written lines. It would also worsen her fear of the camera and her ability to perform in any kind of professional manner. From now on Marilyn demanded even more from herself. Every time she stepped in front of a movie camera (which would become less and less frequent), it became pure torture.

Marilyn soon became a surrogate daughter to Lee and Paula, which upset the balance of the Strasberg family. Lee and Paula already had two children, their seventeen-year-old daughter, Susan, who was already making a name for herself as an actress, and a younger teenage son, Johnny. Often Marilyn would stay for dinner after her private class.

Along with the Greenes, the Strasbergs became her second adopted family in New York. In stark contrast to the outwardly structured and relatively calm life she lived in Connecticut, the Strasbergs' Manhattan apartment was filled with emotional chaos and fractured egos that led to fighting and dysfunction. Marilyn's presence added to this because Strasberg had been more or less neglectful of his two children when they were growing up. Now they saw him treat Marilyn as if she were his only child.

"Come over whenever you like," she was told. Soon Marilyn was going to their apartment very often. Even though this was a hopeful period in Marilyn's life, her darkness always found its way to the surface—and she would try to quelch it with her sleeping medications and champagne.

Before long Marilyn was showing up at the Strasbergs' apartment in the middle of the night, zonked out on sleeping pills, her hair a mess, haphazardly dressed in mismatched clothing—mumbling that she couldn't sleep. Paula might make some tea for her, and later Johnny would give her his bed while he slept on the couch. Lee would cradle Marilyn's head, singing her lullabies, stroking her blond locks. "She didn't get hugged at all when she was a child," he'd murmur to his daughter, Susan, who sometimes watched, confused and hurt, from the doorway. Her father had never treated *her* like that, and she would feel resentful.

Susan had already costarred in the movie version of *Picnic* and had recently been cast in the lead role in the Broadway production of *The Diary of Anne Frank*. But even she paled in comparison to Marilyn, and would admit that she sometimes felt jealous of her. Others who were close to the family say it was Marilyn who was envious of Susan, who was already being taken seriously as an actress.

As a new member of a dysfunctional family, Marilyn indulged her own dysfunctions. The psychotherapy was stirring up her demons, and she let them roam free through the Strasberg household. One night, coming home from the theater, Susan witnessed a heavily drugged Marilyn emerge from her brother's bedroom, where she had been sleeping. Her body was exposed through a flimsy, open robe. She watched as the nation's most adored star crawled sluggishly on all fours, like an injured animal, across the hallway floor toward her parent's room. She slumped in front of the bedroom door mumbling, "Lee, Lee." It was such a disturbing sight: Dear, sweet, delightful Marilyn—so charming during the day—driven by her demons to this pathetic state at night. Eventually Lee came out, half asleep himself, and walked Marilyn back to his son's empty bedroom. Susan stayed in the shadows at the end of the hallway, watching.

Some, like Susan, wondered if there might be sexual feelings between Marilyn and Strasberg. Marilyn understood the reaction she caused in the men who came in contact with her. Almost all of them felt her sexual pull. She wasn't ashamed of sex and on occasion would offer herself to the men in her life who were important to her—she didn't view it as something wrong, as long as it was of her choosing. Sometimes it was as if it were an act she felt was needed to get out of the way so they could get down to the relationship they were supposed to have with her. It might be a way of connecting them even more strongly to her, making them more devoted. Other times it was a way of rewarding them with an especially satisfying prize for being kind. Most friends agree that Lee Strasberg turned her down, but that didn't stop her from teasing him, flirting with him. That was inherent in Marilyn.

At first, she was too shy and afraid to attend classes at the Actors Studio and continued to study privately with Lee at his apartment. Over time she worked up the courage to attend sessions at the Actors Studio on Tuesdays and Fridays.

Peter Bogdanovich, who would go on to become a successful director, encountered Marilyn there and sneaked a few glances. He kept doing so. "She was so extraordinarily wrapped up in every syllable that Lee Strasberg was uttering, not as a student but as a worshipper," Bogdanovich recalled. "She looked like her life depended on understanding everything he was saying. I've never seen such kind of desperation, actually. It was touching."

Marilyn was older than most of the actors in the class, and they did their best to appear uninterested in this superstar among them. They considered themselves serious actors—Marilyn was merely a glitzy film personality.

THIRTEEN

Away from the pressures of actually making movies, Marilyn enjoyed being a movie star. Exhilarated and recharged by all that was happening to her in New York, March 1955, would become one of the highest-profile months of Marilyn's life. The photojournalist Ed Feingersh followed her around for a week in New York, capturing her in her hotel suite putting on makeup before attending the theater, being fitted for a costume for a charity event at Madison Square Garden (where she would ride a pink elephant), and taking a Manhattan subway. It was Feingersh who shot the famous photo of Marilyn dabbing Chanel No. 5 between her breasts.

The perfect event that connected Marilyn with the Actors Studio was the world premiere of *East of Eden,* which had been directed by Elia Kazan and would introduce James Dean to the moviegoing public. The special screening was to be a fund-raiser for the Actors Studio.

Marilyn agreed to be one of the celebrity ushers at the benefit premiere on March 9. Other ushers would include Carol Channing, Eva Marie Saint, and Jayne Meadows. The initial price for a seat at the screening ranged from $50 to $150. But when it was announced that Marilyn Monroe would be an usher, tickets were scalped for three times as much.

The night of the *East of Eden* premiere was charged with excitement, crowds lining the streets hoping to catch a glimpse of Marilyn. After the screening Marilyn's devoted teenage fan James Haspiel waited, hoping to catch a glimpse of Marilyn as she exited the theater to go to the afterparty.

At exactly midnight, the doors reopened and one could see about a dozen policemen with a tousled blonde head in the middle. "It was no small task getting Marilyn across that jammed street," Haspiel recalled. "I remember more than one person suddenly pirouetting out of the crowd, screaming hysterically, 'I touched her!'"

One of the notables attending the afterparty was Arthur Miller. He managed to break through the throngs that surrounded Marilyn that evening and spoke to her very briefly. Through the years they had both kept a line of communication open with notes and letters, maintaining a little flicker of hope that they might one day be able to pick up where they had left off. Later that evening Miller asked Paula Strasberg for Marilyn's number.

In April, Marilyn subleased an apartment at the Waldorf-Astoria Towers, and Miller came to see her there. Milton Greene was still very much a part of her life, but Manhattan was becoming her real home, and she spent less time in Connecticut now. Miller and Marilyn were meeting regularly, and—even though she had the most recognizable face on earth—they managed to keep it a secret: Marilyn had become a master of disguises.

A line could be drawn through Marilyn's life, separating it before her move to New York and after. This was her Renaissance period. Her experience of living in New York City, the people she would meet, the encounters she would have, the knowledge she would acquire would change her forever. As low and desperate as her evenings could be, she managed to face some days with curiosity and exhilaration. Marilyn would usually take a taxi to the Actors Studio classes and her private lessons with Strasberg. She would go around town with a kerchief over her hair and a plain polo coat. Often she would wear jeans and "sensible shoes."

When the weather was good and she wasn't too exhausted, she would walk back to her hotel. It delighted her that often when she walked down the street, guys would whistle at her. "You know she had a walk," Marilyn's press agent, Rupert Allan, noted. Often they didn't recognize her as Marilyn Monroe—and that especially pleased her. She realized she didn't have to be painted and groomed to get men's attention. "She loved it. Never with any vanity. She just thought it was a tribute to her sex."

Marilyn loved to tell the story about the time when—while she was in a taxi on her way to class—she noticed the driver kept looking at her in the rearview mirror. When he dropped her off he finally said to her, "You know, you're a helluva lot prettier than Marilyn Monroe because you don't use so much makeup."

It took many months of observing classes, but Marilyn finally worked up the courage to perform a scene from Eugene O'Neill's *Anna Christie* in front of a live audience. The role was that of a woman who had been left by her sailor father on a farm owned by relatives. Ultimately she flees from the family, which treats her cruelly, and eventually becomes a prostitute. She would be performing the scene with the much-respected actress Maureen Stapleton, who would be playing Marthy—an older waterfront woman she meets in a bar.

One of the rules at the Actors Studio was that after a scene the audience was expected not to applaud. Yet after Marilyn's performance the packed house broke out into spontaneous applause. They were astonished at her skill and her depth. Lee Strasberg himself observed, "It was wonderful. The luminous quality that she had on the screen was, oddly enough, not reduced but in some strange way enlarged in life."

When she wasn't in class or seeing her psychiatrist, she'd spend hours walking the streets, browsing the museums, cafés, and theaters. New York was an adventurous new place to her, and Marilyn never grew tired of exploring the city. Before the move she was often too shy and fearful to venture out, but the complexity, mystery, and earthy charms of Manhattan invigorated her.

She loved everything about New York—the fleeting encounters, the mysteries, each exchange of information with a stranger. In Los Angeles it had always been about networking and climbing and trying to make a connection that might lead to the next break. In New York she learned how to live just for its own sake—there was no need always to be selling herself; she could *be* herself and let people take it or leave it.

In the evenings she'd go out, glammed up in her movie-star-persona, with Milton Greene discreetly, protectively hovering in the background. She had discovered the New York theater scene, and she loved going to Broadway shows; she was fascinated to observe great actors carve out fully sustained performances in the course of one evening—and being able to re-create it night after night. These were real actors to her. During 1955 she saw shows like *Cat on a Hot Tin Roof* (which Tennessee Williams had originally offered Marilyn as a vehicle for her Broadway debut), *Inherit the Wind, Damn Yankees, Teahouse of the August Moon,* and many others. Rex Harrison was surprised and a little chagrined to find Marilyn in his dressing room after a performance of *My Fair Lady.* Harrison couldn't stop himself from staring at Marilyn, who was "doing wondrous things while looking at herself in two mirrors simultaneously."

The sight of Marilyn, lost in her own thoughts, staring into a mirror, was not an unusual one. Often at the studio she'd be discovered sitting naked before her dressing-room mirror "fascinated [by] her own beauty." Once Truman Capote, left at a dinner table in a Chinese restaurant while Marilyn lingered in the ladies' room, finally went to see what was keeping her. He found her gazing dreamily into the mirror. "What are you doing?" Capote demanded. "Looking at Her," Marilyn responded. (The Rostens, too, would notice her staring at the mirror, perfecting her makeup, wanting to—needing to—present "Marilyn Monroe" at times, even in relaxed, casual situations.)

One of her press agents explained: "When she goes to the powder room to wash her hands I have to send someone in to hand her out. She's just standing there before the mirror, transfixed, as if trying to believe the beautiful dame staring back really is Marilyn Monroe." Natasha Lytess also remembered Marilyn's relationship with her looking-glass: "She was naked all day long! And I'm not exaggerating! After breakfast . . . she spent all her days before her mirror, and she put on makeup like a very important surgery."

Actually Marilyn's preoccupation with her reflection was a form of narcissism without vanity. It wasn't so much that she was in love with the image she saw staring back; rather, she was checking for what was wrong with it, perfecting the reflection, doing her best to live up to the mythological creature she had become. That was the only part of herself she could solidly identify. Her beauty was all she had to shield herself. "She was never happy with herself," the press agent Rupert Allan noted. "Give her a mirror and she saw all the flaws. And she'd try to disguise them."

Meanwhile, in an attempt to woo her back to work, Fox bought the rights to *Bus Stop*, the critically acclaimed Broadway play by William Inge. Darryl Zanuck was pulling out his hair over her absence. Every month that went by was another month the studio would suffer the loss of the enormous profits her movies brought in. As he had with *The Seven Year Itch*, he was tempting her back by acquiring the rights to a successful Broadway play with a meaty part for her—that of an uneducated saloon singer who becomes the obsession of a naive cowboy.

"Why do you speak about love? All I could see now is the power she offered me," Arthur Miller wrote in *After the Fall*. When Miller left Marilyn in Los Angeles in 1951, without having had sex with her, he said: "I knew that I must flee or walk into a doom beyond all knowing." Now he was ready to walk into that doom.

By the late summer of 1955 Arthur Miller and Marilyn were secretly in the beginning stages of a full-fledged romance—although he was still married. At last they had a chance to explore the strong feelings that stirred when they first met in 1951. They were both going through great personal changes; it was the perfect time for Miller and Marilyn's initial attraction to blossom.

As Marilyn was taking root in New York City, Arthur Miller was turning forty. His approaching midlife most certainly had an effect on his growing desire to have Marilyn in his life. His marriage had been passionless and static. For the most part he viewed the last few years with Mary Slattery Miller as settling for conformity—for the midcentury idea of what a man should be—a monogamous family man with a devoted wife with a spotless reputation. But it was a cold home they lived in, without passion, without satisfaction. When the writer Jeffrey Meyers confronted Mary Slattery Miller about being repeatedly characterized as "a dull, boring, sexless wife who had been cast off when someone better turned up," she replied simply, "Maybe I was."

Miller had always felt secure and even superior in his talent—but his life was lacking in sexuality. Now his ego was stoked by being loved by the world's greatest symbol of beauty and sex. Miller was no longer in love with his wife, and Marilyn represented the last gasp of a middle-aged man trying to experience carnal delights.

He was also drying up artistically. Marilyn was a compelling woman. Miller looked to her not only to fulfill him personally but to reboot him creatively. "She was full of the most astonishing turns and revelations about people," he said. To him the free-spirited and uninhibited Marilyn offered the kind of adventurous freedom and pleasure he had been denying himself his entire life: She would be both a lover and a muse.

To Marilyn, Miller represented an open door leading to a safe place. Miller was considered one of America's finest playwrights, a great left-wing progressive thinker, and a New York intellectual. He was a god in her eyes. To her he was the right love in the right moment—exactly what she needed while she was struggling to be taken seriously by the public and her critics and Hollywood (her enemies).

His name and reputation would become a shield against the jokes that were aimed at her, a guard against the derogatory comments that people made about her. If a man like Miller respected or even—dare she think—loved her, the public, the industry, and the world would regard her as more than a vacuous sexual ornament. "He treated me as a human being," Marilyn would say. "He was a very sensitive human being, and he treated me as a sensitive person also."

Arthur Miller would say that he and Marilyn "slept with the sword of guilt between them." Presumably he felt guilt for abandoning his wife and family. But he also felt guilt for being involved with a woman with Marilyn's sexual history, which Miller viewed as shameful.

"I keep trying to teach myself to lose you. But I can't learn yet," he said to her.

"Why must you lose me?" she asked, bewildered, stung.

He already knew about her reputation for playing the Hollywood sexual game when he met her at Charles Feldman's party. Then Johnny Hyde had just died, and she went straight into a relationship with Elia Kazan. She also let Miller know she was available. He had heard about other men, too. "I can hate every man you were ever with but I can't hate you," Miller wrote to her. Marilyn's past promiscuity was the real sword between them.

Her sexual history stained all the good Miller saw in her, and she instinctively felt his guilt.

A letter from Marilyn to Miller is revealing: "It's doubly difficult to understand that you, the most different, most beautiful human being, chose me to love." Miller's shame made her feel unworthy of him.

But because they were living in the moment, it was easy for Miller to temporarily block out Marilyn's past and for her to block out his shame. She blinded herself to the problematic nature of a relationship with Miller. For instance, in the beginning Miller seemed to be tenderly teaching Marilyn about the ways of the world, trying to fill in the gaps in her lack of formal education. Eventually, though, it became apparent that he viewed Marilyn as intellectually beneath him.[*] "There is a danger for an artist of becoming a man who sees his role as teaching others and pronouncing judgment on one and all," Elia Kazan stated.

Miller started bringing Marilyn to spend time with his family in Flatbush. "She wanted to be part of our family," Miller's sister, the actress Joan Copeland, observed. "My mother made it comfortable for her, and my dad did. I did. So now she was in heaven because she had a nice boyfriend, she had a father, and a girlfriend. So it made her feel like an ordinary person. A real person who has a family."

"When she'd come to my parents' place in Brooklyn," Copeland continued, "all the kids in the neighborhood would gather outside the house.

---

[*] Eventually Marilyn would view Miller's behavior toward her as patronizing and condescending—she felt that he often judged her as being inadequate. Years after Marilyn's death, the interviewer Larry King asked Susan Strasberg if Marilyn was able to hold her own with Arthur Miller. Without missing a beat Strasberg shot back: "Was he able to hold his own with her?"

They'd bring chairs and stools to stand on and get a good look at Marilyn as she was coming and going. They'd wait for her to come out. My mother would come to the door and yell, 'Go away, children. Go away!' She'd try to scare them away. Marilyn loved it."

During this time Miller was being investigated by the House Un-American Activities Committee (HUAC). Like most of the people with whom Marilyn was surrounding herself now, Miller was a left-wing thinker. Years before, he had attended some meetings with other writers who identified themselves as communists and supported communist ideology. Because of those meetings Miller was a suspected communist. It's hard to convey how much fear there was of communism in America, or "the Red Scare," as it was called in the 1940s and 1950s. Many careers were ruined simply because one was suspected of attending meetings of the Communist Party. Since America was at such odds with Russia, the country lived in a state of fear of anything and anyone associated with communism.

If you were targeted and brought before the committee, one of the things you were expected to do in order to save yourself was to identify other people you saw at meetings or whom you suspected of having ties to the Communist Party. This Miller refused to do, which only made him more of an honorable man in Marilyn's eyes.*

In early 1956, 20th Century-Fox announced to the press that Marilyn would soon be returning to Hollywood to resume her career and make a movie for them. With Marilyn staying away for one year, Fox finally realized that they would have to give in to some of her demands.

Her salary was raised from a weekly check to one hundred thousand dollars per film. She would also be allowed to make one movie a year away from Fox with other studios. Remarkably, she would be contracted to make only four movies for Fox over the next seven years (an indication of how profitable her movies had been).

---

* When Elia Kazan was called before the committee he decided to name the names of his friends who attended communist meetings with him, presumably to save his own career, although it tortured him for the rest of his life. Miller considered this extremely dishonorable, and it severely damaged their friendship.

Most important to her, Marilyn was given director approval—meaning that if Fox was unable to sign a director she approved of, she didn't have to appear in the film. But one major concession Marilyn was unable to get under her new contract was script approval.

The fact that Marilyn was given director approval for her movies was quite revolutionary. No female star up to this point had had so much creative control with her studio. Other stars noted her victory with admiration, and Marilyn set a precedent for their own negotiations in the coming years.

She signed the contract on December 31, 1955. Marilyn's first movie under her new Fox contract would be *Bus Stop*, which would be made in conjunction with Marilyn Monroe Productions. What was most gratifying to Marilyn was that it demonstrated that the dumb blonde was not so dumb after all. "There is persuasive evidence that Marilyn Monroe is a shrewd businesswoman," *Time* proclaimed.

Although Marilyn had demonstrated her power, which was gratifying, it came at a cost. The male-dominated film industry would never forgive Marilyn for her victory. The notion that she had dared to break away and make demands only made her seem ungrateful, impertinent, demanding, and unreasonable. The result was that what she wanted most from her studio—respect as a performer—was not granted. In that way it was not really a victory. If anything, the movie industry now disliked her more than ever for not playing the game by their rules.

Arthur and Marilyn did not specifically talk about getting married, but by now their affair was being whispered about. While Marilyn was in Hollywood making *Bus Stop*, Miller planned on going to Nevada for a few weeks in order to divorce Mary.

In early February, Laurence Olivier and the playwright Terence Rattigan arrived in New York to discuss the movie version of the latter's *The Sleeping Prince*—the first movie to be produced by Marilyn's production company after she completed *Bus Stop*.

They met Marilyn at 2 Sutton Place. It was Milton Greene's Manhattan apartment—where she could live for the time being in order to save the company some money. Olivier and Rattigan patiently waited while, in the bedroom, Marilyn prepared herself to face them. Her delayed appearance was a familiar situation when she was gripped by her inferiority complex and fears of not appearing to be what was expected.

She'd sit in front of her mirror, once again conjuring up the enchanting creature they knew as Marilyn Monroe. By now the recipe had been perfected: a base of her natural magnetism with a mixture of lipstick and lashes and insecurity and perfume and alcohol and exhibitionism. By the time she would appear, at the height of everyone's anticipation, it was in a tizzy of perfume, glamour, powder, and sensuality—there was an air of breathlessness, a slight disarray, a girlish "Hello."

It was decided that Olivier would act opposite Marilyn and also direct the production. Olivier had appeared in the stage play opposite his wife, the two-time Academy Award winner Vivien Leigh.

They announced the project at a press conference held at the Plaza Hotel on February 9, 1956. The assembled media were surprised, amused, perplexed, and grudgingly admiring that Marilyn had managed to snare the great Shakespearean actor Sir Laurence Olivier to star in the very first production of her new company. Just one year before, she had been considered a va-va-voom star who was damaging her career by taking herself way too seriously. Perhaps they had underestimated her.

Yet Marilyn herself, in her own paradoxical way, didn't want to wipe away completely her reputation as a delicious dish. While answering questions—with Olivier, Terence Rattigan, and Milton Greene—Marilyn sat demurely listening, in a formfitting black cocktail dress. At one point she leaned over, and a strap on her dress broke. It caused complete pandemonium in the midst of flashing camera bulbs and general hysteria. A female reporter produced a safety pin, and Marilyn fixed the strap.

Once again she left the press scratching its collective head. Was she a ditzy sexpot who couldn't keep her tits in her dress? Or the head of a corporation producing movies with the world's greatest talents? Marilyn left them to sort it out. The dress strap popping at a key moment would be re-created for the opening sequence of *The Prince and the Showgirl*—almost exactly as it had occurred in the press conference. Marilyn had created a moment that was too good to squander.

FOURTEEN

"A DIFFERENT SUIT"

In February, at a press conference to announce the shooting of *Bus Stop*, a female reporter remarked, "You're wearing a high-necked dress, the last time I saw you, you weren't. Is this a new Marilyn? A new style?"

"No, I'm the same person," Marilyn replied thoughtfully. "But it's a different suit."

Bus Stop was William Inge's Broadway play about a naive young cowboy, Bo, who is in town for a rodeo where he hopes to find himself an "angel" to marry. On his first night out he sees a world-weary singer, who calls herself "Cherie," perform "That Old Black Magic" at the local saloon. Although she is a hillbilly with a tarnished past, Bo sees only her innocence and beauty. But Cherie has ambitions to go to Hollywood—blind to the fact that she doesn't have much talent. Most of the plot revolves around Bo's inept but sincere attempts to win Cherie's heart.

In Cherie, Marilyn saw a role in which she could use the Method techniques she had learned while studying in New York: There were certainly enough parallels with her own troubled life.

The studio secured Joshua Logan, a respected film and stage director, for the movie. He was on the list of directors Marilyn would agree to work with. But when Fox first approached him, Logan's initial reaction was no, because his opinion at the time was that "Marilyn Monroe can't act." After having dinner with her, however, Logan was won over by Marilyn's intense feelings and ideas for the role of Cherie. "She struck me as a much brighter person than I had ever imagined," he said. As they talked, she demonstrated the southern accent she planned to use.

Marilyn had no vanity about playing the character—her goal was realism. When the studio had typically flashy costumes designed for her to wear as Cherie, she instead went to the wardrobe department and rummaged through old costumes for the most worn-out clothes she could find. She chose a flimsy skirt and blouse and a cheap gold lamé coat with a rabbit-fur collar—all in keeping with a second-rate performer's idea of glamour.

As if the clothes didn't look pitiful enough, she pulled off fringe and poked holes in the fabric. The costume Cherie wears in her nightclub act was also realistically tacky—a skimpy green-and-black leotard with a long tail attached, which she wore with fishnet stockings. Marilyn tore at those stockings and had them ineptly darned, as if the costume had been worn and mended by dozens of performers before.

As vice president of Marilyn Monroe Productions, Milton Greene was very much involved with *Bus Stop*. Greene decided to change Marilyn's makeup, creating the ultra-pale appearance that Marilyn was to have in the movie. Greene envisioned Cherie—a performer who worked all night and slept all day—as having skin with the unhealthy pallor of a woman who rarely saw sunlight.

Shortly before filming was to begin, the role of Bo Decker, the lovestruck cowboy who sees the angel hidden within a tawdry saloon singer, went to a twenty-six-year-old screen newcomer, Don Murray. A rising stage actor, he was then winning great reviews on Broadway in *The Skin of Our Teeth*.

Joshua Logan also cast a young fair-haired ingénue, Hope Lange, whom he had seen in a television show, to play a waitress at the bus stop. Lange later found out that Marilyn tried to get her fired. "Even though I was no threat to her in any way, shape, or form," Lange said. Marilyn, with one eye on her image, wanted to be the only blonde in the movie. When Logan didn't fire her, Marilyn insisted that Lange's hair be dyed a shade darker. "But I didn't dislike her," Lange continued. "She was just immensely insecure."

In what was seemingly one of the most callous moves of Marilyn's life, she cut off Natasha Lytess without a word. Natasha reached out to Marilyn over and over, but Marilyn refused even to see her. When Marilyn felt used by someone, she was able to banish that person from her life without ever looking back. She could be very, very strong that way.

Was it the smothering domination Natasha had tried to exercise over Marilyn's life in their years working together? The sexual pressure she had put on her earlier in their relationship? Her greedy demands for more and more money, while trying to persuade her to make inferior movies simply for the salary? Likely all those factors came into play, along with the fact that Marilyn had decided that Natasha's techniques were a fraud.

That doesn't mean that Marilyn didn't need someone on a movie set (other than the director) coaching her. To be with her on this film she had also employed Paula Strasberg as her new drama coach, at the very generous salary of fifteen hundred dollars a week. Whether Paula Strasberg's techniques were any better than Natasha's for Marilyn's acting is not the point. Marilyn simply did not have the self-assurance to perform if she did not have someone she trusted there exclusively for her.

As she had with Natasha Lytess, Marilyn put most of her trust in Paula. As soon as Logan called out "Cut!" it was Paula to whom Marilyn looked for feedback rather than the director. It would be this way on every film Marilyn would make from then on. On the set of a Marilyn Monroe film Paula Strasberg now called the shots.

During the production of *Bus Stop*, a young publicist named Patricia "Pat" Newcomb was assigned to handle Marilyn's press and would briefly enter Marilyn's inner circle. A few years later Newcomb would become one of the major players in the last months of Marilyn's life, but their working relationship on *Bus Stop* was very short-lived and ended badly.

The newspapers and magazines were so crazed by Marilyn's return to filming that her public relations firm, Arthur P. Jacobs Co., Inc., sent the young publicist to handle the media during production on location in Phoenix. Newcomb was young, smart, and fiercely loyal to her celebrity clients. She was also known to have a volatile temper—she would slam her office door so hard that a framed picture of Dean Martin would fall off the wall, shattering the glass "every other day." At first Marilyn and Newcomb became friendly, but after only a few weeks of working on location, Marilyn had Newcomb fired and immediately sent home.

Through the years various reasons have been given for Newcomb's sudden dismissal. Newcomb said it wasn't until years later that she found out why Marilyn fired her. The way she understood it, Marilyn had thought Newcomb was interested in a guy she liked. Newcomb always maintained she wasn't.* Apparently Marilyn was dependent on, and in love with, Arthur Miller but didn't consider it exclusive yet, and she continued to flirt with and see other men.

A different but very interesting version was told to the biographer Donald Spoto by Rupert Allan, who handled most of Marilyn's press relations. According to Allan, Newcomb would take phone messages for Marilyn—many from men wanting to meet her. "Pat intercepted Marilyn's messages," Allan said. "She hogged."

Then, according to Allan, things went too far. Newcomb didn't particularly look like Marilyn, but perhaps with the right lighting and makeup she could pass. Fred Lawrence Guiles wrote in his biography, "Patricia Newcomb was a twenty-five-year-old Mills College graduate who resembled Marilyn physically. They were almost exactly the same height (almost five feet six); her thick hair was medium blond and hung loose to her shoulders."

Rupert Allan asserted that Newcomb went through "a lesbian phase" but also dated men.

Allan heard—and believed—that "Pat passed herself off as Marilyn one night to somebody. And it got back to Marilyn. Marilyn said, 'She's not Marilyn!'" If the story was true, someone trying to pass herself off as Marilyn would certainly infuriate her. "Marilyn couldn't forgive her," Allan said.

Whatever the reason, Newcomb found herself on a plane back to Los Angeles. It would be nearly five years before she and Marilyn would be in contact again. And at that time Newcomb would become one of the most

---

* In an effort to obtain Pat Newcomb's version of any of the events pertaining to her in this book, I wrote two detailed queries to her requesting an interview. Unfortunately she never responded.

important and controversial people in Marilyn's life—known as the keeper of her secrets and one of the last people to see Marilyn on the day she died.

On March 15, 1956, principal photography on *Bus Stop* began on location in Phoenix. The work Marilyn had done the previous year at the Actors Studio with Strasberg *did* make her a better actress, as was revealed in this movie. Everything about her as Cherie comes across as genuine and touching, from the way her body slumps exhaustedly in a chair to the exasperation and anger she displays when Bo pushes her around.

But this new depth in Marilyn's acting came at a price. Now there were demons on the set—her own demons that she called up from her past to use in her acting. The past was with her constantly now because it was part of her work—and the pressures she put herself under were worse than ever.

"She was the most nervous actor I'd ever worked with," Don Murray said. "She would break out into hives and her body would be covered with little red splotches, and they'd have to cover up with makeup."

Because it took Marilyn a long time to get back into character after a scene was stopped, Logan developed a unique way of working with her. Instead of saying "Cut!" he kept the cameras rolling. Sometimes he would simply say, "Begin again." She never broke character as long as the camera was rolling. Marilyn continued acting until she seemed to have exhausted every emotion she could bring to the scene. Only then would Logan stop the cameras.

This was wonderful for Marilyn but frustrating for the other actors, most of who came from the theater and were used to playing as an ensemble with strict discipline through continuous, sustained scenes. But when they saw the edited film, they were astonished. "She was magnificent!" Don Murray exclaimed.

Even with this unorthodox way of shooting, Marilyn would demand many takes if she felt she could do it better. It was already well known that Marilyn was very difficult to work with now; as part of the "new Marilyn" her inability to work in any kind of a professional manner was becoming part of her legend. "She just was out of control," Hope Lange said. "She was like a little baby. When you have an actress who wants thirty and forty takes. It can hold up the set for hours."

When the nights became too unbearable Marilyn would call Arthur Miller. As the production went on, Marilyn became more nervous and began to panic because she feared she wasn't giving a good-enough performance. Miller talked to her for hours as he reassured her: Yes, he loved her. Yes, she had talent. Yes, everything was going to be fine.

When *Bus Stop* was released, it looked as if all of Marilyn's ambitions to be considered seriously were beginning to be realized. The media tentatively began to acknowledge that her talent just might equal her sex appeal. Even Bosley Crowther of the *New York Times*, who before had viewed her as little more than a flashy performer, started his review by declaring: "Hold onto your chairs, everybody, and get set for a rattling surprise. Marilyn Monroe has finally proved herself an actress in *Bus Stop*. She and the picture are swell!"

Marilyn's performance in *Bus Stop* was universally praised and it made money, but ironically it wasn't as big a hit as her previous star vehicles for Fox. Even more disappointing was that she was not even nominated for an Academy Award.* The industry refused to reward Marilyn for anything—even greatness. She had become a star against the odds and then thumbed her nose at them, left Hollywood, lived and studied in New York, and started her own company. In their view she was ungrateful, and they weren't about to reward her for that.

On June 21, 1956, Miller was called to testify in front of the House Un-American Activities Committee in Washington about his alleged association with various communist organizations. Miller claimed that the day before the hearings, Representative Francis E. Walter of Pennsylvania let it be known to his lawyer that if Miller would permit him to take a

---

* "I never understood why she was not nominated for *Bus Stop*," Don Murray said. "That year it was won by Ingrid Bergman—a wonderful actress, there's no question about that—but Marilyn's performance in *Bus Stop* was so much richer, it had so much more variety, and it was so much more interesting than Ingrid Bergman's character in *Anastasia*."

photograph with Marilyn Monroe, he would call off the hearing. Miller said he refused.

Instead he dutifully admitted that he had attended a few Communist Party writer's meetings back in the 1940s. But when they asked him to name some of the colleagues he saw at those meetings, Miller, unlike his friend Elia Kazan, refused to name names. He would eventually be charged with contempt. But after the hearing, when Miller was asked about his future plans, he was willing to name one name that might help him get out of trouble. He announced that he would be marrying Marilyn Monroe. This was big news to everyone—including Marilyn.

Marilyn's friends said sarcastically that it didn't hurt—if you were being investigated by any congressional committee—to be engaged to America's number one sweetheart. It was noble of Miller not to give the names of people who might have been damaged by his testimony. He was, however, willing to use Marilyn's power and celebrity to help him be viewed more sympathetically by HUAC—even though doing so could have damaged her career.

After his brief press conference, Miller called her from Washington.

"I just announced to the press that we're going to be married," he said.

"The press already told me," she replied happily. "They're very fast when they want to be."

Marilyn was really over the moon. In that moment she adored the man and was honored that he would want to marry her. Friends of Miller's commented that she wanted to be married to one of the leading playwrights of the day.

Marilyn still found moments when she filled up with the familiar dread of oncoming doom, the childhood darkness, and in her blackest moments, she wanted to die. The actor Delos Smith, who studied with Marilyn at the Actors Studio, became very close to her. She was always saying to him, "Let's kill ourselves." She'd write it on his notepads during class. "That girl's not going to live," he thought. "I felt the wish, the wish to die. The death wish was strong because it represented freedom, escape," Smith recalled. "Sometimes she had this great bubbly beauty, but dank underwater like she was more submerged than we were, otherworldly, as if she were drowning."*

Very often death was more enticing to her than life, and she chased after it like a dream, like a lover, like sleep. As Miller recounted to actor Frank Langella, "We were hiding out in a little place in Brooklyn. She had just tried to off herself and it had been a nightmare. The press was all over us. So we were secretly holed up in this apartment, and she did it again. I couldn't face another circus. I looked for a doctor in the phone book in the neighborhood and called him. He went into the bedroom and saved her life."**

The doctor promised not to reveal what had happened, and he didn't want any payment. What he did want was Marilyn's autograph, which Miller supplied by holding a half-conscious Marilyn's hand to scrawl a signature on the doctor's prescription pad.

Miller said, "Beneath all her insouciance and wit, death was with her everywhere and at all times, and it may be that its acknowledged presence was what lent her poignancy, dancing at the edge of oblivion as she was."

Death was very much on her mind the day she and Miller made the official announcement of their marriage.

The press conference was to be held outside of Miller's home on Old Tophet Road in Roxbury, Connecticut, on June 22. On the way there, the press tailed Marilyn and Miller, who were driving very fast.

Mara Scherbattoff and Paul Slade, a journalist and photographer from *Paris Match,* following close behind, lost control, and slammed head-on into a tree. Slade was severely injured. Scherbattoff had flown into the car's windshield, her face was smashed. Miller, realizing something had happened, stopped the car and went back to investigate. Within moments Marilyn found herself helping to pull out the profusely bleeding Scherbattoff from the smashed windshield. Her broken and bloodied body was

---

* Susan Strasberg. *Marilyn and Me: Sisters, Rivals, Friends* (Time Warner Paperbacks; First Edition April 1992).
** Frank Langella. *Dropped Names* (Harper; February 26, 2012).

placed on the side of the road, where she lay in great pain—moaning and gurgling, her stomach convulsing.

Miller and Marilyn hurried back to the house to call for an ambulance. When told that it could take up to two hours for medical help to arrive, Miller said, "I think you should know, it's Marilyn Monroe back there on the road, and this will be on the front pages of every newspaper in the world tomorrow!" Because of this fib an ambulance was dispatched immediately. But it was still too late, Mara died on the operating table a few hours later.

Even with the gloom of this tragedy heavy in the atmosphere, the press conference had to go on. In the footage Miller is his usual somber, imperial self. Marilyn is in an emotional fog—hesitant, vague. Clearly something traumatizing had just happened.

On June 22, in a simple four-minute civil ceremony at the Westchester County Court House in White Plains, New York, a judge legally made Arthur Miller and Marilyn Monroe man and wife. Just a few days later, on July 1, the couple had planned a quiet wedding in the home of Miller's agent, Kay Brown—this one a Jewish ceremony for friends and family. (Marilyn had converted when she started to become serious with Miller.) Shortly before walking out among the waiting guests, while sitting in the bedroom with Milton and Amy Greene, Marilyn expressed that she didn't want to go through with the wedding. Greene said, "I'll take care of the guests, just go get in the car with Amy." At the last moment Marilyn said, "No. I better go through with it. After all, all the guests are already here."

Trying desperately to fight off any negative emotions or bad omens, Marilyn scrawled on the back of her wedding portrait: "Hope. Hope. Hope."

On July 6 Miller was granted his passport, which enabled him to travel to England with his new wife to start filming *The Prince and the Showgirl*. The movie's name had been changed from *The Sleeping Prince* to add the Marilyn character to the title and help ensure its success.

FIFTEEN

INNOCENT MONSTER

It should have been the high point of her life. On paper it was. Married to a man she looked up to for his intellect, a man who admired her. She was the head of her own production company, had secured a high-profile film property for herself, and was working with the most respected classical actor in the world. In fact Laurence Olivier was actually under the employ of the former orphan girl.

But instead of being cocooned in security and self-confidence, Marilyn felt enormous pressure to live up to the monster of her image and publicity. She was under the gun to prove herself as a real actress and at the same time maintain the delectable face, figure, and persona of the pinup-queen-turned-Hollywood-goddess.

Everything possible was being done to keep Marilyn calm during the filming. The Millers would be staying at Parkside House, a rented mansion in Surrey, England. It had a dozen rooms and sat on an acre of magnificent gardens. It also had a full staff of servants. The house was about an hour's drive from Pinewood Studios.

The Prince and the Showgirl was set in London, circa 1911. Grand Duke Charles, Prince Regent of Carpathia (Olivier), is taken to see a stage trifle, a comedy called *The Coconut Girl*. Smitten by the sight of her half-exposed bosom when the strap of her gown breaks, he invites Elsie to the embassy for a "late-night supper." Thinking it's a party, Elsie accepts the invitation. When she discovers that dinner is set only for two, she tries to flee. The movie becomes a series of encounters in which Elsie attempts to escape; the regent tries to get her into bed; she meets his approving, eccentric family; melts the prince's frozen heart; and shows a surprising, if naive, intelligence on matters of policy.

By now Marilyn's reputation for erratic on-set behavior was so widespread that Olivier began to worry. Indeed, things got off to a bad start on the first day of rehearsal. Olivier greeted the British cast and crew. These were Olivier's people, with whom he had worked over the course of many years. Then he introduced Marilyn. Already fraught with nerves, she immediately felt he was condescending toward her. In an instant she perceived—and perhaps rightly—that he viewed her as simply a popular Hollywood star for whom professional allowances must be made because, after all, she was not in their league.

Shooting began on August 7. Marilyn might arrive at the studio only an hour or two late, yet it could be hours before she appeared on the set, ready to work. *The Prince and the Showgirl* established the greatest conflict of her career: her desire to be a great artist, and the massive anxiety that overcame her while performing, crippling her with fear.

With the amount of stress she was under—a good deal of it self-inflicted—there was no way for her to get a decent amount of sleep without fairly massive doses of pills. Milton Greene found various ways of getting drugs sent over from America to England. He also rooted out doctors in Europe to supply them with pills. After being knocked out, she would awake depressed and sluggish. Amphetamines came into play to give her energy. Nothing in the scenario was new or shocking to Greene, who was deeply involved with pills to deal with his own demons. It was yet another area in which the movie star and her partner were soulmates.

Each shooting day Beatrice "Bumble" Dawson, a well-respected and much-loved dresser, had a very difficult time getting Marilyn into her costume. Depending on how much she had been eating or drinking, Marilyn's weight fluctuated wildly. (One of her Parkside House maids noted: "There were always empty champagne bottles around.") The costume she wears in the movie had to be made in three different sizes. Marilyn drove Dawson crazy. One day she would come in and her bust would be a size 36, the next day a size 40. To make matters more difficult, Marilyn refused to wear undergarments that could have contained her expanding breasts, belly, and hips. Eventually Dawson would grouse: "I have two ulcers: one is named 'Marilyn' and the other 'Monroe.'"

Even after she was dressed and made up, there were always long gaps before she'd arrive on the set. As the cast and crew waited, Marilyn lingered in the dressing room. There she felt safe and was usually sweet and accommodating. It was on the soundstage that the terrors gripped her and she became difficult. "Sometimes I feel a doom set over me," Marilyn said. "Just as I'm walking on the stage. I don't know why, but I get over it . . . sometimes. Sometimes it lasts all day."

When Marilyn finally did appear on the set, she might appear confused and vague—hungover from barbiturates and another night without sleep. While working, she was unable to follow the actions and lines of the other actors in the scene with her, and she had great difficulty saying her lines on cue.

Olivier claimed that he couldn't understand why Marilyn suddenly turned from the seductive creature he met in New York to this difficult, resentful, spoiled brat of a performer. Although he did concede, "Whenever those cameras rolled you couldn't look at anything else but Marilyn." Perhaps this was another reason for the tension between them. The British actor Robert Stephens once said of Olivier: "His one great fault was a paranoid jealousy of anyone who he thought was a rival."

One morning on the set, Olivier delivered the ultimate insult to Marilyn when, at a loss how to motivate her for a scene, he advised her to "be sexy." As far as she was concerned "sexy" was not something you could switch on or off. It was something you either were or weren't. If the scene called for her to feel sexual, that was one thing. But you couldn't command a performer to "be sexy."

From Marilyn's point of view it was Olivier who was approaching his role wrong—playing the prince too stoic, overly severe, giving the audience no indication that her character could ever break through and make him fall in love with her. She suspected that Olivier's motives were to have the audience focus on him. Arthur Miller wrote that Marilyn felt Olivier was "trying to compete with her like another woman, a coquette drawing the audience's sexual attention away from herself." There may have been just cause for Marilyn's suspicions.

The magic of movies—the magic of Marilyn—was that through all the frustrating waiting, through her anguish, paranoia, and fears, she was absolutely smashing in the rushes. When the cast and crew watched the dailies from the previous day's work, they were collectively astonished at the radiance and joy she projected—along with her expert comic timing.

This also played into Olivier's frustration with her.

Olivier wanted Marilyn to be good. Just not *that* good. "I don't think Laurence Olivier ever forgave Marilyn for being better than him in that movie," Susan Strasberg remarked.

"My hatred for her was one of the strongest emotions I had ever felt," Olivier said years after Marilyn's death.

It was in England that Arthur Miller for the first time got a glimpse into just how damaged and troubled Marilyn was. He was appalled at her unprofessional behavior on the set and how unreasonable she could be. He knew she was vulnerable and sensitive. Those were the reasons he fell in love with her. But now she seemed to be an unpleasant mixture of desperation, insecurity, and irrationality.

In her more lucid moments Marilyn acknowledged that she was not an easy person. "I can be a monster," she said matter-of-factly years later. "When we were first married, he saw me as so beautiful and innocent among the Hollywood wolves that I tried to be like that. I almost became his student in life and literature the way I'm Lee's student for acting. But when the monster showed, Arthur couldn't believe it. I disappointed him when that happened. But I felt he knew and loved all of me. I wasn't sweet all through. He should love the monster too."

Miller never knew when she might change into the accusing, vengeful Marilyn. Marilyn suspected Miller agreed with Olivier that she was an irrational bitch. He wasn't standing up for her. He was just like all the rest. Then she would collapse in despair, her anger replaced by the sorrowful self-lacerating woman. Miller never knew who he was dealing with or if he was dealing with her in the right way.

Fed up with her erratic behavior, negative attitude, and pleas for help,

Miller needed to let his feelings be known. Not wanting to confront Marilyn face-to-face, he wrote about her in his diary. Then he left the diary out in the open on a desk, next to her script—a place she was sure to see it.

Exactly what Miller wrote in the notebook has never been revealed, but reading her new husband's opinion of her was one of the most devastating, catastrophic moments in Marilyn's life. In *After the Fall*, his autobiographical play about their marriage, Miller says she read it in astonishment and then fainted.

Marilyn told friends that it described what a disappointment she had turned out to be. How Miller was embarrassed and ashamed of her in front of his friends. Distraught, she told Lee Strasberg that it had something to do with how at first he thought of her as some kind of an angel, and now he viewed her as a troublesome bitch. (Later she would claim he'd called her a "whore.")

In his play Miller claimed that he had written that the only person he could ever love was his daughter. He goes on to describe how, when they were at their first party as man and wife, he felt ashamed of Marilyn because he didn't know if his new wife had slept with any of the men there. "I swear to you," he reveals, "I did get to where I couldn't imagine what I'd ever been ashamed of. But it was too late. I had written that, and I was like all the others that had betrayed you, and I could never be trusted again."

The diary entry smashed any hope of him saving her from her continuous torment of unworthiness—or of them finding a happy life together. Miller became the embodiment of all the men in her life who took advantage and then looked down on her. He had judged her and found her to be a disappointment.

Although the marriage was shattered, they would spend the next three years trying to put the pieces together again. They tried to put the diary incident aside, and limped forward like wounded animals.

Dressed in formfitting scarlet, Marilyn caused a sensation at the UK premiere of Miller's play *A View from the Bridge*. She was practically mobbed at intermission, and took refuge with a bartender in a small room where refreshments were prepared. She had grown frightened of people staring at her.

Somewhere lost in all of this was Milton Greene. Marilyn was married to Arthur now, and that was putting up a wall between them. They were grappling with how they would fit into each other's lives—and the future of the company. Arthur Miller and Milton Greene had never really liked each other. Each tolerated the other because the common link was Marilyn. Now that Marilyn was married to Arthur, he started to subtly and negatively influence Marilyn's feelings about Milton.

Miller began telling Marilyn that Greene was in over his head with producing her films. In hindsight, this claim seems unfair. Yes, Greene was new, but he had done very well by Marilyn. Spending a lot of time alone with Marilyn, Miller started planting the seeds in her head that Greene was cheating her. Miller writes in his autobiography that Marilyn began to suspect that Greene was buying British antiques and charging them to Marilyn Monroe Productions.[*]

Still, she couldn't deny that the Greenes had supported her and promoted her in the way she wanted to be perceived for a year—when she was basically penniless. Sure they expected to get something from being associated with the phenomenon of the Monroe name—but Milton also seemed genuinely to have the good of her career at heart. Yet Marilyn, always sensitive to people betraying her, began to take on Miller's attitude toward Milton. She started to feel that Greene had been using her all along.

Marilyn was invited to meet Queen Elizabeth at a royal command performance of *The Battle of the River Plate* on October 29. It was to be a glittering event that would combine Hollywood royalty with literal royalty. At a royal command film performance various stars were invited to attend the premiere of a movie chosen by the palace. Whether they were connected to the film or just invited for the viewing, it was a tremendous honor. There was strict protocol with the queen involving "how to curtsey" and specific instructions like "no low cut gowns, no wearing black—because only the Queen can wear black."

---

[*] Although Marilyn was always suspicious of everyone double-crossing her when it came to personal loyalty, she was never concerned with financial matters. It's doubtful she would have suspected Milton of cheating the company (many people skimmed from Marilyn's finances without her batting an eye), and even if she did, she most likely would have simply ignored it.

Jack Cardiff—the cinematographer of *The Prince and the Showgirl* (among many other films)—attempted to give Marilyn some advice before the historic meeting. He explained that Queen Elizabeth had a difficult job—she must remain poised and pleasant without displaying emotion. Cardiff cautioned: "You're so beautiful, so attractive. Everyone will be saying, 'Isn't she wonderful?' So please don't bare your breasts to her. If you have those boobs out they'll all laugh at you." Marilyn listened intently and replied, with a perfectly straight face, "You're so right."

That night, shortly before leaving for the royal meeting, Cardiff witnessed Marilyn coming down the stairs in a formfitting gold lamé gown with her breasts taped up so that they pointed straight forward, almost popping out of the gown—a jaw-droppingly revealing décolletage.*

Just before the assembled celebrities were to be presented to the queen, twenty-two-year-old Brigitte Bardot rushed into one of the powder rooms for a last-minute makeup check. "There we were powdering our noses," Bardot recalled. Staring at each other's reflection, they greeted each other. "She was ravishing," Bardot said. "I will never forget it. She was incredibly lovely . . . like a baby. Fresh, beautiful, and pure."

As for Marilyn, who rarely acknowledged other blondes, she relented for Bardot. When asked about her French rival, Marilyn commented, "I think she is so charming."

The queen regally made her way down the line of guests; when she reached Marilyn they shook hands. While Marilyn curtsied, her bosom was revealed as if it were a serving tray displaying pastries. The queen's eyes flashed for only a moment on Marilyn's exposed breasts before she looked smilingly into her face as the two exchanged pleasantries.

Despite all the tensions, illnesses, hostilities, competiveness, no-shows, lateness, and retakes, *The Prince and The Showgirl* finally wrapped on November 16, 1956. It was eleven days over schedule—but, as Milton Greene liked to point out, under budget. On the last day of filming Marilyn was

---

* Marilyn was slightly plumper now, and would become more so. The weight, to her pleasure, traveled to her bosom. Why hide it? For maximum impact, when she arrived she wore a full-length gold lamé cape wrapped around her—completely covered from the neck down—which gave her a great air of elegance. Once inside she shed the cape for the big "reveal."

actually contrite about her behavior on the film. She addressed the entire cast and crew and begged them to forgive her. She said that she had been ill throughout the filming. Four days later, lovely but windblown and sleepy looking, she flew back to the United States to attempt a happy life with Miller.

SIXTEEN

MARRIAGE

Their marriage hit the iceberg in England, but neither was ready to admit defeat. They sailed deeper into their partnership—somewhat wary and disillusioned but game for an attempt to make it work. Marilyn decided to try to overlook what she read in his diary—life was filled with disappointments anyway. Miller was her current father figure, savior, and lover, and she clung to that, throwing all her emotional resources into it to make it legitimate.

It wasn't that they didn't love each other—it was more that they discovered that they were passionately in love with specific *aspects* of the other, not the full person. Yet there was so much riding on the marriage that they would take the time to nurture the parts of each other that they fell in love with, and try to embrace the various other parts.

As Marilyn turned thirty-one she was very intent on creating something solid to hold on to as she aged. Already she was worrying about her beauty fading. Would that make Miller turn away from her? She feared it was the only thing that had hooked him in the first place. She wrote: "Alas how will I cope when I am/even less youthful—"

In her gratitude to him for loving her, she put her own identity aside and made being Mrs. Arthur Miller her top priority. She adopted a very traditional 1950s housewife's attitude—her husband's career was more important than her own, and her major role was to support him emotionally. "I'll tell you my definition of a good wife: Somebody who feels needed as a wife," she said. "You have to contribute to feel needed. Too many women underrate the responsibilities of marriage. They think once they have the wedding ring they can just sit back and relax."

Unfortunately Miller was not bringing in a lot of money at this time—his plays weren't being produced successfully that often—and what income he did have went to alimony and child support. His financial security mostly fell on Marilyn.

After a brief restorative "honeymoon" in Jamaica, Marilyn and Arthur did their best to settle into a normal, married life. Marilyn leased an apartment in Manhattan at 444 East Fifty-seventh Street in the prestigious Sutton Place area. Ignoring superstition, she accepted an apartment on the thirteenth floor with four bedrooms and four and a half bathrooms. Marilyn set out to decorate the place, furnishing the living room in shades of white. A den was set aside exclusively for Arthur to work in. "I never intrude except to bring him a second cup of coffee," Marilyn told reporters. The couple acquired a basset hound they named Hugo, and the doormen would note them taking him out for evening strolls.

For a while they put the movie business behind them, and their days in Manhattan fell into a routine. Marilyn would try to wake in time to fix Arthur breakfast. Afterward he would go into his den and attempt to do some writing. Marilyn might go shopping for new things for the apartment or clothes for Arthur. Later she would attend classes at the Actors Studio. At night they might see a show, entertain friends, or spend a quiet evening at home.

For a while things seemed to be on the mend. "Please, if I've ever made you cry or made you even more sadder, ever for a second, please forgive me, my perfect girl," Miller wrote to her, probably after a quarrel. "I love you."

Miller owned a house in Roxbury, Connecticut, and Marilyn had grown to love spending time there. Now she bought a house just down the road from Miller's, where the couple could create a home. She planned to have a totally new house built on the property. She employed the architect Frank Lloyd Wright. His elaborate design was a dream house, but an unrealistic one, way out of their budget. They settled on simply modernizing the existing house—which in itself was an expensive endeavor.

In the meantime they rented a quiet cottage in Amagansett, Long Island, for weekends away from the city—taking Hugo with them. It was there that they really enjoyed some of the most idyllic times of their marriage. Marilyn wore no makeup and walked around barefoot—on wooden floors, in the garden, on the beach. She wore shorts and men's shirts that she tied at the waist. She would go horseback riding. They swam together in the ocean and took long drives. She also discovered that she enjoyed gardening. While Marilyn worked in the garden, Miller would spend some time writing.

To free up time from the business of being Marilyn Monroe she hired May Reis to be a personal assistant/secretary and to handle many of her career dealings. May had at one time worked as a secretary for Arthur Miller. More and more, Marilyn's personal and business lives were populated by people from Miller's circle. May turned out to be a very devoted, efficient, and loving addition to Marilyn's life.

One of the things in her business life that had to be taken care of immediately was dissolving her partnership with Milton Greene. Miller kept reminding her that as long as Greene was vice president of Marilyn Monroe Productions, he could be entitled to half of all her earnings. He convinced her that all Greene was after was her money; he was only out to use her.

Greene was surprised to learn (through Miller) that Marilyn did not want him to receive an executive producer credit for *The Prince and the Showgirl*. Lawyers took over. What had started out as Marilyn's glorious artistic liberation from the Hollywood studio system was now in the hands of corporate lawyers. Ultimately Milton Greene settled for one hundred thousand dollars to be bought out of the company. That was basically only a reimbursement for the money he had put into financing Marilyn's sublime year of self-discovery in New York. Even Miller was surprised at the amount Greene settled for. He called it "chicken feed." He told Marilyn that he thought Greene would hold out for a half a million.

Greene said to the press: "It was not my intention to make money on Marilyn Monroe."

The board of Marilyn Monroe Productions was replaced by George Kupchik, George Levine, and Robert H. Montgomery, Jr. These were Arthur Miller's brother-in-law, his boyhood friend, and an attorney from the law firm he used in New York; Miller became vice president.

To further distance herself from Greene, Marilyn started seeing a new psychiatrist, Dr. Marianne Kris, every day. Her office was also conveniently in the building where the Strasbergs lived.

In May, Marilyn traveled to Washington with Miller, where he would be on trial for his contempt of Congress charge. After the weeklong trial, Miller was found guilty on two counts of contempt and immediately launched an appeal. Federal judge Charles F. McLaughlin withheld sentencing.

Standing by her man, Marilyn spoke to reporters, stating in barely a whisper that she was "confident that in the end my husband will win this case." Wearing a brown-and-white knit dress and white gloves, her golden blond hair hanging to her shoulders, Marilyn looked as lovely as she ever would in her life. (Unfortunately she made no films in 1957). She and Arthur then left Washington and headed to their East Fifty-seventh Street apartment.

Miller was well aware of the magic that Marilyn Monroe's presence could produce—and continued to use it to his benefit. In 1957, Paul Libin, a young producer, wanted to revive Miller's play *The Crucible*. Searching for a space for the production, he discovered that the ballroom of the Martinique Hotel at Broadway and Thirty-second Street was available, which he felt would be ideal. However, the hotel manager, Mr. Foreman, did not want the room used for a play. "We set up a meeting, but I didn't have much hope he'd rent me the space," Libin recalled. At the perfunctory meeting, Miller brought Marilyn. Before the men started negotiating, Libin said to Foreman, "I want you to meet Mr. Miller's wife." When Foreman turned and saw Marilyn "he was so flustered he literally melted,"

Libin recalled. Shortly afterward, Libin received a call from Foreman. "When do we make the deal?" Foreman asked. "Marilyn's presence sealed the deal and made the production possible," Libin explained.

Marilyn made very few public appearances that year. She was helicoptered into Manhattan from Amagansett for the opening of the Time-Life Building at Rockefeller Center. She and Arthur attended the April in Paris Ball at the Waldorf-Astoria.

One of Marilyn's most spectacular appearances was for the grand premiere of *The Prince and the Showgirl*, accompanied by Miller. She looked radiant, even in an absurdly structured gold gown that made most of her body look as if it had been encased in metal and then fishtailed out.

The reviews, however, were not rapturous. Bosley Crowther called the two lead characters of the new film "essentially dull." *The New Yorker* said: "Apart from the whimsicality of teaming up England's leading actor with a young lady whose dramatic experience has been largely confined to wiggling about in Technicolor pastries cooked up in Hollywood, it offers little in the way of diversion."

One of the bonus benefits of marrying Arthur was the fact that he came with a family. His family was now officially hers too, and she took it very seriously.

"She loved being in the family," Joan Copeland, Miller's sister, observed, "and the idea of having a family was very sacred to her."

Marilyn felt closest to Arthur's father, Isidore Miller. He had worked hard through the Depression and now, in his old age, had trouble with his feet. When his children grew up, some people said he felt neglected and ignored by the family.

Marilyn, forever on the lookout for father figures, immediately bonded with Isidore. "She was very fond of my dad," Joan recalled. "She was drawn to him immediately and they just had an instant connection. She liked my mother too—my mother would teach her to cook—like borscht—but she adored my father. And he adored her. When she called the house she would say, 'Is Dad there?' She loved saying 'Dad.' She felt it was such a privilege. That was so sweet and poignant." Marilyn called Isidore Miller at least once a week for the rest of her life—even after she and Miller were divorced.

When Miller's parents visited Marilyn and Arthur in Manhattan—which they often did—Marilyn doted on Isidore. She enjoyed doing little things for him like getting him a special chair or propping up his feet.

Once when Marilyn and Arthur went to visit the Miller family for Sunday dinner in Brooklyn, Marilyn wore a new suit. "Dad, what do you think of my new suit?" Marilyn asked, prancing in, turning around, showing it off.

Isidore Miller had been in the clothing business for years and knew good clothes. "That's a beautiful suit, Marilyn," he said. "It looks wonderful."

"But what do you think of the cut, Dad? Do you think it's a well-cut suit?"

"Beautiful," he said.

"Dad, do you like the material? Do you think it's a high-grade fabric?"

"Yes, Marilyn. It's real quality."

"But Dad what do you really think—" And the family watched a little bemused and slightly shocked as Marilyn took her elderly father-in-law's hand and ran it up and down her waist and thigh to get a good feel of the fabric of her new suit.

"To an observer it looked sexual," Joan Copeland said. "But Marilyn didn't mean it in an erotic way. She was acting naturally and completely unaware of it. I mean, I saw her do provocative things deliberately, but this time it was all in innocence. Although it did raise my mother's eyebrows." Copeland feels that some of the happiest moments of Marilyn's life were spent with Miller's family. "But that didn't last too long," she said. "A lot of good things in her life didn't last very long. I think that's another side of her character. She was always searching for something that she never did find. I don't know if anyone or anything could have filled the voids that she had. She would find something temporarily—career, marriage, family—but she would ultimately become disappointed. It was just an unfulfilled hole in her that she was constantly trying to fill."

———

All through this time Marilyn continued to be analyzed, but whether talking to a therapist every day was doing her any good is debatable. Certainly opening up almost daily about her past experiences seemed to be holding her back—she couldn't move on from her childhood hurts and her starlet degradations. The manic-depressive episodes made her unpredictable and even volatile. "She was such a vital, unusual person," Copeland's husband, Dr. George Kupchik, said. "Life left its imprint on her. She had such exuberance. And then sometimes she'd disappear for hours. She was subject to periods of deep depression. She'd snap into these moods very quickly, almost right in front of you. One moment she'd be talking normally and the next she'd be extremely agitated and upset. She was subject to great periods of despondence, probably more intense than most people's. You couldn't predict her moods. There were times we called that she refused to speak to us because she was so depressed. You got the feeling she was on the borderline and she could topple either way."

As she did with Joe DiMaggio's son, Joe Jr., Marilyn took her role as a stepmother to Miller's children very seriously. As Marilyn saw it, they were good kids, traumatized by their parents' divorce and Marilyn desperately wanted to befriend them. Marilyn's press agent, Rupert Allan, claimed that Marilyn confided to him that she was concerned because the eight-year-old boy was dressing up in his sister's clothes. "And the girl, Jane, was dressing as a boy in her father's clothes," Rupert said. Marilyn told Allan, "This isn't normal." Marilyn took both the children, individually, clothes shopping "in the right gender." Although the son went back to dressing in "girls' clothing," Rupert claimed that Miller didn't care. Apparently this was a period of acting out. There is no evidence that Miller's children continued the behavior Allan described.

Marilyn said to the boy, "You have a birthday coming up soon, don't you? Well, I'm going to give you a party."

He said, "A birthday party? I never had one!"

She told him to make a list of all the people he wanted to invite. She called all his friends and invited them. Marilyn was wonderful working the party—giving each child personal attention. She also bought the boy a lot of gifts—including one from Arthur.

———

"When my son went to the hospital with cerebral palsy," Joan Cope-land recalled, "Marilyn went to the hospital and she brought him an enormous television set for the children's ward. And it was a big, big thing. She said, 'This is for Eric and the other children.' And it was so sweet. My son was about ten years old or something like that. She stayed there and she played with them until they had to close up the children's ward. She kissed them all. It was hard for her to leave them. She was such a sweet person. And she loved children. She wanted to have them."

In June, Marilyn learned she was pregnant. As everyone close to her knew, she desperately wanted a baby, and she surely felt that being par-ents would solidify the Miller marriage.

Her joy was short lived. On August 1, while spending the weekend in Amagansett, Arthur Miller heard Marilyn scream out in pain from the garden. An ambulance was called. It was more than a two-hour ride to Manhattan to Doctors Hospital. Once there, doctors discovered that Mar-ilyn's pregnancy was ectopic, meaning that the fetus was developing in a Fallopian tube instead of in the uterus. The fetus had to be removed in order to save the life of the mother.

Miller and Marilyn sat in the darkened hospital room for many days while she recovered. While they were there she called their mutual friend, the photographer Sam Shaw, to come and visit them in the hospital. He discovered Marilyn in bed, and although she was absolutely tortured—no makeup, hair in disarray—he found her remarkably beautiful. Arthur was bearded by now. He hadn't left her side. Marilyn asked Shaw, "Would you take Arthur out for a walk? He's been in here for days."

Shaw and Miller went out into the Manhattan summer. Miller started explaining that he wanted to write something for Marilyn. A movie that would prove what an instinctive and exceptional actress she was. Shaw said, "You wrote a marvelous story in *Esquire* called 'The Misfits.' I think you should work on that as a vehicle for Marilyn."

That gave Miller the idea to turn his short story into a screenplay for his wife. The narrative, about three drifter cowboys, had no female char-acter in the story, but one of the men had a girlfriend named Roslyn, who is talked about. Miller would bring that character front and center for Marilyn for the screen adaptation. He started working on it right away.

Marilyn was released from the hospital ten days later, giving the waiting throngs her beautiful facade, smiling and waving, and vowing that she would eventually have a large family.

The miscarriage sent Marilyn into an extreme depression. She felt somehow that the failure to carry a child was her failure as a woman. Her despair soon led to another suicide attempt, and her stomach was pumped. Her early struggles, goals, disappointments, had battered her down. Marilyn really struggled with day-to-day life. Often, she felt as if the struggle wasn't worth it—better to go to sleep and not wake up. Death often seemed like a more comfortable and viable alternative to all the trouble of existing.

SEVENTEEN

Partly because they needed the money and partly because she needed the spotlight, Marilyn was ready to get back to work and started looking around for a suitable vehicle to return to the movies.

At the time Billy Wilder was collaborating on a new, risqué screenplay with his writing partner, I. A. L. Diamond. The script—which would eventually come to be called *Some Like It Hot*—was a madcap farce that uses classic comedy techniques of disguise and masquerade. In the 1920s musicians Joe and Jerry accidentally witness a mob hit. In order to escape the gangsters, who want to rub them out, they dress in drag, call themselves Josephine and Daphne, and, in their new identities, join an all-girl band heading to Florida by train. Enroute, they both fall for the band's lead singer, the luscious, whiskey-swilling Sugar Kane, who mistakes them for amiable new gal pals.

Since working with her on *The Seven Year Itch*, Billy Wilder had many complex feelings about Marilyn Monroe. "She was a . . . I don't know. A puzzle without any solution," he would say.

Marilyn frustrated the masterful filmmaker: Her constant lateness, no-shows, and delaying tactics, and her insistence on allowing her coach to interfere with his direction, wore down his patience. All that aside, however, he was enthralled by Marilyn and drawn to the idea of another creative collaboration. Before the screenplay was complete, he sent Marilyn a synopsis of the story and waited for her reaction.

It has been written that Marilyn didn't like her role in *Some Like It Hot* and accepted it only for the money. But by this point in her career, Marilyn had developed exceptionally sharp instincts for the art of moviemaking, and with this project she smelled a hit. "Billy Wilder just sent me a brief outline," she explained, when asked why she accepted the project. "If I liked it, he said, he'd finish it—because he was writing it with me in mind. So I read it—and loved it! I told Billy to go ahead—I'd do it without even reading the rest."*

Yes, she would be playing yet another dumb blonde, but she realized that Wilder was one of the best filmmakers in the business and that *Some Like It Hot* was an outrageously funny idea. First-rate material and a superb director were on the top of her list of priorities. *Some Like It Hot* offered both.

From the moment Wilder heard that Marilyn was available for *Some Like It Hot,* he realized there was no other actress in the world for the role of Sugar Kane. Now the title of the movie took on a double meaning. On one hand it stood for the fast, syncopated jazz the 1920s band performed. On the other, it was Marilyn who was "hot"—a sizzling, platinum-blond babe who played the ukulele, sang, and kept a flask tucked in her garter belt—whom everybody had the hots for.

The matinee idol Tony Curtis was already committed to play Marilyn's leading man (and "female" costar), one of the male musicians whom she first meets while he's disguised as a woman.

Wilder's choice for the other male who resorts to drag to save his life was Frank Sinatra. But when Sinatra failed to show up for a lunch meeting with the director, he was immediately crossed off the list. Wilder then approached Jack Lemmon in a restaurant, and while he was eating dinner, the director frantically told him the plot in sixty seconds. Caught up in Wilder's frenzied enthusiasm, Lemmon accepted the role on the spot.

----

* Marilyn's instincts proved to be correct. *Some Like It Hot* became the biggest hit of her career, although no one would have predicted it. Jack Lemmon recalled, "Most of the industry at the time thought Wilder was crazy for trying to make this film, that it would be a disaster. He was trying to make a two-hour movie out of a five-minute burlesque sketch."

Marilyn was not thrilled with the fact that Billy Wilder decided to make it mandatory that all the members of the female band be blond. After all, she was the star of the movie. Shouldn't she be the only blonde?*

Marilyn sent word to the hairdressing department with explicit instructions—every actress was to have her hair at least one shade darker than her own. "We had to stay away from her color," recalled costar Laurie Mitchell. Yet Marilyn was aware of the hair shade of every actress on the set. The honey-blond actress Marion Collier, who was cast as Olga the clarinet player, recalled running into Monroe at the studio a year after the filming. "Do you remember me?" Collier asked.

"Oh yes," Marilyn replied. "You were the only band member who didn't try to have your hair the same color as mine." Marilyn needn't have worried about her costars' hair color. During the production Marilyn discovered that she was once again pregnant, and she looked particularly voluptuous and radiant.

While in production, Billy Wilder decided to replace an actor in one of the smaller roles. Auditions were held and Al Breneman, then seventeen years old, was cast in the small but important role of the horny hotel bellhop with a lech for Tony Curtis dolled up as "Josephine."

"I had been on the set for several days, and there was no sign of Marilyn," Breneman recalled. "One afternoon I was at the studio and Billy Wilder came up to me and said, 'Would you come with me, Al? I want to introduce you to Marilyn.' So he walked me to her dressing room. I was trembling. When I saw Marilyn I didn't expect to have such a reaction. She was mesmerizing. I had never been in the presence of someone with such an overpowering . . . I guess you'd call it charisma. Later when she was on the set, Marilyn displayed a magnetism that I couldn't understand or believe." By the time Breneman was cast in the movie, the main griev-

---

* Marilyn was also distressed to discover Wilder's intention of making the film in black-and-white. "I only make color pictures!" she exclaimed. Wilder explained that Tony Curtis and Jack Lemmon in their drag makeup photographed like green-tinted freaks in color. Marilyn reluctantly said, "Oh, I understand." Wilder appeased Marilyn by telling her, "I'll make you look more beautiful than you ever did before." A promise he would keep.

ance the cast and crew had with Marilyn was that she was consistently late or didn't show up at all—sometimes for days at a time.

Marilyn needed to be pampered, and she turned to Arthur Miller, who flew from New York to be with her. Both sensed the impending end of the marriage. But, for their own personal agendas, each could fleetingly rekindle the feeling of genuine affection they once shared. Miller's presence temporarily soothed Marilyn. Between takes she'd breathe in the sea air, exclaiming, "This will be good for the baby!"

On the inside, however, she was already falling apart. In her troubled state of mind, Marilyn found it impossible to stay away from drugs and alcohol, even though she'd been warned to abstain by her gynecologist, Dr. Leon Krohn. After Miller flew back to New York, Paula Strasberg discovered Marilyn in her hotel room drugged and disoriented. She had overdosed on sleeping pills and champagne. The fact that she had vomited so violently may have saved her life: She was hospitalized for the weekend.

Most of the cast and crew didn't know that Marilyn was pregnant and dealing with disturbing conflicted emotions brought on by having a baby with Miller. She wanted to have a baby more than anything, but her feelings toward Miller were ambivalent, shifting from brief phases of adoration to increasing periods of hostility.

Throughout the shooting day, Marilyn would call for a thermos she would sip from: She said it contained hot bouillon, but it was reported to be vermouth or, as Billy Wilder believed, vodka and orange juice.

Jack Lemmon, although at times vexed by Marilyn's behavior, decided the magic she brought to the film was worth it. "Her lateness, which is legend, was never ever, in my opinion, the slightest bit caused by temperament. Not once," he observed. "It was a literal emotional impossibility for her to come out of that dressing room. . . . She couldn't face it until she got keyed up, psyched up and ready, she knew she wouldn't be able to do it."

There is no doubt that Marilyn was difficult, very difficult, to work with. But because of the embellishments related after the fact about the difficulties of working with her, some of Marilyn's behavior has been distorted and accepted as absolute fact.

One story about Marilyn's work on *Some Like It Hot* that has been described in a myriad of variations is the infamous "Where's that bourbon?" line. It appears in the scene where Marilyn has to walk into the hotel room of her "girlfriends" Curtis and Lemmon. She enters distraught, rummages through the dresser drawers, and asks, "Where's that bourbon?" According to many biographies, Marilyn simply could not remember that line. Supposedly she hopelessly mixed up those few words time and time again.

It became one of Wilder's favorite anecdotes regarding working with Marilyn. "We had eighty-three takes of that one line, 'Where's that bourbon?' that's all she had to say," he told a reporter. "And she had a mental block. She just could not say that line." As Wilder told it, she would say, "Where's the whiskey?" or "Where's the bottle?" or even "Where's the bonbon?" Finally, Wilder said, he resorted to pasting the line on the inside of the drawer.

Ironically, in the finished movie the line is said with Marilyn's back to the camera—which would have made it easy to be dubbed in postproduction. After the movie came out, many stories about Marilyn's bad behavior on the set started to circulate and have since become part of the legend of her troublesome behavior. Gossip columns stated that Marilyn wasn't prepared, she couldn't remember lines, she'd confuse the words.

One witness has a different memory: "I never saw any evidence that she didn't know her lines," Al Breneman said. "I do remember the famous day when we shot the scene when Marilyn comes in and says, 'Where's that bourbon?' I was sitting very close by, watching her. It's true that they did take after take. But I actually feel that history has given Marilyn a little bit of a bad rap for that. It wasn't that she couldn't say the line correctly. I honestly thought Billy Wilder had gotten that take from her very early on. But she kept asking, 'Billy, please, can we do it again?' I don't know what she didn't like about the scene, but she felt it wasn't right, that she could do it better. I always thought it was perfect long before she was satisfied. Billy Wilder was so wonderful with her. He always said, 'Yes, of course, Marilyn.' And he'd shoot it again. Then she'd say, 'I want to do it again, Billy.' He kept doing it again and again for her. When she was finally satisfied, I turned to the assistant cameraman and asked, 'What's the most times you ever shot a scene?' He said, 'You just saw it.'"

It wasn't unusual for Marilyn to request thirty-five to forty takes, stopping in the middle of the performance, which would drive the actors and Billy Wilder crazy. To them the scene seemed to be going fine. But it didn't feel right to her.

Lemmon recalled: "She would stand there with her eyes closed, biting her lip, and kind of wringing her hands until she had it worked out. Now this sounds like selfishness, and I guess it is. But she didn't mean it to be selfish—it was the only way she could work. Marilyn didn't give a damn about the director, the other actors, or anything else. It would seem that she was doing exactly what she'd done in the take before; but for her, something wasn't clicking quite right. I didn't necessarily approve of this tactic; it was not easy working with her, but it was fascinating."

Along with Billy Wilder, Tony Curtis suffered the most. In the second half of the film it was Curtis who had many long scenes with her. Her constant lateness and endless demands for retakes infuriated him, especially since in many of their scenes together he was decked out in a wig, heavy makeup, high heels, and uncomfortable padding under his costume.

One evening some of the cast and crew sat in a screening room watching the day's rushes. Marilyn was not present. The takes that were being screened were from the scene where Curtis and Monroe are on a yacht. Curtis, posing as a millionaire, is pretending to be impotent, which motivates Marilyn to attempt to "cure" him with a series of steamy kisses.

After the rushes finished running, someone joked to Curtis, "You seemed to enjoy kissing Marilyn." Curtis stood up and angrily retorted, "It's like kissing Hitler!" The room fell silent. There was a collective intake of breath. Jack Lemmon, who was in the screening room, cringed in disbelief. When the lights came on, Paula Strasberg was in tears. "How could you say a terrible thing like that, Tony?" she asked.

"You try acting with her, Paula," he fumed, "and see how you feel."*

---

* Curtis (born Bernie Schwartz in the Bronx) absolutely hated working with Marilyn, and by the end of filming he loathed her. His insult was widely reported at the time—and Curtis never once objected. He continued to comment negatively about her after her death, all through the 1960s. But as Marilyn's mythological status grew, Curtis would spend decades denying he ever made the comment. In later years, as his place in movie history was forever linked with Marilyn, Curtis both softened his memories of her and also wildly exaggerated them. Late in his life Curtis went so far as to claim that

Marilyn was bewildered and hurt when she heard the "Hitler" remark. For one thing, Curtis had managed to hide his disdain for her completely while they were shooting. She told Rupert Allan that Curtis would stop by her dressing room before she was making up and say, "I think you're just wonderful! The most beautiful woman I know." She had fallen for it to a degree. She thought Curtis liked her, and she even felt that he might be making a play for her, in spite of the fact he was married, with a new baby daughter.

His malevolent remark touched her deepest insecurities, further proving that she just couldn't trust anybody. People would show her one side, then turn around and stab her in the back.

Although Wilder may have been seething on the inside, he never showed any anger on the set. He was making a frothy comedy, and he did his best to keep the atmosphere relaxed and light. A visiting reporter watching rehearsals noted: "I have never watched a film put together amidst so much hilarity. . . . Electricians, scene shifters, prop men, in fact the entire crew, spent their time roaring with laughter."

The many production stills taken during shooting illustrate a very congenial set. Marilyn is seen laughing with Curtis, Lemmon, and Wilder, posing for publicity shots, or deeply engrossed in conversation. Everyone seems to be getting along and having a good time. "I never saw any signs of the things they said later on in the press and in books," Breneman stated.

When *Some Like It Hot* was released, it caused an immediate sensation. *LIFE* put Marilyn on the cover, playfully nibbling on a rhinestone earring, with the caption, "A comic Marilyn sets movies aglow," setting the tone for the majority of reviews she would receive—some of the best of her career. The movie was daring, sexy, and hilarious—a perfect vehicle for Marilyn at this moment.

Variety, the bible in the world of show business, reported: "To coin a phrase, Marilyn has never looked better. . . . She's a comedienne with that combination of sex appeal and timing that just can't be beat."

---

they had an affair during shooting and that the baby Marilyn was carrying was his. Finally, in 2008 he admitted that he had indeed made the "Hitler" remark but explained that he was simply being sarcastic in response to a silly question.

Hot was one of the most popular movies of the year and went on to gross a fortune. Through the years it has continued to grow in popularity. In 2000 the American Film Institute named it the funniest movie of all time.

"When it was all over I was absolutely drained," Wilder said. "There was a kind of exhaustion and there was a moment of 'never again.' All I can tell you is, if Marilyn were around today I would be down on my knees saying, 'Please, let's do it again.'"

EIGHTEEN

TRUTH

Shortly after filming was complete Marilyn suffered another miscarriage. "I'm sure she would have been a much different person if she could have had a baby," George Kupchik, Miller's brother-in-law, observed. "She loved children so and would play with them on their own level." Marilyn's disillusionment in her marriage, her career, and life in general continued to fester.

Marilyn was angered by *The Misfits*, the screenplay that Miller wrote for her. She was angered by a lot of other things too. But Miller's work was being touted as a gift to her. Despite all her insecurities and self-doubt, she was wise enough to realize that this gift was really to himself: She knew that when they first met he was in Hollywood with Kazan trying to sell a screenplay—a script that never sold. Miller had never had success in the movie industry.

It was unlikely that *The Misfits* would have been produced without her participation. "Marilyn Monroe" was the hook that got everyone interested. She couldn't help but feel used.* Marilyn felt that Miller was merely using her as a conduit to success in the movie industry. Marilyn did not hold in her rage. She let him know it, and as a result she became more impossible to deal with. She upped her pill intake. She upped her alcohol use. Miller, on the other hand, internalized his anger. He couldn't show

---

* Marilyn's intuitions were right. A few years later, shortly after she died, Miller would use her again for one of his last successful plays—writing unflatteringly about their marriage for all to see in his autobiographical play *After the Fall*.

her his frustration, that he needed her to make the movie. But it was there, intensifying.

Marilyn might have been able to overlook everything else if Miller had written something for her that she admired and wanted to play. Unfortunately Marilyn was horrified by what she read in *The Misfits* and she made it known to many people she trusted that she didn't want to play the role of Roslyn.

Her excellent instincts told her *The Misfits* screenplay wouldn't make a good picture—it was too wordy, the monologues were talky and wooden. That's not to say that Marilyn still didn't have the utmost respect for Miller's talent. She simply didn't connect with the script he wrote for her.

They had terrible fights over it. "About rewriting," Sam Shaw revealed. "I think Arthur was wrong. Marilyn felt she couldn't say the dialogue he put in Roslyn's mouth. But Miller refused to take her advice and rework her character," Shaw observed. "It sounds very trite and corny and cliché, but she wanted the truth. Marilyn felt 'Never lie in life. Never lie in a script.' They had trouble. She felt she wasn't telling the truth within the character."

Determined that the movie would be made *with* Marilyn in the lead, Miller pressed ahead. On his own he sent the screenplay to John Huston, a director for whom Marilyn had great respect. Thinking that Marilyn was definitely attached, he agreed to direct it.

Marilyn, however, was much more interested in starring in Truman Capote's *Breakfast at Tiffany's*. She was captivated by the kooky heroine of Capote's novel, Holly Golightly.

A nineteen-year-old actor at the Actors Studio, Michael J. Pollard, was sitting in class with George Maharis (who went on to have a success in TV's *Route 66*) when he looked back and saw a blonde. "That looks like Marilyn Monroe," he said. "That *is* Marilyn Monroe!" Maharis replied. With all the confidence of a twenty-year-old, Pollard approached Marilyn after class. "Would you like to do a scene with me?" he asked. Marilyn didn't hesitate. "Sure," she said.

She suggested they do a scene from *Breakfast at Tiffany's*, and Pollard instantly agreed. Marilyn invited him to rehearse at her Fifty-seventh Street apartment. Walking to the apartment after class, Pollard vividly recalls

pedestrians calling out to her. "People would recognize her when we walked from class to her apartment because she was 'Marilyn Monroe,' and they would call out to her: 'Hi, Marilyn!'"

There was no screenplay for *Breakfast at Tiffany's* yet, so Pollard and Marilyn crafted the scene from the book: Holly climbs through her new neighbor's window: "I've got the most terrible man downstairs," she says, stepping in from the fire escape.

As the day of the scene approached Marilyn admitted, "I'm really worried about the lines." She tore out pages from the book so they could spread them out over the performance area.

For Marilyn, this was a tryout. She was really hoping to snag the lead in the film version, even though it was being done at Paramount. She would have to get Fox to loan her out.

When it was over Strasberg said that it was the best work he had seen from Pollard. Marilyn's own performance was enchanting.

Audrey Hepburn made such an indelible mark on the role that it may be difficult to imagine Marilyn as Holly. But if we erase for a moment Hepburn's delightful and legendary performance, we can see what magic Marilyn might have brought to the character.

George Axelrod, who had a talent for writing quirky dialogue and had adapted two of Marilyn's greatest roles, in *The Seven Year Itch* and *Bus Stop*, was hired to tailor the script for Marilyn specifically, which he did magnificently.

The script was submitted to Marilyn for her consideration in September of 1959 (along with a shooting schedule)—demonstrating that Paramount was strongly considering her.*

When the part went to Hepburn, Capote was furious. "I thought Marilyn Monroe should have played Holly Golightly," he fumed. "She was closer to it than Audrey Hepburn. . . . Holly was a hillbilly named Lula

---

* An interesting factor comes from a memo that was later found with Marilyn's copy of the screenplay. Edward Parone, a writer with ties to Miller, was reviewing potential scripts for Marilyn Monroe Productions. He started off his critique of *Breakfast at Tiffany's* with "I think not." He went on to criticize the script: "I can see Marilyn playing a part like Holly and even giving this present one all the elan it badly needs, but I don't feel she should play it. It lacks insight and warmth and reality and importance." When Marilyn went on to do *The Misfits* instead, Parone was named "Assistant to the Producer."

Mae passing as a sophisticate. She was also an expensive but somewhat innocent call girl. Emotionally, she was very fragile. The tears were very close to the surface."

Capote had used a great deal of the real Marilyn when creating the character, and Holly Golightly would have given Marilyn her most multifaceted and demanding comedy character: a free-spirited modern-day woman with a secret past, who makes her way through the world utilizing her wits and considerable charm while trying desperately to keep some semblance of dignity as she wallows in immorality.

For whatever reasons, Marilyn ended up making *The Misfits* instead. Although she definitely did not feel comfortable with the script, this was a screenplay written expressly for her by her Pulitzer Prize–winning playwright husband. It was a high-profile, high-interest project. The eyes of the entire world would be on the production—just from the curiosity factor alone it seemed like a surefire hit.

That she made *The Misfits* rather than *Breakfast at Tiffany's* was one of the greatest tragedies of Marilyn's career. It would have given Marilyn the opportunity to shine as a charming character who combines wit and pathos. It would also likely have provided her with a smash hit. *The Misfits* gave her neither.

NINETEEN

Before starting *The Misfits* Marilyn had to fulfill her contract and make a movie for Fox. So while Miller toiled away on *The Misfits* screenplay, Marilyn prepared to return to Fox.

Having perfected the deliciously ditzy blonde image for all time in *Some Like It Hot*, it was, in fact, the perfect moment to put a period on it and expand her magic to a different image for the new decade. The year 1959 was a pivotal moment for growth, and had Marilyn been given a good script with a role of substance, she might have been able to transform and transition her image into the 1960s as a beautiful and mature woman living in the real world. *Some Like It Hot* had confirmed that Marilyn was at the top of her game. And she might have stayed there had Fox not put her into the overblown, mediocre musical that was eventually titled *Let's Make Love*.

Reviewing the history of Fox, it's difficult to believe that they hadn't bothered to develop any story exclusively with Marilyn in mind. Instead they assigned her to *The Billionaire*, a trite musical comedy of mistaken identity with a script that was developed as a Gregory Peck vehicle. His leading lady hadn't been cast yet.

The comedic situations in the story would revolve around Peck, playing a fantastically rich tycoon who must learn to become a song-and-dance man to capture the heart of the woman he loves. When he learns that an off-Broadway show plans to spoof his playboy image, he attends a dress rehearsal to check the revue for slander. There he sees Amanda Dell—the female lead in the show—do a dance number, and after watching her perform, he is mistaken for a look-alike actor auditioning for the role of the "billionaire." Because he is so taken with Amanda, he goes along with the charade and accepts the role, essentially agreeing to satirize himself in the production.

When the studio realized they had to put Marilyn to work or risk having another year go by without a Monroe picture, they decided to cast her in the supporting role of Amanda.

The satire in the screenplay derives from the fact that he is a business shark—with no talent—spoofing himself in song-and-dance numbers. Marilyn's role is that of second banana, a noncharacter who is simply a foil for the male lead's comic antics.

Fox secured George Cukor for the movie—one of the directors listed as acceptable in her contract. Well known for bringing out the best in female stars like Jean Harlow, Katharine Hepburn, and Greta Garbo, Cukor was also renowned for his light comedic touch. They also hired Marilyn's favorite choreographer, Jack Cole, to work on her musical numbers.

Now that it was being touted as a Marilyn Monroe film, the title *The Billionaire* was scrapped for the more provocative *Let's Make Love*. Realizing that her supporting role was in no way suitable for a star, the studio—in a supreme miscalculation—hired Arthur Miller to rewrite the script and build up her character. Perhaps they thought it would fire up Marilyn's enthusiasm. Miller, however, had never written a truly comedic line in his career.

In his autobiography Miller attempted to strengthen the legend that he was an all-sacrificing husband willing to do anything to save their marriage. "I went so far as to do some rewriting on *Let's Make Love* to try to save her from a complete catastrophe, work I despised on a script not worth the paper it was typed on," he wrote contemptuously. "It was a bad miscalculation, bringing us no closer to each other. She seemed to take for granted what for me had been a sacrifice of great blocks of time, and it was plain that her inner desperation was not going to let up."

Miller fails to mention that he was paid fifteen thousand dollars for his two weeks of "sacrifice" on the script—money he was happy to pocket although he did not want screen credit for his contributions.

Unfortunately his fingerprints are all over *Let's Make Love*. Amanda's character was suddenly reciting dialogue that could have been rejected lines written for Roslyn, the role he was writing for Marilyn in *The Misfits*. Miller wrote cardboard versions of "Marilyn"—a series of lines that she said in real life or bits of her history that he was incapable of transforming in any way. For example, being a woman with no formal education becomes a major factor in both characters Miller was working on for Marilyn.

In *Let's Make Love* Amanda attends night school in hopes of getting her high school diploma because "I got tired of being ignorant. I never knew what people were referring to." Knowing that Miller felt embarrassed by Marilyn in front of his intellectual friends, one cringes at him putting these lines in her mouth.[*]

Also, Miller's "Marilyn" characters must be ashamed of their past. During a supposedly comedic scene, when the billionaire tries to reveal his true identity to Amanda, in a startling non sequitur, she blurts, "I've done things in my life that are very painful to talk about." What, one wonders, could this carefree musical comedy performer ever have done that's so difficult to talk about? And even more, why are lines like these being recited in what is supposed to be a joyful musical romp?

Gregory Peck, appalled at what was happening to the screenplay, promptly bowed out of *Let's Make Love*. He graciously said that it was because of a scheduling conflict. In a more unguarded moment he said the script was "now about as funny as pushing Grandma down the stairs."

This left *Let's Make Love* without a male star. Rock Hudson, Cary Grant, and Charlton Heston all turned down the role for one reason or another. Satisfied with having Marilyn attached, Fox pushed ahead with the production anyway.

It was Arthur Miller who suggested the French singing star Yves Montand as Marilyn's leading man. Montand had become friendly with

---

[*] In *The Misfits*, Roslyn says, "Me? I never finished high school" (just like Marilyn). When Clark Gable conveys his approval, she is bewildered and asks, "You don't like educated women?"

Miller when he starred in the French production of *The Crucible* with his wife, the French actress Simone Signoret. Although virtually unknown to American audiences, Montand had recently scored a Broadway success in his one-man show, which Marilyn saw with her friend and Manhattan neighbor, Montgomery Clift. Marilyn saw the charisma that made Montand a huge star in France. She wanted him for the movie too. "He sings with his entire body," she cooed.

To almost everyone else involved, Montand seemed like a wrong choice. The original writer, Norman Krasna, saw the character as a gruff "shit kicker." Montand came across as an exceedingly suave gentleman. Since Montand was an accomplished song-and-dance man, all the comedy that would come from a klutz attempting to be a smooth performer would be drained from the story. But Marilyn persisted. She wanted Montand. So Fox agreed.

Another major problem in casting him was that Montand spoke almost no English. It would be difficult for audiences to understand him. Adding to the complications Fox already expected on a Monroe film, the studio hired a speech coach to teach Montand the lines, which he learned by rote.

Though the studio secured Jack Cole's services at great expense, Marilyn's illnesses and pill intake usually made her late or a no-show for most dance rehearsals. On some days Cole waited for hours in an empty rehearsal hall. He was furious and insulted that Marilyn would treat him with such a lack of respect.

After the filming Marilyn regretted her behavior. She sent Cole a note of apology saying it must have been "awful" for him. She included a check for $2,500, suggesting he take a vacation on her. Several days later she sent him another check for $500, advising him to stay "three more days."

On Saturday, January 16, the studio held a press party at the Beverly Hilton to announce the start of filming of Marilyn's latest movie. In newsreel footage of the event Marilyn proved that she could still transform herself into the radiant creature the world expected. She wore a pale silver silk halter dress with a plunging V-neck, body-hugging at the waist and then flaring out in chiffon panels. She sipped her customary champagne and flirted with Montand. When journalists asked what she thought of her future costar, Marilyn said, "Next to my husband and along with Marlon Brando, Yves Montand is the most attractive man I ever met." (Years before, Marlon Brando had been a lover.)

The next day, however, Marilyn's glamorous mask cracked. The star power she had projected at the press party left her feeling exhausted, drained. She called in sick, saying she wouldn't be able to work on Monday after all. Montand was thrown into a panic. He had already spent a great deal of time phonetically learning the lines for his first scene with Marilyn.

Director Cukor was forced to rearrange the schedule to shoot scenes that did not include her—which meant Montand hastily learning new dialogue by rote. Montand was terrified. He had brought a tape recorder to the set so he could read his lines and play them back to himself. Now he had to learn a new scene. Marilyn continued to call in sick for the rest of the week.

The following Monday, Marilyn summoned up enough courage to face the *Let's Make Love* cameras for the first time. Yves Montand was not needed that day. She would start the filming of the "My Heart Belongs to Daddy" number, which she would continue to shoot over the next few days. It was a technically difficult routine because there was a series of poles set up that Marilyn and the male dancers would have to dance around, swing from, and climb. As always, Marilyn used everything she had learned from Jack Cole, and by now she completely owned the number, bringing to it the unique brand of carefree sexuality she was worshipped for.

Dancer Bobby Banas remembered that Cole instructed the male dancers to "get out there and explode! Destroy yourselves!" The choreographer cannily had the dancers reflect the typical male reaction to Monroe. While Marilyn is singing, the guys are jumping and leaping as if her presence pushes a button making this explosion of men happen all around her.

Whereas studio execs viewing the rushes of the scene grumbled about Marilyn's weight, Banas said that Marilyn in person did not appear zaftig at all. "She was voluptuous and beautiful. But in between takes I did hear her wardrobe lady whisper to her, 'Now Marilyn, remember to hold in your stomach.'"

Friday, January 29, was the day Marilyn was scheduled to shoot her first scene with Montand. He observed her from across the set. "Great star that she is—she was trembling, ill at ease, and consuming more coffee than I have ever seen go into anyone's system to steady her nerves."

Shortly before filming their scene she approached Montand and announced sarcastically, "Now you're going to see what it means to shoot with the worst actress in the world."

"So you're scared," Montand replied. "Think of me a little. I'm lost."

This show of vulnerability immediately intensified Marilyn's attraction to Montand. She always responded to someone else's insecurity. Now she had a sense of "We're in this together." She wanted to please him. Of course he realized anything perceived as an insult could instantly send her into a downward spiral. But he also sensed that if he was honest with her he would gain her trust.

He was touched by her and recognized her biggest weakness. It was one he shared: self-doubt, the fear of not being great at all times. Montand informed her, "You look beautiful. But I think you're afraid of acting." He went on to say he recognized her terror in the fact that she could never live up to her own expectations of herself. That's why she was always late.

Marilyn was shocked and impressed that someone she respected was actually calling her out on her insecurities. "Nobody else would tell her that," Montand said. "How could they? They just see this beautiful girl, singing, moving wonderfully."

The more they worked together, the more comfortable they began to feel with each other. Montand saw Marilyn as an enchantress. A beguiling personality with a unique and dazzling combination of sensuality and fragility. When working with her he found himself looking into "those incredibly blue eyes that maintained the clarity other women's only rarely possess." Yet he was determined that he would not allow himself to fall for her. He loved his wife.

Marilyn also became enamored of Montand but—like him—she pushed her attraction aside. The time wasn't right. Miller was obsessed with shooting *The Misfits*. They were both married. There was a movie to be made—and it was being filmed under the ever-watchful eyes of the Hollywood press—which was eager for a Monroe scandal.

At the Beverly Hills Hotel the two couples—the Millers and the Montands—lived across from each other in Bungalows No. 20 and No. 21. In the evening the couples quietly socialized after the day's shooting.

Marilyn would arrive from the set, peek her head into the room, still in studio makeup, and say, "Just let me take a bath and I will join you." A short time later she would join the others for dinner, music, and conversation. "Without makeup and false eyelashes, her face bare, she looked like the most beautiful peasant girl imaginable," Simone Signoret would remember.

Signoret at thirty-seven—heavy and slightly weathered—already had the air of a ruined beauty. But she was a highly respected actress in Europe and was making a mark in America. That year she had played a lonely older woman opposite Laurence Harvey in *Room at the Top* and was nominated for an Academy Award, an honor Marilyn did not receive for *Some Like It Hot*. But Marilyn never displayed resentment or jealousy toward Simone. "You're going to win," she would tell her again and again.

Marilyn—who rarely had women friends—was fascinated by the worldly actress. Simone became an older sister and a mother figure. When Miller left for Ireland to work on *The Misfits* script with John Huston, Marilyn turned to Simone for companionship in the evenings. Plagued by insomnia, Marilyn was terrified of facing her empty bed. Simone told Marilyn how she walked out on her first husband and young daughter in order to be with Montand. "I left my husband and my home, which was bad," Simone explained. "I left my child, which was worse. People didn't like it, but I had to do it." Marilyn was enthralled by this woman who had sacrificed everything for her one chance at true love.

Because of her late evenings, in the mornings, zonked from too many pills and lack of sleep, Marilyn simply could not rouse herself to make it to the studio. Eventually the pace of filming went back to maddening delays. Hours ticked by. The actors were in their makeup. George Cukor stood around. When the morning passed with no sign of Marilyn, Montand would be fuming.

As always, though, many members of the crew forgave Marilyn for her delays. They sensed that she wasn't being malicious or acting like a diva. She really did struggle. A fellow actor found a notebook Marilyn had used for a scene and left on the set. On one page she had written: What am I afraid of? Why am I so afraid? Do I think I can act? I know I can act. But I am afraid. I am afraid and I should not be and I must not be.

"It made her appear more naked than those calendars she posed for," the actor said.

In March the Screen Actors Guild and the Writers Guild went on strike, and all movies shut down, including *Let's Make Love*. The strike was for residual payments for actors when their movies were shown on television. It was such an important issue of the day that no writer would break ranks with the strike to work on the *Let's Make Love* screenplay, which continued to need rewrites.

Astonishingly, because of the strike, Miller flew back from Europe in order to do more work on the troublesome *Let's Make Love* script. Miller's leftist politics decried the plight of the workingman, yet he had no problem crossing union lines in order to make another hefty sum for his work. Marilyn, already long disillusioned with her ideal of Miller, was disturbed by this hypocrisy.

On March 8 Marilyn received a Golden Globe for her performance in *Some Like It Hot* in a ceremony held at the Coconut Grove. She had been snubbed by most of Hollywood, but the town's Hollywood Foreign Press Association, which gave the award, appreciated her in a way that the American entertainment industry still didn't. Wrapped in fur, with tantalizingly exposed shoulders, she languidly sashayed up to the microphone. Her entire speech consisted of "I thank you with all my heart"; a short but heartfelt declaration. Marilyn truly appreciated an acknowledgment for a performance she had worked very hard on. She always made her performances seem so effortless—which was part of her genius.

The Academy Awards were held on April 4. As Marilyn had predicted, Simone Signoret won Best Actress for her performance in *Room at the Top*.

Although she didn't show it, Marilyn was heartbroken at not even being nominated for her acclaimed work in *Some Like It Hot*.

It could be argued that many in the Hollywood industry so resented Marilyn that they were reluctant to endorse anything involving her. The industry still hadn't forgiven her for walking out on her contract in 1954. They forgave her even less now; disliked her even more. Her lateness on sets flaunted her star power and made her seem like a spoiled diva. *Some Like It Hot*—today considered one of the greatest and most influential comedies—received no major Academy Awards.

On April 8 the strike ended, so production on all films resumed. The following day Signoret left for Europe to start a new movie. A few days later Miller flew to New York to continue working on *The Misfits* script. It seems curious that Miller would leave Marilyn alone with Montand when he admitted that his marriage was deteriorating.

Had Miller timed his departure so it would leave Marilyn free to indulge in an affair with Montand—perhaps to assure smooth sailing to the completion of the film and onto *The Misfits* set?

By this point Miller's sole obsession was getting *The Misfits* made. Years later he admitted he was well aware of Marilyn's susceptibility to Montand: "It's true Marilyn was naturally drawn to him. He was a poor boy originally, and as with others, she invested that new person with a selfless interest in her. Personally I was glad he was there. She needed someone like this on the scene at all times, especially when embarking on a new film."

Perhaps Miller saw Montand as a pawn to boost Marilyn's spirits and rouse her energy to finish *Let's Make Love*. *The Misfits* was slated to go into production immediately after this film wrapped. Feeling unappreciated and unloved, Marilyn had nothing to grab on to. Left alone in her bungalow, she grabbed on to Montand.

As for Montand, he succumbed to Marilyn's compelling sexuality—a desire that had been building up in him for weeks. She had been out ill again, and Montand dropped by her room to see how she was feeling. He sat on the edge of her bed and patted her hand tenderly. "I bent over to kiss her goodnight, but suddenly it was a wild kiss, a fire, a hurricane. I couldn't stop," he admitted.

When Marilyn knocked on his door the following night, wearing a fur coat with nothing underneath, the one-night stand evolved into a full-fledged affair. In each other they found a kindred spirit. Marilyn began behaving more professionally.

Instead of conducting a clandestine affair, Montand and Marilyn seemed to be reveling in the attention. With their spouses away, they did nothing to hide their involvement. Marilyn, more social than usual, was seen all over town with Montand. The gossip columns went wild with the Monroe-Montand affair.

As the chaotic production progressed, Marilyn may have seemed more functional on the outside, but emotionally she was a mess. Long-distance conversations with her New York psychiatrist, Dr. Marianne Kris, weren't helping her much either. She made another suicide attempt—which may have been a cry for help. It had happened many times before.

Dr. Kris recommended that she start seeing her colleague in Los Angles, Dr. Ralph Greenson—known as a psychiatrist to the stars (his patients included Frank Sinatra and Vivien Leigh). He would become a central figure in Marilyn's life and a key player on the night of her death.

At first he would describe her as "a woman married to an academic man; sexually frigid; history of promiscuous behavior prior to her marriage to an austere academician." According to one of Dr. Greenson's essays, in which he often used Marilyn as a case study, when the doctor asked her to feel free to talk about herself, she said: "Well, I always get depressed. I think I have been depressed most of my life. At times I do feel good—in fact too good. I know it comes from hating myself or loving myself; the therapist told me so. But knowing this does not seem to be of any help to me."

In subsequent visits she described to the doctor that her latest suicide attempt had been brought on by an affair with a married man, who she felt couldn't give her the attention she craved because of his devotion to his wife.

Dr. Greenson found her unable to stay focused because she "interrupted herself with free association to her childhood miseries, and to other men who had taken advantage of her sexually and otherwise." Greenson began to make arrangements for future visits. They decided to start with sessions three times a week.

When the picture was completed at last in mid-June, the catty columnist Hedda Hopper had summoned Montand for an interview and quoted him saying: "Had Marilyn been more sophisticated, none of this ever would have happened. . . . Perhaps she had a schoolgirl crush. If she did, I'm sorry. But nothing will break up my marriage."

This "schoolgirl crush" comment was quoted repeatedly, much to Marilyn's embarrassment. Montand denied he ever said it.

Marilyn didn't talk about the affair in the press. It wasn't in her character to kiss and tell. But she felt as ardently toward him as ever, and spoke to friends of plans to vacation with Montand in Italy. Apparently he had rhapsodized about the beauty of Florence during pillow talk. Deeply in love with Montand, Marilyn was determined to lure him into her arms.

Back in Europe, Simone Signoret had to deal with the affair by reading about it in front-page headlines. Signoret attempted to put on a stoic facade for the public. To reporters she conveyed a worldly, some might say "French," attitude when defending her husband's dalliance. "Tell me, do you know who could resist if they took Marilyn Monroe into their arms?" At the same time she graciously let Marilyn off the hook: "If Marilyn is in love with my husband, it proves she has good taste, for I am in love with him too."

In actuality Signoret was shattered by the affair, yet for her remaining twenty-five years, she never publicly uttered a negative word about Marilyn. The French actress Catherine Deneuve, a close friend, commented, "She bore Marilyn etched on her face like a permanent scar."*

Montand was aware of his wife's pain and wanted to get back to her as soon as possible to explain and console. He scheduled a flight to Paris immediately after his duties on *Let's Make Love* were complete.

Marilyn intended to keep the relationship alive. But since she was scheduled to go directly into shooting *The Misfits*, she didn't have a plan,

---

* Much later Montand would say that Signoret made him suffer for years to come because of his affair with Marilyn.

or the time to devise one, to complete the seduction. She flew back to New York on June 26 for a brief recuperation period before beginning *The Misfits.*

When she learned that Montand was scheduled to fly back to Europe to patch things up with Signoret—with a stopover and plane switch in New York—Marilyn hatched a scheme. She rented a hotel room near Idlewild Airport and hired a limousine stocked with champagne and caviar. Secure in the knowledge that, using a mixture of her allure and their shared experiences, she could tempt him away from his wife. She headed for the airport. Michael Selsman was sent by Marilyn's press agency to do damage control in case things got out of hand.

Legend has it that Marilyn waited in the limo naked under a fur coat, a trick that had worked for her before. When his flight was delayed because of a bomb threat, Montand did take refuge in the limo with Marilyn. But she was unable to persuade him to leave Simone and stay with her.

As for the finished film, *Let's Make Love* has some moments of charm, but the story really revolves around Yves Montand, and because at this point his English is very bad, he is difficult to understand. The chemistry they conveyed so strongly at the initial press conference did not materialize on screen.

Because of the lackluster box office and her fluctuating weight and appearance in the movie, many in the media began to mark this movie as the start of Marilyn's decline. Although she was still considered one of the world's great love goddesses, the premiere of *Let's Make Love* in 1960 marked a turning point in the way Marilyn would be covered by the press. "Marilyn offers her famous curves, not a little on the fleshy side. Diet anyone?" one review cattily joked.

Her age—thirty-four—was emphasized in almost every article, along with the ticking clock and view that her reign as the leading sex symbol of the day must inevitably come to an end. Some of the more vicious journalists kept a vigilant eye out for any signs of aging.

TWENTY

It is often said that Arthur Miller wrote *The Misfits* as a "Valentine" for his wife.

It's unfortunate and sad that *The Misfits* is Marilyn Monroe's last completed movie. She had reached a mastery of her craft of acting, and her physical appearance in the film, for the most part, is modern and lovely. Miller's basic idea is a good one: three cowboys—all very different personality types—vying for the attention of Roslyn, a beautiful, lost soul in the empty, transitory wilderness of Nevada. The three cowboys make a living by rounding up wild horses in the mountains and selling them for dog food. They reject the idea of having a steady job and the lack of freedom that comes with working for "wages." These cowboys become enamored of Roslyn, who is in town to finalize her divorce. She flirts with all of them but becomes involved with Gay Langland, to be played by Clark Gable.

In the final script the dialogue for these characters is sometimes pretentious and often clumsy. The characters are paper thin—symbols rather than believable people. Whitey Snyder, Marilyn's makeup man, remembered Marilyn's opinion of the script: "She felt that Arthur had written dialogue for her that was totally insignificant and extraneous to the film. She complained that the movie had to do with the cowboys and their horses and had nothing to do with her character."

Despite her dislike of the screenplay, Marilyn hoped that John Huston's vision and direction could transform the material into something exceptional and exciting, while the talent of her costars Clark Gable, Montgomery Clift, and Eli Wallach might somehow bring the characters to life. When Marilyn arrived in Reno to start shooting *The Misfits*, she was ill and dependent on pills.

Though nursing a broken heart and a public humiliation, she was still hoping to continue the affair with Yves Montand. The marriage in which she had put so much hope was over. To make matters worse, most of the shooting would take place during the summer months in the scorching Nevada desert. At the airport on July 21 a throng of fans awaited her arrival. Marilyn was bleary and weary but still game. Determined to live up to her image, she emerged from the plane doing her very best to call up the white goddess. Her beauty is apparent, but—wearing a skintight white blouse, white skirt, and holding a white chiffon scarf—she looks exhausted and slightly bloated.

Regardless of their current feelings for each other, in an attempt to maintain the front of a contently married couple, the Millers took a suite together at the Mapes Hotel—where most of the cast and crew were staying. But it soon became apparent that their union was anything but harmonious. Their violent arguments could be heard through the walls, and other guests began to complain. Eventually they would move to separate rooms.

Very soon after the production began on July 21, the troubles started. "I first noticed her condition when we started production," director John Huston said. "She was very late, and as time went on her condition worsened. Often she would not even know where she was. Her eyes had a strange look. She was definitely under the influence. She had apparently been on narcotics for a very long time. I spoke to Arthur about it . . . it seemed so hopeless."

By now everyone expected there to be delays on a Marilyn Monroe movie, yet shortly into filming it became clear that shooting *The Misfits* was going to be a complete nightmare. "Marilyn didn't show up for hours, sometimes days, while the cast and crew sweated it out in the scorching Nevada desert with temperatures reaching as high as 120 degrees," said Edward Parone, the assistant to the producer. "Some of the luckier crew members could wait in their cars with the air-conditioning running. Others sat around in the dry, dusty heat, waiting and waiting."

Fifty-nine-year-old Clark Gable had it specified in his contract that he wouldn't have to work after 5:00 p.m. because he wanted to spend time with his pregnant wife and stepchildren. His wife, Kay, was pregnant with his first child. But because of Marilyn's continuous tardiness, the producer, Frank Taylor, had to push the time in the morning they'd start shooting to later and later. First he made it 10:00 a.m., then 11:00. Soon the call time for the actors was noon. And Marilyn still didn't show up on time. "When Marilyn finally arrived on the set the work day was almost over— most of the crew was in a state of controlled fury," Parone recalled. "They didn't dare outwardly show their anger, but it turned them against her."

Gable liked Marilyn. He was sympathetic toward her. When they actually did get a scene on film, he was proud of the work they were doing. No matter how late she had shown up on a particular day, often he went against the clause in his contract and worked well beyond 5:00 p.m. If Marilyn was in good shape and the scene was going well, he would stay until 6:00 or 7:30, and sometimes even later if need be.

Some days Marilyn showed up dazed, stumbling around and really out of it, and Huston was lucky if he got a usable take out of her. To counteract her lethargy she would take amphetamines in an attempt to work up the energy to shoot.

It soon became apparent that this was no longer a temperamental perfectionist determined to appear on the set only when she was ready to give her very best. Nor did her lateness stem exclusively from being a self-critical narcissist in fear of disappointing herself and her public: Marilyn had become a woman dangerously close to the edge—psychologically damaged, drug addicted—with pills being flown to her by various doctors. There was no longer an illusion that she was able to sustain the schedule of a normal, functioning, professional movie actress.

The dangerous cocktail of drugs she was taking, combined with the pressure of filming, started unleashing uncharacteristic bitchiness in Marilyn. Crew members like Angela Allen became disgusted with her behavior. Allen was shocked when Marilyn aggressively confronted her on the set. "I hear you're Arthur's new girlfriend," Marilyn accused the younger woman. "Are you enjoying it?" Allen was incensed. It was known on the set—having been widely reported in the press—that Marilyn had had an affair with Yves Montand and was still pursuing him. She was the one committing adultery. There was certainly nothing going on between Miller and Allen. "But she could never be the one doing wrong, you see," Allen explained. "She had to believe that Arthur was the one having an affair to make herself the victim."

Marilyn waited for Allen's response.

"If you have so much inside information then you must know if I'm enjoying it or not," Allen shot back. "Because I certainly don't know what you're talking about. And I think you're being very rude with your ac- cusations." Marilyn sauntered off to the safe haven of her entourage.

Later Huston took Allen aside. "Don't feel bad about that," he advised her. "She's not normally like that. That's not Marilyn talking. It's the pills."

At other times Marilyn was the consummate actress, letter perfect to the script and ready to work. Gable said of her admiringly, "When she's there, she's there. All of her is there! She's there to work."

Dawn Wells, who later went on to fame as Mary Ann in TV's *Gilligan's Island*, was then a Nevada high school student cast as an extra in a crowd scene. She happened to witness Marilyn working at her best. On a scorching day, Wells watched Marilyn do take after take with the cast. "What struck me was her fragility,' Wells remembers. "I didn't get a sense of the sex symbol I had seen in previous movies. She was beautiful, yes. Glowing. But I got the feeling that men would like to put their arms around her and protect her rather than take her to bed." Indeed, Wells noticed that both Gable and Clift were very attentive, very gentle with Marilyn between takes. She also noticed Arthur Miller, dour and passive, observ- ing on the sidelines. Wells did not see a disoriented, difficult actress. "On the one day that I was on the set, Marilyn was working. She knew her lines and was working like a true professional."

Huston continued to demand rewrites of a script he intuitively knew was not working. Marilyn and Gable were each handed difficult new scenes to learn the night before shooting. Never a quick study, Marilyn disliked the rewrites even more than the originals. Miller was still grappling with mixed feelings of enchantment and repulsion toward Marilyn—his weird combination of lust and disgust: He couldn't get past her past. He was ashamed of and fascinated by Marilyn's humble beginnings, her lack of education, her childlike neediness, and most of all her sexual history— all of which he kept working into the lines.*

It has been suggested that Marilyn found the script painful to perform because it was based on her life, and the character was too close to her "true self." This is not the case. Marilyn wanted nothing more than a good dramatic role. She resented that Miller could not bring Roslyn—a one-dimensional character—to compelling life.

Miller would have been better served writing a character with qualities he knew Marilyn to possess—vulnerability, naïveté, sensitivity, even suppressed anger—but also changing her character into a totally different woman rather than his caricature of Marilyn. Roslyn is a cardboard cutout of Marilyn plopped down in Nevada. He simply used lines that Marilyn had actually spoken and bits of biographical information, with only the slightest alterations attempting to disguise her. But it's not done in any kind of creative or transformative way.

Any number of excellent writers would be moved by Marilyn's unsettled personality—her vulnerability, her hazy sensuality, her paranoid outbursts—to write a complex and compelling character with Monroe's qualities.**

But Miller continued to grind out scenes that never conveyed a deep

---

*   Miller's true feelings would be conveyed in his revenge play *After the Fall*. By the time it was produced, Marilyn was dead. Elia Kazan directed the play, and it can be argued that it also displayed *his* disparaging feelings for Marilyn. Traces of Miller's truer feelings for Marilyn can be found in all the characters he allegedly based on her after her death. Most of them are unhinged or whores or both (*After the Fall, Some Kind of Love Story, Everybody Wins, Finishing the Picture*).

** Jules Feiffer with the character of "Bobbie" in *Carnal Knowledge*, played by Ann-Margret. Woody Allen's "Nola" in *Match Point*, played by Scarlett Johansson. Also David Cronenberg with "Claire" in *Dead Ringers*, played by Geneviève Bujold. All these writers brilliantly managed to accomplish what Miller could not: creating psychologically complex Monroe-like characters—beautiful, neurotic, seductive, and emotionally fragile women.

exploration of Roslyn. The rewrites made Marilyn more hostile. Continuously now, she felt Miller was using her, just like almost everyone else. Yet Marilyn was trapped in the movie, and she worked hard in an attempt to bring nuances and shading to a character that lacked depth, using the Method style of acting—often painfully searching through her past to bring realism to her character.

Marilyn's physical presence on the set caused contradictory feelings. The script supervisor, Angela Allen, asked some of the male crew members if they really thought Monroe was the ultimate standard of feminine beauty and sexuality. Fed up, grumpy, and exhausted, a number of the men shouted out "No!" in unison. Perhaps they were put off by her inconsiderate lateness, but some of them insisted they found her zonked-out, Rubensian presence unappealing.

Others thought her preternaturally beautiful. The pills, the lack of sleep, the unstoppable anxiety did nothing to diminish Marilyn's astonishing radiance. While visiting the set for *Esquire* magazine, journalist Alice McIntyre marveled: "She is like nothing human you have ever seen or dreamed of. . . . She is astonishingly white, so radically pale that in her presence you can look at others about as easily as you explore the darkness around the moon."

After seeing the first screening of rushes, Angela Allen suddenly understood the fantastic hoopla surrounding the legend. "On the set she was exasperating. But the mythology surrounding her, the legend, all made sense when you saw her up there on the screen . . . she had an absolute luminous, magical quality."

Marilyn, well aware that half of the production crew had turned against her, wanted to show them her celebrated body. It was something important she could add to the movie, she felt. As always, her nudity was the most valuable thing she thought she had to offer.

In a bedroom scene where Marilyn and Gable's characters have spent the night together for the first time, Gay comes into the room and kisses Roslyn. Marilyn stretches languorously and the sheet drops, exposing her breast. The entire set perked up with excitement. Huston, however, said condescendingly, "I've seen 'em before." He wanted a retake. They shot the scene again, this time without the sheet slipping.

There was a great debate as to whether or not the nude take should be used. Frank Taylor, Miller, Gable, and Marilyn all wanted it used. Taylor, who felt it was the best take of the scene, thought Huston was being prudish. Marilyn said, "I love doing things the censors won't pass." Huston was against showing Marilyn's bare breast, not because he was afraid of censorship, but because the nudity was gratuitous in the scene. "Believe me, he was the last person who would be afraid to challenge the censors," Angela Allen stated.

The argument raged on for several days, and was much more heated and contentious than previously reported. Huston was adamant it would not be in the film, and ultimately his decision was the final one. Taylor, exasperated at the thought of the take being lost forever, kept the actual film.

For years it has been believed that the exposed-breast take from *The Misfits* had been destroyed and that Marilyn's only existing nude scene on film was in her last, uncompleted movie, *Something's Got to Give*. However, the unused take from *The Misfits*, including the sound, still exists. Today the nude scene is in Curtice (Frank Taylor's son) Taylor's possession in a locked filing cabinet.

Determined that her body be showcased in the movie, Marilyn continuously wandered around the set, vague and druggy, murmuring in her breathless voice, "When are we going to shoot the bikini scene?" As in *Let's Make Love*, Marilyn's weight fluctuated through the filming. Huston was holding off on the scene, waiting for her to drop a few pounds. Ultimately the scene could be put off no longer, and there is in the film a fleeting shot of a particularly plump Marilyn running from the sea toward Gable, who is waiting for her with an embrace.

In the evenings, after trying to memorize Miller's rewrites—revisions that even Huston considered "pedestrian"—she would be too wound up to sleep. In desperation she was taking up to four Nembutals a night. To make them work faster she would stick a pin in them, sometimes licking the powder from her palm.

Marilyn's good friend and masseur Ralph Roberts would massage her into drowsiness. The following day Whitey Snyder would make up her face while she was flat on her back in bed to allow Marilyn precious time to rest before she had to face the cameras.

With each passing day, Marilyn's pill intake was increasing to alarmingly dangerous doses. An ambulance was called in twice to pump Marilyn's stomach. "There were most definitely at least two serious suicide attempts during the production," Angela Allen recalled. Whether these were serious suicide attempts or accidents is uncertain. Each time she was saved because she managed to make a phone call while she was quickly falling under. The chatter on the set began to focus not only on if she'd show up for shooting, but if she would live through it.

One day, as the cast and crew were waiting, Huston approached Miller. "This has to stop," Huston warned. "Marilyn has had only two afternoons in front of the camera in a week." A few days later a car pulled up to the set. Huston witnessed Marilyn being helped out of the car. The crew watched helplessly as she staggered around. She didn't seem to know where she was. Later, when she was in front of the camera at last, the cameraman, Russell Metty, approached Huston: "I can't film her like this," he said. "Her eyes won't focus."

The production had reached a breaking point. Dr. Ralph Greenson, the psychiatrist who had treated Marilyn during *Let's Make Love*, was called in again to help. Huston made the decision to shut down the production for a week or two. If she didn't complete *The Misfits*, it was unlikely she'd ever be insured on another movie, and if Marilyn was going to complete the film, it was necessary to get her off narcotics.

On Saturday, August 27, Marilyn was flown to Los Angeles by private plane so she could enter Westwood Hospital. She was escorted by her secretary, May Reis, and Paula Strasberg.

While she was in the hospital, Dr. Greenson and an internist, Dr. Hyman Engelberg, started giving her smaller doses of Nembutal and substituting a milder drug. Meanwhile Marilyn stayed busy on the telephone trying to reach Yves Montand and taking calls from Marlon Brando and Frank Sinatra.

After her hospital rest, Marilyn returned to the set on September 5: "I'm looking forward to getting back to work. I'm feeling much better. I guess I was just worn out."

On October 24 *The Misfits* crew returned to Los Angeles for studio work needed to complete the film. She and Miller moved into the Beverly Hills Hotel, where Roberts witnessed a loud argument between them— they had already decided to divorce.

The last day of shooting was on November 4, 1960. At the end of the movie Marilyn and Gable reconcile. "How do you find your way back in the dark?" she asks him as they drive into the night toward their home. It is the last line Marilyn uttered in her final completed film. Privately Huston said of Marilyn, "I'll be surprised if she lives for another year."

As the movie wrapped, Gable saw a rough cut of *The Misfits*. He was very moved by the film and proud of his performance. He announced that he thought it was the best thing he'd done since *Gone with the Wind*

Two days later Marilyn was shaken by the news that Clark Gable had suffered a heart attack and was in the hospital. At first he seemed to be doing well and was on the road to recovery. Gable's wife, Kay, who was staying at the hospital in a nearby room to be close to him, told reporters: "He finished shooting *The Misfits* with Marilyn Monroe on Friday, and he said he never felt better in his life. He spent most of Saturday rolling around on the floor wrestling with his stepchildren." Marilyn traveled back to New York to start preparations for her divorce from Miller.

She had completed her Valentine to her husband.

TWENTY-ONE

A WOMAN ALONE

With the making of two pictures back-to-back, a frantic affair with Yves Montand, and the dissolution of her long-troubled marriage to Arthur Miller, when Marilyn returned to Manhattan in the fall of 1960 she was a diminished, lost woman.

In New York, a city of millions of people, it was easy to get lost in the comfort of anonymity. "I restore myself when I'm alone," she said. Marilyn needed time to learn how to define herself, her career, and an image that was fast becoming obsolete. In New York she could be just one more displaced person trying to find her place: There was a certain comfort in not having the constant expectations of filmmaking and professionalism placed on her. Yet her solitude often turned into loneliness.

She sequestered herself in the dark bedroom of her apartment, where she slipped into depression. She longed to sleep, but she once again found it impossible, except with heavy doses of medication. It was easy for her to lose track of the amount she took before falling under. She'd wake disoriented and lethargic and put on a stack of records—mostly Sinatra's blues ballads.* Naked, she'd spend hours sipping champagne, gazing at herself trancelike in the floor-to-ceiling mirrors that covered the walls. For the first time she was scrutinizing the changes in her body, specifically the result of her steady weight gain over the past few years. Although she had

---

* Sinatra's music was a tremendously important part of her life. She often listened to it in the privacy of her bedroom, and played his records in her dressing room before shooting to get herself in the right mood for a scene.

begun to diet shortly before completion of *The Misfits*, the changes she saw troubled her.

Some of the reviews of *Let's Make Love* commented that she appeared fleshy, not at all like the Marilyn from her prime. The movie magazines, which she read, were also reporting on her weight gain.

Hedda Hopper, the powerful gossip columnist, who had been a failed actress before becoming a reporter, took to her poisonous pen and published a shockingly venomous "open letter" to Marilyn. Disguised as a helpful bit of advice titled "Marilyn, Don't Drink It Won't Bring Back the Baby."

In the article Hopper scolds Marilyn for drinking gin as a way to cope with her miscarriage. It goes on: "Being overly sensitive about your weight and doing nothing about it makes no sense. You're a star and must know you can't have your cake and eat it too." Hopper continued to chastise: "When you do a scene that doesn't come up to your expectations, is it fair to blame the cameraman when your rushes are a disappointment because you are too heavy?"

For a woman as vain as Marilyn, it must have been devastating. However, she wasn't turning a blind eye to her body now. She had already begun to lose weight—and she was seeing the results. Marilyn, approaching thirty-five, knew that she was still considered beautiful, but it was time to start fighting more seriously to protect the part of her image that had given her the only real security she'd ever felt.

On the rare occasion that a friend managed to get her on the phone, her voice was drained of emotion—defeated and faraway. Sometimes, when overwhelmed with anguish, she would phone Yves Montand, who was in Paris trying desperately to repair the relationship with his wife. Marilyn begged him to come see her in New York. When he refused she threatened to fly to Paris to visit him. Montand didn't respond.

Like many women of the era, Marilyn was desperate to have a man to love her, comfort her, affirm her. "A woman can't be alone," she commented. "She needs a man. A man and woman strengthen and support each other . . . she just can't do it by herself." Or Marilyn couldn't.

It wasn't that there was a shortage of suitors. Soon after her separation from Miller, her phone began ringing. Ralph Roberts, who knew her as well as anyone at this time, recalled that a lot of guys were pursuing the newly available Monroe—including Frank Sinatra and John F. Kennedy. Kennedy's invitations would often come through messages passed on by Peter Lawford or Pat Newcomb, but Marilyn wasn't interested in him at this point. She was wounded, unsure—hurting over the end of her marriage and still pining for Montand. The thought of getting involved with someone new seemed daunting.

Pat Newcomb was a name from Marilyn's past—the press agent who had worked briefly on *Bus Stop*. Marilyn felt Newcomb had betrayed her and promptly sent her packing. Newcomb entered Marilyn's life again, but this time the two would work well together and become close.

Marilyn's primary press agent, Rupert Allan, decided to move to Europe to represent Princess Grace of Monaco, who was a good friend. The head of Marilyn's public relations firm, Arthur Jacobs, recommended she give Newcomb another try. With Allan gone, it was necessary for Newcomb to travel to Nevada to talk some business with the star. Marilyn, who was especially vulnerable, was warm during the conversation. When she was headed back to New York, Paula Strasberg suggested that Newcomb fly with her because she was about to announce the separation from Arthur Miller and somebody had to do it.

Worn out and feeling defenseless, Marilyn was apparently able to put aside the previous antagonism that had developed when she believed Newcomb had passed herself off as "Marilyn Monroe" on a date, while handling her press during the shooting of *Bus Stop*. Evidently the very smart and hardworking Newcomb convinced Marilyn that she would be devoted to her.

Those who knew Marilyn well in her last years say that the two women would become extraordinarily close. Rupert Allan and Ralph Roberts (among others) would come to believe that Pat Newcomb became obsessed with Marilyn as she became more and more a part of her famous client's life.

———

On November 16 Marilyn was awoken by the phone and, in her half-sleep state, was informed that Clark Gable had died. He died of a coronary thrombosis while recuperating in the hospital from a heart attack. In childhood she had fantasized that Gable was her father. He behaved tenderly and protectively toward her during the harrowing months they spent making *The Misfits*. Now she had lost another connection to a father figure. Marilyn was overwhelmed with despair.

To make matters worse, she worried that perhaps her frustrating absences during the shooting had contributed to Gable's death. His widow made statements to the press suggesting that the maddening delays in making *The Misfits* had contributed to his heart attack. Kay Gable never mentioned Marilyn by name, but the implication seemed clear: "That picture helped kill my husband. It wasn't the physical exertion that did it; it was the horrible tension—that eternal waiting. He waited around forever, for everybody. He'd get so angry waiting."*

It must be noted that Gable had crash-dieted before shooting started in order to be in better shape for the film. He was a three-pack-a-day smoker and had been for decades. Gable also insisted on doing the extremely strenuous stunts involving the capturing of the wild horses—one of which had him being dragged across the desert.

Still, in the court of public opinion, the blame was placed on Marilyn, and she couldn't help but feel some guilt. "Murderer!" strangers would call out as she hurried down the city streets. How easily they could turn. Her public, her people, her fans, the ones who always called out, "Hiya Marilyn, how're you feeling today?" were now shouting, "How does it feel to be a murderer?"

Outside the claustrophobia and deadness of her bedroom, the city was more alive than usual. The holidays can be crushing, especially for the lonely, and Marilyn was feeling it that season. Surrounded by people who were doing things, traveling, embracing their relationships with

---

* Later, when pressed, Kay Gable refused to put any blame on Marilyn for Clark's death. Kay remained fond of her, and sent her a warm invitation to her baby's christening, which Marilyn accepted.

friends and family, Marilyn had no one with whom she wanted to share Christmastime.

Marilyn spent Christmas Eve quietly in her apartment with her new public relations agent, Pat Newcomb. For a present, Marilyn gave Newcomb a mink coat. It was an extravagant gift for a recent employee—and someone she had clashed with and mistrusted in the past. Perhaps it was Marilyn's way of saying she had been wrong about her initial impression, but it's also poignant to think that Marilyn felt she was valued by her friends and employees only when she was giving them valuables.

That evening, however, she received a "forest of poinsettias" from Joe DiMaggio. He sent them, he explained, because he knew she would call to thank him, which of course she did. "Besides," he added when he had her on the phone, "who in the hell else do you have in the world?"

She invited him to visit her, and they did spend Christmas night alone together. They quietly began seeing each other again. Always very discreet, DiMaggio would visit her at her apartment. He would arrive late in the evening, use the service elevator, enter through the kitchen door, and leave by dawn.

They continued seeing each other for several weeks until he was called back to Florida on business. DiMaggio remained concerned not only at the apparent wasteland of Marilyn's emotional life but her increasingly haggard appearance. Food was something she rarely thought of anymore.

An unhappy break in the monotony of Marilyn's misery came on January 20, 1961, when Marilyn flew to Mexico with Pat Newcomb and her attorney, Aaron Frosch. Newcomb wisely chose the day of President Kennedy's inauguration to deflect attention—and headlines—from the Monroe-Miller divorce.

On that day Kennedy walked into his wife, Jackie's, bedroom while she was having her hair done for the inauguration by the stylist Rosemarie Sorrentino. When Jackie mentioned that Sorrentino also did Marilyn Monroe's hair on occasion, Kennedy casually asked if Marilyn—whom he had not yet met—was as temperamental as her reputation. Neither woman thought to ask why the soon-to-be president was interested in Marilyn Monroe's temperament.

Meanwhile Pat Newcomb remembers that she and Marilyn watched the inauguration at the Dallas airport while between flights. In the Mexico court Marilyn pleaded "incompatibility of character." She requested an immediate divorce. It was granted without incident, and she was back in the safety of her apartment four days later.

It seems that nobody was aware of just how sick Marilyn really was. Fox announced that they planned to cast her in the lead of *Goodbye Charlie*, by George Axelrod, which had been a Broadway flop starring Lauren Bacall. The plot revolved around a callous playboy, Charlie, who is killed by a lover's jealous husband and instantly reincarnated in the body of a gorgeous woman—to be played by Marilyn.

Although Charlie materializes in glorious female form (karmic retribution for the way he treated women), his/her mind and mannerisms remain those of a male. The studio was eager to collect the last picture Marilyn owed them on her contract and thought the novelty of Marilyn Monroe playing a man trapped inside her famous curves would be a box-office bonanza.

Marilyn, however, was appalled at the idea of having to butch it up. She couldn't bear the thought of her femininity being questioned. Obsessing over homosexuality during a psychiatric session with Greenson, Marilyn had expressed rage when he informed her that there was something feminine and masculine in both genders, and she became mortified that anything masculine might be perceived in her. Now she was being asked to act masculine on screen for laughs.

"The studio people want me to do *Goodbye Charlie*," she fumed to the press. "But I'm not going to do it. I don't like the idea of playing a man in a woman's body, you know? It doesn't seem feminine."

In early 1961 she seized on an offer of a project she thought could move her career in a new direction. It was announced in the press with great fanfare that Marilyn would star in a high-profile television production of *Rain*.

The play, based on Somerset Maugham's short story, is about a prostitute named Sadie Thompson and the obsessed preacher who tries to reform her. Exercising total control over Marilyn's confidence in her acting abilities, Lee Strasberg inserted himself into the project from its beginning, spotlighting his role in her life as a way of reflecting his own importance. Strasberg thought the role of the prostitute in *Rain* was ideal for her—and he wanted to be involved: Sharing a screen credit with the Actors Studio's biggest cash cow was irresistible.

NBC offered Marilyn $150,000 to star in a ninety-minute adaptation of the play. Maugham was delighted with the idea of Marilyn in the role. "I'm so glad you're going to play Sadie in the television production," the legendary author wrote her. "I'm sure you'll be splendid."

But Marilyn wanted Strasberg to direct, something NBC would not approve because of his lack of experience. Negotiations for the project would continue for months to come, and whenever interviewed, Marilyn would confidently proclaim that the role of Sadie Thompson in *Rain* would be her next project.

Although the public was aware that Marilyn was troubled, they had no idea just how ill—emotionally and physically—she was in 1961. The death of Clark Gable certainly had a great deal to do with her emotional distress. But there were many other contributing factors to her downward spiral—the end of her marriage to Miller and the hopeful affair with (and ultimate rejection by) Montand.

The release of *The Misfits* also devastated her. Before its premiere she had tremendous hopes that this performance might be the start of a turning point in her career. So much effort had gone into it. So much was riding on it.

Glamorous, dressed to the nines in black, smiling radiantly, hopefully, and escorted by Montgomery Clift, Marilyn attended the premiere on January 31. Arthur Miller was there, but he and Marilyn didn't acknowledge each other and sat at opposite sides of the theater. There was a small party set up after the screening, but when the movie ended, Curtice Taylor, the son of the film's producer, Frank Taylor, remembers Marilyn rushing out of the theater with Clift without saying a word to anyone: "Clearly she was distraught and not happy with the film."

The reviews echoed her opinion. In spite of the many months of anticipation and hoopla building up toward the world's greatest sexpot finally proving herself a serious dramatic actress, the finished picture was a letdown. Despite a few excellent reviews, the critics' opinions leaned toward the negative.

Bosley Crowther, in the all-important *New York Times*, said: "Miss Monroe—well, she is completely blank and unfathomable as a new divorcée who shed her husband because 'you could touch him but he wasn't there.'" He went on to say, "There is really not much about her that is very exciting or interesting."

Now Marilyn's dreams of being taken seriously as an actress seemed as far away as ever. She had let down the Strasbergs. She had let down her fans. She had let down herself.

She confided to Ralph Roberts that her smothering depression made her feel as if she couldn't go on any longer. Citing her guilt feelings regarding her possible contribution to Gable's heart attack, Marilyn looked out the window of her thirteenth-story apartment. She considered hurling herself to the pavement.

"I remembered reading somewhere that people who fall from heights lose consciousness before they hit the ground," she remarked. The thought of a loss of consciousness and then oblivion seemed welcoming to her. She climbed out on the ledge. She was going to throw herself down. It would have only been a matter of moments before someone looked up and noticed her there. But just before she made the plunge, she saw a woman wearing a brown dress walking on the sidewalk.

Marilyn recognized her. The woman stopped and waited for the bus. "I was afraid if I jumped, I could splatter all over her. So I couldn't," she said. The attention to detail and the sudden reality of such a messy death in front of someone she knew snapped her out of the fantasy of jumping.

At their next appointment, Marilyn's psychiatrist, Dr. Kris, was disturbed by the drug-addled, washed-out-looking woman who sat before her. In a tiny voice Marilyn recounted the suicide attempt. Dr. Kris was alarmed. Like most people who were close to Marilyn, the doctor was well aware of her famous patient's preoccupation with suicide. Arthur Miller once confided to Pat Newcomb that Marilyn had tried to jump out of that

TWENTY-TWO

On February 7 Dr. Kris herself drove Marilyn to New York Hospital. Although the staff knew who their new patient was, the just-divorced Marilyn Monroe signed herself in as "Miss Faye Miller," so it wouldn't be leaked to the press that she was being hospitalized.

Once the forms were signed, however, everything changed. Marilyn immediately knew something was wrong. It was as if the staff, the doctors and the nurses, had been told some inside information about her condition that she wasn't aware of. They took her by the arms and, in a fast-moving blur, she was escorted down an ominous system of hallways through New York Hospital to a psychiatric wing known as the Payne Whitney Clinic.

Because she was admitted as a patient who had threatened suicide and could possibly harm herself, she was locked in a bare, cell-like room. It was only moments until she realized she was in a psychiatric ward. "Cement blocks and all," Marilyn later revealed to Dr. Greenson.

What had haunted her all her life had become a reality—the fear of the fate of her mother's insanity, the terror of a madhouse. There were bars on the windows. Patients were locked in their rooms—but there was a window on every door so she could be gawked at by any passerby like a bug under a magnifying glass. Marilyn would be allowed no privacy—and thus no dignity.

Stripped of any power, stripped of her clothes, it was as if she had signed same window on Fifty-seventh Street during their marriage, and that "he pulled her in."

Dr. Kris made the decision that Marilyn should be hospitalized. She assured Marilyn that the best thing for her would be some rest and relaxation under medical supervision. Undoubtedly thinking of the pampering she had been given while hospitalized in Los Angeles when *The Misfits* shut down, Marilyn thought that perhaps it was a good idea.

away her rights as well as her identity. "I felt I was in prison for a crime I hadn't committed," Marilyn stated. As a child she had often been placed in situations where she was at the complete mercy of those around her. Panic was gripping her, but—like a child, like an orphan, like a ward of the state—she sensed that her best defense was to try to remain calm, follow orders, and respond rationally.

The first thing she was ordered to do was bathe. She took her bath under supervision. Afterward a psychiatrist whom she did not know arrived to give her a full physical examination, including a breast exam, checking for lumps. Marilyn attempted to explain that she had been given a complete physical less than a month before. Without comment the psychiatrist continued his probing. She felt violated but was afraid to be perceived as violent, so she allowed the examination to proceed.

In her locked room she noticed the markings on the wall, scratchings, cries for help, from patients who had inhabited the room before her. She would not scratch. She would remain calm. Finally a nurse entered; it was she who confirmed to Marilyn that she was on a psychiatric floor for very disturbed and depressed patients.

Meanwhile the screams of other patients echoed through the halls. "They screamed out when life was unbearable for them, I guess," Marilyn mused. Even amid this chaos, Marilyn's mind was churning with empathy and compassion, sympathizing with the confined women around her. "I felt an available psychiatrist should have talked to them. Perhaps to alleviate even temporarily their misery and pain—I think they [the doctors] might learn something even—but all are only interested in something from the books they studied. . . . Maybe from some live suffering human being they could discover more."

Eventually several doctors came in to evaluate Marilyn's state of mind.

"Why aren't you happy here?" she was asked.

"Well," Marilyn replied reasonably, "I'd have to be nuts if I liked it here."

Since it was the part of the day when occupational therapy took place—when some of the patients mingled—they urged Marilyn to socialize. Marilyn wondered out loud what she could possibly do. They suggested she knit, or play cards or checkers. The absurdity of a panicked Marilyn Monroe playing cards with mental patients was lost on these professionals, although it was not lost on Marilyn.

"The day I do that you will have a nut on your hands," she retorted.

"Why do you think you're different?" she was asked, as if she were the average woman on the street. Later Marilyn would say of the Payne Whitney doctors, "They should all have their heads examined." For now, still playing along, she said simply, "I just am."

They had misunderstood. She didn't think she was better than anyone else, or deserving of special treatment—Marilyn was simply very much aware that she wasn't regarded as the average person. Still, she did try to socialize a bit and soon encountered a woman who described herself as having a "mental condition," confiding that she had tried to cut her throat and slash her wrists "either three or four times."

This piteous woman observed that Marilyn "looked sad." She suggested that Marilyn call a friend—maybe it would make her feel less lonely. Marilyn explained that she had been told that there were no phones on this floor. The woman led Marilyn—shaken that the staff had lied to her—to a phone, but as Marilyn started dialing, a security guard grabbed the receiver from her hand. "You can't use the phone!" he snapped.

Marilyn grew more desperate. She returned to her room and sat on the bed trying to think of what to do next.

Her fame could not shield her here. Nor could her beauty or wit. It was a defenselessness she hadn't experienced for a long time. Marilyn went into panic mode. She sat on the bed for the moment, her thoughts divided between trying to continue to cooperate and play along or doing something dramatic as a way to force them to let her out of there. Marilyn asked herself: "What would Marlon [Brando] do if he was put in my position? That kept my sanity because I knew he'd do a lot more."

She decided to turn to her career—which was a success—to help her get out of the situation. She would approach the experience as an improvisational acting exercise. Her Method-trained mind went back to *Don't Bother to Knock*, the film she had made just when she was on the brink of superstardom. In the movie she portrayed a troubled young woman who, when confronted by the authorities, held up a razor, threatening to hurt herself. Marilyn acknowledged to herself that the idea to try that in this place was "corny"—but she couldn't see any other way to get them to listen to her.

In order to get a piece of glass, she picked up a chair and threw it against the window. To her surprise the glass didn't shatter. It was thick, unbreakable. It would take a lot of work—but she was determined. With all her strength she kept at it, hurling the chair against the glass until a small, sharp shard cracked off.

When two burly doctors, along with two hefty nurses, arrived at her room, she startled them by holding up the glass, threatening, "If you are going to treat me like a nut I'll act like a nut." Marilyn had no real intention of cutting her skin or harming herself. She was, after all, an actress.

But they took the threat seriously. She told them to let her out of there. They refused. The situation became surreal. They asked her to come with them quietly, but since she had no reason to trust that they had her best interests in mind, she refused to cooperate. Marilyn continued to sit there, broken glass in hand. The four of them pounced and seized her by the wrists until she dropped the glass. They then grabbed her arms and legs and carried her—facedown and sobbing—to the elevator.

She was brought up to the ominous seventh floor—reserved for patients who were violently disturbed and dangerous. The first thing she was ordered to do by the nurse was to disrobe and take a bath. She was growing suspicious and upset about the focus on her body. Marilyn explained that she had already been given a bath on the sixth floor. She was told sternly that every time a patient changed floors they were required to take a bath.

After her second bath, a dour hospital administrator—Marilyn wasn't even sure if he was a doctor—began questioning her about her movie work. "How can you work when you're depressed?" he wanted to know.

She tried to articulate that depression was not so cut-and-dry, black-and-white. Many artists suffer from depression from time to time and still manage to create. "Didn't he think that perhaps Greta Garbo and Charlie Chaplin perhaps and perhaps Ingrid Bergman they had been depressed when they worked sometimes but I said it's like saying a ball player like DiMaggio if he could hit a ball when he was depressed. Pretty silly."

"You are a very sick girl," he informed her, based on their short exchange. "And you have been for a very long time."

By now word had leaked out to the media that Marilyn had been hospitalized, but no one on the outside was quite sure why. Her hospitalization caused widespread speculation, and reporters camped out in front of New York Hospital. Her press rep, John Springer, released a benign statement allowing that Marilyn had been admitted "for a period of rest and recuperation following a very arduous year in which she completed two films in rapid succession and in which she has had to face marital problems."

That explanation satisfied no one, and the media kept their vigil outside the hospital. Lewd stories were being leaked out: Marilyn had ripped off her hospital gown in front of gaping doctors and nurses.

A resourceful journalist, Chiari Pisani, an American correspondent for the Italian publication *Gente*, called a doctor she knew at the hospital and asked him if he could possibly get her any information on Marilyn's condition. Pisani soon heard a physician from the clinic give his diagnosis of Marilyn: "Miss Monroe does not have any symptoms of schizophrenia—she is only psychiatrically disconnected in an acute way because she works too hard—two movies in one year—and the recent divorce."

Pisani discovered that Marilyn had been placed in a padded room—and, for a time, in a straitjacket—where she was kept in a trancelike sleep for three days.

The remoteness and secretive demeanor of the staff, the seclusion of her rooms, and the constant exposure of her body made each passing moment seem more sinister and dangerous to Marilyn. She was afraid to be left alone because some of the employees were not to be trusted. After she was sedated, they removed the straitjacket but restrained her arms.

Marilyn would later reveal to her friend Gloria Romanoff, the wife of restaurateur Michael, that she was indeed kept semisedated—but not so medicated that she wasn't aware of what was going on around her.

Of course her presence in the sanatorium caused corruption.

During the evening a procession of hospital personnel—doctors, interns nurses, orderlies—all in uniform, would come into her room, pull down the blankets, and, transfixed to be in the presence of this legend, violate her body. "There I was with my arms bound," she told Gloria Romanoff. "And—you'll find this hard to believe—they came into my room and touched my private areas. I was unable to defend myself. I was a curiosity to them, with no one defending me or having my interest at heart." She felt that, knowing how people reacted to her, the hospital should have provided a guard at the door. Marilyn added that it was mostly the women who came in and probed her body. "Probably lesbians," she added.

Romanoff believed her completely, commenting that Marilyn had no reason to reveal this "except it was a bit of a nightmare for her." She vividly remembered Marilyn quietly but intently telling the story. She told her about this horrifying episode at the hospital with stoic resolve, as if she were lecturing, "See? These are the things that can happen to you."

"It was a shattering thing to hear," Romanoff recalled many years later. It enforced what Romanoff had always thought about Marilyn. That she really needed someone around to protect her at all times. "She was just so vulnerable to this kind of thing."

Finally a sympathetic nurse managed to get a pencil and paper to Marilyn and allowed her to write a short letter. Out of all the people she knew in the world, it was the Strasbergs she reached out to for help. "I'm locked up with all these poor nutty people," she wrote. "I'm sure to end up a nut too if I stay in this nightmare. Please help me. This is the last place I should be."*

At last Marilyn was able to get to a phone. The one person she could think of who might be able to help her was Joe DiMaggio. Joe was in St. Petersburg, Florida, sitting in front of the television when he received the call from a sobbing Marilyn. "That was all he needed to hear," remembered DiMaggio's friend Stacy Edwards. "He jumped on the very next plane."

---

* Not being family members, the Strasbergs were unable to do anything about Marilyn's situation.

DiMaggio arrived at the hospital that very night. In the face of the staff's formal, no-nonsense, unyielding demeanor, he was like a wild animal unleashed. "I want my wife," he demanded at the front desk. Taken aback at the sight of an enraged Joe DiMaggio, no one dared remind him that Miss Monroe was no longer his wife and he had no authority to have her released.

DiMaggio was informed, however, that he needed to get permission from Dr. Kris to have Marilyn released. "I don't care who does it!" DiMaggio bellowed. "But if somebody doesn't get her out of here I swear to Christ I'll take this hospital apart brick by brick!"

The next day Marilyn was taken to the hospital's basement, where a labyrinth of passageways led to another door, outside which a car with Ralph Roberts and Dr. Kris was waiting for her.

Once they were safely in the car, Marilyn released all the bottled-up anger and fear that had been festering in her for four days. "Marilyn began screaming at the doctor as only she could," Roberts recalled. "She was like a hurricane unleashed. Dr. Kris was very frightened and very shaken by the violence of Marilyn's response at their meeting. I wound up driving the doctor home. There was a lot of traffic, so we inched down the West Side Highway overlooking the river, and Dr. Kris was trembling and kept repeating over and over, 'I did a terrible thing, a terrible, terrible thing. Oh, God, I didn't mean to. I didn't mean to, but I did.'"

Marilyn was transferred to Columbia Presbyterian Hospital in upper Manhattan. This was the kind of hospital Marilyn had originally had in mind. She was allowed to have visitors and, after a while, was even allowed to leave on a pass for short periods of time. Most important, Joe DiMaggio promised to stay in town until she felt safe.

She stayed at the hospital for three weeks. DiMaggio, who had to return to Florida for business, flew in once a week to visit her for a couple of days. She received visitors, telegrams, flowers, and notes, one from her good friend and former lover Marlon Brando:

Dear Marilyn,
   The best reappraisals are born in the worst crisis. It has happened to all of us in relative degrees. Be glad for it and don't be afraid of being afraid. It

*can only help. Relax and enjoy it. I send you my thoughts and my warmest
affections.*

—Marlon

Marilyn made sure that everyone at Columbia Presbyterian knew she
was coherent and sane. She did not emerge from her room without being
properly groomed, coiffed, and made up. One doctor, who spoke with her
often, found her "incredibly beautiful, but very troubled. I had no idea if
what she told me was the truth or not. It was fascinating, but deeply disturbing."

Time, on the other hand, was impressed with Marilyn's public "nervous breakdown" and subsequent treatment and wrote, "In seeking help,
she may have done more than the psychiatrists to win popular acceptance
of a more modern view of mental illness and treatment for it."

On March 5, looking rested and healthy, Marilyn checked out of
Columbia Presbyterian and, supported by Pat Newcomb, emerged into
the obligatory throng of waiting reporters—a greedy, aggressive, out-of-
control mob. Amid the pandemonium she paused in front of the micro-
phones being thrust at her, giving simple quotes like, "I feel wonderful,
thank you," before moving on to the safety of a waiting car.

Her loyalty to the Strasbergs remained strong. Marilyn still looked
to Lee Strasberg as the link to an important dramatic career. He was her
confidence. To show her allegiance to him, on March 13, just a week after
her release from the hospital, she attended a benefit to raise money for
the Actors Studio, held at Roseland Dance City in Manhattan.

The stress of the hardships of the previous year showed clearly on her
face that night. She looked ravaged and empty, as if she had sent her tired
body to attend the function without her soul inhabiting it. It was one of
her few public appearances where nowhere in sight was her special spark,
her magic. She drank continuously throughout the evening.

In photographs it looks as if she would prefer to be anywhere else.
Especially considering the fact that sitting at her table briefly was, of all
people, Vivien Leigh. The *Gone with the Wind* star had just finalized her
divorce from Laurence Olivier, and surely she and Marilyn were looking

back on their regrets and the misery of *The Prince and the Showgirl* shoot. Only one photo of this survives. At one end of the table there is Monroe, wrapped in her furs, pale, thin, lost. On the other end Leigh is smiling and smoking a cigarette. In the center is Susan Strasberg, staring straight into the camera, looking stunned.

At the end of March it was once more DiMaggio she turned to.* She decided to visit him for a recuperative vacation in a secluded resort in Redington Beach, Florida. Although she loved DiMaggio dearly, she was not "in love" with him any longer. They would have to settle on a special friendship for now. Their relationship had become what might be today called "loving friends with benefits."

When Marilyn returned refreshed from her vacation with DiMaggio, she started seeing Frank Sinatra—who had begun to pursue her months before. She had known him through the years—they had a lot of conversations—but up to this point they'd never had an affair. Now she was excited, giddy, and nervous at the prospect of a romance with the legendary crooner. The only time Ralph Roberts saw Marilyn drink vodka was when she was going on her first real date with Sinatra, who was staying at the Waldorf. Marilyn asked Roberts to drive her there.

"I always had a flask of vodka in my glove compartment," Roberts remembered. During the drive Marilyn started having an anxiety attack and finally asked him if she could take a sip. Roberts replied, "Sure, but I don't have a cup." Marilyn didn't care. She took a sip from the flask and "almost vomited." Roberts recalled that, most of the time, Marilyn couldn't bear hard liquor. "It did something to her."

The date, however, was a success, and they discreetly started seeing each other. Sinatra presented Marilyn with a white Maltese-poodle crossbreed so she wouldn't feel so alone. Marilyn teasingly named the dog "Maf Honey" because of Sinatra's alleged ties to the Mafia.

---

* DiMaggio told Marilyn that he was a changed man—and that it was partially due to her. He said he had taken her advice to go into psychotherapy after the divorce and that it saved his life. He saw the errors of his ways—that he had been remote, distant. He told her that if he had been Marilyn, he would have divorced him too. But if he was hoping for a total reconciliation, a remarriage, Marilyn had other ideas.

When Marilyn mentioned Sinatra's name to Dr. Greenson, he frowned through his mustache and looked up at the ceiling. (Sinatra had been a patient of Greenson's before Marilyn.) Obviously the doctor didn't think that the singer would be a good influence on Marilyn, but she defended him in a letter. "He has been (secretly) a very tender friend," Marilyn wrote. "I know you won't believe this but you must trust me with my instincts. It was sort of a fling on the wing. I have never done that before— but now I have—but he is very unselfish in bed."

The affair would go on to be more than a "fling on the wing" but Marilyn was hesitant to get involved seriously. She was still smarting from her divorce from Miller and hurting over the relationship with Yves Montand. In the letter to Greenson she added: "From Yves I have heard nothing—but I don't mind because I have such a strong, tender, wonderful memory."

Marilyn's outlook seemed to be turning more positive. Directly quoting Brando's note to her, Marilyn told *Look* magazine, "I'm not afraid to be afraid anymore." The winter had been bleak; the gray weather, with a lot of rain and snow, had mirrored her moods. Now, more aware than ever of the passing of time, she decided to go back to the West Coast. She looked forward to getting back to the sunshine of Los Angeles, and to the business of being Marilyn Monroe.

TWENTY-THREE

MANIC-DEPRESSIVE

No one close to Marilyn in the last two years of her life doubts the importance of Pat Newcomb to Marilyn. "It's Pat Newcomb who knows more about Marilyn Monroe than anyone else," Jeanne Martin (Dean Martin's wife) commented. "But one has never been able to get anything very revealing out of her."

In Monroe biographies, the shadowy Pat Newcomb often comes across as being a not very forthcoming person, mostly because of her silences and dodges when it comes to discussing Marilyn in her very few interviews. Yet many people talk of her as being a very smart, loyal, and attractive woman with a marvelous sense of humor.

Newcomb and Marilyn had psychological traits in common. Jeanne, who socialized with both women, observed that Newcomb, like Marilyn, "had highs and lows." Both of them used prescription drugs, especially sedatives. Both women relied heavily on their psychiatrists. Newcomb is an accomplished, complex individual who has had many decades to evolve after Marilyn's death—it's understandable that she doesn't want her reputation to be associated only with Marilyn Monroe. But for the purpose of this biography she is examined in the framework of that relationship.

Newcomb was at Marilyn's side at almost every major event in 1961–62, hovering discreetly, protectively on the sidelines. When not working, the two women socialized together, and it was through Newcomb that Marilyn reacquainted herself with Peter Lawford and his wife, Pat Kennedy Lawford, the sister of John and Bobby Kennedy. Newcomb would often stay at Marilyn's apartment when she was in New York and—at times—at her home in Los Angeles. At the scene of Marilyn's death, a devastated Newcomb asked gathering reporters: "How would you feel if your best friend died?"

Newcomb was the primary person in charge of Marilyn's publicity, but the relationship went way beyond that. People who were around at the time go so far as to say that Newcomb became obsessed with Marilyn.

Because of Newcomb's feverish dedication to Marilyn, her intentions began to confuse the star. Marilyn both craved this devotion and feared it (coming from a woman). Some say Newcomb wanted more from Marilyn than she was prepared to give. But—at this stage in her life—without a husband or steady lover, Marilyn needed someone who extended complete dedication, unconditional love. This is what Newcomb offered.

In return—as she did with anyone who was devoted to her—Marilyn made extreme demands. If Marilyn tried to call Newcomb at home and got a busy signal, she would become hysterical. When she finally got through she would scream and yell. Eventually Marilyn had a separate phone line installed in Newcomb's apartment so she could reach her at all times. Marilyn was the only one who had the number. "And she'd call and call," Newcomb remembered. "I tried to do everything I could, but sometimes it was just too much."

As always, Marilyn would do her best to repay Newcomb's loyalty. After she complained that her car wasn't working well, Marilyn gave Newcomb a new Thunderbird. She gifted her with a mink coat. And after wearing them a few times, Marilyn gave Pat a valuable pair of emerald earrings Frank Sinatra had given her.

But after Marilyn's death, Newcomb seemed to want to distance herself from their intensely personal and multilayered relationship. In 1992 Newcomb told Donald Spoto: "All of these publications calling me 'her best friend, her closest friend.' It wasn't like that. I mean, she told me a lot of things. . . . But she never told anybody everything. But I think of a friendship as a two-way street. And since she is not anyone I would have ever called on as a friend, I don't consider it a friendship in that way. It was a professional relationship. I cared about her as a person."

In spite of what Newcomb had to say after the fact, all the evidence shows that she and Marilyn were close. Very close. Rupert Allan became annoyed when, after talking to Marilyn at the office, Newcomb suggested that if he wanted to know what was going on with Marilyn, he should go through her. Allan snapped back that he had been a friend of Marilyn's for a long time.

Michael Selsman, who also worked with Newcomb at the Arthur P. Jacobs agency, claims that there was a lot of talk about a possible lesbian relationship between Marilyn and Newcomb—and it wasn't coming from the show-business community. The rumors spread among people in Marilyn's circle "who knew her and worked with her."

Whether their relationship eventually became sexualized or not, it definitely became one of mutual dependency that was unhealthy for both women.

Newcomb was possessive of Marilyn, building a barrier around her client—someone described Marilyn as "a caged animal"—no one could get to Marilyn without going through Newcomb. "Pat Newcomb was the closest confidante to Marilyn," Milt Ebbins, Peter Lawford's agent and friend, who was part of Marilyn's social set, commented. "Was there something sexual between them? I have no proof of that, but they were very, very close. Constantly together. Marilyn loved her, she was very fond of her. I don't know what their association was. I hesitate even to read something into it."

Newcomb asserted to the author Lois Banner that there was no lesbian relationship between her and Marilyn. Yet Susan Strasberg made the distinction that "the adrenaline rush that came from Marilyn's involvement with Pat Newcomb became somewhat sexualized." Strasberg would say that Marilyn had nicknamed Newcomb "Sybil," implying friendly "sibling rivalry." But as their relationship intensified, Marilyn's feelings grew more complicated, with paranoid undertones.

In those pre-sexual-liberation days, what had come to terrify Marilyn was the confusing of genders. For her there was a clear line of masculine and feminine behavior. She was paranoid about anyone finding anything masculine in herself.

Marilyn began discussing Newcomb in her sessions with Greenson, with homosexuality a major concern. "She could not bear the slightest hint of anything homosexual," Greenson wrote. "She had an outright phobia of homosexuality* and yet unwittingly fell into situations which had homosexual coloring, which she then recognized and projected onto the other, who then became her enemy."

Was Marilyn afraid of developing sexual feelings for Newcomb, or did she simply resent Newcomb for pressuring her into something she wanted no part of—shades of Natasha Lytess? "Marilyn's mother was schizophrenic," Susan Strasberg observed. "As a result Marilyn's feelings toward women were complex and ambivalent."

In his correspondence Greenson gave an example of Marilyn's relationship with a girlfriend named "Pat," who had put a blond streak in her hair, close to Marilyn's color. Marilyn interpreted Newcomb's emulation as an attempt to "take possession of her," feeling that identification meant "homosexual possessiveness." Greenson wrote that Marilyn "burned with fury against this girl," accusing her of trying to "rob her most valuable possession."

So much of Marilyn's identity, her public persona, was being the sexual desire of men. Her whole projection of herself was based on that. She once stated, "I don't mind it being a man's world. As long as I can be a woman in it." Newcomb's perceived passionate feelings threatened her. But—with everything in her life becoming more confusing and unclear—she pressed ahead with the relationship.

"She could be very touching," Newcomb recalled. "I always felt a kind of watching out for her. But deep down at the core she was really strong, much stronger than all of us. And you'd forget it for a while because she seemed so vulnerable." But sometimes Marilyn's suppressed angst surfaced, and she would say something "quite cruel," Newcomb revealed. "She could be quite mean."

Milt Ebbins would witness Marilyn's "meanness" toward Pat on a flight

---

* Just the idea of being suspected of homosexuality frightened Marilyn. As the world's sex symbol, the desire of all men, she couldn't stand the idea of her sexuality being in question. Revered as the ideal woman, she was terrified of anything of a masculine nature being detected in herself, although homosexuality in others generally didn't bother her. Certainly she had many gay friends that she loved and respected, including Montgomery Clift, Rupert Allan, Truman Capote, and Jack Cole.

from Los Angeles to New York. He was sitting behind Marilyn and New-comb. Marilyn started yelling at Newcomb. "She was really screaming at her," Ebbins recalled. Even in the airplane with the motors running, Ebbins could hear Marilyn's angry voice hysterically lashing into Newcomb. "Marilyn's vocabulary included words I'd never ever heard of, and she wielded them like a sailor with no embarrassment," Susan Strasberg once said. "She had quite a temper when she lost control." Ebbins leaned over the seat and saw that Newcomb was in tears. Just sitting there crying—taking it. Ebbins said, "Marilyn, cool it.'" Then Marilyn turned around and gave Ebbins a sly, cat-that-ate-the-canary grin.

As the months went on, Marilyn's love-hate relationship with Newcomb—and sibling rivalry—would grow more extreme. It would crescendo on the last mysterious day of Marilyn's life.

Marilyn entered a manic phase that was all about shedding the past four years. She wanted something new in her life: a movie, a lover, a hairdo. With a renewed vitality, she lost weight, gushing to the columnist Jonah Ruddy, "I'm on a high-protein diet and I weigh 123 pounds, which is right for me. I feel absolutely wonderful."

With her shaky new confidence she consulted a hip young hair stylist, George Masters, who went to meet Marilyn at the Beverly Hills Hotel.

"Do me any way you want. I don't care," Marilyn told him, as he assessed the freshly washed hair hanging limply to her shoulders. Masters couldn't believe that this huge star would give him free rein over her legendary blond locks. But in the moment, sipping champagne in a ripped terry robe, it really seemed as if she couldn't care less.

He went to work on her, cutting her hair shorter and teasing it out. When he finished he gushed, "Miss Monroe, you look absolutely *killing*." Marilyn loved it and called to tell her newspaper columnist friends about her new look; they labeled Monroe's new hairstyle the "killer cut."

As if to project a new hopeful attitude and youthful vigor, Marilyn started dressing in very bright colors—Pucci became a favorite designer. Gone were the polo coats and baggy checkered slacks of New York. In previous years she had preferred neutral colors—black, white, and nude tones. Soon her closets were filled with clingy Pucci dresses of fuchsia, powder blue, hot pink, lime green, and orange—which showed off her newly svelte figure. She bought colorful patterned blouses she contrasted with fitted white shantung pants and spike heels. She looked marvelous.

However Marilyn was also experiencing the physical effects of entering her midthirties. As she lost more weight, her breasts became smaller. A few years earlier Billy Wilder had commented: "She has breasts like granite, they defy gravity." Now they were becoming less perky.

Still, she liked to be provocative and give the illusion of being braless with high, firm breasts. Marilyn's longtime makeup artist, Whitey Snyder, disclosed that—in those days before breast implants—Marilyn came up with an ingenious trick: Under her clothes she started wearing a flimsy bra. To give the impression that she was braless she had a pair of breast pads created. These were thin padded cups with a slight bump in the middle—which suggested a nipple—that fitted over her bra cups. When Marilyn put on one of her tight jersey dresses or a silky top over the bra and breast pads, it appeared she was braless with firm breasts and a hint of nipple peeking through.

In 1961 Hollywood friends were delighted to have her back on the scene. The bad times of the winter had left her feeling isolated and estranged from the world. Now she attempted to join in and found herself at times happier than she had been in years.

She became good friends with the much-older esteemed poet Carl Sandburg. They were both thrilled to find they had so much common ground. They talked of their admiration for Abraham Lincoln and Charlie Chaplin. Most of all they shared a love of poetry. Sandburg gave her a volume of his complete poems, and she sought his opinion on poems she had written. "She had faith in me," Sandburg would say. She sensed he wasn't impressed with her celebrity but wanted to know her as a person. Marilyn would often throw her arms around him or squeeze his hand while he was talking. Obviously he had become another father figure—she confided in him. "He's so pleased to meet you," Marilyn said. "He wants to know about you, and you want to know about him." Sandburg was moved by her tragic story. "The first sixteen years of her life was [*sic*] enough to floor most of us," he said. He added, "I had great respect for her as an artist and as a person." She was a lovely girl. He thought she "was a good talker." "There were realms of science, politics, and economics in which she wasn't at home, but she spoke well on the national scene, the Hollywood scene, and on people who are good to know and people who ain't. She sometimes threw her arms around me like people do who like each other very much. Too bad I was forty-eight years older—I couldn't play her leading man."*

By now Marilyn was openly dating Frank Sinatra, which conflicted both of them because Sinatra had been such a close friend of DiMaggio's. Marilyn still cared for Joe, but she was definitely in the market for a new lover. She and Sinatra dined together, she was his guest in Palm Springs, they attended a swank party for Billy Wilder at Romanoff's, and she visited him at his recording studio.

Considering that Monroe and Sinatra were two of the most charismatic entertainers of their time, it was only natural that they would eventually become romantically involved. Even Sinatra's daughter Nancy felt that an attraction was inevitable: "I met Marilyn only once, very briefly, at Lee Strasberg's house," Nancy recalled. "I remember she was glowing, no make-up, wore a babushka and had a definite aura. Three people had that aura: Elvis, Marilyn, and my father. I've met a lot of celebrities in my lifetime, and these were the only three who glowed."

The relationship brought her to the center of an exciting circle of friends, which included the now infamous "Rat Pack." These were the hard-drinking, chain-smoking, tough-talking celebrity A-listers who flaunted their fame and wealth and were out for a swinging good time. Sammy Davis, Jr., Dean Martin and his wife, Jeanne, and Peter and Pat Lawford were the core of the group. Pat Lawford, in the coming months, would become one of Marilyn's closest friends.

These luminaries expected Marilyn to be witty, gorgeous, and fun. Everyone knew she had this beguiling side to her personality, and she enjoyed presenting it. When she was "on" and sparkling, there was no one like her—the aura, the magic.

----

* Sandburg expressed great sadness over her death in *Look*. "I wish I could have been with her that day. . . . I believe I could have persuaded her not to take her life."

She had indulged her demons in New York. Now she would deal with her dark side, mostly in sessions with Greenson. She alternated jet-setting with her celebrity friends and spending days at a time consulting with her psychiatrist—who disapproved of most of her friends and, in an attempt to help her, began involving himself in her life.

When she was in Los Angeles she would see Dr. Greenson regularly— almost daily—and he was working in conjunction with Dr. Hyman Engelberg, who would confer with Greenson and then write the prescriptions the two doctors agreed on.

"We knew that she was manic-depressive, which is now called bipolar personality," Engelberg said in a rare interview many years after her death. "I think the term manic-depressive is better. It's more descriptive. And that always meant that there were emotional problems and she could have big swings in her moods."

Unfortunately, by this time Marilyn's psychological problems were so deep that she could only muster the joyful, happy girl for brief periods. To bolster her courage and try to maintain a lighthearted demeanor, she almost always drank champagne and popped pills throughout social events, usually ending up wasted. She would then discuss these events with Greenson.

In her private sessions with Greenson, she would do a reversal regarding how she felt about her Hollywood friends. Marilyn knew a great many people, but on the inside she felt she hardly knew anyone at all. Or at least they didn't know her. Sometimes she would say that they were all out to use her and that she was being manipulated. She would become "paranoid," a word that came up often when friends and colleagues described Marilyn.

Depression as a genuine mental illness was not talked about socially in the early 1960s. Even in the psychiatric world they didn't have the knowledge of bipolar disorder that has come to light in the decades following Marilyn's death. The antidepressants that might have stabilized her moods certainly were not as advanced or available to that generation. For the most part the best her doctors felt they could do for Marilyn was prescribe tranquilizers to calm her manic periods and sleeping pills in an attempt to help her find the ever-elusive sleep.

Marilyn took stabs at overcoming her depressive episodes, but usually she self-medicated with alcohol—the thing that was most readily available to her. Many of her friends didn't understand the melancholy periods when it was difficult for her to leave the cocoonlike safety of her bedroom. Oh, they knew of her tortured past—everybody did. But they couldn't understand why she couldn't get over her childhood, get over everything she'd been through, get tough—be happy. Dean Martin was always very gentle and kind with Marilyn, but behind her back he would say things like, "We all had it rough at one time or another. Why can't she get over it?"

Milt Ebbins once asked Marilyn why she was depressed. "You're the goddamn biggest star in the business," he said. "You're a legend. You're beautiful. You have everything." Instead of viewing herself as a woman the world fell in love with, Marilyn replied, "Listen, the only people who love me are the guys who jerk off in the balcony."

She continued to socialize, with varying degrees of success. Whether at an informal party at Peter Lawford's beach house, or a glitzy nightclub, she could appear in turns elegant and clever or sloppy and vague. She attempted to compartmentalize the social part of her life, the therapy part, and the professional part—aiming to be what was expected in each situation. That's why so many have different ideas of who Marilyn was.

Physically Marilyn still was not feeling well, and on May 26 she was admitted to Cedars of Lebanon Hospital for a gynecological procedure that was intended to ease the excruciating pain of her endometriosis.

She bounced back from that surgery quickly and was feeling well enough to be Frank Sinatra's guest at his June 7 opening at the Sands Hotel.* It was a special performance in celebration of Dean Martin's forty-fifth birthday.

---

* A memo was sent out to the hotel staff stating: "Marilyn Monroe will be Mr. Sinatra's guest. It is Mr. Sinatra's intention that Miss Monroe be accorded the utmost privacy during her brief stay here at the Sands. She will be registered in Mr. Sinatra's suite. Under no circumstance is she or Mr. Sinatra to be disturbed by telephone calls or visitors before two pm."

At the concert Marilyn sat ringside with Elizabeth Taylor and her then-husband Eddie Fisher. Taylor and Monroe were undoubtedly the biggest female stars in the world. Contrasting sex symbols, the epitomes of dark versus blond beauty. But that night it was Elizabeth who receded.

"All eyes were on Marilyn," Eddie Fisher recalled. "She swayed back and forth to the music and pounded her hands on the stage, her breasts falling out of her low-cut dress. She was so beautiful—and so drunk."*

At the Vegas party after the performance, the actress Ruta Lee vividly recalled Marilyn walking in on Sinatra's arm: "She had a glow around her. A built-in klieg light that followed her everywhere. As beautiful as Elizabeth Taylor was, Marilyn stole the show." But when Sinatra noticed that Marilyn had drunk too much, he immediately had her escorted back to their room. Not understanding the fear and insecurity that caused her to drink, he disapproved of her when she was intoxicated.

Sinatra especially adored Marilyn when she was beautifully turned out and sparkling. But he also knew her deep-rooted problems. Her inherent hurt and loneliness often made it difficult for Marilyn to function without alcohol and pills to subdue her demons. At times she overdid it and became wasted, a mess. This side of Marilyn's personality frightened Sinatra.

Once, at a party, when she suddenly became morose and began talking about some childhood trauma, Sinatra called out, "Oh no! Not that again, Norma Jeane!" Marilyn was crushed, but she understood what he meant: Men liked her best when she was happy and gay.

Rupert Allan observed, "I always thought of Frank and Marilyn as star-crossed lovers. In a different time and place, they would have been together. He loved her a lot. However, by 1961, she was in so much turmoil, I think he was annoyed with her a lot of the time. He just thought she should have worked harder to pull herself together, so, yes, sometimes she pissed him off."

Marilyn deeply touched something in Frank—in a way no other

---

*   When Earl Wilson reported in his column that Marilyn held her highball glass on the railing—while Sinatra sang to her—Marilyn was quick to call and correct him. "It was not a highball glass," she protested affably. "I was drinking champagne on the rocks— and it was a champagne glass."

woman could. He responded to her damsel-in-distress quality by fiercely wanting to protect her. Gloria Romanoff was always impressed by the great concern he showed for her. She observed that this was very different from his relationships with other women.

As an example of Sinatra's devotion to Marilyn, Milt Ebbins recalled the time when Sinatra missed a luncheon at the White House because he couldn't find her. A special Italian menu had been prepared at the request of President Kennedy, but Sinatra canceled, claiming that he "had the flu." Months later Ebbins discovered through Sinatra's secretary, Gloria Lovell, that Marilyn had been staying at Sinatra's house and "just walked out without a word." Sinatra didn't know where she was. He became frantic when he couldn't find her and opted to stay in Los Angeles to look for her. "I'm telling you, he was hung up on this girl," Ebbins stated.

As for Marilyn, she loved Sinatra. His confidence and power made her feel safe. No one, no Hollywood big shot, would dare mess around with her, try to take advantage, or push her around with Sinatra in her corner. She, however, realized that at this point in his life he was a womanizer.

Soon the movie magazine headlines were asking: "Marilyn Monroe, Frank Sinatra: Is it a fling? Or is it a thing?" It was actually something in between.

It seemed that for the time being they settled on an open romance— they both dated other people and waited to see where it might lead. But Marilyn counted on Sinatra's devotion and protection for the remainder of her life.

TWENTY-FOUR

AGE THREE FIVE

But age stalked Marilyn like a demon. She had always managed life's complexities because, as long as she was young and beautiful, she could bewitch a savior to lift her up. She worried terribly about what would happen when she lost that.

On June 1 Marilyn celebrated her thirty-fifth birthday. Her telegram to Dr. Greenson on the same day, although also trying hard to project optimism, has a dark element: "In this world of people I'm glad there is you. I have a feeling of hope though today I'm three five.*

As for her career, Fox still hadn't offered Marilyn anything she felt was worth doing. Her next picture was already being called "a comeback." Desperate to get Marilyn back to work, Fox offered her a screenplay then titled *Celebration!* based on another flop play, *A Loss of Roses,* by William Inge. It is a dreary drama about an aging loser—a failed dancer named Lila—and her relationship with a younger man. This was not the sort of story Marilyn was in the market for.

With no interesting film projects coming from her studio, Marilyn turned her attention back to *Rain,* the television spectacular still on the table at NBC. She felt that with her star power she'd be able to exercise much more control in a television production. In 1961 it was a rare occurrence for a motion picture star to appear in a television drama, and for months *Rain,* starring Marilyn Monroe, was touted as a major upcoming

---

* By now Marilyn sometimes had trouble even saying her age.

event. The Hollywood studio system despised Marilyn. The television industry felt damn lucky to have her and was willing to bend over backward to please her.

Deteriorating health kept getting in the way of Marilyn's plans. On June 28, back in New York, she was rushed to Polyclinic Hospital with what was first described as "a mild intestinal disorder." It was discovered that her condition was much more serious: Her entire gall bladder was inflamed and had to be removed in a two-hour operation. The diseased gall bladder had been the cause of much of the physical pain she had been in for many of the previous months.

When she woke up, it was with Joe DiMaggio at her side. The operation left a five-inch angry-looking scar on the right side of her lower abdomen—which she hadn't seen yet but was aware of because of the size of the bandage and the amount of pain she was in. Marilyn needed coddling. Once again her career was put on hold while she concentrated on her health. She wanted a family around her. Weak and fearful, she asked her half sister, Berniece Miracle, to fly in from Florida and stay with her at the apartment while she recuperated: "I need you to be with me," Marilyn pleaded.

In actuality the two women weren't close. They were in each other's presence only a handful of times during their lives. But this visit wasn't about nostalgia, curiosity, or sentimentality.

The day Marilyn was released from the hospital, reporters and fans waiting outside jostled her, tearing her scar open. Even though Marilyn was used to assertive crowds by now, this time she was really shaken. "That was a little rough because I just had a gall bladder operation and my side opened up," Marilyn recalled. "The crowds pushed and there went my side! So when I got home . . . they sent a young doctor with me, and they had to put clamps and tapes and I don't know what else. But that didn't help it any."

In her vulnerable condition, Marilyn appreciated Berniece coming, but it was obvious that these two women, who shared a mother, had little in common. Still, they tried to connect. Berniece remarked on Marilyn's tastefully decorated apartment. Marilyn complimented her half sister for her white teeth. They tried on each other's clothes and experimented with makeup. They had breakfast and dinner together—often joined by DiMaggio and his friend George Solitaire.

But even as she convalesced, getting back to her career was never far from Marilyn's mind. Berniece noticed that, upon rising in the mornings, the first thing Marilyn did was take the newspaper into her bedroom so she could go over the entertainment section. With "getting on with it" a top priority, Marilyn decided to move back to Los Angeles on a more permanent basis.

The two main reasons for Marilyn's return to Hollywood that August were to revive her career and to return to therapy with Dr. Ralph Greenson. She hoped Greenson could help her to lift the mask of "Marilyn Monroe" and live simply as Marilyn.

Once again in need of a savior to believe in, she referred to Greenson as "My Jesus." It's frightening that at this stage in her life Marilyn was still looking to another person to ease the pain of her troubled past, her restlessness, her mounting dissatisfactions. Almost immediately she began to see Greenson on a daily basis.

Marilyn began looking for a place of her own and discovered that the modest apartment on Doheny, where she had lived briefly in 1954, was available again. It seemed like a good omen. Marilyn moved back into her old digs and started "fixing it up."

Now Marilyn asked Ralph Roberts, her close friend and masseur, to move to Los Angeles with her. "Rafe," as she called him, was devoted to Marilyn, and she cherished their friendship—referring to him as "the Brother." Indeed, people in Marilyn's circle noted that at times they seemed as close as brother and sister. His expert massages helped her relax as much as any of her tranquilizing medications. If all else failed, Roberts would say, she'd "fall asleep when I was massaging her feet." But more than anything he was a trusted friend who seemed to want nothing more from Marilyn than to be part of her life, to help her. Within weeks Roberts had his own apartment, nearby on (the ironically named) Norma Place.

Living in the same complex as Marilyn was Sinatra's secretary, Gloria Lovell. Marilyn became good friends with Lovell, a good-natured, heavy-drinking woman. It was said that Sinatra also rented an apartment in the Doheny complex, so it was a place where Marilyn felt especially safe.*

Marilyn always felt more comfortable in small spaces, but the Doheny apartment was downright gloomy. Determined to make the space work, she attempted to transform it into a sanctuary of sleep. It seems she wanted to cocoon herself in a womb-tomb. (When she took her sedatives she told Greenson they made her feel "womb-y" and "tomb-y.") She was extremely sensitive to ambient noise and light—they exacerbated her insomnia. Taking over the living room to use as a bedroom, she blanketed the sliding glass doors—which opened to the outside—with very heavy blackout drapes. "She didn't want a crack of light coming in," Roberts explained. "But," he would often say, "I could massage her in the dark because her body gave off light."

In an effort to further re-create her womb-tomb experience, Marilyn liked to keep her room very warm. She would sometimes use an electric blanket while Roberts massaged her to sleep, afraid that the sweat dripping from him while he massaged her in the hot room might set off a shock from the electricity in the blanket.

Her entire life revolved around sleep, and how to find new ways to do so.

Thinking that the sound of gently flowing water would help lull her into slumber, Marilyn also had a fountain built just outside the glass doors that led out of the room. She loved the sound of trickling water, like a running stream. Unfortunately, when it was finished it was a big, cement thing, and the trickle was a loud, booming gush. "This fountain has cost a fortune, and all I wanted was a little trickle," Marilyn complained. "And they can't get it right . . . they gave me a roar."

Without much going on in her life beyond therapy, Marilyn spent more time brooding behind the darkened drapes of her Doheny apartment. In an attempt to keep up a social life, however, she began making frequent

---

* After she died Sinatra would lease her old apartment unit, probably out of a combination of sentimentality and convenience. Sinatra had the apartment soundproofed at a cost of seven thousand dollars.

visits to the home of Peter Lawford and his wife, the president's sister, Pat Kennedy Lawford.

The Lawford house was a beautiful 6,416-square-foot Mediterranean-style home on the beach in Santa Monica. Originally built by MGM's Louis B. Mayer, the place had five bedrooms, thirteen bathrooms, wood-beamed ceilings, wrought-iron balconies, and a huge outdoor swimming pool. When Jack was a senator, and after he became president, he would often visit his sister and brother-in-law at the beach house, which became known as a sort of quintessential Hollywood party house— sometimes quite decadent—that entertained some of the biggest players in show business. Kennedy spent so much of his time at the house that it was dubbed "the Western White House."

At social gatherings there might be anything from a casual game of volleyball on the beach and a barbecue to a formal sit-down dinner. The house was also infamous—it was said that there were sex parties there and that Jack would use it to rendezvous with various actresses. Dean Martin's wife, Jeanne, who was part of that crowd, said that she saw Peter and Pat Lawford in the roles of pimps for John Kennedy.

Marilyn was pulled into this crowd by a combination of her mental illness, drugs, pressure from friends, and loneliness. The 1960s were becoming more sexually liberated—and Hollywood was on the cusp of that liberation. We know that Marilyn was apprehensive about getting involved because she talked to her doctor about it. Greenson disapproved of her becoming entangled with this crowd; he felt himself falling into the role of a parent of an unruly adolescent.

Now that she was basically single (Marilyn's romance with Sinatra continued to be on-again, off-again) and living in Los Angeles, President Kennedy put out the word that he wanted an introduction. He told Senator George Smathers, who had been best man at Kennedy's wedding, that he had to meet her.

It was easy for Marilyn to merge into this social set. She knew Peter Lawford from her starlet years, when they dated briefly. Sinatra was a big part of the scene, and Pat Newcomb was very friendly with the Lawfords. Both she and Judy Garland (a former client) would attend the poker parties at the Lawford home.

Marilyn liked Pat Lawford, and Pat adored her. Marilyn was in awe of Pat's pedigree, her wealth, her extended family, her education, the power of the Kennedy name. Like so many others, Pat was seduced by Marilyn's glamour, her famous wit, her irresistible childlike quality. Some of her friends said that Pat became "infatuated" with Marilyn,

The two women indeed became very close friends. Marilyn's housekeeper, Mrs. Eunice Murray, said that Pat Kennedy was Marilyn's "best friend," and that she would always take a call from Pat no matter what she was doing. Ralph Roberts said that Marilyn liked Pat much more than she ever liked Peter.

Lawford became a part of the Kennedy family when he married Pat in 1954, shortly after John F. Kennedy became a senator. He was part of the clan during Kennedy's fantastic rise from senator to president, with his brother Bobby being named attorney general. Bobby Kennedy was also a frequent guest at the Lawfords'.

Pat Newcomb remarked that she knew the Kennedys long before she started working for Marilyn. "They were friends of mine," she liked to say. Interestingly, Pat Newcomb and Peter Lawford—both of whom were attached to Marilyn—seemed very intent on setting her up with the president. After she first broke up with Arthur Miller, Ralph Roberts noted that Kennedy started pursing Marilyn. Mostly he would try to get in touch with her through Pat Newcomb or Peter Lawford.

Often people introduced their friends to Marilyn as a gift. That's how legendary, how fascinating, she was. By now the same could be said of John F. Kennedy. There was something very modern, very sixties about it—but also something mythical. The handsome Kennedy—who looked like a Hollywood playboy, took drugs, loved beautiful women, and became the most powerful person in the world by the age of forty-three—matched up with Monroe, the goddess, the sex symbol, of the generation. Wouldn't it be exciting if these two dynamos got together? A meeting was set up at a party at the Lawford house.

There is no documented evidence of when Marilyn first met Jack Kennedy at the Lawfords'. They most likely met at a dinner party there on Sunday, November 19.

At first John F. Kennedy was "smitten" with Marilyn. Senator Smathers stated that Kennedy later introduced him to Marilyn at a Washington party. Smathers also claimed that Marilyn sometimes went sailing with Kennedy on the presidential yacht on the Potomac River. He added that she never stayed at the White House (as has been rumored) but at a nearby hotel. "She always handled herself like a lady, as far as I'm concerned," Smathers said.

Marilyn also met Bobby Kennedy casually at the Lawfords'. Pat Lawford had been gushing to Marilyn: "You've got to meet him, Marilyn. You'll never know anyone like my brother." Milt Ebbins remembers seeing Marilyn at an informal buffet dinner there—but he didn't notice any interaction between the two. In coming months they became friendlier.

Bobby Kennedy's press aide, Edwin Guthman—a Pulitzer Prize–winning journalist—recalled meeting Marilyn at a Lawford party in October 1961, after the attorney general gave a speech in Oregon. Guthman remembered being at the party with "a lot of the Lawfords' friends—including Marilyn Monroe. By around midnight she was very drunk." It is likely that Marilyn had once again felt insecure in a big social gathering, and had overdone the champagne on top of pills.

Bobby told Marilyn: "You can't get home by yourself. I'll drive you." He then asked his press aide to come along. Guthman thought the reason was obvious: He didn't want to be seen . . . going off in a car at night alone with Marilyn Monroe.

"We drove her home," Guthman recalled later. "We put her to bed, and we left. It was a two-person job. She wasn't 'passed out' but she was pretty close." Guthman and Bobby left feeling that Marilyn was very sweet and very sad.

Marilyn remained very much a romantic, still hoping to meet that one special man she had been searching for all her life. But she played the field a lot in her final season—in retrospect somewhat desperately.

A blow to her ego came when Marilyn learned that Sinatra had become engaged to the beautiful dancer Juliet Prowse. The two did date, but on January 17 the gossip columnist Dorothy Kilgallen wrote that the engagement was "a marvelous publicity stunt" Sinatra pulled to help raise Prowse's name recognition.

Now, however, Marilyn was acquainted with both Jack and Bobby Kennedy—men as dynamic—and even more revered—than Frank Sinatra. No one saw anything overt or untoward between Marilyn and either of the Kennedy brothers at this point, but by that fall the first rumors of a romance between Marilyn and the president were just beginning in their inner circles.

What was unusual for her—and troubling to others—was that some of her affairs overlapped. In spite of her flurry of activity and attempts at socializing, Greenson noted: "She was terribly, terribly lonely. As a consequence she became involved with people who only hurt her and who evoked in her this feeling of mistreatment which had paranoid undertones to it."

TWENTY-FIVE

DOCTOR-PATIENT RELATIONS

"I took over a patient that Marianne Kris had been treating for several years, and she has turned out to be a very sick borderline paranoid addict, as well as an actress," Greenson wrote to his psychoanalyst friend Anna Freud (Sigmund's daughter). "You can imagine how terribly difficult it is to treat someone with such severe problems and who is also a great celebrity and completely alone in the world. Psychoanalysis is out of the question and I improvise, often wondering where I am going, and yet have nowhere else to turn. If I succeed, I will have learned something, but it takes a tremendous amount of time and also emotion."

Greenson had dealt with famous people before, but in Marilyn he found an entirely different kind of personality. Perplexed by the paradoxes of her extreme fame and loneliness, her beauty and lack of self-worth, and her undeniable power offset by her feelings of helplessness, he had apprehensions about what exactly was the best way to treat her. First of all—explaining that it was to protect her privacy—he conducted sessions with her at his home rather than at the office.

Although he was a Freudian, he decided not to treat Marilyn "on the couch," which was Freud and his followers' favored method of dealing with patients. In therapy Freud would have his patients lie on the couch and free-associate, talking about whatever came into their heads.

Greenson felt that Marilyn's mind was too muddled for free association. She could go off on tangents, into the past, into dreams, or ruminate on fantasies that would lead nowhere. He felt it was best to sit face-to-face with her, keep her in the moment, keep her focus on the here and now—that way he could better keep her functioning on a day-to-day basis.

As a Freudian analyst, Greenson also firmly believed that socializing with patients was absolutely wrong. But somewhere along the line, sitting across from her, sharing her intimacies, hearing her stories, remembering her in her movies, observing her at her worst, he got lost in Marilyn Monroe: The myth and the patient began to merge.

In a highly controversial decision—one that brought him much criticism through the years—the doctor took Marilyn into the fold of his personal life, involving the movie star with his family and friends. "There was something very lovable about this girl," he wrote, "and we all cared about her and she could be delightful."

There is evidence that—like the many men before him—he fell under Marilyn's charismatic spell while keeping up the front that he was professionally in control of this unusual doctor-patient relationship. Greenson started the socializing by inviting Marilyn—along with friends—to his house on evenings to hear him play the violin with a group of chamber musicians. Greenson had crossed a line by introducing a patient to his circle of friends.

He was uneasy about it, but while improvising the therapy, he was trying out new ways to help her overcome her paranoia, depressions, and feelings of isolation.

Marilyn also felt that there was something not quite right about these social invitations. She told Ralph Roberts she didn't even like chamber music. But she had so much faith in the doctor, was so much in his thrall, that she decided to attend these gatherings—and gradually become a part of his world outside the therapy sessions. In the coming months her relationship with Greenson and his family would become much closer—and much more dangerous.

Lee Strasberg had begun the eradication of her ego by convincing Marilyn that her great stardom was nothing, really. Only *he* could make her an actress. Indeed, she took his opinions to heart—and put a lot of her worth as an actress in his hands and the hands of his wife. But she was still powerful and young enough to exercise her own willfulness.

LEFT: Marilyn knew Charles Stanley Gifford only from this photograph her mother showed her when she was a little girl, stating, "This is your father." Marilyn would spend her lifetime looking for him in other men. She once confided a fantasy in which she anonymously met her father in a bar and seduced him.

ABOVE: Norma Jeane on an outing to the beach with her mother, Gladys Baker, in the late 1920s. At the time, the child was living with foster parents, the Bolenders, and she would live with her mentally unstable mother for only a brief period before Gladys was institutionalized.

LEFT: Norma Jeane, about age seven. She was living in foster care.

RIGHT: For the first time in her life, twelve-year-old Norma Jeane felt loved when she was placed in the foster care of Ana Lower, whom she would call "Aunt Ana."

LEFT: Norma Jeane married twenty-one-year-old James Dougherty in 1942, a few weeks after she turned sixteen. The choice was either to marry or go back to an orphanage.

ABOVE: Before getting her first movie contract and changing her name to Marilyn Monroe, Norma Jeane found steady work as a model while her husband was in the Merchant Marines. She would divorce Dougherty when he objected to her career.

ABOVE: Shortly after her divorce, Marilyn had a rare lunch with "family." Clockwise from left to right: her half-sister Berniece Miracle, niece Mona Rae, foster mother Grace Goddard, Grace's sister Enid Knebelkamp, Marilyn, foster mother Ana Lower, Marilyn's mother Gladys Baker (flower in hair).

ABOVE: In 1952, with her career on the rise, Fox decided to try Marilyn out in a dramatic role in *Don't Bother to Knock*, playing a psychotic babysitter. The vulnerability and fragility that made audiences want to love and protect her was already abundantly evident.

ABOVE: A lifelong dream came true when Marilyn was asked to put her hand- and footprints in cement in front of Grauman's Chinese Theatre with her *Gentlemen Prefer Blondes* costar, Jane Russell.

RIGHT: Baseball great Joe DiMaggio became Marilyn's second husband in 1954. Although the marriage lasted only nine months, he remained close to her throughout her life. "No woman in the world will ever be loved the way he loved her," a friend said.

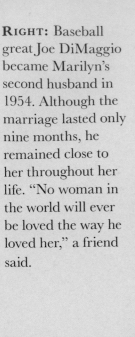

ACTORS STUDIO

LEFT: Disillusioned with the kind of roles that Fox was giving her and fearing she would always be cast as sexy dumb blondes, Marilyn walked out on her studio and spent a year studying at the prestigious Actor's Studio in New York.

LEFT: After a year of study with Lee Strasberg, Marilyn returned to the screen in 1956, costarring with Don Murray in *Bus Stop*. With this performance critics finally began to acknowledge she had acting talent that went beyond a dynamic sexual allure.

ABOVE: *The Prince and the Showgirl* with Laurence Olivier was the first and only movie produced by Marilyn's production company. There was high tension on the set because of her constant lateness and Olivier's fear she was stealing the picture.

LEFT: On October 29, 1956, Marilyn was presented to Queen Elizabeth for a Royal Command Film Performance. The Queen's eyes curiously went up and down Marilyn's tight, revealing gown before she smilingly extended her hand in greeting.

RIGHT: Marilyn with her third husband, playwright Arthur Miller, at the premiere of *The Prince and the Showgirl* in 1957. They each fell in love with aspects of the other but were never able to fully grasp or accept the full person.

LEFT: Marilyn poses on the set of *Some Like It Hot.* Her constant lateness and absences caused friction with costars Tony Curtis and Jack Lemmon, as well as director Billy Wilder. But the movie would go on to be the greatest hit of all their careers.

ABOVE: Marilyn's marriage was already in trouble when she started an affair with French film star Yves Montand during the making of the ironically titled *Let's Make Love.* Here they are at a press conference announcing the start of filming in 1960.

ABOVE: Marilyn performing in the "My Heart Belongs to Daddy"
number in *Let's Make Love*, a bright spot in an otherwise dismal film.
Some critics marked this movie as the beginning of a decline in her career.

LEFT: Marilyn was physically and emotionally ill when she arrived—tired and slightly bloated—in Reno to start shooting *The Misfits* in July 1960. Nevertheless, a great crowd greeted her at the airport and she did her best to project the expected movie star image.

RIGHT: Although Marilyn looked stunning when she attended the premiere of *The Misfits* in January 1961 with costar Montgomery Clift, she was close to an emotional breakdown. A week later she was committed to a psychiatric hospital.

LEFT: In a year plagued by illness, Marilyn was released from Manhattan Polyclinic Hospital in July 1961 after having her gall bladder removed.

RIGHT: Feeling rejuvenated, Marilyn looked every inch the movie star when she left for a trip to Mexico in February 1962 to buy furnishings for her newly purchased house.

LEFT: At a high-spirited press conference in Mexico City, Marilyn sipped champagne and wittily answered questions. She is wearing the green Pucci dress she would be buried in.

RIGHT: A tipsy Marilyn falling into the arms of Rock Hudson, after she was presented with the Golden Globe Award in March 1962 for being the Female World Film Favorite. She was gratified to get this particular award at a time when some people in the press were speculating that her career was finished.

ABOVE: After losing more than 20 pounds, Marilyn was excited to show off her svelte body in *Something's Got to Give.* In the wardrobe and makeup tests for the film, her beauty seems to have reached its zenith.

RIGHT: Marilyn looked lovely and was giving a very tender performance in *Something's Got to Give,* because of deepening psychological problems and a fear of facing the camera, she rarely showed up for shooting. The film was never completed.

LEFT: The air was swirling with gossip and innuendo when Marilyn was escorted into Madison Square Garden with press aide Pat Newcomb on May 19, 1962. Marilyn was there to sing "Happy Birthday" to President John F. Kennedy. Her sexy, breathy serenade caused a sensation.

RIGHT: Marilyn made her last public appearance with Angels center fielder Albie Pearson at a charity event at Dodger Stadium on her thirty-sixth birthday, June 1, 1962. It was also the last day she filmed a scene for a motion picture. The final weeks of her life were fraught with illness, intrigue, and mystery.

All insert photos courtesy of Photofest.

Greenson got her when she feared that her beauty and power were fading. When he wrote to Dr. Kris disapprovingly about Marilyn's affair with Sinatra (or other sexual relationships), he compared her to a child disobeying a parent. Clearly that feeling of a lost child is what she brought out in people. Previously, however, enough of the canny adult remained within Marilyn for her to function. Now she was weakening emotionally, and the only thing she had to secure her—her career—seemed to be slipping away.

Her desperation was so palpable that it acted on Greenson almost as an aphrodisiac. That thing she brought out in everyone—*I have to save her!*—was now far more seductive than her reputation as a sex symbol. Indeed, if all Greenson had wanted was to have her physically, she might have survived, because she knew how to deal with men who wanted that. It's probable that Greenson was not malevolent but vastly unwise—and, like Strasberg and Miller, essentially condescending toward "this poor thing."

Once the social door was open, Greenson became more and more preoccupied with his beautiful but deeply troubled patient. And, in an attempt to save her, he took control of her. Dr. Richard Litman, who had been a student of Greenson's and later investigated her death, told the Monroe biographer Lois Banner, "He was 'in love' with her. Not sexual love. But love. It sometimes can happen with a patient whom you become especially attached to."

According to Ralph Roberts, Greenson persuaded Marilyn to push away people she was close to if *he* felt she was becoming too dependent on them. "He wanted her to drop all her old friends—he felt that we were all bad influences—and put herself in his hands," Roberts observed. But because of their close bond, their brother-sister relationship, Roberts never dreamed that Marilyn could be persuaded to shut him out.

One morning on the phone she confronted her friend: "Dr. Greenson thinks you should go back to New York," she said hesitantly. Greenson had told Marilyn, "Two Ralphs are too many in your life." Marilyn had been dumbfounded. She was very attached to Roberts. "But you're a 'Ralph' and he's a 'Rafe,'" Marilyn sobbed to Greenson. But the doctor insisted Roberts had to go. "I wish she had picked the right Ralph," Pat Newcomb said years later.

Marilyn made her choice. She told Roberts that she promised Greenson that she would ask Rafe to go back East. Alarmingly Greenson had advised Marilyn to employ another old friend of his family to take Roberts's place as her driver and also to act as a housekeeper. Fifty-nine-year-old Eunice Murray, or Mrs. Murray as everyone came to know her (even Marilyn addressed her as Mrs. Murray), would take a more and more significant role in Marilyn's life—even though Marilyn never warmed to her.

Crushed, Roberts left for New York City that very night. The following day he called Gloria Lovell to let her know that he had arrived in Manhattan. She told him that since he left "it's been horrible." She said that she could hear Marilyn screaming all night long. She simply couldn't bear the loss. "What will Marilyn do?" Gloria cried. "Whatever will she do?"

"I realized after the fact that I was trying to create a foster family for her, my own, but a good foster family who would not throw her out like all the others had," Greenson said. "In addition I was her therapist, the good father who would not disappoint her and would bring her insights, and if not insights just kindness."

Through the years Greenson's family members have attempted to explain how Marilyn first started to become a part of the Greenson family. As much as she respected Greenson, she didn't at first change her habit of being late for their appointments—which were scheduled as his last for the day, usually at 5:00 p.m. After she showed up late for a number of appointments, Greenson reprimanded Marilyn: "If you come late this means, consciously or unconsciously, you don't respect or trust me."

His words hit her hard. To demonstrate that she was dedicated to her therapy, she started arriving at his house early—so early that Greenson wasn't even back from his office. She'd pull up in front of the Greenson house in a large black limousine, ring the bell, and Greenson's wife, Hildi, would answer, telling the famous movie star that the doctor wasn't in yet and asking if she'd like to come in or wait outside.

"Outside," Marilyn would respond uneasily.

Greenson suggested that perhaps his twenty-one-year-old daughter, Joan, could go out and say hello and walk with Marilyn so she wouldn't be so alone. Soon Joan and Marilyn were walking back and forth across a nearby reservoir.

Eventually Marilyn was staying for dinner at his house after sessions, socializing with his family. Later Greenson's family would become somewhat defensive about Marilyn staying for dinner. Mrs. Greenson explained that it was a natural progression, since Marilyn was Greenson's last appointment: Discovering she had no plans for the evening, he would invite her to eat with them.

Greenson was concerned that her solitude might put her in danger of getting involved with somebody or something that could be harmful to her. For instance, he discovered that once Marilyn invited a taxi driver into her home to have supper with her. Because Greenson felt she was so desperately lonely, he wanted to be certain she wouldn't get into trouble. So very often she would eat with his family. Afterward they would all sit around and talk or listen to records, and then someone would drive her home.

Eventually Marilyn made sure they were well stocked with her favorite champagne, Dom Pérignon. She enjoyed a glass or two on certain evenings as they talked or listened to music. Joan Greenson remembers her banging merrily on the countertop, slightly tipsy, proclaiming: "I am an atheist Jew!"

Marilyn became close to Greenson's wife, Hildi; their son, Daniel; and particularly their daughter, Joan, who was twenty-one at the time. Joan would describe it as a big-sister, little-sister relationship. Marilyn taught Joan how to dance, how to apply makeup, and gave her dating advice. Joan was studying art, and they would spread out her latest drawings for Marilyn to critique.

But some who were close to Marilyn at the time, like Whitey Snyder, Susan Strasberg, and Pat Newcomb, didn't think her sessions with Greenson were doing Marilyn any good. Ralph Roberts said that the more he found out about Greenson, the more he felt *he* was the one who should be analyzed, not Marilyn. Although his family contended that Greenson encouraged Marilyn to have friendships, her inner circle felt that Greenson was using his influence over Marilyn to build a protective fortress around her—keeping her old friends out while bringing in his friends and family—and they resented it.

Dr. Greenson's treatment of Marilyn was wrong, bringing her into his family was a mistake because she, of course, was a grown woman—and a powerful one. Yet he opened the floodgates, and Marilyn came pouring in. Although she was as dependent on him as a problematic adolescent, her age, fame, and power allowed her to act out rebellions. All he could do was stand back, let her take over more of his life, and send her the bill.

Meanwhile Fox still wanted Marilyn back at work.[*] In fact they needed her back. At this point the almighty 20th Century-Fox was almost bankrupt. Darryl F. Zanuck, who cofounded Fox in 1935, had left the studio to become an independent film producer in Europe. Fox president Spyros P. Skouras took over the decision making regarding new productions, but he didn't really understand the art of filmmaking the way Zanuck had.

Still, it seems unlikely that the best thing that Fox had to offer Marilyn in 1961 was a screenplay they were calling *Something's Got to Give*. The script, based on the 1940 farce *My Favorite Wife*, starring Cary Grant and Irene Dunne, revolves around a woman who—after being stranded on a tropical island for five years—is rescued and returns home to find that she has been declared legally dead and that her husband has remarried on that very day. Even by 1961 standards, the script was dated, and Marilyn was not optimistic about it.

Fox executives were in no mood to accede to Marilyn's demands. They were in desperate need of a blockbuster, and Marilyn was one of the few stars they had under contract who they felt could deliver one. At this point the studio had invested almost all of its money in the epic *Cleopatra*, starring Elizabeth Taylor, which by now was way over budget.

Marilyn was shrewd enough to realize that her next film needed to be something that lived up to—and revitalized—her legend: sharp, sexy, and

---

[*] Because of constant delays and setbacks, NBC finally canceled any plans for a production of *Rain* starring Marilyn.

daring. From the start it was clear to Marilyn that *Something's Got to Give* was not, and never could be, such a vehicle.

Adding insult to injury, Fox had originally intended the movie to be made with Jayne Mansfield, a buxom blond actress the studio had brought in to replace Marilyn when she was being "difficult." Fox's idea was to have Mansfield team up with Joan Collins,* who would play the new wife. But by 1961 Jayne Mansfield's box-office appeal had waned—she was not a "new" Monroe, and Fox lost interest in producing the movie with her. Joan Collins says that she was never even notified about the project—Fox was already revamping it with a totally new cast in mind.

Now they offered the shopworn vehicle to Marilyn, and she certainly felt it was beneath her. To Marilyn, the studio represented fifteen years of struggle to be viewed as an artist who deserved respect. Fox viewed Marilyn as a troublesome diva, a demanding bitch, a star who was most unpleasant to deal with. They felt a tremendous amount of resentment toward her. These executives still wanted a puppet; a performing doll who did what they said and brought in the money. Marilyn was filled with rage— not just because of the way the studio was treating her but for other things as well. To have struggled and fought for so long and still be exactly where she was at the beginning of her career affected her psychologically, assaulted her physically, and wore her down.

But if Marilyn refused another film, Fox could legally keep her off of the screen in projects for other studios for a long time. A stall in her career was the last thing she wanted at this stage. Peter Levathes, who was then in charge of production at Fox, called Marilyn into his office for a meeting.

Greenson was now also advising her on career decisions. To help Marilyn deal with the studio, he brought in his brother-in-law—the brilliant Hollywood lawyer Mickey Rudin—to represent Marilyn on the negotiations for *Something's Got to Give*. Rudin was a big deal—a high-powered, no-nonsense, tough-talking attorney who had worked for Frank Sinatra for years.

The question Rudin was facing was "Can Marilyn perform?" She needed the money, but she also needed the self-esteem of being able to

---

* The two sex symbols had costarred in *The Wayward Bus* in 1957.

finish a picture. The validation of being able to function was as important as the money. Rudin thought she was in no condition to make the movie and needed at least a year. "Look, you're pushing her to go ahead," Rudin told the Fox executives. "I wish you wouldn't. Give it more time. You may be finishing her. Not the picture."

Peter Levathes was desperate for a success. "No, no," he said. "We've got to go." He sensed that Rudin was trying to weasel out of the film and maybe planning to go to another studio for a more lucrative deal for Marilyn. "I wasn't playing games," Rudin recounted. "Her problems were obvious. She wasn't really prepared."

But Fox was adamant. So while she knew the movie was not a career changer, she also needed to get back on screen and then be free to take more artistic control over her projects. On September 26 Marilyn reluctantly agreed to make *Something's Got to Give* at Fox.

Once the decision was made to go ahead, Greenson and Rudin had to do everything possible to see that Marilyn finished the picture. First and foremost Rudin fought for certain things that her contract didn't give her but at least made her feel important. Rudin got her cast approval, and she would ultimately demand Dean Martin as her leading man.[*]

The studio approached George Cukor, on Marilyn's list of approved directors, who also owed them a movie on his contract. Even though *Let's Make Love* had resulted in a failure, the studio was willing to take a chance on another teaming of the director and actress.

In the meantime the star still needed to get through day-to-day living. Marilyn's new paid companion, Mrs. Murray, brought in by Greenson, was extremely soft-spoken, often speaking in whispers, with a deceptively timid demeanor. She was a mysterious woman who always seemed to be lurking around corners.

In the coming months Mrs. Murray would go from being a housekeeper who did some errands to what she would describe as a "devoted assistant." She did anything Marilyn needed—fielding phone calls, marketing, al-

---

[*]   The studio had originally wanted James Garner for the role.

tering clothes, preparing meals, helping Marilyn dress for special occasions, and driving her to appointments. Although she kept her own apartment, Mrs. Murray would sometimes spend the night at Marilyn's place, even though Marilyn never felt completely at ease with her.

Some of Marilyn's friends felt that Mrs. Murray was acting as a spy for Greenson. Even though she wasn't a nurse, Mrs. Murray had a history of taking care of people under Greenson's care. In this position she would witness Marilyn's actions behind the heavy blackout drapes of the Doheny apartment—her behavior during some of her most private moments. It's terrifying to think of the amount of trust Marilyn was putting into Greenson and the control he exercised over her life: Greenson now had his hands on Marilyn's mind, home, and career.[*]

Greenson was also nudging Marilyn to make another momentous decision, because he didn't feel that Marilyn's tiny apartment was a place for a celebrity of her magnitude, and suggested she find a more suitable space. "I suggested to her that she look for a little house of her own, a piece of ground which was hers and she could therefore stop being an orphan and a waif and homeless," he wrote. As a result Mrs. Murray's first assignment was to help Marilyn find a house. Dr. Greenson also suggested the area: some place in his neighborhood.

---

[*] Although Greenson may have had good intentions in surrounding Marilyn with people he knew and trusted, it appears suspicious in the eyes of history that he felt the need to have his own personal relationship with all the people he was bringing into Marilyn's fold, extending his influence—some might say control—in her life.

PART 3

CLOSE TO CAMELOT

TWENTY-SIX

In early December a party was thrown in John F. Kennedy's honor at the Park Avenue apartment of the Manhattan socialite Mrs. John "Fifi" Fell. Peter Lawford arranged for Marilyn to be a special guest at the dinner—she was flown into New York specifically for the occasion. It was a very swank affair—black-tie, cocktails at eight with dinner to follow. A famous French chef was hired for the evening. Of course the main course at any party was Marilyn Monroe.

The Lawfords' manager, Milt Ebbins, was put in charge of getting Marilyn to the party on time—a noble challenge but impossible feat. He remembered it as one of the most excruciating nights of his life. "I arrived at her apartment a little before seven," Ebbins recalled. Marilyn was in her bedroom getting her hair done by the world-renowned Mr. Kenneth Battelle.

"By eight o'clock I still hadn't seen any signs of her," Ebbins said. A maid came out of Marilyn's bedroom: "Miss Marilyn is almost ready."

Lawford was calling every five minutes, "Where is she?"

Ebbins kept assuring him. "She's almost ready. I'm just sitting here. I haven't seen her yet."

"Well, hurry her up!"

Twenty minutes later the maid came out again. "Kenneth is doing the final touches. She'll be a few more minutes." Then the maid left for the evening.

At nine fifteen an exhausted Mr. Kenneth emerged from the bedroom.

He was leaving for the night too. The phone rang again: "Where the hell is she? Everybody's waiting!"

Ebbins said, "She's still in her bedroom."

Lawford screamed into the phone, "Well, go in there and get her! Everyone's waiting!"

There was no one else in the apartment now. Ebbins walked into her bedroom. There Marilyn sat, at her vanity table staring dreamily into the mirror. "Marilyn, come on!" Ebbins implored. "We've got to go." Suddenly Ebbins noticed that she was completely naked. Ebbins was so flustered he nearly fainted.

Marilyn stood up. "Will you help me get dressed?" she asked breathlessly, stepping into her shoes. Marilyn handed Ebbins a white beaded dress and lifted her arms, saying, "Watch out for my hair."

Ebbins began pulling down the dress, which was like donning a glove two sizes too small.

"Oh, careful of the beads!" Marilyn said.

"Now I'm on my knees pulling down the dress over her hips. My face is a few inches away from her crotch. I couldn't believe it! Talk about temptation."

Ebbins finally got the dress on her. "Oh, she looked like a dream!" he said.

Trying to push her out the door, Ebbins was surprised to see that Marilyn paused again to put on a red wig. She had just had her hair done. Then she put on a scarf around the wig, dark glasses, and threw on a mink coat. "They'll never know me," she told Ebbins.

"What do you mean?"

"You'll see."

When they arrived in the lobby of the apartment building, the place was swarming with photographers. Marilyn was right. No one recognized her. She and Ebbins walked through the crowd and went up the elevator. When they arrived at the floor, the Secret Service men—who recognized Ebbins—started laughing. They knew the redhead in the mink was Marilyn. Methodically she took off the scarf, wig, and glasses and jammed them all into the pocket of the coat, which she handed to Ebbins. Then she fluffed out her platinum hair, and they knocked on the door.

Marilyn walked into the room, and Kennedy spotted her immediately. "Finally, you're here!" the president gushed. "How good to see you!" Ebbins watched them talking intimately for a few minutes. "I was standing there, and she turned around and gave me a wink and then turned and walked away from him." The actress Arlene Dahl was one of the guests: "I had seen a lot of celebrities be the center of attention," she said. "But I never saw anyone enchant a room so quickly. She was magic to watch."

After five minutes in her presence all the guests had forgotten that they had been waiting for her for more than two hours. Apparently they also forgot about eating dinner. The food was ruined, Milt Ebbins recalled. "Nobody ate. The French chef tried to jump out the window. No kidding. He tried to commit suicide." His prized dinner remained untouched. Marilyn, perhaps, did not.

"They say that afterwards she spent the night with Jack at the Carlyle Hotel," Ebbins said in his usual evasive way when discussing Marilyn and Kennedy. "I couldn't say one way or another. I had left by that point."

Soon after the holidays Mrs. Murray found a house for Marilyn on Fifth Helena Drive in Brentwood, about a mile from the Greenson residence. It was a 2,900-square-foot, one-story, L-shaped Spanish colonial-style home—very modest by movie star standards. It sat at the end of the street in a cul-de-sac or, as Marilyn called it, "a dead end."

But she fell in love with the house at first sight and—in typical Marilyn fashion—wanted to make arrangements to buy it immediately. Her first step was to call Joe DiMaggio to ask him to come back out to look the house over. Purchasing her first home was a big step, and she wanted someone she trusted to help her.

True to form, DiMaggio flew out to Los Angeles to survey the property. She walked DiMaggio through the gate, past the garden, up the red tile walk to the entrance of the house.

Embedded in the concrete at the front door was a tile with a coat of arms and a Latin inscription: *Cursum Perficio*, which translates to "End of my journey." She was aware of the meaning, but it didn't bother her. On the contrary she told a journalist, "I hope it's true."

She described it as "a cute little Mexican-style house with eight rooms, and at least I can say it's mine"; it was "a fortress where I feel secure." DiMaggio approved of the property. After offers and counteroffers went back and forth between the owners and Marilyn's lawyer, she was able to buy the house for $57,500. It was a substantial amount, but for a movie star of Marilyn's magnitude certainly not exorbitant. Still, at the moment she was strapped for cash and had to borrow $5,000 from Joe DiMaggio to make the down payment

Marilyn's spending habits remained the same when she was a major celebrity as when she was a struggling starlet—she spent what she had when she had it and borrowed when she didn't. "When I try to balance my budget," she sighed, "somehow I'm always overdrawn."

It wasn't that she was broke, exactly. She had some very big money coming in from *Some Like It Hot* and residuals from other projects. Plus she still could command a huge salary for television appearances and with other studios. But Marilyn never seemed to be able to hold on to money— and often had very little to show for her substantial earnings. Marilyn's more affluent friends knew she earned big money, yet she didn't have expensive jewels or cars. She owned no property. She didn't travel. She often wore a favorite dress repeatedly.

Famous for saying she didn't care about money, Marilyn actually lived up to that statement. Yet she spent indiscriminately, generously, and impulsively. She never went over the accounting of her bills, which made her fair game for just about everyone. Vendors had a way of making Marilyn feel that she should pay more for her success. "They think I'm rich," she sighed. "Everyone is begging me for money."

It's also accepted fact that Marilyn simply loved to give her money away. She presented Susan Strasberg with a Chagall drawing for her birthday. Jane Fonda recalled lunching at New York's Sardi's restaurant with Marilyn, Shelley Winters, and Lee and Paula Strasberg. Marilyn gifted Lee and Paula ten thousand dollars to travel to Europe to attend a Stanislavski festival. That was an enormous amount of money in the day— almost double the average annual salary.

So when Marilyn signed the papers for her new house, she did so with money borrowed from her ex-husband and a mortgage that would extend over the next fifteen years. At the signing, Marilyn abruptly burst into tears. "I couldn't imagine buying a house alone," she said. "But I've always been alone so I don't know why I couldn't imagine it."

On Thursday, February 1, Peter and Pat Lawford threw a party for Bobby and Ethel Kennedy, who in a few days would be leaving on a world tour starting in Japan. Marilyn was one of the carefully selected guests, and for this meeting she wanted to be sure she had a lot of important political topics to talk to the attorney general about.

This glitzy, formal dinner was filled with some of the best and brightest in Hollywood circles, including Judy Garland, Angie Dickinson, Dean and Jeanne Martin, Tony Curtis and Janet Leigh, and Michael and Gloria Romanoff. Marilyn knew beforehand that she would be sitting on one side of Bobby Kennedy, with Kim Novak on the other. Pat Kennedy thought it would be cute to seat her brother between two of the screen's most beautiful blondes. She probably knew that Bobby had been fascinated with Marilyn for years.

Marilyn always wanted to live up to expectations, and now that she and Bobby would have an extended period of time getting to know each other, she prepared to make an indelible impression. She asked Danny Greenson—a very politically savvy young man—to help her compose a list of political questions she could discuss with the attorney general.

Marilyn had met Bobby before on several occasions, but she seemed to consider this a date. Of course she wasn't planning on dazzling Bobby with her intellect alone: Before the party Marilyn called in George Masters to do her hair and makeup. As Masters understood it, this was a "first date," even though Bobby's wife, Ethel, would be there. "I did an extra-special makeup job on her. When I finished she looked like a fawn, innocent and wide-eyed but supersexy."

At the party Kennedy was at first impressed with Marilyn's questions and then amused when he caught her peering at the crib notes tucked in her purse. This could be the night that the serious spark between Bobby and Marilyn started. (Ethel Kennedy was as excited about meeting Marilyn as anyone else.)

The party became lighthearted. When Chubby Checker's "Let's Twist Again" was played on the phonograph, they got up to dance, and Marilyn taught Bobby how to do the Twist. Later he asked her to phone his father, Joseph Kennedy, because the elder Kennedy would get a kick out of a phone call from the generation's greatest love goddess—and she was happy to oblige.

The following month, while talking about the evening with Fred Field, a friend she met on a shopping trip to Mexico, Marilyn revealed that at one point she and Kennedy had slipped away from the party into the den and had a very long, very political talk. What went on within the den walls was known only to Marilyn and Bobby.

Jeanne Martin characterized the Kennedy brothers' behavior at parties as "sophomoric . . . high school time." She told the author Anthony Summers that their wives could be in another room—while they were jumping around with a woman. She recalled having a friend who was in the library with Bobby, and before she knew it, the door was locked and he had thrown her on the couch.

The author Larry Tye interviewed Ethel Kennedy decades later: "Ethel has lived with the rumors for over fifty years, and she says she long ago stopped listening to or reading them," Tye relayed. "She tried to block them out then, too, although they must have hurt. She never disclosed any suspicions." However, Ethel also acknowledged that there was "no tradition of monogamy in the Kennedy clan. She loved her husband more completely than she dreamed possible . . . and she knew he always came home. Not just to the kids but to her."

For her own reasons Marilyn talked to some as if this was her first meeting with Bobby. She was an expert at subterfuge when she wanted to be. "Marilyn had known him before," Joan Greenson said, "but she was really excited that he was going to be sitting next to her. I don't think she knew him that well."

To Arthur Miller's son, Robert, she wrote: "I had to go to this dinner last night as [Robert Kennedy] was the guest of honor and when they asked him who he wanted to meet, he wanted to meet me. So, I went to the dinner and I sat next to him, and he isn't a bad dancer either. But I was mostly impressed with how serious he is about civil rights."

———

In the coming weeks Marilyn called Bobby Kennedy at the Justice Department. Some of the telephone records are available, showing how many times (and for how long) Marilyn called Bobby from her home phone. Much has been made of this—and the reasons for the calls have been the subject of much speculation. It is also possible that she called him from pay phones. Also unknown is how many times Bobby called Marilyn.

An undated letter to Marilyn from a Kennedy sister, Jean Smith, sent sometime that year, seems to acknowledge some sort of relationship between Marilyn and Bobby—and that Marilyn was known, and well liked, by the entire Kennedy family, including the parents, Rose and Joseph Kennedy. Marilyn had probably sent Joe Kennedy a get-well message. He had suffered a stroke in 1961 and continued to recover for months to come. Jean responded with a letter:

> *Dear Marilyn—Mother asked me to write and thank you for your sweet note to Daddy—He really enjoyed it and you were very cute to send it. / Understand that you and Bobby are the new item! We all think you should come with him when he comes back east! Again thanks for the note. / Love, Jean Smith*

Soon after the Lawford dinner party, Joan Greenson visited Marilyn's new house. As they sat chatting in the guest room near the daybed, the subject turned to boyfriends. Joan knew that Marilyn was seeing someone new, and she asked her about it. Marilyn told Joan that there was a new man in her life who was "really terrific and cute," but the man was "so important" she didn't want her to know more than that.

"She didn't want to burden me with knowing who it was, so she was going to call him 'the General,'" Joan recalled. They both laughed. Marilyn seemed to enjoy the intrigue.

TWENTY-SEVEN

In keeping with Greenson's own home decor, Marilyn decided to furnish her house with authentic furniture and accessories. A trip to Mexico was planned. Mrs. Murray was sent first to scout out stores and to do some advance shopping (she had done Greenson's interior decorating), and Marilyn would follow a week later with Pat Newcomb and her hair and makeup man, George Masters.

Evidence of Marilyn's continuing popularity can be found in the incredible excitement on her arrival in Mexico City on February 20. Newcomb arranged a press conference in the Grand Ballroom of the Continental Hilton Hotel.

Though surrounded by media hysteria, she appeared serene. As Whitey Snyder said: "No matter what you saw on the surface, underneath was always nerves and uncertainty." Yet with assurance and grace, she walked toward the throng of two hundred reporters. She slowly turned, showing off her newly slim figure, clad in a clingy green Pucci dress—a recent favorite of hers (in a few months it would be chosen for her to wear in the casket). The Mexicans were fascinated by her blond beauty, her golden radiance.

Marilyn drank champagne steadily throughout the press conference as she continued to answer questions and pose for photos. Toward the end, it seems, Marilyn had imbibed a bit too much. Some of her elegant control had left her, and she was emboldened to strike some campy poses—almost in a self-parody, demonstrating the Twist and climbing up on the

back of a couch. The Mexican press didn't seem to mind. They were en-
raptured by Marilyn, and images of her from this appearance would be
on magazine covers for months to come.

All along Marilyn had planned to combine this trip with a shopping
expedition and a minivacation. On the social front, two of Marilyn's Connecticut friends arranged an introduction to Frederick Vanderbilt Field
and his Mexican wife, Nieves. Field (who had been heir to the Vanderbilt
fortune but was disinherited by his family because of his politics) became
more than just another man on Marilyn's ever-growing list of left-wing
friends. There was an instant attraction between Field and Marilyn. Almost immediately after meeting, they started an affair. He was happily
married, but of course that hadn't stopped Marilyn in the past. She even
befriended his wife, and the three of them socialized together.

Marilyn may have become hastily involved with Field because she was
deeply disturbed when a few days before, she received news of Arthur
Miller's wedding to Inge Morath (a photographer he had met on the set
of *The Misfits*). Marilyn was insulted by Miller's quick remarriage. Was
she so easily replaced? Marilyn probably didn't know yet that Morath was
already pregnant with Miller's child.[*]

Field was a longtime communist and a dedicated Marxist. He had
left America in 1953 and was part of a circle of Mexican communists. In
an era when hostilities between America, Russia, and the rest of the world
were reaching dangerous new heights, even casual associations with someone with communist tendencies were classified as dangerous by the FBI.
Because of this relationship Marilyn became the subject of a new file
opened by the agency. It shows that Marilyn's activities in Mexico were
being monitored very closely indeed. Informants reported to the FBI that
a "mutual infatuation" had developed between Field and Monroe, which
"caused concern among some in her inner circle."

More alarming, one of the informants in the FBI files seems to be
Eunice Murray (wrongly identified as Eunice Churchill), who said: "The
subject was much disturbed by ARTHUR MILLER's marriage on

---

[*] Greenson was worried about her escalating promiscuity. Marilyn had entered a phase
of sexually searching, exploring—almost in a desperate way—for someone to rescue
her with intimacy.

2/20/62 and feels like a negated sex symbol." Surprisingly, it was also alleged in this document that the "subject reportedly spent some time with ROBERT KENNEDY in the home of PETER LAWFORD in Hollywood"—confirming that the FBI was already aware of Marilyn's acquaintance with Bobby.

Simultaneously Pat Newcomb fixed Marilyn up with José Bolanos, a sexy, twenty-six-year-old screenwriter with one film credit to his name, *La Cucaracha*, about a woman soldier. The meeting was Newcomb's way of encouraging Marilyn to go on some casual dates with a handsome, uncomplicated Latin-lover type.

They did see each other a few times, but by all accounts (except Bolanos's), this was a very casual vacation flirtation. Mexico proved to be a lovely distraction for Marilyn. Other than the furniture she purchased, it had nothing to do with her future plans.

Back in Los Angeles, Marilyn had received word that the Golden Globes planned on naming her as the Female World Film Favorite at a showy Hollywood ceremony on March 5.

She talked with Pat Newcomb about who should be her escort to the event. "I guess I'll go with Sidney Skolsky," Marilyn said, settling on her columnist friend. "Why don't you surprise them all?" Newcomb suggested. "Show up with José Bolanos!" Newcomb cannily predicted it would further enhance Marilyn's modern image to appear with a dark, handsome Latin. Marilyn by no means considered Bolanos a serious romance, but she liked the idea of being seen with a mystery man and invited him to the event. He gladly flew in to be Marilyn's date.

The media would be there in full force, some expecting an aging, overblown sexpot. It would be an ideal time to reveal to the American paparazzi her trim figure, her new white-on-white beauty, and to demonstrate that her appeal was stronger than ever. It was expected that Marilyn would appear at an industry event in a gown that was in some way provocative. As George Masters explained, she was "so concerned with her cleavage and the crack in her rear end that she would stand for hours while seamstresses sewed her into her sequined sex come-ons with all her curves showing." This time Marilyn was sewn into an emerald green gown by Norman Norell, a top American designer.

As always, her patience paid off. When she arrived at the event held at the Beverly Hilton Hotel, her appearance—with her exposed back and teased, pillowcase-white hair—caused absolute pandemonium. There was no sign that fascination with Monroe was in any way waning. Among the biggest names in the business, the crowd of photographers and fans were clamoring to get to her—a beam of light in emerald sequins—impossible to look away from. Once again, though, Marilyn needed alcohol to coax out the astounding "Marilyn Monroe" who stunned and seduced.

Susan Strasberg remembered that Marilyn arrived "four sheets to the wind and proceeded to go for five." Even so, Strasberg confessed that Marilyn's entrance "knocked me out. There was a room full of the biggest stars in the world, and when Marilyn walked in and made her way slowly to the table, her dress was so tight she could hardly move, some people in the room stood on chairs just to get a look at her, like kids. I'd never seen stars react to another star like that."

But the adoration did not reassure her, did not relieve her anxiety. "I sat near her." the columnist James Bacon observed. "She gulped wine by the glassful. When her name was called, she had to be helped out of her chair onto the stage."

Handing out some of the awards that year was Stefanie Powers, then a young starlet chosen to be a presenter. "She was giving them the image they wanted," Powers remarked. "You have to understand that in that time, Marilyn was still kind of a joke in the industry, still not being taken seriously—which is what she really wanted at that point. Even this event, the Golden Globes, was not a serious ceremony back then. It was a poor man's Academy Award. But as she approached to receive the award, she was glowing. The closer she got, the brighter she glowed. I mean, you understood why in a room filled with the biggest stars it was Marilyn that was the focus. We—the photographers, the celebrities, the guests—all just circled around her. She was the center. It seemed to just happen naturally with her."

The award was presented to her by Rock Hudson. Marilyn's acceptance speech was exceptionally short: "Thank you," she whispered, slurring the words. "I'm grateful to you all." Bacon said that she accepted the award almost in a caricature of herself. An opinion Susan Strasberg shared: "Didn't she know she was better than this?" Susan lamented. "Worth more than this?" Charlton Heston, who was on the stage when she accepted the award, wrote in his diary: "Monroe was absolutely smashed, unable to say a word. Probably just as well."

Photographs from the evening show the ambiguities in Marilyn's beauty in 1962. In some of the pictures, taken early in the evening, she looks vibrant, stunning, ageless. But as the evening wore on (and the wine continued to flow), Marilyn at times appears messy and brittle.

Still, the lovely and much younger Susan Strasberg was envious of Marilyn. "Even drunk, barely in control, overly made-up, she still exuded innocence and a vibrant life force that surrounded her like an aura."

John F. Kennedy was planning on spending a weekend in Palm Springs—the beautiful resort town in the desert, one hundred miles southeast of Los Angeles. Many celebrities had weekend homes there, and Kennedy intended to spend his visit at the home of Frank Sinatra, but eventually the plans were changed so he could stay at Bing Crosby's house. The attorney general didn't want the president associated with Sinatra because of his mob ties.

The president thought it would be nice to at last have some uninterrupted time with Marilyn, and he invited her to be his date for the weekend. He had probably thought about her since their last encounter, in her white beaded dress and tousled hair, at the Fifi Fell dinner party.

The Palm Springs weekend was planned in an atmosphere of secrecy and high drama that appealed to Marilyn. She agreed to join him. It was arranged that she would fly from Los Angeles to Palm Springs in disguise, escorted by Peter Lawford. This was where the training of Norma Jeane took over. She could take refuge from grim reality in a fantasy world of her own devising, playacting, becoming one of the dramatic heroines she saw on the screen. Interludes with the president were taking on a fantasy quality—a temporary escape from her encroaching problems. It was fun for him, and it was a pleasurable distraction for her. The problem was,

Marilyn wanted it to last. She wanted Kennedy in her life. Strong men were her protectors. They were, in fact, her father.

It's alarming to consider how intertwined the sexual and social lives of these high-profile players were. Marilyn was now entangled—to varying degrees—in the attentions of John Kennedy, Bobby Kennedy, and Frank Sinatra.

It's no wonder that in her therapy sessions with Greenson—when she was feeling lethargic and depressed—she confided that she felt that she was being used. Yet the ego boost that these powerful associations gave her was worth the risk for the time being. In her manic periods, she loved the collusion, the temporary feeling of being in control of her own life.

On Saturday, March 24, Peter Lawford arrived at her place to drive her to the airport so the two of them could catch the president's Conair plane, which would take them to Palm Springs airport. As she had with other meetings with Kennedy, Marilyn avoided any chance of being recognized by covering her fresh hairdo with a black wig and wearing dowdy clothes. Lawford got a kick out of Marilyn looking very unlike "Monroe." To take the masquerade a step further, he told everyone they encountered during the trip that Marilyn was his secretary.

Once they were safely sequestered at the Bing Crosby estate, hidden away in the desert of Palm Springs, Marilyn and Kennedy could casually stroll the grounds, have long talks, and socialize—with a few select, very trusted friends—without the tension of being found out.

An affair between Marilyn and the president wasn't exactly unheard of. By now talk was swirling that Marilyn and Kennedy were seeing each other. To those who saw them together that weekend, it was just confirmation. At the Crosby estate, the two stayed in one of the cottages, where they were met by a loyal group of Kennedy's friends and Secret Service men.

This is the one time that is generally accepted by all investigative journalists that Marilyn Monroe and John F. Kennedy had a sexual encounter. The reason is a phone call Marilyn made—from the bed she was sharing with the president—to her good friend Ralph Roberts. She even put Roberts on the phone with Kennedy.

With the president lying next to her, Marilyn had decided to use some of Roberts's massaging techniques on the president. Kennedy notoriously had a bad back. Somewhere in the course of their pillow talk, the conversation turned to anatomy—a subject on which Marilyn was very knowledgeable and had been for a long time: The human body was one of her main fascinations.

Marilyn sang a little bit of the classic gospel song "Dem Bones," with the lyric "Hip bone connected to the back bone." Meanwhile she wanted Kennedy to understand the importance of the soleus muscle—which Marilyn used for her famous walk.*

Hence the call to Roberts—all the better for him to explain the soleus muscle to Kennedy. Roberts knew that Marilyn was rendezvousing with the president that weekend; she had told him beforehand ("Pat Newcomb was in on it," he said), but he wasn't expecting a phone call. Still, soon Roberts was on the phone listening to the unmistakable voice of the president of the United States. Afterward Kennedy thanked him.

Philip Watson, a Los Angeles County assessor, one of the select guests at the Crosby property that weekend, was brought into the cottage Marilyn and Kennedy were sharing. He observed Kennedy casually attired in a turtleneck sweater and Marilyn even more casually dressed in her usual choice for relaxing—a robe. He noticed that Marilyn had had a lot to drink. "There was no question in my mind that they were having a good time," Watson said. "It was obvious they were intimate, that they were staying there together for the night."

After the weekend was over, Roberts casually asked her how the president was. "Well," Marilyn replied coyly, "I think I made his back feel better."

There was something almost Shakespearean about Marilyn's saga in her final year. She was the beautiful, mad, aging queen, referring to her mirror and then turning to the mighty king and his ambitious brother to make sure she was still desirable, her position safe.

---

* She learned this from an exercise that she got from *The Thinking Body* by Mabel Elsworth Todd. This was a book that she first read as a very young starlet and usually carried around with her from place to place.

When the Kennedys moved into Marilyn's orbit, who can estimate the significance she put on their attentions? Marilyn's delicate frame of mind—the crushing loneliness, her fear of fading and losing her beauty, power, and ability to be loved—made her more fragile and needy than ever.

Evidence of Marilyn's relationship with the Kennedys is mostly anecdotal. Yet the number of people who witnessed them together, and friends whom Marilyn told bits and pieces about the affairs, is substantial. By taking the time to read and listen to all accounts as objectively as possible, and study what evidence there is—and there is an exhaustive amount—the existing data point to the conclusion that Marilyn had some amount of romantic involvement with both Kennedy brothers.

The definite number of times they were in one another's company and what exactly they felt for one another can never be known. Marilyn's affair with John F. Kennedy is more famous and spectacular because they were two people in politics and show business about whom the public was extremely curious. They both entered into an affair with different intentions. Jack—who also had a public persona and a very private self—was married to the elegant and much-loved Jacqueline Bouvier Kennedy, and they had a young daughter and son. But that didn't stop him from engaging in numerous flings, with White House interns, call girls, movie stars, and friends, all simultaneously. In the meantime Kennedy had the world to run.

Her relationship with Bobby Kennedy was more serious—at least to Marilyn—and it lasted longer. It is apparent now that Marilyn put much more expectations and hope in these relationships than either of the brothers did. History has shown that both Kennedys indulged in affairs—John much more indiscreetly and frequently than Bobby. "I'm not saying they were saints in any way," Pat Newcomb said of the Kennedys. "But who wants to know saints?"

When we look for tangible evidence of Marilyn's affairs with the Kennedys—photos, documents, letters—there is little to be found. At least not yet. Some of it has most certainly been destroyed.* Also, it was a

---

* For example, the respected medical researcher Mathilde Krim stated that all of the

different world in the early 1960s. Today we have computerized systems
of checks and balances that didn't exist in 1962. There were no video
cameras recording every movement. There were no cell phones that could
discreetly capture a moment for posterity. It wasn't unusual to pay for
things with cash rather than traceable credit cards or checks. It was much
easier to be clandestine and deceptive in the days when things were documented mostly by hand.

We all have private lives, and share only parts of ourselves with certain people. This was most certainly true of Marilyn, who normally was
living several lives at once. "Marilyn Monroe never told anybody everything," Pat Newcomb famously said of her. "She would slip off and do this.
Then she would slip out and do that. None of us really knew everything."

It was much easier to compartmentalize your life in the early sixties.
It is well known that Marilyn could move around easily without being recognized. She was a master of disguise. When she didn't want people to
know she was traveling, she would do so in a black or red wig, a kerchief,
dark glasses, and under a different name.

Today, many decades after Marilyn's last months, people are no longer afraid to go on the record with the information that they know about
her relationships because they no longer fear retribution.

For example, a Hollywood hostess, now elderly, whose husband was a
well-known actor (and a good friend of Marilyn's) had a dinner party
Marilyn and Bobby Kennedy attended—together. "After dinner Bobby
and Marilyn went out for a walk," she recalled. "But when they didn't
return my husband said he was going to go out and look for them. I said,
'Never mind. I'll go. I'll go look for them.' While I was walking down the
driveway I saw Bobby and Marilyn in a parked car."

The hostess turned on her heels and went back to the party. Marilyn
and Bobby returned a little while later. "I never told the story because my
husband was close with Marilyn," she told this author. "During his life-

---

photos taken of Marilyn and both Kennedy brothers at her celebrated party on the
night of May 19, 1962, were "borrowed" by officials and never returned. Also Marilyn's
phone records of the last week of her life were confiscated the day she died and never
seen again.

time, Marilyn's affair with Bobby was whispered about but never confirmed. It seems today it's well known and accepted."

The esteemed photographer Murray Garrett, who had known Marilyn before she was a star, was working for Time Inc. in 1962. He and other photographers would hang out at New York's Cock and Bull Bar—across from *Time*'s offices—where they would discuss the major photo ops of the day. Garrett recalled a night in the spring of 1962 when all the photographers were saying: "The big story is to catch Monroe either with JFK or Bobby at the house Lawford has in Santa Monica right near the beach."

One of them asked: "If you told me that I could get a picture of them making it in the backyard what would I do with it?" Garrett explains: "The only place you could sell a photo like that was to one of those insane gossip magazines. No legitimate publication would touch it. *LIFE, Parade, Look*—they'd say 'Come on. Are you kidding me with that stuff? We can't print a picture like that! And you can't take it. You can't do that.'"

In that time there was an unwritten rule that serious journalists didn't report on politicians' extramarital affairs. Garrett continued, "Today you could do it. But then there was a self-imposed area of silence that you had to understand. Like a wall of silence that you wouldn't cross. There were some things that were taboo that you wouldn't cover."

Susan Strasberg, whose family was close to Marilyn for years, said that Marilyn told her mother, Paula, that there was an affair first with John F. Kennedy and then with Bobby.

Marilyn's life was compartmentalized. Because so much of her was publicized, she carefully boxed away segments of her life that she shared with very few—and even to those she gave only bits and pieces. So much of her belonged to the public. She wanted to keep a piece of herself to herself—it was a way to survive. That's what makes her such a fascinating puzzle.

TWENTY-EIGHT

STARTING SOMETHING

Meanwhile 20th Century-Fox was committed to getting Marilyn in front of the cameras. By now, in addition to Dean Martin, the glamorous Cyd Charisse had been added to the cast of *Something's Got to Give*, playing Martin's other wife. Since there was no script anywhere near completion, the production couldn't realistically begin until sometime that spring. In the coming months, as the start date continued to be delayed, five writers worked on the story, but none of their versions pleased Marilyn. She still felt something was missing—the spark, the wit that would make it a "Marilyn Monroe" movie. In desperation the studio hired Nunnally Johnson, who had written *How to Marry a Millionaire*, one of Marilyn's great hits.

While preparations for the movie plodded on, a huge boost to Marilyn's ego arrived in the form of an invitation to sing "Happy Birthday" at an elaborate celebration for President John F. Kennedy to be held in New York's Madison Square Garden that May. She called her current favorite designer, Jean Louis, and told him she wanted a dress that "only Marilyn Monroe could wear." In response the designer came up with a concept that would be both elegant and racy. A transparent, flesh-colored gown, covered with crystals that would give the illusion of nudity. Marilyn was delighted and started fittings with Jean Louis.

When Nunnally Johnson sent his reworked script to Marilyn, she was pleased. All the previous adaptations she had been shown did not have the feel of the star vehicle she was looking for. She liked that Johnson had added bits like a hula dance—she could make that kind of thing her own. She felt it was an excellent draft and that it just needed a few more jokes added.

When Cukor saw the new script, however, he hit the roof. He felt it was too different from the original movie—which of course was the point. Marilyn wanted an updated, modern comedy written exclusively for her. Cukor, on the other hand, felt that the original script, although dated, had "charm." To demonstrate his own power, Cukor hired a new writer, Walter Bernstein, to totally revamp the Johnson version in two weeks' time.

Director and star had completely different visions of what kind of movie it should be. A compromise was reached: Bernstein would work on rewrites of the Johnson screenplay on different-colored paper so Marilyn could evaluate the changes he was making.

The public hadn't seen Marilyn on screen for more than a year, and in this film, scheduled to be released in October 1962, she would be introducing a new version of herself. She was slimmer than she had been in years, her hair was white-blond, teased out, and flipped. The Jean Louis costumes, while formfitting and sexy, were also stylish and elegant. The look would introduce an up-to-date, more sophisticated Marilyn.

On Tuesday, April 10, 1962, the day of the filmed costume and makeup tests, Marilyn Monroe's beauty reached its zenith—as if all her other looks had been experiments to reach this ravishing pinnacle.

If there was any question in Hollywood's eyes of Marilyn's continuing charisma, her absolute ability to light up the screen, this footage—had it been seen by the public at the time—would have put any doubts to rest. Parading a variety of looks, she walks back and forth across the set modeling her costumes, elegantly flaunting her perfectly proportioned body. Regaining her figure has clearly given her renewed confidence. Marilyn has never appeared more in command of herself, or more exquisite on film. All the adoration and betrayals and love and hate and failures and triumphs of her life have fed into this moment, filling Marilyn with a complicated beauty that is thrilling to watch.

The following day, however, Marilyn failed to show up for a meeting to discuss the tests. The producer, Henry Weinstein, eager to share his excitement about her appearance, rushed to her house and was horrified to discover Marilyn in bed in a drug-induced coma. Greenson and Engelberg were called to what was by now a familiar and worrisome scenario. Marilyn was rescued once more.

Weinstein was so troubled by Marilyn's overdose that he went to the studio executives and, like Mickey Rudin, asked them to postpone the production. He argued that Marilyn's mental state was too unpredictable. Determined to get a Marilyn movie into theaters, they called Weinstein "melodramatic." The Fox heads declared that production would continue as scheduled.

On April 18 Marilyn received Bernstein's revised version of the script on blue paper. Marilyn was not amused by his pedestrian dialogue and was dismayed at the gooey lines he wrote in an attempt to make her character more likable to the children, who don't recognize her as their mother. In a razor-sharp criticism, Marilyn contemptuously scrawled across one page: "Too flat. It's painting black on black so to speak. We don't have to worry about heart. I have one, believe it or not."

With the script still unsatisfactory to Marilyn, Cukor postponed the start of shooting until April 23. This would give Bernstein another week to rewrite. A few days later Marilyn received new pages on pink paper. Soon after that, yellow pages with more rewrites arrived. The script was now a mess of different colors, ideas, and styles.

That Monday 104 crew members reported to soundstage 14, ready and excited to start filming, even though the script was still incomplete. Marilyn called in sick. By now no one could have been expecting an easy production involving Marilyn Monroe. All the studio could do was schedule a start day and hope for the best. Marilyn continued to call in sick for the rest of the week. The familiar pattern of rearranging schedules and shooting around her had begun. The studio doctor confirmed that Marilyn was sick with a fever and chest congestion, and suggested production should be postponed for one month. But by now it was a case of a movie star who had cried wolf too many times. No one believed she was ill.

What was really going on with Marilyn that spring? Was it a power play? Hypochondria? A simple fear of facing the camera? Was she truly sick? The answer, according to her internist, Dr. Engelberg, was that her illness was most likely a combination of all of these things.

"She was easily disturbed by the pressures of work, although she worked hard," Engelberg explained. "When she was depressed her resistance dropped to infection. There's a phrase that is used by doctors, Psyche and Soma, which means psychological and emotional things and the bodily things. They affect each other."

Elizabeth Taylor's delays on the astronomically overbudget *Cleopatra*, now in its last days of filming in Rome, had created severe financial problems for the studio. Marilyn, just starting her movie, would bear the brunt of it. Fox had everything invested in the Taylor extravaganza and needed immediate cash. It was well known—and widely reported—that the studio was less patient with what they considered Marilyn's shenanigans because of *Cleopatra*.

20th Century-Fox treated its two biggest stars quite differently. To Fox, Marilyn Monroe was a disturbed marshmallow they could push around and appease by submitting to a few of her demands and making her feel important. Elizabeth Taylor was nobody's fool: a no-nonsense, tough-talking businesswoman who knew what she wanted and demanded it—or else. If she was sick, they better damn well wait it out. Unlike Monroe, Taylor cared a lot more about getting her money than being wonderful. Although she often managed to do both.

Because of Fox's treatment of her, Marilyn viewed the studio as the enemy, which made it even more difficult for her to show up. They were using her. They were disrespecting her. They were treating her like a "machine." It made her more belligerent regarding the studio heads, and it intensified her illness.

On Monday, April 30, a week after production had begun, Monroe showed up at the studio to shoot her first scene for *Something's Got to Give*. She arrived on the set looking slim and lovely but still complaining of a fever. She shot scenes around the house where her character returns after five years of being stranded on a tropical island. There was no dialogue, but in close-up Marilyn powerfully conveyed a range of tender emotions when she first sees her children.

The next day hopes sank again when Marilyn showed up at 7:00 a.m. only to collapse under a hair dryer at 7:30. She was sent home. She didn't work for the rest of the second week. Marilyn was so ill that she missed an opportunity to meet the visiting shah and empress of Iran.

By Thursday, May 10, Marilyn was still calling in sick. In the midst of panic and disorder, Greenson left for a four-week trip to Europe with his wife. It was a planned trip, and part of Marilyn's illness stemmed from her dread of Greenson going away. "I told her that I would return if it was necessary," Greenson said. The doctor would be leaving her in the care of his colleague Dr. Milton Wexler. At this point Marilyn had worked one day in the three weeks of filming. He seems to have made Marilyn dependent on him; now he was leaving her at a time when she needed support the most.

At last on Monday, May 14, Marilyn returned to work. She picked up shooting the scene where her character first returns home. Her actions involved her lingering by the pool, interacting with the children. In spite of the mawkish dialogue, Marilyn found in the scene—a mother at last being reunited with her children—an emotional and psychological gold mine to draw on. They finally seemed to be making progress when Marilyn showed up for work the next two days.

What is fascinating about *Something's Got to Give* is that almost every moment filmed for the movie survives. Because this movie was never completed, the footage was boxed and locked in a warehouse where it remained unseen for three decades. When discovered it was a revelation. In the unedited footage we get an excellent view of the shooting days on the set of *Something's Got to Give* and an unprecedented look at the working Marilyn Monroe.

For years her studio, her directors, and her costars had attempted to portray Marilyn as a difficult, exhausting actress who screwed up lines, demanded retakes, and acted like a troublesome, uncooperative diva. Yet this unedited footage tells a different story. Even between takes, as the camera rolled, we see a Marilyn who is focused, agreeable, pleasant, and working hard. It clearly illustrates how some in the industry were against her: There is no monster in Marilyn here.

Even though Marilyn was working hard and well, there was tension. Her many absences had put everyone on edge, and Cukor in particular was now on the brink of despising her—although the actress and director put up a pleasantly polite working facade, when watching the rushes you can sense the strain between them. Cukor got back at her by ordering many takes of the same scene even after it seems to have been flawlessly performed in the first few takes.

Cukor wasted almost an entire day of shooting a scene between Marilyn's character and the family dog, because the trained dog refused to bark on cue. Marilyn, kneeling by the pool in heels, remains in good humor while the director insists the scene be shot again and again—slowing down a production that was already moving at a sloth's pace.

Although she showed up on time once again on Thursday, a helicopter landed on the studio lot after lunch with the intention of picking up Marilyn and—along with Pat Newcomb, Peter Lawford, and his agent, Milt Ebbins—flying her to the airport to catch a plane to New York so she could perform at the president's birthday celebration that Saturday night.

When the studio heads objected, Marilyn countered that she had told them six weeks earlier that she was going—which was true—but that was before they knew the extent of the absences she would have racked up by then. Now they were horrified that she would even consider walking out during a workweek.

As far as Marilyn was concerned, missing President Kennedy's birthday fete was out of the question. It was one of the biggest honors of her life to be asked to sing "Happy Birthday" to the president of the United States. Here was a woman who constantly questioned herself, and now she would be associated with the world's most powerful man. With a remarkable gown already designed, she intended not only to perform for the president but also to affirm to the world—and herself—that Marilyn Monroe was still in every way a phenomenon.

TWENTY-NINE

Marilyn was actually quite terrified of singing the simple "Happy Birthday" in front of a massive crowd. She started practicing weeks before. "I remember sitting on the bathtub, listening to her singing as she was putting on makeup," Joan Greenson said. "She would sing to me. As it got closer to the time of her going, she got more and more nervous about it. I gave her my copy of *The Little Engine That Could*. It was very strange to me, a twenty-one-year-old art student saying to Marilyn Monroe, 'Oh I know you can. Get out there and do a good job.'"

Marilyn found comfort in the tale of the little train's bravery and perseverance and took the book with her to New York as a talisman.

In Manhattan, on the evening before the gala, Ralph Roberts dropped by Marilyn's Fifty-seventh Street apartment to watch her rehearse. Pat Newcomb and Paula Strasberg were there, along with the Broadway lyricist Richard Adler. Adler was staging and producing the event, and came to get a sneak preview of her performance.

As she did when rehearsing for her show for the troops in Korea, Marilyn worked tirelessly at perfecting her act. "I went to the apartment about eight or nine o'clock and there was a pianist there," Ralph Roberts recalled. "They rehearsed 'Happy Birthday' over and over again. As the evening progressed, Marilyn's rendition of the song became more and more suggestive, and the show's producer became increasingly perturbed. "Richard Adler was very upset with her interpretation," Roberts recalled.

Marilyn knew that Jackie Kennedy wouldn't be in the audience next to her husband; the first lady had chosen to be at a horse show in Virginia with her children.

Marilyn began the song yet again, and Adler approached Roberts, whispering urgently, "We cannot do this to the president of the United States!" Adler then slipped out of the apartment to call the president to warn him that Marilyn couldn't do it. It was too sexy.

Kennedy laughed. "It'll be fine. Everybody'll love it."

The day of the event Marilyn transformed herself into the bigger-than-life icon people expected. In those hair-obsessed days, Marilyn had Mr. Kenneth style her hair into a mega-bouffant with an exaggerated wing on one side. Her semitransparent gown of flesh-colored silk—soufflé gauze covered with more than 2,500 crystals—had to be sewn onto her naked body so that it became a top layer of skin. Of course it was impossible to wear any underclothes beneath such a garment—although it did have an invisible zipper in the back so that she wouldn't have to be cut out of it as she had been with other gowns.

She left her apartment and arrived at Madison Square Garden with Pat Newcomb, very late. Her date for the evening was Isidore Miller, her ex-father-in-law, whom she still loved very dearly, and whom she continued to look to as a father figure. She brought him because she wanted to give him the gift of meeting the president.

Capitalizing on the barrage of press Marilyn was receiving about always being absent or late on the set of her new movie, Peter Lawford made her introduction a running gag throughout the show. He kept introducing her, only to find himself gesturing, with a drumroll, to an empty spotlight.

"I think we were all holding our breath because we knew she was extremely nervous," Diahann Carroll recalled. "I mean really just petrified. But we weren't worried about the dress. We knew the dress was almost lacquered onto the body."

Finally Lawford begins to introduce her again, this time even referencing his wife, Pat Kennedy: "Mr. President, because in the history of show business, Pat says, in no one female who meant so much, who has done more . . ." At this point Marilyn appears, seeming to metaphysically materialize out of the darkness as she climbs several steps and teeters across the stage, her ermine wrap giving brief flashes of the delights underneath.

When she stands at the podium side by side with Lawford she pulls the stole tightly around her until he says, "I'll take that." Then Marilyn does the big reveal. When she removes the white fur and hands it to Lawford, the audience of fifteen thousand people gasps collectively. The sheer silk material of the gown seems to have melted away under the lights, and Marilyn's magnificent body appears to be nude, covered only by hundreds of sparkling crystals.

Lawford exits, leaving her alone onstage. "When she came down with that flesh colored dress without any underwear on you could smell lust," reported Hugh Sidey, who covered John F. Kennedy for *Time*. At the podium Marilyn takes her time. Standing there she is the culmination of everything Marilyn Monroe was mythologized for—dreamy, sexual, fuzzy, glittering, naked—unworldly in her beauty.

Marilyn flicks the microphone. She shields her eyes from the lights to gaze out at the audience. She smiles. She looks around. She lets out a deep sigh, which elicits more screams and whistles from the crowd. She hesitates, allowing the sex slowly to fill up in her. Then she begins: "Happy Birthday to you. . . ."

A giant birthday cake is wheeled out; the glamorous president takes to the stage to thank all the performers, ending with: "Miss Monroe left a picture to come all the way East. And I can now retire from politics after having had 'Happy Birthday' sung to me in such a sweet wholesome way."

Marilyn's sultry serenade to the president electrified audiences at the time and continues to fascinate today. "It was mass seduction," Richard Adler declared, even though he had been scandalized by her rehearsal the night before. Dorothy Kilgallen, one of the journalists who suspected an affair at the time and dared to hint at it, wrote: "It seemed like Marilyn was making love to the President in the direct view of 40 million Americans."

After the performances an exclusive party was held at the Manhattan residence of the entertainment lawyer Arthur B. Krim and his wife, the medical researcher Mathilde Krim. Marilyn chatted and laughed, but Susan Strasberg noticed that she seemed totally lost. When she hugged Susan, she felt Marilyn's nails nervously dig into her arms as if she were trying desperately to hold on to something. When it came to Marilyn, there was always something going on underneath.

"I watched President Kennedy watching her," Susan said. "Those two glittering, charismatic Geminis were fascinating together, and apart. . . . I wondered if she was going to rendezvous with the president as she had before." Marilyn may also have felt Kennedy watching her.

The pollster Lou Harris, who was friends with John F. Kennedy, remembers that the air at the Krims' party was filled with sexual innuendo and flirtations. Harris was especially aware of the erotic atmosphere because he watched Henry Fonda talking intimately to his wife on the couch for a long time. Susan Strasberg was appalled when Vice President Lyndon Johnson put his hand up her dress, inviting her: "Come sit on my lap, little girl."

Amid all this, it was impossible not to notice Marilyn. That night she was the moon. Everything and everyone was viewed through her incandescence. "The image of this exquisite, beguiling, and desperate girl will always stay with me," Kennedy historian Arthur Schlesinger wrote in his journal. "I do not think I have seen anyone so beautiful; I was enchanted by her manner and her wit, at once so masked, so ingenuous, and so penetrating. But one felt a terrible unreality about her—as if talking to someone under water. Bobby and I engaged in mock competition for her; she was most agreeable to him and pleasant to me, but one never felt her to be wholly engaged." Then Schlesinger watched, fascinated, as Marilyn "receded into her own glittering mist."

At one point, it seems, Marilyn led Bobby to believe that he had won the "mock" competition. "Jack had already been with Marilyn more than once before," Lou Harris said. "I know because he told me. So it was curious to see Bobby flirting with her—and she was flirting back." When asked if he thought it might be a ploy by Marilyn to make the president jealous, Harris replied: "I was aware that there was sometimes a competitive thing going on between the two brothers—particularly when it came to women. Marilyn may have been playing up their rivalry."

According to Harris, at one point in the pretend competition, Marilyn briefly pressed Bobby up against the wall. "I thought that was brazen of her," Harris stated. "And Jack certainly witnessed it since he rarely took his eyes off of her. But the next moment she could act very demure . . . alone in the world, belonging to no one. That made her all the more attractive to everyone."

Because of Marilyn's sexy performance that night, and the rumors that were circulating about an affair between them, it has widely been assumed that the two had a sexual encounter after the party. Susan Strasberg, who had kept a curious eye on both of them, witnessed them leaving separately, although she did notice that Marilyn's "exit was uncharacteristically reserved. She slipped out—no grand farewells." Kennedy was staying at his favorite Manhattan hotel, the Carlyle.

Two reliable sources have gone on record with contradictory accounts of seeing Marilyn after the Krims' party. James Haspiel, who had been following Marilyn around New York since 1955, and whose accounts of her have proved to be trustworthy, said that she arrived at her apartment alone in a car at exactly 3:50 a.m. Earlier he had been at Madison Square Garden and had watched his idol's dynamic performance. As was usual for him, he waited in front of her apartment building for Marilyn to arrive home.

She pulled up in front of the building in a black limo. He noticed that her hair was not in the carefully lacquered style she had worn at the gala. It looked "as though she had combed it out" like "white spun gold." And she was not wearing her shoes. He also noticed that Marilyn was fatigued and visibly upset. When she saw Haspiel she said something to him, a comment that he chose not to reveal but that angered him and prompted him to reply, "Oh, go to hell, Marilyn." That was the last time Haspiel ever saw her.

Ralph Roberts gives a different time frame. Encased in the security of her apartment, Marilyn was far too hyped up to sleep and she phoned Roberts, waking him, asking him to come over and give her a massage. "She called me as soon as she got home," Roberts said. He arrived at her place within minutes "because I lived three blocks away from her."

Roberts estimated the time to have been about two o'clock, but he could be confused; his approximation was made after being roused from a deep sleep and hurrying to Marilyn's place. It is unlikely she could have been home by two considering the length of the event at Madison Square Garden and the time she spent socializing at the Krims' party.

Haspiel claimed to have seen Roberts enter the building—which would put the time at about four. Haspiel was not as close to Marilyn as Roberts was, but he was friendly with the star and, in his way, as devoted. Although he was not directly involved in her life, he often knew her schedule and discreetly followed her around town for years, sometimes documenting their encounters with photos, sometimes not. At times he interacted with her, and at others he simply observed her. Haspiel often knew her secret activities and meetings better than the press.

The time of her arrival at her apartment is important, and it depends on which witness you believe. If Marilyn arrived home near four, that would have given her enough time to rendezvous with Kennedy at the Carlyle—something that was widely assumed at the time. If Marilyn did meet the president at the hotel, it was a brief encounter. But this would not be unusual for Kennedy, who notoriously didn't engage in sexual foreplay.

Jackie Kennedy confessed that her promiscuous husband was "a flop as a lover." She told a friend that he "just goes too fast and falls asleep." Milt Ebbins commented: "Jack was a hit and run with women. We know that from the women. Bing! Up and out. And I asked him about that once, and he said, 'You gotta take it fast when you don't have much time.'"

Angie Dickinson who, like Marilyn, often socialized with the Rat Pack and was also having affairs with Frank Sinatra and John Kennedy, described making love with Kennedy as "the best twenty seconds of my life."

Pamela Colin—then a socialite and an editor at *Vogue*—guested at the White House and knew of many society woman who were having affairs with the president. The future Lady Harlech revealed: "Then there was the famous Angie Dickinson who used to go up and down in the lift at the Carlyle Hotel, you know, at the back, the service lift."

It's possible that Marilyn had been whisked up the service elevator to where an exclusive group of friends had gathered. Then Marilyn and

Kennedy could have slipped away for a quick tryst before she was driven the short twenty blocks back to her apartment—where Haspiel observed her emerging from the car barefoot and upset. It would also make sense that Marilyn's hairdo would have been combed out at the hotel—her hair is intact in all the photos at the Krims' party, and it is unlikely she would have mussed it there.

When Marilyn showed up for work on the Fox lot on Monday morning, the studio executives were not feeling any excitement over her much-talked-about performance. They were in fact furious that she had missed more work because of the event. She did nothing to appease their allegations of her being difficult. Pleading exhaustion, she wouldn't do close-ups. The following day, because Dean Martin had a cold she refused to work with him. All Cukor could do was shoot retakes. The movie had been in production for weeks, and Marilyn was still working on her first scenes.

On Wednesday, however, she showed up for the third day in a row with a "Marilyn Monroe" tactic that never failed to sway everyone back into her corner. She was scheduled to film a swimming scene in which her character, Ellen, tries to entice her husband, Nick, into telling his new wife that she has returned. The scene required Marilyn to swim naked by moonlight and squeal in delight until her husband comes out to confront her. In keeping with the morals of the era, the swim would be only a tease: The costume department had created a flesh-colored net bikini for Marilyn to wear in the water.

After Marilyn conferred with Cukor, she decided to make it a genuine nude scene. She later explained, "Honestly, if I had done those scenes in a flesh netting it really would have looked phony, and I am convinced that false nudity is much more obscene than the real thing could ever be."

Although she had the set cleared of unnecessary bystanders, Marilyn did allow two photographers, Lawrence Schiller and Billy Woodfield, to document the scene. Even while Marilyn was performing naked, swimming, splashing, and kicking in the water, the scene was lit in such a way that one really couldn't see much nudity. But every frame of film is filled with Marilyn's peachy playfulness. "I think I am an actress," she later told a reporter, "and as such in order to act nude I had to feel nude."

After coming out of the water, she sits poolside, her exquisite back facing the camera, as she dries her hair. Then she stands and languidly wraps her naked body in a plush blue robe. In one take the robe slips open, very briefly exposing a breast and firm derriere. These naked flashes allowed the film's publicity to announce that it was the "first true nude scene done in an American film by a major movie actress."

Photos of Marilyn frolicking naked would surely make global headlines and be worth a fortune. When Woodfield and Schiller asked what Marilyn wanted in return for allowing them to sell the photos, she casually informed them that she wanted the pictures to knock Elizabeth Taylor off worldwide magazine covers.

Not only did the still photographs result in a sensation, Fox and the entire *Something's Got to Give* company were thrilled. The mundane little comedy now had a bona fide "Marilyn Monroe" scene, and because of the skinny-dip scene, it had a highly inviting hook to attract audiences. The rushes were viewed as being right up there with some of the greatest moments of Marilyn ever captured on film.

The psychological contradictions were not lost on Marilyn: posing nude, flaunting playful sexuality, while wanting to be taken seriously as an actress. In the coming decades this would not be impossible for an actress, but in 1962 a woman past thirty-five was expected to act in certain ways, and appearing naked in a motion picture was not one of them.

THIRTY

Marilyn continued to show up for work for the next two days. However, she phoned in sick on the twenty-seventh and twenty-eighth because of an ear infection. Once again morale sank. By now everyone was almost out of their minds from waiting for Monroe.

The crew and studio executives weren't the only ones reaching the breaking point with Marilyn. Her lawyer, Mickey Rudin, was getting fed up with her causing one disturbance after another. "Every day, coming on the set was a challenge. Every day she'd find reasons not to do it. I mean, she'd have to screw up the courage to come out of that dressing room! That could have been a cinch for normal people, with sane people. You don't judge the actions of a disturbed person by standards of normality. She was not sane. Nobody seems to accept that fact."

That Wednesday, Marilyn did show up to—at last—shoot her very first scene with leading man Dean Martin. Marilyn starts off strong in the opening takes of the scene but seems to be fading by the end of the day. Flubbing lines and low on energy, she was sent home early.

The following day Marilyn seemed energized, her performance rising above the mundane writing. In a scene that takes place in a fancy shoe store, the dithery comic actor Wally Cox—best known for his TV series *Mr. Peepers*—plays a nerdy shoe salesman she wants to pass off to her husband as the man with whom she was stranded on the island. Marilyn had one more day of shooting left in her.

Marilyn filmed the last scene of her life on June 1, 1962—her thirty-sixth birthday. If she was feeling down or panicked that day, it didn't show in her performance. She arrived on time and filmed an entire day with Martin and Cox. The scenes captured are some of Marilyn's best work in the film. As she was busy shooting, flowers and cards arrived all day at the studio.

At the end of the workday, a cake adorned with sparklers was wheeled out. In spite of the cake and champagne, the celebration seemed forced: The smiles were fake. The underlying mood was grim. Still, there was no way of anyone knowing that this would be the last day of shooting.

After the on-set celebration, Marilyn took Dean Martin's son to a baseball game at Dodger Stadium. The Angels were playing the Yankees. Her appearance was a fund-raiser for muscular dystrophy. Marilyn was scheduled to walk onto the field, throw out the first pitch, and accept the check for the worthy cause.

Albie Pearson, the Angels center fielder, was waiting to walk her to home plate for the pregame presentation. Pearson was excited and nervous to meet Marilyn Monroe, and he asked, "Well, where is she?" He was surprised to see one of the biggest stars of the era alone in the corner of the dugout. Marilyn was wearing the elegant beige fur-trimmed suit and mink beret she had worn earlier in her scene at the studio, but she was "pale, nervous and shaking."

Pearson did not encounter the Monroe he was expecting. "I was shocked," he said. "I expected her to be flashing a big smile, and instead I got this sober look."

In spite of the expert makeup, the glamour, the exquisite form, he "looked at the most famous yet loneliest person I ever saw in my life," Pearson recalled. "She was a beautiful shell." Pearson remained silent as he and Marilyn walked out of the dugout, but he was astonished at her transformation once she was in front of the crowd. She instantly turned on—smiling and waving—giving them exactly what was expected. When Pearson walked her off the field, her persona no longer needed, her smile vanished instantly.

The distress, the emptiness, the loneliness that Albie Pearson recognized in Marilyn were reflections of real suffering, a culmination of hopelessness that had been building up in her for some time and may have been exacerbated by the mere fact of another birthday, a year older, the ever-ticking clock.

Also, word had reached Marilyn that President Kennedy, once smitten with her, now felt it necessary to distance himself. Her performance at his birthday gala had brought too much whispered speculation of a possible affair between them.

Others had warned Kennedy that tongues were wagging—that behind her deceptively self-assured sensuality she was terribly vulnerable, impossibly needy, and in fact unstable. At first Kennedy wasn't concerned. He felt tremendously protected by both the Secret Service and the press. But when he was confronted by the one person he knew he could not refuse— his wife—he understood he had to put a stop to anything further developing between him and Marilyn.

Although his indiscretions hurt her terribly, Jackie Kennedy had long ago come to terms with her husband's infidelities. She learned to accept his affairs as long as they did not touch her—or her family. But she viewed his dalliance with Marilyn differently from the others for a number of reasons. It wasn't that Jackie felt threatened by Marilyn—she was too assured of her importance in Kennedy's life—but she understood the fascination that surrounded the blond star.

More than anything Jackie understood that her family would be publicly disgraced if it somehow came out that her husband was having an affair with Marilyn. Plus, Jackie felt a great deal of empathy for her. She knew that Marilyn was a deeply sensitive, troubled woman. "This one is different, Jack. Have some pity on her," she warned. "I want you to leave Marilyn alone."

Kennedy realized that Jackie was right. Though he felt revelations about his sex life had been protected by a press that, for the most part, adored him, gossip regarding himself and Marilyn could spread to the mainstream press, causing serious harm.

Kennedy sprang into damage-control mode. He approached a former journalist, William Haddad, who was now inspector general of the Peace Corps, and asked him to go to the media and squelch any budding rumors regarding him and Marilyn.

Some stories linking the president to the sex goddess were already in the works in gossip columns as blind items. "See the editors," Kennedy demanded. "Tell them you are speaking from me and that it's just not true." Haddad believed him. Years later, however, Haddad felt betrayed by Kennedy. Eventually he came to believe that the stories regarding an affair between Kennedy and Monroe were true. "He lied to me," Haddad said. "He used my credibility with people I knew."

Along with having the press taken care of, Kennedy knew that Marilyn herself had to be dealt with. Senator Smathers, a close friend of Kennedy's, confirmed that Kennedy asked him to get Marilyn to stop talking to her friends. Smathers said, "So I called someone I knew. A friend of Marilyn's I knew I could trust, and I said, 'Look, I need you to put a bridle on Marilyn's mouth and stop her from talking so much about what's going on with Jack. It's starting to get around too much.'"

With Greenson still out of the country that weekend, a distraught and drugged Marilyn called his adult children, Joan and Daniel, and asked them to come visit her at her home. When they arrived, they were drawn into a disturbing scene. It was the middle of the afternoon, but the heavy blackout drapes were tightly drawn. They encountered Marilyn sitting up in bed, naked under a sheet, wearing a sleeping mask over her eyes "like the Lone Ranger." But unlike what might be expected from a seminude Monroe in her bed, Daniel Greenson described it as "the least erotic sight you could ever imagine. The woman was desperate."

As they sat with her, every depressive thought that inhabited her mind poured out in a litany of anguish. "She talked about being a waif, that she was ugly, that people were only nice to her for what they could get from her, nobody loved her," Daniel recalled. She also expressed remorse about not having children. "She said life wasn't worth living anymore."

Soon their father's colleague, Milton Wexler, arrived and confiscated the multitude of pills at Marilyn's bedside. But it was apparent that this was no passing depression: Marilyn was in serious need of help.

Pat Newcomb was so concerned about Marilyn's dreadful state that she slept at the foot of her bed. Marilyn, in no condition to work, phoned in sick once again. When she failed to show up on Tuesday—the production was once again at a standstill—studio executives were realistically considering the possibility that they had to take drastic action. Fox had already started contacting other major stars to replace Marilyn. Both Kim Novak and Shirley MacLaine turned down the role.

Greenson was contacted in Rome by Mickey Rudin, who informed his brother-in-law that, on top of Marilyn's awful condition, he believed the studio had had it. "I think they're about to bounce her," he said.

"I'll come back," Greenson said. "I'll interrupt my trip." Greenson told Rudin to let the studio know that he would get Marilyn back to work. Leaving his wife in Europe, Greenson headed back to Los Angeles.

Because there was no way that the public could see the material that Marilyn had already shot, stories started circulating that her performance was no good. She was distracted and disconnected. George Cukor himself fanned the flames of these rumors.

Cukor called Hedda Hopper with an exclusive interview, hinting that Marilyn was over the hill, although he insisted his comments not be credited to him. In a column headlined "Marilyn to Be Replaced, Is She Finished?" Hopper referred to Cukor as "one of the most knowledgeable men in the industry." Then she quoted him: "I believe it is the end of her career. She wants to do the picture but she has no control of herself. Her performance is not good. It's as though she's acting underwater."*

Greenson arrived on the evening of June 6 and went directly from the airport to Marilyn's house. He was concerned but he was also angry—although some of this anger should have been directed toward himself. Throughout the year, while proclaiming he was working to get Marilyn more independent, what he had succeeded in doing was the opposite. He made her more reliant on him, more dangerously vulnerable, instilling in her a neediness and dependence on him that was impossible to fill. Marilyn had become a huge responsibility. She had taken over his life while losing control of her own. Marilyn Monroe had become a barely functioning mess, partially of his making.

---

* We know now, because the footage is available, that Cukor was not telling the truth. He had no idea it would someday be available, and it shows Marilyn giving a fine performance.

He returned to Marilyn's house the following morning. That day he brought a disheveled Marilyn, with black-and-blue marks under her eyes, to the Beverly Hills plastic surgeon Michael Gurdin. The doctor noted that Marilyn was obviously heavily medicated and that she had hastily attempted to cover the bruises with makeup. Greenson told Gurdin that Marilyn had taken too much medication and had slipped in the shower. After taking an X-ray he determined her nose was not broken.

On Friday, June 8, Greenson met with executives at Fox to persuade them he could have her on the set the following Monday. He did not mention her injuries; instead he attempted to insert himself more deeply into the production of *Something's Got to Give*.

Although Marilyn's lawyer, Mickey Rudin, sat in on the meeting, it is disturbing that a star's psychiatrist was negotiating with her studio. Also in attendance was Fox's vice president of business operations, Phil Feldman, who took extensive notes. He recorded Greenson boasting that he would "be able to get his patient to go along with any reasonable request and although he did not want us to deem his relationship as a Svengali one, he in fact could persuade her to anything reasonable that he wanted." Making a huge leap of faith, Greenson assured the studio representatives that he could have Marilyn on the set, ready and eager to work that Monday.

Rudin didn't share Greenson's optimism. "I did my best. I was trying to keep that project alive," Rudin said. "Not because I personally believed it would get done. If you're defending a client in a murder case you try everything. To me this was it: There was going to be a Marilyn Monroe or there wasn't going to be a Marilyn Monroe. She had to finish that shitty picture."

No matter how much influence Greenson had over Marilyn, however, he did not have any impact on her studio's assessment of her. Later that day 20th Century-Fox announced that Marilyn Monroe had been fired.

Lee Remick, a pretty twenty-six-year-old actress who was under contract with Fox, was announced as Marilyn's replacement in *Something's Got to Give*. Since she was the same size as Marilyn, she could fit into her costumes. She was rushed to the studio that day to pose happily with Cukor, while going over the screenplay. It seemed as if it had all been orchestrated to humiliate Marilyn, to show the star that she was actually dispensable.

By the end of the day the studio had filed a $750,000 lawsuit against Monroe. Marilyn, already in a terrible emotional state, was devastated by the news that she was fired. She was incensed that the studio didn't believe that she was ill, and distressed that they dismissed her so publicly and cruelly.

THIRTY-ONE

ELIZABETH AND MARILYN

"You know, don't you, that they fired me because of Elizabeth Taylor?" Marilyn asked Ralph Roberts. "It's not her fault; it's the company's fault. But they fired me because of Elizabeth Taylor." The studio already had too much time and money invested in *Cleopatra* and Taylor could not be replaced. A Fox spokesman had said to the press: "No company can afford Monroe and Taylor."

The media was constantly trying to instigate a feud between Monroe and Taylor, though their screen images and physical appearances couldn't have been more different. In reality they barely knew each other, and the two had no animosity toward each other.

Taylor, in Rome finishing her last weeks on the trouble-plagued set of *Cleopatra*, saw the angry headlines declaring that Marilyn had been fired by the studio to which they were both under contract. She immediately felt a kinship with the troubled star.

In 1962 Marilyn's beauty, emotional problems, loneliness, illnesses, and advancing age were good copy for magazine articles, while Taylor's over-blown, passion-fueled exploits seemed specifically created for lurid cover stories.

Taylor's public image was that of a lusty, big-bosomed man-eater—a dark femme fatale who went after her passions with gusto, got them, and then dug in for more. Audiences simultaneously condemned and admired her—and they hungrily gobbled up any scraps of information about her latest doings.

But those close to Taylor knew that, in her private life, she was a fiercely loyal friend with an extraordinarily big heart. She always responded to wounded souls. It was common for Taylor to come to the aid of someone she felt sympathy for, and she never sought out press coverage or bragged about it to other people in a self-aggrandizing way.

The director Mike Nichols, who worked with Taylor and knew her well, commented: "There are three things I never saw Elizabeth Taylor do: Tell a lie; be unkind to anyone; and be on time." The third trait is probably something Taylor and Monroe could have bonded over. Like the rest of the world, Taylor read of Marilyn's firing from Fox on the front pages of newspapers.

One unknown fact is that immediately after Marilyn's firing, Elizabeth called Marilyn from Rome and offered to help her in any way possible. Taylor didn't often talk publicly about the good deeds she did in her private time, but on some nights, when she was in a chatty mood, she might tell some of her stories.

Kimothy Crues, who became close with Taylor years later when she was making her Broadway debut, remembers, "I worked with Elizabeth Taylor on *The Little Foxes* on Broadway in 1981. We stayed friends pretty much up until her death. Through the years we spent a lot of time both in New York and then in Los Angeles after Elizabeth bought her house in Bel Air. We had various discussions about any number of subjects.

"There was a night that publicist Chen Sam, Elizabeth, and I were sitting around, a couple of sheets to the wind—Elizabeth hadn't gotten sober yet—and I asked her about her studio years. It was a subject she would talk about sometimes and other times she preferred not to. But on this night she started talking about the *Cleopatra* experience."

Taylor told Crues that it was really the studio's own mishandling that was causing them to have serious financial troubles. "They started shooting the movie while I was ill," she said. "They shut down the production in London. They started over in Rome and had to rebuild the sets at a great cost." She was not happy with some of her behavior but also horrified by how she was treated by the studio and by the press. Crues felt comfortable enough to ask Taylor about Marilyn Monroe.

"Well," Taylor replied, "I didn't know her well. In many ways we were sort of pitted against each other by the press. But in 1962 I was being blamed for bankrupting 20th Century-Fox, and then Marilyn started a movie and Fox and the press started going after her. She was ill and missing shooting days. Then I heard Fox had fired her. I could only imagine how humiliating that was for her."

Elizabeth had had enough. She revealed to Crues, "I actually called her. I got her on the phone, and I said, 'I know we're not friends, Marilyn, but what's happening to you now has been happening to me for a long time over this *Cleopatra* situation. The financial problems that are going on with the studio are not the fault of either one of us—but they need to put the blame on someone for their desperate problems and they seem to be using the two of us. So I wanted to tell you, if you're in a bad position and you need any help financially I will send some money to you.'"

More surprisingly Taylor told Marilyn that she was willing to publicly demonstrate her solidarity with her. Taylor was in the last weeks of a chaotic two-year ordeal with *Cleopatra*, but the studio still needed some key shots for her to complete the movie. "If this gets any uglier than it already is," Taylor went on, "I can stage a walkout. I will walk off this picture and go to the press and say, 'They are trying to put the blame on Marilyn for their troubles just as they tried to put the blame on me.'"

Marilyn was flabbergasted and very moved by Taylor's kindness toward her, but she didn't want to make matters worse for either one of them. "Well, thank you so much, Elizabeth," Marilyn said. "I'm okay financially. I don't need money, although I really appreciate the offer. And I don't want you to walk out of the movie. Neither one of us should damage our career any more than the studio already has."

Aware of all the bad press being heaped on Marilyn, Taylor (who knew her own share of scandals) offered her some advice: "No matter what they write about me, Marilyn, I never deny it. I never confirm it.

I just keep smiling and I just walk. I just keep walking forward. You do the same."

Taylor ended the conversation by saying, "If there is anything you need—anything at all—call me and you will have it within twenty-four hours."*

---

* Crues elaborated: "Having known Elizabeth well for a number of years, I repeatedly saw her, without any fanfare and very privately, stand up for a lot of people, saying that she would put herself on the line for them in various ways. I often recall that discussion with her and think that it's something that no one really knows about—the situation that both those women were put in by 20th Century-Fox."

THIRTY-TWO

LAST SITTINGS

Being fired brought up all Marilyn's lifelong fears of being unwanted and rejected. She was devastated. She spent her days without structure. She might go to the Lawford's beach house, often spending the night there. Everyone could feel her despair.

She had never been fired before, and now she felt that her good name in the industry had been tarnished and she might never be hired for another movie. If she looked too deeply into the future, she saw those doors slamming in her face. In an attempt to numb her fears she was drinking heavily, living mainly on a diet of champagne, potent tranquilizers, and sleeping pills.

Marilyn was well aware that John F. Kennedy was shutting her out. When she felt his affection slipping, she felt her emotional stability going with it. She needed someone or something to anchor her. Robert Kennedy wasn't the most powerful man in the world—but as attorney general he certainly had power. And he had the illustrious Kennedy name. Marilyn found that he had a sensitivity that John didn't. He was more receptive to her, and more touched by her combination of beauty and vulnerability. Bobby was a man she could love and, she hoped, who could love her—rescue her.

Marilyn's phone records show eight calls to Bobby Kennedy at his office between late June and early July. Kennedy's private secretary said that whenever Marilyn called he would take it if he was in the office; if not he would return it immediately.

She was invited to a party being thrown by Bobby and Ethel Kennedy for Peter and Pat Lawford. Instead of calling, Marilyn sent a weird telegram on June 13, which has often been misquoted.

UNFORTUNATELY I AM INVOLVED IN A FREEDOM RIDE PROTESTING THE LOSS OF THE MINORITY RIGHTS BELONGING TO THE FEW REMAINING EARTHBOUND STARS. AFTER ALL, ALL WE DEMANDED WAS OUR RIGHT TO TWINKLE.

On June 27 Marilyn saw Bobby, who was in Los Angeles for a meeting regarding a movie adaptation of his book, *The Enemy Within*, at Fox. After the meeting was over, Kennedy drove to Marilyn's house. The official reason for this visit was that her kitchen was being remodeled and he wanted to see it. Later Marilyn went over to the Lawfords' house for a dinner party with Bobby.

Simultaneously Marilyn did her best to keep her career going. She attended meetings at Fox; they were already seriously discussing rehiring her and bringing the movie back into production. Dean Martin had rejected Lee Remick as a costar, stating that he had signed to do a movie with Monroe and only Monroe. After the studio lost Monroe—well, after they fired her—they started to realize what a valuable commodity they had actually let go. There was really no one who could replace her. They wanted Marilyn back. Meanwhile, Marilyn also set out to do something that had given her reassurance for most of her life (most of her adult life, that is): facing the still camera. To demonstrate to the media, Fox, and the world who still had the power, Marilyn agreed to do various photo shoots. Marilyn was especially excited about a scheduled sitting with *Vogue*. The photographer would be a hot young photographer from New York named Bert Stern.

Marilyn's dismissal from Fox allowed the press to sensationalize the current hook in their "Monroe" stories: The world's most popular sex symbol was fading fast, her once-sensational career was all but washed up.

As she had done many times, Marilyn set out to prove the establishment wrong. In spite of the unflattering headlines, she remained very much in demand and was in negotiations for upcoming projects. She was in talks with Frank Sinatra about costarring with him in two movies: an acerbic comedy, *How to Murder Your Wife,* and a musical version of *Born Yesterday.*

In addition to planning these projects, Marilyn was staying in close contact with Marlon Brando. Ralph Roberts said that she had "rediscovered" her friendship with Brando that summer and was closer to him than ever before.* She had not given up on her dream of one day acting as Lady Macbeth opposite Brando. The emotionally confusing nature of the summer, the onslaught of nasty press, intermixed with the lovely images of her movie-set skinny-dip on magazine covers and offers of provocative new projects, pulled Marilyn in different directions, forcing her to take action and to make her voice heard.

In mid-June Marilyn entered a hypomanic phase of activity, socializing and publicizing herself. To combat the ongoing negative publicity of her dismissal from *Something's Got to Give,* Marilyn had Newcomb set up in-depth interviews with *Redbook* and *LIFE.* Marilyn also agreed to a photo layout for *Cosmopolitan.*

Marilyn was desperately trying to convince the public—and herself—that she was more than a sex symbol. The interviews she gave to magazines that summer clearly illustrate her divided mind. "I'm not only proud of my firm bosom," she told Alan Levy for *Redbook.* "I'm going to be proud of my firm character."

It was Bert Stern's idea to shoot Marilyn for *Vogue.* At thirty-two Stern had risen up the ranks in photography, starting his career in advertising. Ironically he had just returned from Rome, where he had shot Elizabeth Taylor on the set of *Cleopatra.* Stern had become so successful that he had the opportunity to make his own assignments for *Vogue.*

At this vulnerable crossroads, a *Vogue* spread must have seemed like a reassuring coup for Marilyn. She had never appeared in the fashion magazine so highly regarded for its style and sophistication. She immediately

---

* She was also good friends with Brando's longtime buddy Wally Cox, who was costarring with her. Marilyn was amused by Cox's cautious driving. "Driving along the freeway with Wally is like sitting in a parked car," she joked.

agreed to do it. The important sitting was set up for June 23, less than three weeks after she had been fired by Fox.

But like most people on the planet, the photographer was still thinking "Delicious." Many years later Stern admitted that what he really wanted was "to get Marilyn Monroe alone in a room, with no one else around, and take all her clothes off." Stern felt that there wasn't one great photo that defined Marilyn Monroe. Stern wanted to be the photographer to take it—that was his major goal: "How else could it be the definitive photo of Marilyn Monroe if she wasn't naked?"

Feeling that it might be difficult to get Marilyn to pose nude in a formal studio setting—he wanted something more personal—Stern secured a secluded suite at the Bel-Air Hotel. He covered the walls with seamless white paper and brightly lit the entire space so Marilyn would be free to move around and be spontaneous. He asked *Vogue* to send over a selection of filmy, see-through scarves designed by Vera Neumann, and assorted jewelry for her to play with while posing. Marilyn asked him to provide three bottles of Dom Pérignon champagne for the session. Stern knew better: He ordered a case.

The shoot was set for 2:00 p.m. Stern's assistant, Leif-Erik Nygårds, arrived, then Marilyn's hairdresser, George Masters. The time ticked by, but Stern wasn't concerned. By now "waiting for Monroe" was part of her legend. At 7:00 p.m. Marilyn strode in—alone. As with many people before him, Stern was quite taken with the living, breathing Monroe up close, in the flesh—no makeup and her hair in a scarf. "You're beautiful," he blurted.

"Really!" Marilyn said with a smile. "What a nice thing to say." Stern meant it. "I didn't expect her to be so beautiful."

The bedroom of the suite had been reserved as her dressing room, and she began applying makeup. Stern wanted stunning pictures, but he also wanted to reveal something new in the most photographed woman of the generation. "I picked up my Nikon and watched her through the eyepiece," Stern remembered. "My eye roved over her face, but I couldn't find the secret of her beauty in any one feature."

When Marilyn leaned forward to the mirror to apply lipstick, her eyes caught sight of the scarves and glittering jewelry carefully laid out on the bed. Marilyn went over to inspect them. When she lifted a scarf to cover her face she could see right through it. She understood now. "You want me to do nudes?" she asked.

Stern was rattled that Marilyn had seen through his plan so quickly. "Uh, well"—he stammered—"that's a good idea."

Marilyn hesitated. She felt nervous and wanted to know how much would show. He replied to her vaguely that it depended on how he lit the shots. Looking back on it, Stern said, "I got the feeling she was delighted to do nudes—but she felt like she should be talked into it."

Imagine her confusion: One day she was on the phone with Brando talking about *Macbeth*; the next *Vogue* was asking her to pose naked. Marilyn was flattered, horrified, honored, excited, offended, and elated—all at the same time. Marilyn delighted in showing her body, but wasn't she supposed to be working on a new image?

Unsure, she called to her hairdresser, "George? What do you think about these scarves and doing nudes?"

"Divine," he said.

That was the reassurance she was looking for, even though it was everything she was fighting against.

She turned back to Stern. "What about my scar?" she asked. He hadn't been aware that she had one—nor was the public. She explained that there was a scar on her torso from her gall-bladder surgery. "Will it show?" she asked.

"If it does we can always retouch it," he assured her. But Stern, who disliked retouching photographs, saw that she wasn't completely convinced. "It took a little bit more coaxing," he admitted. He assured her they wouldn't be full nudes. "I said, 'I really don't think too much of anything will show through the scarves with the colors and the designs. I can light it in a way that suggests nudity more than showing it.'"

"All right," Marilyn said, less anxious.

Stern was ecstatic. He had set out to photograph Marilyn Monroe nude, and within fifteen minutes she had agreed to do it. He hurried off to check the lights. "I wanted these pictures soft but sharp," he explained. "A sharp Marilyn floating in light."

When asked to elaborate by this author about what he most wanted to capture in Monroe, Stern responded: "I wanted to discover and expose the secret to her beauty. Unlock the mysteries to her appeal. What set her apart? What made Marilyn Monroe *the* woman among millions of women?"

Marilyn walked onto the set carrying a glass of champagne, covered in a sheer orange striped scarf, with her waistband rolled low. Stern saw the scar now on the right side of her midriff. "An imperfection that only made her seem more vulnerable and only accentuated the incredible smoothness of her skin," he wrote.

Marilyn's age was very much on her mind. "How's this for thirty-six?" Marilyn asked Stern, lifting the scarf to reveal her naked breasts. A few weeks earlier when a reporter mentioned her age, Marilyn retorted: "Thirty-six is just great when kids twelve to seventeen still whistle." Stern declared he saw something in her: "Divinity. God. Living. Passion." But at the time he responded, "I'm not afraid of you, Marilyn."

As always when working, Marilyn gave the camera her all. Under Stern's often unforgiving lighting, she played with the scarves and beads, teasing the photographer, draping the scarves over her bosom, wrapping and unwrapping them around her body, hanging them from her teeth, raising them over her head. She held two chiffon roses up to her breast. That night she was on—alive with hope and desperation—fueled by champagne.

In retrospect Marilyn wasn't only attempting to resurrect her career—she was trying to save her life. At one point Pat Newcomb stopped by with Peter Lawford—the two had been out to dinner. "She had practically nothing on," Newcomb recalled. "'This place is going to be barraged in the morning if you don't get some clothes on,'" she joked. "'What's going on here?' By then he'd taken all those nudes."

For hours Stern probed every inch of Marilyn Monroe with his camera, sometimes under lighting that would have been unflattering to a sixteen-year-old. Because of Marilyn's exquisite bone structure and flawless features, her beauty was never in doubt. But as the night wore on and the champagne flowed more freely, her exhaustion set in. Stern's camera continued clicking.

The sitting lasted until 7: 00 a.m.

The resulting photos from the June 23 session are as bipolar as Marilyn's mind was that chaotic month. The pictures are alternately beautiful and creepy. They show her at her very best—a number of these photos are some of the most beautiful and timeless ever taken of her—and also at her most drunken, fragile worst. In these one-of-a-kind nude studies, Marilyn looks fresh, upbeat, vibrant, and gorgeous—and exhausted, pale, boozy, and somewhat weathered—a glamorous phantom.

Eve Arnold, a photographer and friend who had photographed Marilyn many times, was appalled when she saw the resulting seminude pictures. "They were wild and almost out of control when he shot them," Arnold said. "I don't know whether she was hyped up from sheer excitation or whether she'd been drinking, or what had happened to her. But she was absolutely wild during that session."

In the softer-lighted shots Marilyn appears at her loveliest, and Stern's mastery of the camera shines through. It is most likely how she looked in everyday life, in flattering lighting. Through the sheer scarves and gaudy jewelry, Marilyn exudes a palpable yearning to reveal her true self that is breathtaking and poignant. Never before was Marilyn's beauty more fragile, vulnerable, indefinable.

When Stern used sharper lighting and his camera moved in close with a stark approach, the results were at times unflattering, and could be considered an exploitative examination. Stern seems to be attempting to penetrate and expose the enigmatic phenomenon that was Marilyn Monroe, to demystify her beauty.

The bright lighting he chose at times exaggerated her laugh lines, pores, freckles, bleach-damaged hair, and the soft down on her face. Often one's eye goes to the scar on her belly; the angry slash that she was so self-conscious about and was assured would be retouched was never retouched. "And it was a nasty scar," Stern remarked years later.

In addition, some of Stern's seminude photos explicitly show the effect of her continuing weight loss. In the weeks since her naked skinny-dip, Marilyn seemed to have shed even more pounds.

Always a healthy eater, by June, Marilyn would barely eat one meal a day, if at all. Mrs. Murray remembered her skipping many meals altogether. George Masters recalled her often existing on champagne and hard-boiled eggs. It's impossible to say if Marilyn was developing an eating disorder, and her loss of appetite may have come from her depressions. But also, her obsession with weight loss stemmed from the fact that the voluptuous bodies of the 1950s—an ideal she helped create—were considered nostalgic by 1962.

On seeing the photos after Marilyn's death, the literary critic Diana Trilling said: "Her body looked ravaged and ill, already drained of life." When Marilyn peeked over her shoulder, the spine in her beautiful back appeared more pronounced. Depending on the angle of her body and the pose, her breasts—which had helped propel her during her rise to stardom—sometimes appeared modest but perky, and in other shots they seemed deflated and a bit saggy.*

To a number of Marilyn's fans, these are their favorite photos of her because they reveal her flaws in a way that hadn't been exposed before. They bring the goddess image down to earth, within reach. To some, the pictures only make her beauty more remarkable. That is Stern's considerable achievement.

Marilyn wanted to see the photographs before their expected publication. Shortly before her death, Stern mailed her some of the pictures as a courtesy. "She hated a great many of them," Eve Arnold said. Marilyn angrily tried to destroy some of them. Arnold explained: "What she returned to him had been gouged with some sort of a sharp instrument, a hairpin or something like that." Marilyn also crossed many of the images of herself out with a red magic marker to make sure they'd never be seen.

Her anger stemmed from the fact that some of the shots, harshly lit and extremely close up, clearly showed a more mature Marilyn Monroe. "The pictures that she was upset by were the ones that didn't project her image of herself," Stern said. Surely she saw that in many of the shots she

---

* To a modern person living in the days of breast implants, they simply appear to be the natural, unremarkable breasts of a thirty-six-year-old woman.

was sensual and lovely but she had passed the age of strawberries and cream.

When Stern got back the photos with her angry marks destroying them, he was furious. After her death he published all of the photos—every single one taken that night—and he featured them in several books. Eve Arnold strongly disapproved: "I feel that it is a kind of invasion. If somebody lends you their face, you owe them a courtesy."

Stern felt justified. "Just because she scratched them out doesn't mean she is the ultimate purveyor of my work. I hadn't signed any deal that she could destroy pictures she didn't like. They are *my* pictures." And since they were his pictures he didn't feel it necessary to honor their agreement. "Well, we had a verbal agreement about me retouching her scar," Stern countered when confronted. "But it was my understanding that they were to be retouched if they were to be used in *Vogue*, which these particular photos weren't. Besides, after she died the verbal agreement became null and void." He was blunter when asked by the columnist Liz Smith about his refusal to retouch: "She was dead, why bother?" But these were not to be the last photos Stern took of Marilyn for *Vogue*. But first she would do an important session with another photographer.

Energized by the session with Stern, the following weekend Marilyn turned to the camera once again for reassurance—this time for a series of photos that were to be used along with an in-depth interview for *Cosmopolitan*. She did two long days of shooting on June 29 and 30 with the photographer George Barris. In her brightly colored Puccis, Marilyn posed in and around the house of real estate magnate Walter Tim Leimert, a friend of Barris.

The next day she did wonderful shots on a windy beach, frolicking in the waves and posing in the sand, sipping champagne or wrapped in a blanket. As usual that summer, she looked anywhere from a carefree, fresh-faced twenty-five to a troubled woman in lovely early middle age.

After the all-night Stern session at the Bel-Air Hotel, Stern flew back to New York and showed the pictures to *Vogue*'s artistic director, Alexander Lieberman. He immediately started examining them with a loup. Describing the photos as "marvelous," he explained to Stern that they also must be shown to Diana Vreeland, the whimsical new editor in chief, then in her first year at *Vogue*. But before Stern had even arrived back at his own office, Lieberman had left a message: Vreeland wanted a reshoot.

It's probable that *Vogue* simply wasn't satisfied with Stern's first set of photos. They didn't suit the magazine's style. Though they wanted an issue that featured Marilyn between their covers, they also wanted a new session where the editorial staff would exercise more control of the way Marilyn would appear—in high fashion. When she was reached in Los Angeles, Marilyn agreed to do additional photographs (she had yet to receive Stern's proofs from the first sitting). Three more sessions were set up for July 10, 11, and 12.

Astutely observing the new phase of Monroe's beauty, Diana Vreeland wanted to see Marilyn in couture. Vreeland would later describe Marilyn as "the greatest chameleon that's ever lived. She was enticing! She was appetizing! You wanted to take a bite out of her. That effect." Vreeland was eager to see how the chameleon would adapt to *Vogue* fashions.

An entire entourage was flown to Los Angeles from New York to oversee these sessions. A much larger, three-room bungalow at the Bel-Air Hotel (number 96) was reserved. A fashion editor, Babs Simpson, was present; Marilyn's press secretary, Pat Newcomb, came along to supervise; and the renowned hairdresser Kenneth Battelle was there. Also present was Marilyn's makeup artist, Whitey Snyder.

This time dozens of beautiful Christian Dior haute couture garments had been supplied, along with evening gowns, furs, and diamonds. In addition a large assortment of shoes, hats, gloves, and coats had been sent. Since hairpieces were becoming extremely chic, a brunette wig was provided.

This session seemed to be more in tune with the direction in which Marilyn hoped her image was going—stylish and sophisticated. Though she had posed for many of the great fashion photographers during her career, it was rarely about the clothes, and she never tried to compete with the sophistication of high-fashion models. Now Marilyn understood the value of fashion as part of her new maturing image. She worked hard at making the couture clothes work in a contemporary way.

Marilyn had obviously done her homework by studying what was happening in the pages of *Vogue* and *Harper's Bazaar*. "In frame after frame, from her second *Vogue* session, she twists and contorts her body in an evocative ballet of exaggerated movement," the photo archivist and curator David Wills stated. "In other photos from the shoot, she dons a black flipped wig with a diamond-shaped beauty spot that eerily suggests a fast-forward to 1964 or '65."

Stern was taking the Marilyn high-fashion session with equal seriousness. With his high-fashion compositions and original use of backlighting, there is little trace of Lorelei Lee in any of Stern's images of Monroe. Marilyn's reinvention from sex symbol into fashion goddess was complete. In Stern's fashion studies, Marilyn was decked out in gowns, furs, and towering architectural hairdos constructed with swirling hairpieces of platinum Dynel.

Babs Simpson was also impressed with Marilyn. "She was absolutely perfect," Simpson recalled. "But there was this awful hairdresser who kept giving her ice water that turned out to be vodka." Once again she became inebriated.

After six hours of posing in the formal clothing, Marilyn began to lose patience, becoming bored, disinterested.

"She was combative in a way, confrontational," Stern said.

"What's your premise?" Marilyn asked him coldly as he knelt in front of her, camera in hand. "Don't you have any ambitions to do anything more?"

"Yeah," he replied. "I want to get you into bed."

Drunk now, and tired of all the high fashion, Marilyn informed the people in the room that she wanted to do shots wearing a frilly, translucent bed jacket, and stormed off to change. Sadly, after hours of demonstrating that a chic and lovely Marilyn Monroe could be just as potent and intoxicating as a sexual one, Marilyn felt the need to go back to the cheesecake-type photos that had started her career fifteen years before. She emerged wearing the bed jacket, with a towel wrapped around her waist.

Stern said, "Could everyone leave us alone?" The entourage moved into the adjoining room. Stern suggested that Marilyn take off the bed jacket and just cover herself with a sheet.

As with the other important events in recent months, when plied with enough alcohol, Marilyn regressed to her sex-symbol image. A friend had recently revealed to a magazine that Marilyn's two outstanding traits were "a need for love and a need to seduce." Intent on seducing, Marilyn rolled around on the bed, laughing and flirting with the camera, letting the sheet drop a bit, hanging one leg off the corner of the bed, sipping champagne.

Marilyn didn't mind teasing seminudes, but under no circumstances was she about to give Stern what he wanted—full frontal. "I wondered how far he'd dare to push her," Stern's assistant, Nygårds, recalled in *Icon* magazine. "The atmosphere between Stern and Marilyn got worse and worse. She said 'no' and he kept going."

Finally, when Stern and Marilyn were left completely alone in the room, Marilyn seemed to fall asleep. He leaned down to kiss her. The moment she felt his lips touch her, she turned her face away. "No," she said without opening her eyes.

Exhausted and hungover, Marilyn did not show up for more photos the following day. On Thursday, July 12, she returned to complete the *Vogue* sittings.

The resulting high-fashion photos, rarely seen for decades, show a glimpse of the ravishing Marilyn Monroe who was on her way. The actress who might have been.* Complex. Mature. Elegant. Breathtaking.

---

* *Vogue* rejected all the nude photos Stern took of Marilyn. The magazine chose to publish only the black-and-white fashion shots. The editors saw the value in the direction Marilyn was heading. In most of the photographs she is wearing haute couture—looking moody and sublime. Marilyn, however, would never see the layout. She was dead before the issue hit the stands.

doing and talk to her—sometimes go to her. She would call in the middle of the night and announce, "I haven't slept." Or she would tell him about something that had happened to her. At this point he was her only real lifeline.

The depression that enveloped her in 1962 was like nothing she had ever experienced before. It was soul crushing. It paralyzed her.

As a result her life became messy. On occasion, when socializing, she ignored things—like personal hygiene and grooming—that in the past had been important to her. Friends looked away sadly when she sometimes showed up at the Lawfords' house in a drugged fog, her hair wrapped in a scarf, unkempt fingernails, with menstrual spots on her white Capri pants. "She would get wobbly," a guest who encountered her there said. "She did drink champagne and take pills at the same time. I'd seen her very out of it. All of us had. I mean, really stumbling around."

Some felt Marilyn was slowly going mad that summer, and the people around her recognized it, but if she disgusted them they were seduced by her too. It was intoxicating to be near someone who was so beautiful and famous and by turns needy and demanding or brilliant and hopeful. Marilyn sometimes seemed to be existing in a place between life and death.

To combat loneliness she would spend the night at the Lawfords' house in Santa Monica. There she might appear completely out of it. Attempting to quash her pain with drugs, she would wander into the couple's bedroom in the middle of the night, without knocking on the door, and stand at the foot of their bed, staring down at them. Lawford would pretend to be sleeping and watch her through slitted eyes. His marriage was actually crumbling by this point, but Marilyn had no clue. "Why can't I be as happy as you two?" she would ask. Some mornings they would find menstrual blood on the sheets in her bedroom.

William Asher was in the process of writing a movie about a train heist for Marilyn that would have had her starring with Sinatra and other members of the Rat Pack. Encountering her at the Lawford beach house, he observed, "She was trying to sleepwalk through life. She'd reach that point, where she was going through the paces and not really being there. Going through it and not really making contact. It was a bad period."

THIRTY-THREE

SLEEPWALKING

By mid-July President Kennedy told Bobby to end the relationship with Marilyn for the same reasons he had—there was too much talk going around; the risk was too great. Bobby was not only jeopardizing his own career, he was putting the entire Kennedy White House and legacy in danger. Bobby started distancing himself that July. Not cutting her off completely, as his brother had done, but definitely pulling back and letting Marilyn know they couldn't go on the way they had been.

Marilyn was hurt and confused and furious. It was one blow too many that summer. Perhaps if there was a family. A man who loved her completely and accepted her with all her complexities. Or a baby. Or parents. But Marilyn had none of these things as the summer days moved on. It was awful to feel that she didn't fit in anywhere, that she didn't belong.

She lashed out and brooded and raged because she felt unwanted and used: She had always felt this way—these were the ongoing themes of her life. But she was helpless in responding to her feelings or resolving them because ultimately she felt she was unlovable—and that being used is what she deserved.

Desperate, grasping, and searching—she still had hopes that she could win Bobby back. Perhaps if they met again she could be beautiful enough, witty enough, sparkling enough, to make him risk everything for her. She continued to call him.

Marilyn also called Greenson at all hours. She would be overcome with anxiety and despair, and he would have to drop whatever he was

Yet she was still able to glue herself together on occasion and show up as the stunningly beautiful, assured woman everyone wanted—although it was becoming more and more of a burden for her. On Wednesday, Marilyn attended a Fourth of July barbecue at the Lawfords', where Robert Kennedy was one of the guests.

In early July she met with Richard Meryman several times for a long profile in *LIFE*. Also, sometime between July 5 and July 7, there was a party in Marilyn's honor—another orchestrated event to counter all the bad publicity insinuating that she was a fading sex symbol on a downward spiral—this one for the people in her Hollywood circle. Most likely the party was on Friday, July 6.

During the recorded interview, Meryman asked her how long it took to get into her persona and "appear" for such an event. Marilyn replied: "Well, that ordinarily wouldn't take very long. It's just that [the press] sort of slandered me, saying that I'm depressed and I'm in some kind of a slump, and hidden away—all those kind of things. So then I take a little extra time with my hair, a little extra flip of the hair. A little extra eyeshadow around the eye. A little more glitter. It's just my way of saying 'HA!'" Then Marilyn and Meryman broke up laughing (along with Pat Newcomb, who was sitting in on the interview).

Marilyn was determined to show her friends that she was still optimistic for the future and at the top of her game, even though she was filled with mistrust. "It's a private party but a lot of people will be there who are sort of concerned about my welfare—they claim," she added. With her increasing paranoia it was difficult for her to believe that anyone, even her friends, truly cared.

Death was certainly on her mind that July. Marilyn very much wanted to change her will. Mickey Rudin, who was convinced that Marilyn was dangerously unstable, kept putting her off. He said he could not sign a document that stated Marilyn Monroe was of sound mind. If Rudin had had his way, he would have declared Marilyn incompetent. "She could have a crisis over what she was having for lunch," he groused. He felt she should be institutionalized: "After she was fired that was the only hope."

Marilyn had a great fear of going insane—especially after her Payne

Whitney experience. Being put in an institution again would have been torture for her, but her lawyer said he felt she should have been. Rudin's problem being her attorney—as he saw it—was that if he went to court asking for her to be declared incompetent, he'd be "thrown out on my ass and make a fool of myself." In addition Greenson felt, and Rudin agreed, that institutionalizing Marilyn would have been worse than death for her.

The amount of medication Marilyn was taking cannot be overlooked. Greenson's family said that he was trying to wean Marilyn from her dependency on the barbiturate Nembutal by prescribing chloral hydrate, a sedative he felt was milder and not quite as addictive. "He was trying to get her to exist," Rudin said. "He didn't have control. He wasn't her guardian. He couldn't tell her not to associate with Pat Newcomb so they could exchange pills."

Newcomb admitted that she and Marilyn shared pills at times. Today people point to Marilyn's prescription-drug intake as if it were something extraordinary and unusual. Although there is no doubt that she took an enormous number of pills, in Hollywood circles and in the upper echelons of society, casual pill taking was surprisingly common in the 1960s. "Everybody was taking pills," Newcomb said. "Everybody tried everything." Newcomb named a famous actor whose poker parties she'd attended, where they used "all kinds of sleeping pills for chips." Rudin said of the show-biz set of the era, "I might bring a good bottle of wine to somebody's dinner—they'd bring pills."

But even by those standards, Marilyn was different. She had much more access to pills because of the number of doctors she saw, the variety of pills they prescribed, and the amounts she consumed because of the tolerance she had built up. Newcomb recalled that Marilyn had some strong stuff on her nightstand. "One time I just wanted to relax, and there wasn't valium and she gave me a pill and I was knocked out," Newcomb said. "I was so detached. I was scared. So I don't know what the doctors were loading her up with."

Engelberg was also giving Marilyn injections, shots that he later claimed were vitamins and liver extract. It is likely that he was also alternately injecting her with stimulants and sedatives, depending on her needs. Nothing made her feel any better.

Friends picked up on her distress signals. Most of them, however, didn't understand the depths of her sickness and despair. Surely she couldn't have imagined that a relationship with John F. Kennedy could ever have become serious. And if she was feeling neglected by Bobby Kennedy, they thought the solution was to keep her close, show her a good time, help her snap out of it. A weekend at the Cal-Neva resort lodge—owned by Frank Sinatra—might give her some relief, some relaxation, music, games, a few drinks.

Marilyn didn't want to go. She wasn't feeling well mentally or physically. Peter and Pat Lawford, who were going to be there that weekend, tried to persuade her to come along. Whatever was going on with her—and no one was 100 percent sure—Sinatra was worried too. He wanted her there. One of his long-term assistants had told him that Marilyn was in a state of depression because she had recently had an abortion. (This was another hush-hush rumor going around industry circles at the time regarding Marilyn that could never be proved or disproved.)

Others claim that Marilyn simply had one of many gynecological procedures—more corrective surgery trying to relieve her agonizing periods. Still, there were enough rumors and controversy swirling around Marilyn to make Sinatra seriously concerned.

Eventually Pat Lawford persuaded her to go to Cal-Neva—but the Lawfords had their own agenda. The couple were doing their best to cheer Marilyn—and to get it through her head that it was time to move on. There was no future with Bobby Kennedy—he would never leave Ethel.

Sinatra had his private plane pick them up and deliver them to the resort for the weekend of July 28–29. The Cal-Neva lodge got its name because it was located exactly on the state line that divided California from Nevada. One of its novelties was that gambling was allowed on the Nevada side of the resort. The other side had a beautiful main room for live entertainment, where Sinatra's friends would often perform. It also included about twenty furnished cottages. When staying there, Marilyn was always given Chalet 52, a place of honor for special guests.

On this weekend Frank Sinatra would be performing in the main room at the lodge while the singers Buddy Greco and Roberta Linn would be playing in the lounge.

On arrival, Marilyn presented her mask on cue—the expert celebrity, the practiced smile. "When she arrived you'd never believe that she had a care in the world," Greco said. "I was sitting with Frank [Sinatra], Peter Lawford, and a bunch of other people, outside of Frank's bungalow, when a limousine pulls up and this gorgeous woman in dark glasses steps out. Before I realized who it was, I thought, 'My God, what a beautiful woman.'" But after a while Greco saw that underneath the assured pretense, the woman was crumbling. "She was shaky, fragile, almost what I would call breakable," he added.

The few surviving photographs—the last-known photos taken of her alive—show her wearing a scarf over her hair, tied under her chin. Her face is clean of makeup, and she is wearing dark sunglasses. She is thin and wan—wearing Capri pants and a clingy Pucci top. She looks thinner than ever before, and in spite of her automatic smile, the photos exude an atmosphere of delicacy and illness. She in fact looks like a woman going through the motions of being Marilyn Monroe.

Still, at this early stage of the weekend she seemed game. She cozied up to Greco, turning her back to the camera, showing a tiny derriere through the slacks, face turned to look at the lens. Sinatra, sitting a few feet away, probably not knowing he was in the frame, looked up quizzically, protectively, an expression that seems to ask, "What is she doing now?"

When the Lawfords and Sinatra joined Marilyn in her chalet, her mental anguish was palpable. Joe Langford, a Sinatra security employee, recalled that the head chef at Cal-Neva was ordered to prepare the ailing Monroe special meals. At one point a steak dinner with baked potato and cheesecake was served. "I know that the meal was sent to her chalet. Mr. Lawford opened the door in Marilyn's room. The waiter never saw her. Then the tray was sent back to the kitchen about two hours later. The only thing that had been eaten was the cheesecake, and someone said that Mr. Sinatra had eaten that." Food was no longer something Marilyn was concerned with.

The weekend would only go downhill from there. Pat Lawford was livid to discover that Sam Giancana was also staying at Cal-Neva that weekend. Giancana was one of the kingpins of the underworld, one of the best-known mobsters in the world. To have him there, hobnobbing with the president's sister and brother-in-law and Marilyn Monroe, was very dangerous indeed. One wonders what was going through Sinatra's head when he made arrangements for the ingredients of this deadly social cocktail.

As the day went on, Marilyn continued to self-medicate to distance herself from her pain. Numbed by pills, champagne, and eventually vodka, she reached the point where she didn't care—or was unable to do anything—about her appearance. Guests remember a blond mess in a Pucci dress. She did attend Sinatra's show that evening. Betsy Duncan Hammes, a guest at the lodge for the weekend, observed Marilyn watching Sinatra perform looking "completely out of it."

"I couldn't understand how the smiling woman who arrived a few hours earlier had disintegrated so quickly," Buddy Greco remarked. "The porcelain doll had smashed."

Cami Sebring was also a guest that weekend because her husband at the time, the celebrity hairstylist Jay Sebring (later a victim of the Manson killings along with Sharon Tate), cut Sinatra's hair. Cami, who attended Sinatra's show, remembered seeing some ushers carrying out a woman who was clearly inebriated. They had her under the arms, her feet were dragging. They seemed to have some concern, but were moving very, very fast—as if they had been told to remove her as quickly and inconspicuously as possible. Cami was sitting by the door and they passed right by her. "It was then," she recalled, "when she was right in front of me, that I realized that this woman was Marilyn Monroe."

They deposited her in Chalet 52. Marilyn passed out with the phone off the hook—perhaps she dropped off while dialing a friend, perhaps she kept it off the hook on purpose as a lifeline. The operator working the switchboard could hear her breathing. At some point Pat Lawford decided to check on her, and, entering Marilyn's room, she realized that the star had once again overdosed.

Pandemonium ensued. Ted Stephens, who worked in the kitchen, remembered getting a phone call from Peter Lawford in the middle of the night. "'We need coffee in Chalet 52!' he screamed into the phone. He sounded frantic. No less than two minutes passed and it was Mr. Sinatra on the phone screaming, 'Where's that goddamn coffee?' I learned later they were walking Marilyn Monroe around, trying to get her to wake up."

Betsy Hammes said that, although they didn't call an ambulance and Marilyn's stomach wasn't pumped, they did "roll her over a barrel," meaning that they forced Marilyn to vomit in case she had taken too many pills.

Gloria Romanoff, another guest that weekend, heard the following morning that they had plied Marilyn with coffee and walked her around until she started to come to. Gloria recalled this being the second time Marilyn had overdosed at Cal-Neva. The next morning Cal-Neva guests and staff were abuzz with the news that there had been a close call in Chalet 52, where Marilyn Monroe had overdosed.

Some witnesses say that at one point, Sam Giancana got into Marilyn's room. Photos were said to exist of Giancana degrading Marilyn (supposedly because of her involvement with Bobby Kennedy). At a Marilyn Remembered fan club meeting, Lily Woodfield told this author that she had seen photographs (in the possession of her husband, the photographer Billy Woodfield) of Sam Giancana in Marilyn's room. Both were fully clothed, but Marilyn was on all fours and Giancana was sitting on her back, like children playing "horsie." It would have been a remarkably degrading position for a world-renowned celebrity.

Sinatra was distraught at Marilyn's behavior. He saw to it that she went back to Los Angeles with Peter Lawford in his private plane. "We all wondered what happened to her," Buddy Greco said. "But it was obvious Frank was too upset to talk about it. When Frank was upset you didn't push it."

According to legend, Sinatra had asked that those photos be destroyed. But Delores Swann, a friend of Sinatra's first wife, Nancy, said that Sinatra kept at least one photograph taken of him and Marilyn during that "lost" weekend. "I saw it in his home," Swann said. Frank told her, "That was taken the weekend before she died. Every time I look at it I want to cry. She was a beautiful, beautiful woman." Then he added, "But she was weak. She was so goddamn weak."

Fox's head of production, Peter Levathes, came to talk to Marilyn about going back into production with *Something's Got to Give*.* She wanted to finish the movie, but with a new script and director. The executive was charmed by Marilyn's ideas for some physical comedy. She thought of a scene where Ellen, who has been eating with her hands on the island for five years, tries to remember how to use utensils gracefully, and keeps kicking off her shoes because she's used to being barefoot. Later, after they agreed the film would be completed with her suggestions, she showed him some of the fashion photos from the *Vogue* shoot. She laid the pictures out on the floor and asked him to pick out some that he liked.

Sometime that week Marilyn learned that Bobby Kennedy was going to San Francisco to give a speech to the American Bar Association that Monday. She hoped to see him, and called Pat Lawford and found out that he would be at the St. Francis Hotel with his wife, Ethel. Marilyn focused on trying to get Bobby to make a detour to see her. She started by leaving messages at the hotel, and attempting to persuade Peter and Pat to get him to come to the beach house for another visit. She was desperate to try again.

"Men grow cold/As girls grow old/and we all lose our charms in the end," Marilyn sang nine years earlier—in one of her most glorious moments on the screen. Now that the truths of the lyrics from "Diamonds Are a Girl's Best Friend" were becoming perilously close to reality, she found herself astonished—terrified. Thirty-six hit Marilyn like a punch

---

* Fox was also offering her another movie, at a salary of a half-million dollars, tentatively titled *I Love Louisa*. The movie would eventually be made as *What a Way to Go!* with Shirley MacLaine.

to the gut, winding her, filling her with fear. The thought of reaching the age of being slightly past her prime had been tormenting her for years.

Two days before Marilyn died, Natalie Wood and Warren Beatty encountered an agitated Marilyn, preoccupied with her age, at a small party at the Lawford beach house. "Thirty-six, thirty-six. It's all over," Wood heard Marilyn mumble obsessively.

"Her beauty, charming wit, and joy of life seemed paradoxical to the tense loneliness which she faced in her life, and was to me, clearly apparent," Wood remarked.

In 1982 Beatty told Anthony Summers that he had seen Marilyn "the night before she died." Most likely it was Thursday night (two nights before), since Marilyn had dinner with Pat Newcomb on the evening before she died. In 2016 Beatty was more forthcoming with *Vanity Fair*, revealing that he had been invited to Peter Lawford's for a night of tacos and poker. Marilyn was there. "I hadn't seen anything that beautiful," he recalled. Marilyn's dress was so clingy—probably one of her Puccis—it was clear she wore nothing underneath. They went for a walk on the beach, which he described as "more soulful than romantic."

Yet according to Ralph Roberts—whom Marilyn told about their meeting—Beatty made his intentions known. Marilyn responded, "Warren, you are 'two five,' and I am 'three six.'" Beatty felt it was difficult for Marilyn even to say her age to him, not wanting to bring the two numbers together. Later she sat next to him at the piano while he played, and they talked a little more.

Leslie Caron, a longtime lover of Beatty's, remembered him expanding on his encounter with Marilyn. "He had been very moved by her, and the night haunted him." After a while at the piano Marilyn turned to Beatty and again softly brought up her age. "You know I'm three six and I'm frightened," she said.

Beatty was taken aback by Marilyn's abrupt declaration, her stark honesty, the naked pain in her voice. He related to her fear. Beatty was just becoming well known in Hollywood as a notorious lady-killer, but he also had a tenderhearted nature that especially responded to women in distress. "Warren was a very sensitive man. Like Marilyn he was shy and uncomfortable in social situations," Caron said. "But because of his exceptional looks and natural sex appeal, he learned how to project the consummate playboy image in public. He approached that role as if it were an acting job and eventually he became expert at it."

Marilyn, who was very much the same, seemed to pick up on the vulnerabilities masked by Beatty's facade and felt compelled to confide to him things she had been trying to keep concealed from the public. She was "alone and lost," she told him. She confessed that she was having trouble sleeping at night and difficulty waking up in the day. She confided that as time went on, she was getting less and less sleep and becoming more and more disorganized. She had tried many different things in an attempt to get her life on track, without much success. "I don't know what to do about it anymore," she said.

"It affected Warren so much," Caron recalled. "Marilyn felt comfortable pouring out her psychological secrets to Warren because she recognized a kindred spirit. He can get anything out of you because he's so warm and compassionate—in France we have a saying, 'He can get the worms out of your eyes.' Actually, he was very much like Marilyn. He related to her. Warren was so shaken up by what Marilyn said because he saw her future for himself. Warren was very beautiful, but he was afraid of losing it one day. He was frightened too. He was a frightened child, like her. This is what was happening to him psychologically. But Marilyn, that night, was feeling it intensely."

Caron remembered thinking, "That poor woman. She was only thirty-six and already afraid of getting old. But that's what this business does to you when you're known primarily for your beauty and sex appeal."

On Friday afternoon, August 3, 1962, Marilyn filled two prescriptions at a pharmacy on Wilshire Boulevard in Beverly Hills. One was for Phenergan, a drug used to treat allergies, and the other for Nembutal. Greenson and Engelberg had been weaning Marilyn off of Nembutal for weeks, substituting the milder drug chloral hydrate. Marilyn would take that with a glass of milk before bed. But Marilyn fibbed, telling Engelberg that Greenson said it was okay for him to write her a prescription for Nembutal. It was twenty-four of these pills, from this prescription of twenty-five, that would be the main cause of her death.

That evening Pat Newcomb had dinner with Marilyn in a Santa Monica French restaurant, whose name she can't remember. When talking to Donald Spoto she said, "Afterwards we came back to the house. We just sat around—"

Then Newcomb indicated the journalist's tape recorder, stating, "I want to shut this off."

THIRTY-FOUR

ANGER AND DESPAIR

On Saturday, August 4, 1962, Marilyn Monroe woke up angry. She'd been angry the night before—and for much of the previous week. And she remained angry well into the evening, when—because of medication and resignation—anger turned into despair.

"The day she died?" Pat Newcomb recalled decades later when the tape recorder was turned back on. "She was furious."

Mrs. Murray arrived Saturday morning to find the house quiet. Marilyn and Pat Newcomb were still in their bedrooms. Marilyn, however, was already awake. Behind her closed bedroom door she was involved in a series of phone calls that were adding to her rage—although in the hours remaining to her she would not fully discuss with whom these phone calls were or what they were about.

At 9:00 a.m., Marilyn emerged from her bedroom—wearing her favorite white terry robe. She drank a glass of grapefruit juice and informed Mrs. Murray that Pat Newcomb had spent the night and was still sleeping in the guest bedroom. She explained that Newcomb had not been feeling well and was going to spend the day "baking" by the pool. Other than that, Mrs. Murray found Marilyn quiet, contemplative.

Marilyn had no definite schedule for the day. She had tentative plans of going to Peter Lawford's house for dinner in the evening. Pat Lawford was visiting back East, but Peter was having a few people over for a casual supper. Some say that Robert Kennedy had planned to make a quick trip from San Francisco to attend the party, specifically to talk to Marilyn.

By now he knew Marilyn wanted a face-to-face meeting. But that morning nothing was definite.

It has been reported that Newcomb was so sick with bronchitis that she considered checking herself into the hospital that weekend, but instead—at Marilyn's urging—she spent the night at her house in order to get a good night's sleep and, during the day, use the sun lamp by the pool.

Newcomb was ill, but the real reason that she wanted to check herself into a hospital was not because of the severity of her bronchitis. She wanted to sequester herself in a hospital room to escape Marilyn's fury. All that week, Newcomb said, Marilyn had been "a pain in the ass." Marilyn was acting so disagreeable that Newcomb felt it was necessary to take a break from her. "Sometimes you just have it up to here," she explained. "I was trying to get away. That's why I wanted to go to the hospital. I had my doctor book me a room for the weekend."

Pat Newcomb finally woke up Saturday around noon. Mrs. Murray sensed conflict between the two friends. At one point she heard them bickering. Still Newcomb didn't leave. What were the two women fighting about? "I don't know what she was really upset about," Newcomb said. "But everything about her was angry that day." Newcomb always maintained she didn't know what was upsetting Marilyn deep down. But Marilyn's anger was relentless. She held on to what was making her angry in a way that only Marilyn Monroe could.

Legend has come down through the years that Marilyn's foul mood toward Pat was because she had been able to sleep for twelve hours straight while Marilyn slept very little. That's probably partially true. However, there was something else going on that Pat Newcomb has been silent about for decades. Many years later Milt Ebbins evasively said that Newcomb was party to many secret things regarding Marilyn in her last months.

The reason for Marilyn's fury the last week of her life is that she had come to believe that Pat Newcomb had become romantically involved with Bobby Kennedy—an involvement that would have overlapped with the time frame in which Marilyn had been seeing him. After Marilyn came to believe that she and her friend had shared a man, she was beside herself.[*]

---

[*]   This information comes from a highly respected and reliable source who was interviewed

We can only imagine Marilyn's rage and confusion. Bobby's desire for her, his love for her, is what was going to make the thirty-six-year-old love goddess feel relevant. Pat Newcomb was an attractive, sexy, intelligent woman who was four years younger than her. But she wasn't Marilyn Monroe. If Bobby did have an intimate entanglement with Marilyn's assistant/press agent while Marilyn was relying on his affection, she must have felt worthless. When you're fragile, empty, and lonely—as Marilyn was that summer—any slight or rejection becomes amplified. It can feel fatal. The end.

It was Newcomb, along with Peter Lawford, who had gotten Marilyn involved with the Kennedys in the first place. Now Marilyn felt betrayed by someone she considered a trustworthy friend. She had been demanding explanations and details about the affair from Newcomb all week. Newcomb did admit that she saw Bobby Kennedy shortly before Marilyn died. She could not remember the exact evening but revealed: "I had dinner with him, but it was just before that night."

And as Joan Greenson observed, Marilyn could be very vehement on subjects. For Marilyn anything that had shades of gray was very difficult. Everything was black or white. Friend or foe. God forbid you did something that got on her bad side. It would be difficult, if not impossible, to get back into her good graces.

Dean Martin's wife, Jeanne, has said that "Pat was deeply in love with Bobby. It took her many years to get over it." There was something deeper to their relationship than friendship. It certainly would have been better for all concerned if Marilyn didn't hear of it. But she suspected. And now she demanded explanations. She grappled with the notion of Pat Newcomb possibly being involved with Bobby—at once so loyal but at the same time seemingly desperate to take "possession" of her. Was an involvement with Bobby, in some way, a maneuver for Newcomb to be more enmeshed with Marilyn? Marilyn thought so, feeling a "sibling rivalry" kind of relationship had developed between them in the two years they had been closely associated with each other.

---

by the author and wishes to remain anonymous.

Mrs. Murray, who had young daughters, said that Marilyn and Newcomb's quibbling often reminded her of teenage girls. If we are to believe Rupert Allan's account, we know that Newcomb, in her fascination with Marilyn, had allegedly tried to pass herself off as Marilyn to a man six years earlier, when she briefly worked as her press agent on *Bus Stop*. When Marilyn discovered the deception, she was so upset that she had Newcomb fired.

Marilyn had accepted her back, and now it seemed to her that history was repeating itself, only this time there were strange twists and deeper emotional complications. But now Marilyn was in a much more delicate frame of mind. She was also very close with Newcomb, and if she was not in love with Bobby, she was at the very least deeply infatuated. Marilyn felt betrayed by both of them.

Newcomb spent the night with the irate, disagreeable Marilyn because she realized Marilyn was feeling deceived and used—two emotions that were traumatizing to her. That day Newcomb decided to stay and try to work things out with Marilyn. In return Marilyn attempted to control her simmering sexual jealousy. But most of the morning she was having violent mood swings. One moment she appeared calm, and the next she would erupt in hostility.

The two friends spent much of the morning avoiding each other—neither knowing how to start the confrontation again—or how to end the animosity. Newcomb sat by the pool under the heat lamp while Marilyn attempted to get on with life: talking on the phone, signing for furniture that was delivered that afternoon, and working in the garden. At one point Mrs. Murray fixed Pat an herb omelet for lunch. Marilyn did not join her—she had no appetite. She would eat nothing all day, something that Mrs. Murray said by now wasn't unusual.

Early in the day Marilyn talked to Ralph Roberts. She wanted to know if he could have a record made from the master tape of the unpublished album of their friend, the singer-actress Janice Mars. Marilyn was still hoping to get a deal for Mars, so that the record could be released commercially. She had spoken to someone at Sinatra's office, and she wanted to give him a copy the following week. It also seems that Marilyn was having second thoughts about going to the Lawfords' place that evening for dinner. She talked with Roberts about grilling some steaks in the backyard for supper. They planned on touching base later in the day.

Sometime that day Isidore Miller called Marilyn. Mrs. Murray told him that "Marilyn is dressing." But she never called her former father-in-law back—which was highly unusual for her. Later he would say, "I'm so sorry I was not out there to be with her. She must have been very lonely and afraid."

There are two versions of Bobby Kennedy's whereabouts on Saturday, August 4. There are reasonable witnesses on both sides of the story, and wildly conflicting accounts. One version has him staying with friends in Gilroy, California, which is sixty miles south of San Francisco, for the entire day with Ethel and several of their children. The other version has him flying to Los Angeles for at least part of the day—to see Marilyn.

Whether Bobby Kennedy was in Los Angeles for part of that Saturday has been a subject of speculation for decades. Officially Bobby was staying in Gilroy that entire weekend. As Marilyn had learned the previous week, he was scheduled to give a speech to the American Bar Association in San Francisco on Monday. At first he was booked into the St. Francis Hotel for the weekend. When Marilyn discovered he was staying there she began to call the hotel switchboard, leaving messages for Bobby. He did not return these messages.

Since the attorney general was traveling with his wife and some of his children—and didn't want to take the chance of Marilyn showing up unexpectedly—it was decided that he would instead stay with a family friend, the respected attorney John Bates, and his wife, at their ranch in Gilroy.

Over and over again through the years, John Bates claimed that Bobby was with him for the entire weekend and was rarely out of his sight. That Saturday, he said, they went horseback riding, played touch football, and went swimming. After a "full active day" they had an early dinner, and then the Kennedy family retired for the evening. He has photographic proof of Bobby Kennedy and his family during the day. There are also photographs of the Kennedys attending mass that Sunday morning at 8:00 a.m.

Bolstering Bates's assertion that Bobby did not go to Los Angeles at all on Saturday, Pat Newcomb told Donald Spoto: "I have pretty good reasons to think he was not down here that night." The "pretty good reasons" Newcomb has for her beliefs could have been given to her by Bobby himself when she had dinner with him several nights earlier.

The other version of Bobby Kennedy's whereabouts that day has him in Los Angeles. According to some, he took a private helicopter to see Marilyn. He stayed part of the time at the Beverly Hills Hotel. There are witnesses who say Bobby left his family behind with his host and flew down to Los Angeles to confront Marilyn—to try to soothe her, reassure her.

Chief of Police William Parker told several people that Bobby Kennedy was in Los Angeles the Saturday that Marilyn died. He relayed this information to Mayor Sam Yorty and homicide detective Dan Stewart, among others on the L.A. police force.

Another witness to Bobby being in Los Angeles was Ward Wood, Peter Lawford's next-door neighbor in Santa Monica. Wood stated: "The car drove up, the people got out, and they went from the car to the house. I said, 'Oh, there's Bobby Kennedy.'" Having a view of the front of Lawford's house from his window, Wood was used to seeing the Kennedys coming and going. When interviewed, he was asked if he was sure it was Bobby. "Oh, I know it was Bobby Kennedy," he replied.

After many years of telling conflicting stories, late in life Mrs. Murray stated that Bobby Kennedy did indeed come to Marilyn's house that Saturday afternoon—and that she witnessed it. But listening to audiotapes of Mrs. Murray's interviews from the 1980s through the 1990s, or seeing her in documentaries, she often becomes forgetful and vague and then suddenly becomes sharp and clear: The most consistent thing about Mrs. Murray's interviews is her inconsistencies.

The reason for Bobby to come to Los Angeles would be to see Marilyn and, most likely, break off their relationship in person. Senator Smathers, a close friend of John F. Kennedy, said: "I heard about her seeing Bobby, and Jack told Bobby to break it off." Greenson said that Marilyn did expect to see Bobby that Saturday evening at Peter Lawford's, but was disappointed to learn that he wouldn't be there after all—which is why she would cancel her plans to go there. And it's also the reason she made no plans to glamorize herself that day.

There is a two-hour period in Marilyn's day that is more or less unaccounted for, and—like so many events in her life—it is surrounded with mystery: Between twelve and two o'clock Mrs. Murray was out doing some shopping.

If Bobby Kennedy visited Marilyn at her home that afternoon, it would have been an unexpected visit because she was not dressed for visitors—especially a love interest. This would not have been the seduction scene she had planned for later on that evening at the Lawfords': Her hair was a mess. She had been working in the garden—her feet and nails were dirty. Her face was clean of cosmetics.

This version suggests that Bobby quarreled with Marilyn—telling her that the relationship was over for good. There was no chance of it reviving. It was becoming too dangerous to his political career—and to the future of the president—to be involved with her.

If the confrontation did happen, Pat Newcomb would have still been at the house. In one of her last accounts of that day, Mrs. Murray said that when she came home from shopping Bobby was indeed there. But since her story about that day changed so many times, she is not a reliable source.

What we know for sure, however, is that by 4:00 p.m., Marilyn was in such a despondent state that she called Greenson to ask him to come to the house to see her for a therapy session.

When he arrived Greenson observed: "She seemed somewhat depressed. Somewhat drugged." Greenson ensconced himself with Marilyn in her bedroom for an intense therapy session. He would later tell the Suicide Prevention Team that Marilyn was in a jealous rage over Pat Newcomb, without, however, specifying the reason for her jealousy. Several days later, with time to start establishing scenarios, he would write to a colleague that one of the reasons for her depression and fury—on that day—was that Pat Newcomb had slept for fifteen hours and Marilyn—as usual—had had such a troubled night. This was the first time that the "lack of sleep" reason was put forth as one of the excuses for her anger. But there was more to it than that. After Marilyn's death Greenson planned to take a trip to New York to see his friend, the physician Max Schur (who had been a friend of Sigmund Freud), "where I can say certain things which I cannot say to anybody here."

It was during this last session with Greenson that Marilyn complained that "here she was, the most beautiful woman in the world, and she didn't have a date on Saturday night." Greenson, of course, knew that Marilyn was involved with the Kennedy brothers. She told him she had been expecting to see Bobby that evening. He would later disclose that Marilyn had been expecting to see one of the "important men in her life" that night and was disappointed when the expected visit was called off. Marilyn died, Greenson said, "feeling rejected by some of the people she had been close to."

Suddenly Marilyn told Greenson that she wanted Pat Newcomb out of her house. The doctor stepped outside her bedroom, found Newcomb, and said, "I'm going to talk to her now. I think it would be better if you go."

Mrs. Murray said that Newcomb sprang up and left without saying a word, not even a good-bye. Since Marilyn remained in an agitated state, Greenson asked Mrs. Murray to spend the night—which she normally did not do, especially on weekends.

Greenson continued talking to Marilyn. The doctor realized that Marilyn would not, could not, accept it if he didn't take her side completely. She wanted him to be furious with Newcomb too. To soothe her, Greenson agreed, but she sensed that his agreement wasn't wholehearted. Now her anger spread to include Greenson.

During the session Ralph Roberts called to ask Marilyn if he should still come over that evening for dinner. He was taken aback when Greenson answered the phone. When Roberts asked to speak to Marilyn, Greenson replied curtly, "She's not in," and abruptly hung up.

It is unknown if Greenson ever told her that Roberts had called.

Marilyn apparently had changed her mind about grilling steaks anyway; by this time she wasn't up to seeing anybody. Now she announced to Greenson that she would like to take a walk on the beach. The doctor discouraged her, feeling that she was too groggy to go walking. Instead he suggested she drink a Coke and go for a drive up the coast with Mrs. Murray.

When he left Marilyn at seven fifteen, Greenson thought she still seemed "somewhat depressed but I had seen her many, many times in a much worse condition." He went home to prepare for a dinner party.

Shortly after Greenson left, Marilyn received a phone call from Joe DiMaggio, Jr. After her divorces, she maintained a warm relationship with all her stepchildren. Joe Jr. wanted to share the news that he had broken off his engagement. Marilyn—who didn't think that they were a good match—was delighted that the twenty-one-year-old had decided not to get married yet. Marilyn sat down with the phone on some cushions on her bedroom floor. Mrs. Murray remembered Marilyn's voice rising with enthusiasm and laughing with delight.

After this phone call Marilyn called Greenson, now in the middle of dressing for his dinner engagement. She told him that she had had a nice conversation with Joe Jr., and expressed how happy she was that he was breaking up with his fiancée.

It was during this call that she told Greenson that she had decided not to take a drive with Mrs. Murray after all. In spite of sounding more cheerful, before she hung up, Marilyn asked Greenson, "Did you take my Nembutal?"

Greenson became alarmed. He had been weaning Marilyn off Nembutal and had Engelberg prescribe her the milder chloral hydrate for sleep instead.

"I didn't know you were taking Nembutal," he told her.

Marilyn didn't press him about the missing drugs. "Oh, forget it," she said.

Since she had been disoriented that day, Greenson didn't make much of the notion that Marilyn was asking about Nembutal. But it turned out to be a significant factor in her death.

———

Those in Marilyn's circle understood that Engelberg had made a deal with Greenson: Whenever the internist prescribed pills for Marilyn, he would let Greenson know. That way Greenson could keep track of the amount of pills Marilyn had in the house—and might keep her from doctor shopping. "I mean, here's somebody who everybody knows is capable of suicide," Pat Newcomb stated.

Also, if on a house call Greenson noticed too many pills on Marilyn's nightstand, he would pour some out and put them in his pocket, leaving Marilyn with a supply that would enable her to get some sleep but not enough to be lethal.

During a visit with Engelberg on Friday, Marilyn told him that Greenson had said it was okay for her to take some Nembutal and—believing her—he wrote her a prescription. Unfortunately, during this period, Engelberg was having problems with his wife, and—preoccupied with marital troubles—he forgot to tell Greenson that he had prescribed twenty-five Nembutal for Marilyn.

This miscommunication took a dangerous turn. The previous night, with Marilyn in an ornery mood, Newcomb—who admittedly shared pills with her—took Marilyn's Nembutal from her bedroom nightstand and brought them to the guest room, where she swallowed one. (That's why she had the solid fifteen-hour sleep that so ticked Marilyn off.)

When Greenson was having the therapy session with Marilyn in her bedroom, there was no Nembutal on her bedside table. When he left her in her depressed state, he felt assured that there was no Nembutal in the house: "She had stopped taking barbiturates for three weeks," he said. Now Greenson was relieved to hear that Marilyn was feeling a little better—although still depressed—and ended the call by saying, "I'll talk to you in the morning."

Marilyn walked through the house looking for her bottle of Nembutal and eventually found it on the nightstand in the guest room, where Pat Newcomb had left it the night before. Marilyn carried the bottle back to her bedroom and began taking her nighttime dose on top of the tranquilizing medication she had been taking all day. There were twenty-four capsules left. When the pill bottle was confiscated several hours later it would be empty.

"I think I'll turn in now, Mrs. Murray," she told her housekeeper. Then she closed the door. That's the last time anyone ever saw Marilyn alive.

THIRTY-FIVE

MISCOMMUNICATIONS

Rather than being tired of living, she was tired of dying.

Her private phone was in the bedroom with her—it had a long extension cord so, when she felt like it, she could wander all over the house while she was talking. The telephone cord snaked under the closed door to an outlet in another room.

Naked in her bed, Marilyn called Peter Lawford to inform him that she wasn't going to attend his dinner party. "Peter, I'm tired," she said. "I'm going to have a sandwich and take a couple of pills. Then I'm going to go to sleep. Please forgive me." In reality she wasn't interested in food. She hung up with Lawford and swallowed some pills.

Her hair was in disarray—perhaps there was a hint of roots growing in. She needed a manicure and a pedicure. Marilyn loved to go barefoot, and she had worked in the garden earlier—her feet were dirty. In the coming days all these details of her appearance would be reported to the press by the morticians who attended to her corpse, for even in death she wasn't permitted to be viewed as a normal woman. "She didn't look good, not like Marilyn Monroe," a coroner's man, Guy Hockett, who a few hours later removed her body from the bed, remarked. "She looked just like a poor little girl that had died." Which—at the time of her death—is what she was.

Alone, abandoned and angry, Marilyn thought—as she often did in the nighttime—about where her life was. When her fears and problems looked bigger than her accomplishments and hopes, the world closed in on her—her petite body, her overbleached hair—in her tiny, cluttered rooms, with her mirrors, her makeup, her breast pads, and a wardrobe of brightly colored clothes. What some considered vanities were really just a way of life for her; it was what she knew, what she thought was expected of her. Other Hollywood stars served up illusion too, but they had lasting loves, families, and confidence, things that never materialized for her. By this time Marilyn felt all she had to stand on was a fantasy, an illusion that was becoming harder to maintain.

Marilyn was blessed with qualities other than her physical perfection. A lively intelligent mind. A hunger to know more. Kindness. Empathy for those who had been held down or hurt. A love of children. A keen sensitivity that made her genuine talent unique. But all these wonderful qualities seemed useless to her if people didn't find her beautiful.

The lust of men was what had always given her confidence. She mostly saw her worth through their eyes. These men—some kind, but mostly cruel—were a manifestation of the father she never knew and the love she never felt strongly enough. The more powerful the man, the more worthy she felt. John and Bobby Kennedy were the biggest prize. But they, too, proved to be temporary.

The hack writers who had built her up wanted to see her career in ruins now because they thought it might make a few headlines. Before she was fired, Marilyn gave an interview to *Photoplay* about her nude swim scene. It was one of the few publications that did not praise her still-perfect proportions. Instead it accused her of despairing, exploiting her final years of beauty. "Desperate Monroe Poses Nude" declared the headline on the magazine's cover.

She thought her magic was leaving her, but really it was just transitioning. But she was too tired now to believe that, to believe in anything. Instead of embracing the transformation she willed things to stay as they were.

Feeling the effects of the drugs, Marilyn continued dialing. She reached her New York friend Henry Rosenfeld, and they talked about an East Coast visit, but eventually the call turned into a diatribe against Pat Newcomb.

Around eight o'clock Peter Lawford called her again. He tried to persuade her to come to his house. It was clear to Lawford that she was very drugged.

She faded out. Peter waited for her to say something more, and when she didn't he said sharply, "Marilyn! Are you okay?" Suddenly she came to for a moment and said, "I'm fine. I just wanted to let you know that everything you've done for me is beautiful. I can't thank you and Pat enough." And her voice became very low, and her last words to him were, "Say good-bye to Pat and Bobby . . . say goodbye to the president . . . and say goodbye to yourself because you're a nice guy . . ." and her voice trailed off once more.

He tried to awaken her with what he later called "a verbal slap in the face," screaming into the receiver, "Marilyn! Marilyn! *Marilyn!!*"

She was silent. Lawford hung up. After trying the line several times, he called Milt Ebbins. It was approximately eight fifteen.

Ebbins agreed to try and get through to Marilyn. He called the operator, who checked Marilyn's line and informed him the phone was off the hook. In those days of busy signals, no call-waiting, and no caller ID, Marilyn had two phones. A white one that only her close friends had the number to—a sort of "hotline," and a pink "house" phone for business calls and secondary people. Lawford had only the number of the white phone that Marilyn was holding.

When Ebbins informed Lawford that Marilyn's phone was off the hook, Lawford became hysterical. "Let's go over there. I want to go over there right now," he demanded. Ebbins had a more guarded response, "Wait a minute, Peter! You're the brother-in-law of the president of the United States. What if something happened? You'd see headlines all over the place." Ebbins offered to call Mickey Rudin—Marilyn's increasingly impatient lawyer. Ebbins thought it was best to get advice legal advice before they made any kind of move.

The alarm bell had been rung. On a social Saturday evening in Hollywood, while Marilyn lay dying, people were being called, tracked down, and discussing options, as crucial minutes were ticking away.

————

At approximately eight forty-five p.m., Mildred Allenberg—the widow of Frank Sinatra's agent—interrupted her dinner party to call Mickey Rudin to the phone. Rudin was not pleased that the caller was Ebbins. He was further irritated when he heard that the reason for the call was that Marilyn Monroe was, perhaps, in the middle of yet another crisis.

"Mickey," Ebbins said, "Peter was talking to Marilyn, and the phone went dead. Peter's worried—he wants to go over to her house. He's adamant about going over there now. I don't think he should."

Rudin, a gruff man often described as an exceptional attorney, recalled it being mentioned that Marilyn had made distressed calls wanting to talk to Bobby. "She could have been hysterical or something," Rudin commented. He also realized the potential problem with John F. Kennedy's brother-in-law being seen at the home of Marilyn Monroe on a Saturday night. "I think you're right. Let me check it out. I'll get back to you."

Mrs. Murray was in her guest bedroom reading when she heard the house phone rang. It was Rudin, calling from Mrs. Allenberg's dinner party.

Rudin asked Mrs. Murray if Marilyn was all right.

"As far as I know everything is fine," Mrs. Murray replied.

Rudin said, "Do you think anything's wrong?"

According to Rudin she replied, "No. She's done what she does every night. She takes her pills. She goes in. She puts on music. She locks the door. She calls somebody, and she drops the phone."

That was enough for Rudin—in his opinion Marilyn was simply having one of her "despondent moments." He called Ebbins back. "Don't go over there," he said. "She's driving me crazy. Tell Peter not to worry about it."

Of course Rudin could have called Greenson to find out if Marilyn had been in any kind of distress, but his sympathy was with his brother-in-law, not with Marilyn. "He spent most of the day with her," Rudin explained. "He was upset." He wasn't about to go tracking Greenson down because, as he later explained, he wanted "the poor guy to have one dinner without being interrupted"—a decision that would trouble him for the rest of his life.

Through the years Mrs. Murray maintained that had there been more urgency in Rudin's voice she would have made it a point to bang on Marilyn's door. But knowing that Marilyn was in a foul mood, Mrs. Murray didn't want to take a chance of waking her up for no reason.

Ralph Roberts was having dinner with a friend, but he was wondering about Marilyn. Why hadn't she returned his call? He had completed the errand of getting a copy made of the Janice Mars record she wanted and never heard back from her regarding dinner plans.

Because of the high content of barbiturates in her liver, the coroner could conclude that Marilyn died slowly. The drugs had had a chance to be absorbed. At 10:00 p.m. the phone was still beside Marilyn on the bed, and she dialed Ralph Roberts's number, but the call was picked up by Roberts's answering service. Marilyn did not leave a message. The following day Roberts would be told simply that he had received a call from a woman with a "slurred voice." The operator had no way of knowing that it was one of the last phone calls made by the dying Marilyn Monroe.

Though Lawford became more and more inebriated, he continued to call Ebbins throughout the night—getting drunker with each phone call. Then Ebbins got angry. "Get in the car and go! If you can't drive, get one of those guys there and go! You don't need me." The last time the two men talked was about two in the morning.

Very drunk now—and beginning to realize that Milt Ebbins wasn't going to cave in—Peter Lawford began calling other friends to try to get them to go over to Marilyn's house with him. One of the people he may have tried was Pat Newcomb. "I was out to dinner that night," Newcomb said. "I wasn't even home."

Eventually Lawford got through to William Asher and asked if he would drive with him. Asher was irritated that he called in the middle of the night, wanting to go over to Marilyn's.

After telling him there was no way he would go, Asher suggested he call the "old man"—meaning Joe Kennedy, adding, "If we go over there and find something, I don't know if you should be there. Call Mr. Kennedy and ask him what you should do."

Asher was well aware of the inside rumors of Marilyn being involved with both Kennedy brothers. "I blush to admit now," Asher said later, "I've thought about maybe . . . had I gone. It might have been different. That makes you crazy."

At 4:00 a.m. Eastern Daylight Time, 1:00 a.m. in Los Angeles, Lawford called the White House. Obviously he wanted to talk to John F. Kennedy about his extreme concern for Marilyn, perhaps the dangerous consequences of something happening to her. Lawford was unable to reach the president this time. The log for the call says Lawford was calling about plans for a vacation in Maine.

Lawford was losing coherence. At last—his mind sufficiently numbed to avoid the thought of Marilyn in peril—he retired to his bedroom, pulled the phone jack out of the wall (as he did every night), and passed out in bed.

By this time it didn't matter. Marilyn Monroe was already dead.

THIRTY-SIX

"WE'VE LOST HER"

Mrs. Murray had retired to the guest room early; in retrospect she thought it was about eight thirty. In interviews she would always explain that she was never really aware of the time that night—she simply wasn't paying attention to it. What could be taken from the number of stories she told is that sometime after midnight she woke up with the sense that something was wrong.[*]

Mrs. Murray got out of bed to do a quick check of the house. The first thing she noticed was that the phone cord was still snaking into Marilyn's room from under the door. This was unusual and sent an "electric shock" through her body. Marilyn never slept with a phone in her room. Normally, before her drugs kicked in, she would take her private phone into the spare bedroom next to the house phone, and cover them both with pillows and blankets to muffle the sound of their ringing.

Since Marilyn had such a preoccupation with sleep, Mrs. Murray didn't dare call out to her or even try the lock on the door. But she was concerned enough to call Greenson. The doctor instructed her to try the door. It was locked. Rather than rush back to the doctor, Mrs. Murray went outside to the front window that looked into Marilyn's bedroom, while Greenson waited on the phone.

The window itself was open, but it was protected by heavy Mexican

---

[*] The accounts vary wildly as to the time—anywhere from shortly after midnight to 3:30 a.m. It seems all the major players wanted her body to be discovered later than it was, because there was a delay in notifying the police.

grillwork, and Marilyn's blackout drapes prevented her from seeing in. Mrs. Murray couldn't reach the drapes with her hand so she rushed back in for a poker from the fireplace to stick through the grillwork and part the drapes.

"I saw Marilyn lying on the bed, facedown, nude. The light was on. So everything was wrong," Mrs. Murray explained. She ran back inside in a panic. She picked up the phone and gasped, "Come quickly!"

When Greenson arrived at the house a few minutes later, he retrieved the poker and broke into another window, which also opened into Marilyn's bedroom. He climbed through.

Greenson saw that Marilyn's body was cold and blue. The phone receiver was still in her hand. She was clutching it so fiercely, so strongly, that at first he could not remove it. It took some time for him to pry the receiver out of Marilyn's dead hand. Other than that there was nothing he could do. "He knew it was hopeless," Mrs. Murray said. "No one could help her." Greenson opened the door and whispered to Mrs. Murray, "We've lost her."

He instructed Mrs. Murray to call Engelberg—who arrived at the house in a matter of minutes. Although the following events get very muddled, with each of the participants giving different accounts, it is likely that Greenson called Rudin, his brother-in-law and Marilyn's attorney, who also came to the house immediately.

One thing these three early-morning players realized is that one of the most popular and beloved women in the world was dead and they all had a hand in it—some amount of culpability. Though overwhelmed by loss and grief, at the same time they were racked with guilt as well as panic about what their place would be in the history of—and responsibility for—the death of Marilyn Monroe. For instance, when examining Marilyn's bedside table Greenson discovered the empty pill bottle that had contained the twenty-five Nembutals prescribed by Engelberg the day before.

"My God, what is this?" Greenson exclaimed.

Engelberg said: "Oh my God, I forgot to call you!"

The two doctors and Marilyn's attorney—each filled with private remorse—were well aware of the level of fame of the woman who lay dead in the bedroom. Ralph Greenson, Hyman Engelberg, and Mickey Rudin spent a long period of time before they notified the police. Just how long they took has never been, and can never be, said with certainty. Mrs. Murray stated many times that she had no idea what these men discussed over Marilyn's dead body. She felt they were professional people and had good reason to say what they had to say to one another.

They were also well aware that there would be a firestorm of publicity surrounding this death. The level of their involvement would be questioned—and possibly condemned. None of them, however, could ever have imagined the extent of the fascination with the mystery they were helping to create. There would be questions regarding the statements they gave that night. And from those statements through the years, offshoots of questions and theories about Marilyn developed that would lead only to more mystery. For the rest of their lives—and beyond—the narrative of Marilyn Monroe's life and death would grow beyond the story of a very popular actress of her generation and become an enduring enigma, a true icon of American culture.

Because of the inquiring phone call he had received about how to handle Peter Lawford's profound concern, Rudin also called Milt Ebbins.

"Milt—" he began.

"Mickey!" Ebbins exclaimed. "What are you doing up so late?"

He said, "We've got problems."

Ebbins asked, "How's Marilyn?"

Rudin replied, "Not good. Her doctors and I broke into the bedroom . . . they just pronounced her dead, and we notified the police. You're the first one who knows about it."

Next, to handle the first onslaught of media regarding Marilyn's death, Rudin called Pat Newcomb.

"There's been an accident," he said. "Marilyn's taken an overdose of pills."

"Is she okay?" Newcomb asked.

"She's dead," the attorney informed her.

Once these phone calls were made, and the police notified, it was a matter of minutes before Marilyn's small courtyard was filled with curious neighbors, police cars, reporters, and a coroner's vehicle.

Mrs. Murray would always remember hearing Pat Newcomb's screams, coming through the crowd. "Keep shooting, vultures!" she yelled at the reporters who continuously snapped her picture. Being in public relations, she knew some of them. "How would you feel if your best friend had died?" she plaintively asked them. She wanted them to make way for her, to let her get through. Marilyn's body wasn't removed until about five o'clock in the morning. "I didn't want to see it," Newcomb said. She would recall sitting in the living room with a bunch of people around. She couldn't remember who was there. But she most certainly did not want to go anywhere near the bedroom.

Part of the silence surrounding Marilyn's death through the years has been because people who were still alive could be hurt by the information about her affairs with John and Bobby Kennedy. But also Marilyn's feeling of neglect, her loneliness, her sweetness—made everyone feel they wanted to help her. Because so many failed, there were enough guilty feelings to go around for the major players to feel partially responsible for her death. This added to the fog of secrecy that has surrounded Marilyn's last days, hours, and the aftermath.

Mrs. Murray, Greenson, Rudin, Engelberg, Peter Lawford, Pat Newcomb—they all had played inadvertent roles in Marilyn's death. No one was guilty, except of poor judgment. But each of them probably dreaded being associated with that horrible night.

It is safe to assume that none of them wanted any kind of blame for Marilyn slipping away, when a few extra steps, some precautionary measures, might have saved her—at least that evening.

Pat Newcomb does not appear to have ever disclosed everything she knows about Marilyn's last days. She apparently had some sort of romantic feelings toward Bobby Kennedy at the same time Marilyn was trying to redefine her own complicated relationship with him. It added to her turbulent emotions. Had Marilyn lived, the two friends might have worked through their difficulties, and Marilyn might have overcome her anger and moved on. But she died that night, forever immobilizing the friendship in the center of the intensity of the jealousy and rage she was feeling that early August.

It was Newcomb who took Marilyn's Nembutal bottle into the spare bedroom. Had it been on Marilyn's nightstand, Greenson would have likely taken the pills away, concerned about Marilyn's depression that evening.

Mrs. Murray displayed her regrets about that night with her constantly changing story. Being an assistant to Marilyn Monroe was the highlight of her life. The fact that Marilyn succumbed while Mrs. Murray was spending the night to keep an eye on her well-being was a heavy burden to bear. She constantly adjusted events to appear less culpable.

Rudin had his own grudging feelings of guilt. Had he taken Ebbins's phone call more seriously, had he believed there was a reason for Lawford's deep concern, he might have suggested that someone drive over to the house to check on Marilyn, or at least requested Mrs. Murray to knock on her bedroom door.

Lawford was eaten up by guilt feelings over Marilyn for the rest of his life. He was one of the main reasons Marilyn was involved with the Kennedys at all. He orchestrated most of their clandestine meetings. He would never forgive himself for not going over to Marilyn's house that Saturday night. What she had said to him in their last phone call alerted him to the fact that she was in a desperate state of mind, beyond suffering. Had he requested one of his guests to drive him there after the phone went silent, he might have arrived in time to save her.

Engelberg shared part of the blame because he forgot to tell Greenson about the Nembutal he had prescribed Marilyn the previous day. Because of the difficulties he was going through in his marriage, it slipped Engelberg's mind to confirm with Greenson that he had okayed the prescription.

And of course there's Greenson, who had his own feelings of inadequacy and culpability because his decision to treat Marilyn in an unorthodox way—a way that went against everything he believed in regarding his therapy—had failed. Hildi Greenson said her husband was "devastated" by Marilyn's death. His patient had died, despite his efforts to make her feel part of a family. Instead he increased her dependence on him, rendering her unable to function on her own. He was also tortured by his knowledge of Marilyn's relationship with the Kennedy brothers—her current terrible frame of mind caused by Bobby—and he had to keep quiet about it.

In 1964, when William Woodfield called Greenson to try to get more details on Monroe's death, the doctor said: "I can't explain myself or defend myself without revealing things I don't want to reveal. You can't draw a line and say, 'I'll tell you this but I won't tell you that.' It's a terrible position to be in to have to say 'I can't talk about it because I can't tell the whole story.'" Then Greenson said to Woodfield: "Listen, talk to Bobby Kennedy."

None of these people is responsible for Marilyn swallowing a fatal amount of drugs. Yet they all had their personal guilt feelings for not having done more for a woman as emotionally disturbed and fragile as Marilyn was that summer. Perhaps they could have been a little more vigilant, but ultimately no one could have saved her.

By the early-morning hours news of Marilyn's death was being broadcast on the radio and breaking in on television shows. The reports brought on a feeling of profound sadness and loss across the world—the kind of collective mourning that a famous person's death brings only a handful of times a century. People were shocked and heartbroken by the thought that someone who had brought them so much joy was no longer with them. The feeling that Marilyn brought out in a multitude of people was "If only I had been there, I could have saved her." In the days following her death, people from all walks of life committed suicide.

"Her death has diminished the loveliness of the world in which we live," *LIFE* cried.

EPILOGUE

Marilyn Monroe died just before the advent of feminism and the blossoming of the civil rights movement. She lived in a generation when people were categorized, where roles were strongly defined and stringently observed. There was very little crossing over lines. She had to find an identity early in her career, and she found one "self" that became beloved beyond her wildest imagination, leaving her other selves looking desperately for a way of expression.

First she was a delicious blonde. That was okay. They understood that. Still, there were so many other sides to her wanting to get out and display themselves. Then she presented herself as an orphan, a fragile girl, someone who needed to be protected. The public was confused but intrigued, and her star rose. Next she wanted to be seen as a serious actress—and now the media started viewing her as a woman who wanted too much. When she started her own production company so she could exercise more control over her career, they began to think of her as ludicrous.

Marilyn was trying to be accepted as all these things. "Marilyn Monroe" confused Hollywood, the media, studio executives, and the public. And in their confusion some of them became angry. Although they didn't really know what they were angry about, it was easier to just view her as a slut who took herself too seriously.

After Marilyn became successful for one thing, unlike many other people of the day, she wanted desperately to cross the line—to be accepted as many things. But alas, the generation she was born into wouldn't allow that. And that's partially what killed her.

Such acceptance became her motivation, her goal. She tried to develop other aspects of her personality, but her power to seduce was always so potent that she eventually began asking herself, If people don't find me beautiful, do I really deserve to be here?

Today we realize that the beautiful Marilyn Monroe was a remarkable woman in so many ways that we simply cannot forget her. Her spectacular, indefinable radiance still lingers here on earth—and we never want to lose it.

As her friend Ella Fitzgerald said, "She was an unusual woman—a little ahead of her times. And she didn't know it." Now she is recognized as an unusual woman for all times.

Yet throughout her life, Marilyn's self-doubts, her fears, her lingering questions left her constantly chasing after a sleep that always managed to elude her. On August 4 Marilyn Monroe retired to her bedroom and—her head filled with a myriad of secrets—closed the door.

Naked, sleeping pills flowing through her bloodstream, her face pressed into the pillow, a hand clutching a phone with no one on the other end, Marilyn Monroe—who never told anyone everything—died. What her thoughts were as she drifted toward the death that had always fascinated her, she kept to herself—creating forever her final and most confounding mystery.

Loved by millions but feeling let down and alone, on a warm summer night, she went out as the most sensational movie star of the twentieth century. She is perfected and frozen in time: beautiful, vulnerable, impenetrable, delicious—forever our white goddess.

She left us what she needed to leave. We stand back, mouths agape: judging, adoring, questioning. For eternity Marilyn's skirt billows over a subway grating, she reclines nude against a red velvet backdrop, she slinks around a chorus of tuxedoed men singing the praises of diamonds, she is mobbed on her way out of the hospital, she sings a breathless "Happy Birthday" to our thirty-fifth president, or she says into a tape recorder, slightly high: "I guess I'll settle for what I am."

Leaving each of us to decide exactly who she was.

ACKNOWLEDGMENTS

I would like to thank my parents, Gloria and Ralph, who gave me everything.

I am grateful to my agent, Tom Miller, who believed in this project and encouraged me from our first meeting in his office until the last sentence was written. I was fortunate enough to have Charles Spicer as my editor at St. Martin's Press—his instincts and guidance were invaluable. Thanks also to April Osborn for her assistance.

For this biography, I had contact with many individuals, each with special qualities, who added to the book in different ways. Because Marilyn Monroe's life was a mosaic, each person led me to a piece of the puzzle in some unique way (whether they are quoted in the text or not). I am grateful to the extraordinary Joan Copeland, who was generous with her time talking about Marilyn—her sister-in-law through Arthur Miller—and who gave me rare, firsthand insights. Photographer Murray Garrett—who took ravishing and revealing photos of Marilyn at many public events—stunned me with his perception into the dichotomies of the public Monroe and also about the relationship between the media and celebrities in the 1950s and '60s. I also enjoyed talking with Michael J. Pollard, who studied and performed with Marilyn at the Actor's Studio, and became a friend.

I was fortunate enough to share a meal with Angela Allen (John Huston's script supervisor), who was perfectly lovely and forthcoming with her memories of Marilyn on the set of *The Misfits*, even while planning her own memoir. Curtice Taylor could not have been more welcoming when we discussed the relationship his parents (Frank and Nan Taylor) had with Marilyn and his own experiences knowing her. The gregarious Hap Roberts, nephew of one of Marilyn's greatest friends, Ralph Roberts, added another level of understanding to that multifaceted friendship.

Three gentlemen were particularly enlightening on three different periods in Marilyn's life: Al Carmen Guastafeste arranged Marilyn's music and played piano for her when she entertained troops in Korea in 1954. Al Brenneman worked with Marilyn on the classic comedy *Some Like It Hot* in 1958. Kimothy Cruse had fascinating information regarding Marilyn after she was fired from *Something's Got to Give* in 1962. Their interviews added greatly to Marilyn's life story.

For their time and input into this biography I would like to thank Allan Abbott, Bobby Banas, Leslie Caron, Marion Collier, Joan Collins, Rhonda Fleming, Buddy Greco, Joshua Greene, Joan Greenson, Betsy Duncan Hammes, Lou Harris, Kathleen Hughes, Christian Larson, Paul Libin, Roberta Linn, Chris Lemmon, Bob Mardesich, Edward Parone, Stefanie Powers, Michael Selsman, Nancy Sinatra, Eric Skipsey, Lena Tabori, Lisa Immordino Vreelend, Dawn Wells, Bette Westcott, Ken Wescott, and David Wills. There were also several important sources who asked to remain anonymous.

For valuable insight into mental illness and therapy I would like to give my sincere thanks for interviews granted by Jared Seltzer, Psy.D. Licensed Psychologist. And Douglas Kirsner, Ph.D., author of the enlightening essay "Do As I Say, Not As I Do: Ralph Greenson, Anna Freud, and Superrich Patients."

Biographer James Spada shared long talks with me and divulged new information he had uncovered regarding Marilyn Monroe. I will always cherish the memory of James.

I am grateful to the Margaret Herrick Library, Academy of Motion Picture Arts and Sciences. The entire staff made it one my favorite places in the world. They are gracious, knowledgeable, and actually go out of their way to be helpful. I would particularly like to thank Jenny Romero, Louise Hilton, and Marisa Duron for all their good-natured assistance.

The Margaret Herrick Library houses three collections which were extremely helpful in my research. I would like to thank three wonderful writers who donated their extensive research on Marilyn Monroe. Sources who were close to Marilyn who are dead or no longer available are heard in these pages because of the work of these impressive authors:

Lois Banner Collection. Notes on interviews for her book *Marilyn: The Passion and the Paradox.*

Donald Spoto. Oral interviews for his biography *Marilyn Monroe: The Biography.*

Anthony Summers. Oral interviews for his biography *Goddess: The Secret Lives of Marilyn Monroe.*

I also consulted the Guido Orlando papers regarding Marilyn's relationship with Natasha Lytess.

The Newberry Library houses the Ben Hecht Collection. Hecht was Marilyn's ghostwriter for her early memoir *My Story.* Samantha Smith was especially helpful to me in comparing what is in the published version of *My Story* and Hecht's unpublished notes.

My research of Marilyn Monroe started as a child when I became fascinated with a photo I saw of her in a magazine. I have been following a trail ever since. As an adult, through my work as a writer, I had an opportunity to cross paths and interview people who were connected to Marilyn in a variety of ways. In 1997–99, when I was working on a totally different Marilyn Monroe project, I interviewed Bert Stern, Bill Asher, Jeanne Martin, Milton Ebbins, Arthur James, and Gloria Romanoff, and I've now been able to incorporate those conversations in the text. I am thankful to them. Through my longtime friendship with Los Angeles cult personality and public access talk show host Skip E. Lowe, I met and got to know Susan Strasberg, Cyd Charisse, Jack Larson, Shelley Winters, Carol Lynley, and Jane Russell. These lovely personalities indulged my interest in Marilyn and patiently answered my questions while sharing their own memories and observations, which are woven throughout the book.

I joined the group Marilyn Remembered in 1999, founded by the wonderful Greg Schreiner (an affable man who is always generous with his time and insights regarding Marilyn), and regularly attended meetings through 2005. These meetings led to many interesting, in-depth discussions about Marilyn with knowledgeable, sensitive individuals, some who knew and worked with Marilyn and some of them Monroe scholars. One thing they taught me is how passionate people can be about Marilyn Monroe, how attached they are to their beliefs, what a hold she continues to have, and how there is a different Marilyn Monroe for all of us. My friends there included George Barris, Evelyn Moriarity, Gene Allen, George Chakiris, Ernest Cunningham, Stanley Rubin, and Lily Woodfield.

One of the big breaks in my life happened when I first moved to Los Angeles and met and befriended the renowned biographer J. Randy Taraborrelli. I became a member of his team for a number of his celebrated books. Through the years I learned a lot from working with him. Randy is not only a blockbuster biographer but a blockbuster friend, and my affection and thanks go out to him.

I am also grateful to B. Harlan Boll, Harrison Held, Alison Martino, and Evan MacDonald for their assistance. The agency Photofest was an enormous help to me in gathering the photos that illustrate this book.

A second pair of eyes was so helpful in editing down Marilyn's complex life story. I am enormously grateful to my red rose, Rossana Scotto-divettimo Weitekamp, who greatly assisted me with her intelligence and skill—above and beyond the call of friendship.

Laughs, understanding, and support are the greatest gifts a friend can give. In that regard, I have been very gifted with the friendship of Jeff Dymowski. My dearest friend and a kindred spirit.

I am extremely grateful for the friendship, support, and wisdom of Denis Ferrara. Not only a brilliant writer (and Marilyn scholar) but also a friend who is dear to me.

The writer Vincent Curcio has been a longtime encourager and friend whom I value. He often pointed me in a direction that yielded gold.

When occasionally lost in a world of words, it's wonderful to have someone to turn to for some clarity. At various times I was fortunate enough to be able to turn to Lily Acevedo, Tricia Civello, and Mary Gaitskill. Each of them mean a lot.

Sometimes friends and family contribute to a work without even knowing they're contributing. A shoulder to lean on, not telling me to shut up when I can't shut up about my subject, being light when I'm dark, or just being. I have been very blessed in the family and friends department: I love John Rechy, period. And Scott Lesko, Rick Brooks, Marcella Winn, Lisa Santucci, Frank Perry, Mike Prestie, Sally Kirkland, Steve Curtis, Isaac Rodriguez, Debra Tate, Stewart Penn, Jacqueline Michelle, Greg Veneklasen, Bernie Guzman, Tony Frere, David Sloan, and Marc Wynn. And Anthony and Marlene Casillo, Anthony Jr., Joseph, and Adrianna.

NOTES

Prologue

1   See Anthony Summers, *Goddess: The Secret Lives of Marilyn Monroe* (Macmillan, 1985). See also Anthony Summers, "Marilyn's Darkest Days Laid Bare," *The Sunday Times,* July 29, 2012.

1–2   record of her calls that night: David Marshall, *The DD Group: An Online Investigation into the Death of Marilyn Monroe* (iUniverse, Inc., 2005). See also *Say Goodbye to the President*, British Broadcasting Corporation, 1985.

1. Mama

6   "went nuts and then went to God": J. Randy Taraborrelli, *The Secret Life of Marilyn Monroe* (New York: Grand Central Publishing, 2009).

6   "Mama liked men": Donald Spoto, *Marilyn Monroe: The Biography* (New York: HarperCollins, 1993).

7   lewd and lascivious: Adam Victor, *The Marilyn Encyclopedia* (New York: Overlook Press, 1999).

8   "loose morals": Maurice Zolotow, *Marilyn Monroe* (New York: Harcourt, Brace, 1960).

2. Struggle for Survival

13   police were called: *The Legend of Marilyn Monroe* (1966), documentary directed by Terry Sanders, interview with Ida Bolender.

13   "Manic Depressive Psychosis": Los Angeles death certificate of Della M. Monroe.

13   "because we loved her": *The Legend of Marilyn Monroe*, documentary directed by Terry Sanders (1966), interview with Ida and Wayne Bolender.

13   "in the world": Michelle Morgan, *Marilyn Monroe: Private and Confidential* (New York: Skyhorse Publishing, 2012).

14   ". . . with a leather strap": Marilyn Monroe, *My Story* (Lanham, MD: Taylor Trade Publishing, 2007).

14   "I was hard on her for her own good": J. Randy Taraborrelli, *The Secret Life of Marilyn Monroe* (New York: Grand Central Publishing, 2009).

14   "churchgoers not moviegoers": Monroe, *My Story.*

14   "afraid and ashamed" of her genitals: Marilyn Monroe, *Fragments: Poems, Intimate Notes, Letters* (New York: Farrar, Straus and Giroux, 2010).

15   "and they would look up at me": Monroe, *My Story.*

16   "Hello Mama": Maurice Zolotow, *Marilyn Monroe* (New York: Harper & Row, 1990).

3. Be a Good Girl

21   screaming and laughing: Marilyn Monroe, *My Story* (Lanham, MD: Taylor Trade Publishing, 2007).

22   "Oh, I feel it in my bones": Maurice Zolotow, *Marilyn Monroe* (New York: Harper & Row, 1990).

23   count was ten including the orphanage: Marilyn Monroe audiotape interview with Georges Belmont, editor of *Marie Claire* magazine, 1960.

24   "forgive the sins of others": Monroe, *My Story.*

24   "protect ourselves": Marilyn Monroe audiotape interview with Georges Belmont, editor of *Marie Claire*, 1960.

24   "she wasn't a virgin": Donald Spoto interview with Lucille Ryman Carrol, Donald Spoto Collection, Margaret Herrick Library.

25   "It was pretty terrible": Elsa Maxwell, "I'll Never Be the Same," *Modern Screen*, July 1956.

27   "not even my mother's best friend": George Barris, *Marilyn: Her Life in Her Own Words: Marilyn Monroe's Revealing Last Words and Photographs* (New York: Citadel Press, 2001).

28   "can really know": Arthur Miller, *Timebends: A Life* (New York: Grove Press, 1987).

4. The World Became Friendly

31   "it opened up to me": Marilyn Monroe interview with Richard Meryman for *Life*, 1962. Taken from audiotapes for the interview (in private hands).

32   "us to know about": Charles Casillo interview with Bette Wescott, February 8, 2016.

33   out of state: *The Many Loves of Marilyn Monroe*, interview with James Dougherty, E! True Hollywood Story documentary, 2001.

33   high school football captain: *Los Angeles Times*, James Dougherty obituary, August 18, 2005.

33   "very important to her": *Inside Edition* interview with James Dougherty; the 1990s clip is on YouTube.

34   what was expected of her: Marilyn Monroe audiotape interview with Georges Belmont, editor of *Marie Claire*, 1960.

34   "and be Norma Jeane again": From a James Dougherty interview posted by "The Marilyn Monroe Archives" on YouTube on May 29, 2012.

35   "wanted me to look into": *The Discovery of Marilyn Monroe*, documentary interview with Bebe Goddard (who reads the letter on camera).

36   "the cute way she said it": Charles Casillo interview with Christian Larson, July 30, 2016.

37   "radiated sex": Clark Kidder, *Marilyn Monroe: Cover to Cover* (Iola, WI: Krause Publications, February 2003).

38   "that was related": Marilyn Monroe audiotape interview with Georges Belmont, editor of *Marie Claire*, 1960.

39   "supply and demand": *The Legend of Marilyn Monroe*, documentary narrated by John Huston, 1966.

5. "A Stray Little Kitten"

41   "love me": Donald Spoto interview with Lucille Ryman Carroll, Donald Spoto Collection, Margaret Herrick Library.

42   "oldest profession": Charles Casillo interview with Susan Strasberg, 1999.

43   "only chance at stardom": Donald Spoto interview with Lucille Ryman Carroll, Donald Spoto Collection, Margaret Herrick Library.

43   "little kitten": Ibid.

44   at this indignity: Peter Bogdanovich, *Who the Hell's in It: Portraits and Conversations* (New York: Knopf, 2004).

45   "for your soul": Marilyn Monroe, *My Story* (Lanham, MD: Taylor Trade Publishing, 2007).

45   "I was never kept": George Barris, *Marilyn: Her Life in Her Own Words: Marilyn Monroe's Revealing Last Words and Photographs* (New York: Citadel Press, 2001).

47   "Louder": Archive interview with Natasha Lytess on YouTube, unsourced, in French with English subtitles.

49   "fair to her": Monroe, *My Story*.

50   "I didn't want to": Barris, *Marilyn: Her Life in Her Own Words*.

6. Rising

51   tiny as the rest of him: Frank Rose, *The Agency: William Morris and the Hidden History of Show Business* (New York: HarperCollins, 1995).

53   "meant it in the nicest way": Carl Rollyson, *Marilyn Monroe Day by Day: A Timeline of People, Places, and Events* (New York: Rowman & Littlefield, 2014).

54   "nude on red velvet": Marilyn Monroe audiotape interview with Richard Meryman for *Life* magazine, 1962. In private hands.

55   "more of the blonde": Rollyson, *Marilyn Monroe Day by Day*.

57   "she was trying to fill": "Bette and Marilyn: A Matter of Diction," blog .everlastingstar.net, May 8, 2014.

57   "whose girl is that?": Sandra Shevey, *The Marilyn Scandal: Her True Life Revealed by Those Who Knew Her* (New York: William Morrow, 1988).

59   "It shook everyone": Fred Lawrence Guiles, *Norma Jeane: The Life of Marilyn Monroe* (Vadnais Heights, MI: Paragon House, 1993).

7. Important Meetings

61   "at odds with her sadness": Arthur Miller, *Timebends: A Life* (New York: Grove Press, 1987).

61   "heroines in one": Elia Kazan, *The Selected Letters of Elia Kazan,* ed. Albert J. Devlin (New York: Knopf, 2014).

62   "starved for sexual release": Elia Kazan, *A Life* (New York: Knopf, 1988).

63   "'I'm very sincere'": *Marilyn on Marilyn*. British Broadcasting Corporation.

63   "God, the hypocrisy": Arthur Miller, *After the Fall* (New York: Viking Press, 1967).

63   "lose myself in sensuality": Miller, *Timebends*.

63   "the history of this country": Georges Belmont and Jane Russell, *Marilyn Monroe and the Camera* (Munich: Schirmer/Mosel, 2007).

63   "nor ever change": Martin Gottfried, *Arthur Miller: His Life and Work* (Boston: Da Capo, 2004).

63   "I never had one": Ibid.

65   "this is Marilyn Monroe": Georges Belmont and Jane Russell, *Marilyn Monroe and the Camera* (Munich: Schirmer/Mosel, 2007).

65   "big tits": Patrick McGilligan, *Fritz Lang: The Nature of the Beast* (New York: St. Martin's Press, 1997).

66   "It did her no good. . . . It broke her heart": J. Randy Taraborrelli, *The Secret Life of Marilyn Monroe* (New York: Grand Central Publishing, 2009).

66   "nuts or not": Sandra Shevey, *The Marilyn Scandal: Her True Life Revealed by Those Who Knew Her* (New York: William Morrow, 1988).

8. The Talk of Hollywood

69   "It's Joe DiMaggio": Maurice Zolotow, *Marilyn Monroe* (New York: Harcourt, Brace, 1960).

70   "lonely character": Bernie Miklasz, "Shy, Private Baseball Icon," *St. Louis Post-Dispatch,* February 17, 1991.

72   "What should I do?": Marilyn Monroe interview with Aline Mosby, syndi-
      cated, March 1952.

73   "retreated into her shell": James Bawden and Ron Miller, *Conversations with
      Classic Film Stars: Interviews from Hollywood's Golden Era* (Lexington: Univer-
      sity Press of Kentucky, 2016).

9. Melting the Screen

78   "I *am* the blonde": Marilyn Monroe audiotape interview with Richard Mery-
      man for *Life* magazine, August 1962. In private hands.

79   satin strapless: Andrew Hansford and Karen Homer, *Dressing Marilyn: How
      a Hollywood Icon Was Styled by William Travilla* (New York: Goodman, 2011).

79   "sleepy eyes of hers": Adam Victor, *The Marilyn Encyclopedia* (New York: Over-
      look Press, 1999).

80   "quite a lousy childhood": *Larry King Live* interview with Lauren Bacall,
      CNN, May 6, 2005.

80   "only for her": Lauren Bacall, *By Myself* (New York: Knopf, 1978).

81   "melts the screen": Ariel Rogers, *Cinematic Appeals: The Experience of New Movie
      Technologies* (Columbia University Press, 2013).

82   "to make it": Charles Casillo interview with Murray Garrett, July 30,
      2016.

82   "Including herself": Ibid.

10. Dissatisfactions

88   "be happy just being Marilyn Monroe": Michael Sheridan, "Marilyn Doesn't
      Believe in Hiding Things," *Screenland*, August 1952.

88   "great name of medicine": Marilyn Monroe, *My Story* (Lanham, MD: Tay-
      lor Trade Publishing, 2007).

91   "She was sparkling": Charles Casillo interview with Albert Carmine Guas-
      tafeste, March 13, 2016.

91   "Nobody minded that": "Marilyn Monroe Shatters Quiet on Korean Front,"
      Herald Journal, February 18, 1954.

91   "then we all did that": Casillo interview with Guastafeste, March 13, 2016.

92   ran out of film: "Monroe Exhausts Korea Film Supply," *The South Missou-
      rian*, February 19, 1954.

92   "I want to be a dramatic actress": Casillo interview with Guastafeste,
      March 13, 2016.

92   "loud as they can cheer": Ted Schwarz, *Marilyn Revealed: The Ambitious Life of
      an American Icon* (Lanham MD: Taylor Trade Publishing, 2009).

11. "Elegant Vulgarity"

95   "with a baseball bat": Earl Wilson, "Now You Get Marilyn with Music,"
      The Miami News, July 4, 1954.

95   "I didn't know it had": Erskine Johnson, in Hollywood NEA syndicated col-
        umn, *Statesville* (North Carolina) *Record and Landmark*, March 25, 1955.

96   "embarrassing to behold": Bosley Crowther, "There's No Business, Etc.; And
        Musical at the Roxy Sets Out to Prove It," *The New York Times*, December 17,
        1954

97   "I think was very important": Cameron Crowe, *Conversations with Wilder* (New
        York: Knopf, 2001).

97   "Marilyn Wiggles In": Barbara Leaming, *Marilyn Monroe* (New York: Three
        Rivers Press, 2000).

97   not wearing stockings: Leonard Lyons's syndicated column, September 14,
        1954.

98   "public streets": Earl Wilson's syndicated column, September 9, 1954.

99   "the look of death": Donald Spoto, *Marilyn Monroe: The Biography* (New York:
        HarperCollins, 1993).

99   "important than any career": Earl Wilson's syndicated column, Septem-
        ber 15, 1954.

100   "she didn't have any foundation": *The Many Loves of Marilyn Monroe*. E! True
        Hollywood Story documentary, 2001.

100   "anything at all": Spoto, *Marilyn Monroe*.

12. Marilyn Inc.

102   "You're a movie star": Donald Spoto interview with Amy Greene, Donald
        Spoto Collection, Margaret Herrick Library.

103   "he gave me great help": Clark Kidder, *Marilyn Monroe: Cover to Cover* (Iola:
        WI, Krause Publications, 2003).

103   "the way the character does": Sharon Marie Carnicke, *Stanislavsky in Focus:
        An Acting Master for the Twenty-First Century*. Routledge Theatre Classics (Abing-
        don, UK: Routledge, 2008).

105   "when she was a child": Susan Strasberg, *Marilyn and Me: Sisters, Rivals, Friends*
        (New York: Time Warner Paperbacks, 1992).

107   "It was touching": Clive James interview with Peter Bogdanovich, *The Guard-
        ian*, November 30, 2004.

13. New York Actress

108   "I touched her": James Haspiel, *Marilyn: The Ultimate Look at the Legend* (New
        York: Henry Holt & Co, 1991).

109   was Arthur Miller: Charles Casillo interview with Joan Copeland, June 9,
        2016. Copeland witnessed them talking.

110   "a tribute to her sex": Donald Spoto interview with Rupert Allan, Donald
        Spoto Collection, Margaret Herrick Library.

111   "two mirrors simultaneously": Rex Harrison, *Rex: An Autobiography* (New
        York: William Morrow, 1974).

111   "looking at Her": Truman Capote, *Music for Chameleons* (New York: Random House, 1979).

111   "really is Marilyn Monroe": Keith Badman, *Marilyn Monroe: The Final Years* (New York: St. Martin's Press/Thomas Dunne Books, 2012).

111   "a very important surgery": Interview with Natasha Lytess on YouTube, unsourced, in French with English subtitles.

113   "maybe I was": Jeffrey Meyers, *The Genius and the Goddess: Arthur Miller & Marilyn Monroe* (Champaign: University of Illinois Press, 2010).

113   "sensitive person also": Marilyn Monroe audiotape interview with Georges Belmont, editor of *Marie Claire*, 1960.

113   "guilt between them": Frank Langella, *Dropped Names* (New York: Harper, 2012).

113   "Why must you lose me?": Arthur Miller, *Timebends: A Life* (New York: Grove Press, 1987).

114   "I can't hate you": Letter from Arthur Miller to Marilyn Monroe, 1956.

114   "one and all": Elia Kazan, *A Life* (New York: Knopf, 1988).

115   "Marilyn loved it": Casillo interview with Copeland, June 9, 2016.

116   a shrewd businesswoman: *Time*, January 1956.

14. "A Different Suit"

119   "She was just immensely insecure": *Larry King Live*, interview with Hope Lange, 1997.

121   "every other day": Donald Spoto interview with Rupert Allan, Donald Spoto Collection, Margaret Herrick Library.

121   a guy that she liked: Donald Spoto interview with Patricia Newcomb, Donald Spoto Collection, Margaret Herrick Library.

121   "she hogged": Donald Spoto interview with Rupert Allan, Donald Spoto Collection, Margaret Herrick Library.

121   "Marilyn couldn't forgive her": Ibid.

122   "with makeup": Michele Farinola, *Backstory: The Making of Bus Stop*, AMC Productions.

122   Only then would Logan: Joshua Logan, *Movie Stars, Real People, and Me* (New York: Delacorte Press, 1978).

122   "She was magnificent": Leo Verswijver, "Don Murray: 'I never understood why Marilyn Monroe was not nominated for "Bus Stop"'" *Film Talk*, December 11, 2014.

123   "It can hold up the set for hours": Michele Farinola, *Backstory: The Making of Bus Stop*, AMC Productions; *Larry King Live*, interview with Hope Lange, 1997.

123   "She and the picture are swell": Bosley Crowther, *New York Times*, September 1, 1956.

15. Innocent Monster

128   "champagne bottles around": J. Randy Taraborrelli, *The Secret Life of Marilyn Monroe* (New York: Grand Central Publishing, 2009).

129   the next day a size 40: Charles Casillo interview with Leslie Caron, January 14, 2016.

129   she became difficult: Jack Cardiff, *Magic Hour: A Life in Movies* (London: Faber & Faber, 1997).

129   "lasts all day": Marilyn Monroe audiotape interview with Georges Belmont, editor of *Marie Claire*, 1960.

129   "anything else but Marilyn": Casillo interview with Leslie Caron, January 14, 2016.

129   "thought was a rival": Philip Ziegler, *Olivier* (London: MacLehose Press, 2015).

130   "attention away from herself": Arthur Miller, *Timebends: A Life* (New York: Grove Press, 1987).

130   "better than him in that movie": *Marilyn Monroe—Life After Death*, documentary, United Artists Theatre Circuit, 1994.

130   "monster too": W. J. Weatherby, *Conversations with Marilyn* (Vadnais Heights, MI: Paragon House, 1992).

131   called her a "whore": Charles Casillo interview with Denis Ferrara, February 3, 2017.

133   "She was ravishing": Online interview with Brigitte Bardot, Witnify, February 28, 2014.

133   "I think she is so charming": Liz Smith, "Bardot," *Q Magazine*, Spring 2016.

16. Marriage

135   "even less youthful": Marilyn Monroe, *Fragments: Poems, Intimate Notes, Letters* (New York: Farrar, Straus and Giroux, 2010).

136   "sit back and relax": Radie Harris, "The Empty Crib in the Nursery," *Photoplay*, December 1958.

136   "I love you": "Marilyn Monroe's Lost Love Letters to Be Auctioned," (AP) Hollywood Reporter, November 11, 2014.

138   Miller became vice president: Barbara Leaming, *Marilyn Monroe* (New York: Three Rivers Press, 2000).

139   "made the production possible": Charles Casillo interview with Paul Libin, March 4, 2016.

140   "That was so sweet and poignant" Charles Casillo interview with Joan Copeland, September 27, 2016.

140   "constantly trying to": Ibid.

141   "topple either way": *Marilyn Monroe: Her Last Untold Secrets* (Interview with Dr. George Kupchik for this tribute magazine, 1962, publisher unidentified).

141   "I never had one": Donald Spoto interview with Rupert Allan, Donald Spoto
       Collection, Margaret Herrick Library.

141   "including one from Arthur": Ibid.

142   "she wanted to have them": Charles Casillo interview with Joan Copeland,
       June 9, 2016.

17. Marilyn Gets Hot

145   "reading the rest": Radie Harris, "The Empty Crib in the Nursery," *Photo-
       play*, December 1958.

146   than her own: Peer J. Oppenheimer, "Look Who's Back—Marilyn," *Family
       Weekly*, February 22, 1959.

146   recalled costar Laurie Mitchell: Mike Thomas, *The Making of* Some Like It
       Hot. Documentary, 2006.

146   "color as mine": Charles Casillo interview with Marion Collier, March 20,
       2016.

146   "or believe": Charles Casillo interview with Al Breneman, March 6, 2016.

147   for the weekend: Thomas Larson, "The White Mask: Marilyn Monroe and
       the Hotel Del Coronado," *The San Diego Reader*, September 4, 2003.

147   reported to be vermouth: Chris Hatcher, "Is Marilyn Monroe Ruining Her
       Life," *Movie Mirror*, August 1960.

147   vodka and orange juice: Barbara Leaming, *Marilyn Monroe* (New York: Three
       Rivers Press, 2000).

147   "be able to do it": *Cinéma Cinémas*: Jack Lemmon—Hollywood Juillet 1987.
       Documentary directed by Claude Ventura.

148   inside the drawer: Billy Wilder interview, MSNBC news, April 30, 1984.

148   "You just saw it": Charles Casillo interview with Al Breneman, March 6,
       2016.

149   "it was fascinating": Don Widener, *Lemmon: A Biography* (New York: Mac-
       millan, 1975).

151   can't be beat: *Variety*, February 25, 1959.

151   "let's do it again": Mike Thomas, *The Making of* Some Like It Hot. Documen-
       tary, 2006.

18. Truth

153   the script he wrote for her: Norman Rosten, *Marilyn: The Untold Story* (New
       York: Signet, 1973).

153   "Never lie in a script": Donald Spoto with Sam Shaw, Donald Spoto Col-
       lection, Margaret Herrick Library.

154   "'Hi Marilyn!'": Charles Casillo interview with Michael J. Pollard, Novem-
       ber 11, 2015.

155   "very close to the surface": Boze Hadleigh, *Marilyn Forever: Musings on an American Icon by the Stars of Yesterday and Today* (Lanham, MD: Taylor Trade Publishing, 2016).

19. Making Love

157   "going to let up": Arthur Miller, *Timebends: A Life* (New York: Grove Press, 1987).

161   "hold in your stomach": Charles Casillo interview with Robert Banas, January 28, 2016.

161   "I'm lost": Barbara Leaming, *Marilyn Monroe* (New York: Three Rivers Press, 2000).

161   "afraid of acting": Yves Montand and Jeremy Leggatt, *You See, I Haven't Forgotten* (New York: Knopf, 1992).

161   "moving wonderfully": Mervyn Rothstein, "For Montand at 66, the Passions Burn, the Memories Endure," *The New York Times*, April 25, 1988.

161   "only rarely possess": Montand and Leggatt, *You See, I Haven't Forgotten*.

162   "girl imaginable": Simone Signoret, *Nostalgia Isn't What It Used to Be* (New York: Harper & Row, 1978).

162   "I had to do it": Pamela Andrioakis, "At 57, Simone Signoret Decides 'It Is Useless to Hang onto the Branches of Youth," *People*, June 12, 1978.

163   "she posed for": Richard Gehman, "The Big M," *The Milwaukee Sentinel*, May 1, 1960.

164   "a new film": Fred Lawrence Guiles, *Legend: The Life and Death of Marilyn Monroe* (New York: Stein & Day, 1984). See also Montand and Leggatt. *You See, I Haven't Forgotten*.

164   "I couldn't stop": Montand and Leggatt, *You See, I Haven't Forgotten*.

166   times a week: This segment and quotations are based on the 1978 paper "Special Problems in Psychotherapy with the Rich and Famous," Dr. Ralph Greenson (in private hands).

166   "into their arms": Rothstein, "For Montand at 66."

166   "a permanent scar": Montand and Leggatt, *You See, I Haven't Forgotten*.

167   stay with her: Charles Casillo interview with Michael Selsman, July 15, 2015.

167   "Diet anyone?": *Hollywood Citizen News* review by Lowell E. Redelings, as quoted in Adam Victor, *The Marilyn Encyclopedia* (New York: Overlook Press, 1999).

20. An Unfit Misfit

169   "it seemed so hopeless": Ted Schwarz, *Marilyn Revealed: The Ambitious Life of an American Icon* (Lanham, MD: Taylor Trade Publishing, 2009).

170   "waiting and waiting": Charles Casillo interview with Frank Parone, September 10, 2015.

170   "against her": Ibid.

171   "It's the pills": Charles Casillo interview with Angela Allen, October 24, 2015.

171   "true professional": Charles Casillo interview with Dawn Wells, August 23, 2015.

173   "Rubensian presence unappealing": Casillo interview with Allen, October 24, 2015.

173   "around the moon": *Esquire*, March 1961.

173   "magical quality": Casillo interview with Allen, October 24, 2015.

174   "the censors won't pass": Ibid.

174   more heated and contentious than previously reported: Charles Casillo interview with Curtice Taylor, October 19, 2015.

174   locked filing cabinet: Ibid.

174   "shoot the bikini scene?": Casillo interview with Allen, October 24, 2015.

174   Huston considered "pedestrian": Patricia Bosworth, *Montgomery Clift: A Biography* (New York: Harcourt Brace Jovanovich, 1978).

175   "suicide attempts during the production": Casillo interview with Allen, October 24, 2015.

176   "just worn out": Michelle Morgan, *Marilyn Monroe: Private and Confidential* (New York: Skyhorse Publishing, 2012).

21. A Woman Alone

178   "because you are too heavy": *Motion Picture*, July 1960.

178   didn't respond: Yves Montand and Jeremy Leggatt, *You See, I Haven't Forgotten* (New York: Knopf, 1992).

178   "can't do it": *Look*, February 19, 1979.

179   "wasn't interested in him at this point": Donald Spoto interview with Ralph Roberts, Donald Spoto Collection, Margaret Herrick Library.

179   (among others) would come to believe: Charles Casillo interview with Michael Selsman, July 21, 2015.

180   "He'd get so angry waiting": "What Really Happened When They Were Filming *The Misfits*," *Screen Stories*, May 1961.

180   "Murderer!": Berniece Baker Miracle and Mona Rae Miracle, *My Sister Marilyn: A Memoir of Marilyn Monroe* (Chapel Hill, NC: Algonquin Books, 1994).

181   as temperamental as her reputation: Thurston Clarke, *Ask Not: The Inauguration of John F. Kennedy and the Speech That Changed America* (New York: Penguin, 2010).

182   "It doesn't seem feminine": Margaret Parton, "A Revealing Last Interview with *Marilyn Monroe*," *Look*, February 9, 1979.

183   "not happy with the film": Charles Casillo interview with Curtice Taylor, October 19, 2015.

184 "very exciting or interesting": "Gable and Monroe Star in Script by Miller," *The New York Times*, February 2, 1961.

184 snapped her out of the fantasy of jumping: Fred Lawrence Guiles, *Legend: The Life and Death of Marilyn Monroe* (New York: Stein & Day, 1984).

22. Nightmare

188 "I just am": Marilyn Monroe. *Fragments: Poems, Intimate Notes, Letters* (New York: Farrar, Straus and Giroux, 2010).

190 "you have been for a very long time": Monroe, *Fragments: Poems, Intimate Notes, Letters*.

190 trancelike sleep for three days: George Carpozi, Jr., "Crack-Up: Tragic Report on Marilyn's Nervous Breakdown," *Motion Picture*, April 1961.

191 "kind of thing": Although I quoted from Anthony Summers interview with Romanoff tapes for the book *Goddess* at the Margaret Herrick Library, Romanoff told me essentially the same story when I interviewed her in 1999 for my novel *The Marilyn Diaries*.

191 "poor nutty people": Monroe, *Fragments: Poems, Intimate Notes, Letters*.

191 "on the very next plane": J. Randy Taraborrelli, *The Secret Life of Marilyn Monroe* (New York: Grand Central Publishing, 2009).

192 "I didn't mean to but I did": Strasberg, *Marilyn and Me*.

193 "my warmest affections": www.lettersofnote.com, published July 19, 2010 (along with a scan of the typewritten letter).

193 "but deeply disturbing": Charles Casillo interview with Denis Ferrara, January 27, 2016.

193 "view of mental illness and treatment for it": *Time*, February 17, 1961.

194 "it did something to her": Donald Spoto interview with Ralph Roberts, Donald Spoto Collection, Margaret Herrick Library. See also Charles Casillo interview with Hap Roberts, March 16, 2016.

195 "unselfish in bed": Monroe, *Fragments: Poems, Intimate Notes, Letters*.

195 "to be afraid anymore": *Look*, April 1961.

23. Manic-Depressive

197 became obsessed with Marilyn: Donald Spoto interviews with Rupert Allan and Ralph Roberts, Donald Spoto Collection, Margaret Herrick Library. See also Casillo interview with Selsman, July 21, 2015; interviews with Jeanne Martin, Arthur James, and Susan Strasberg, in 1998.

197 than she was prepared to give: Newcomb's alleged lesbian relationships are mentioned in Richard Burton, *The Richard Burton Diaries*, ed. Chris Williams (New Haven, CT: Yale University Press, 2013). Donald Spoto interview with Rupert Allan, Donald Spoto Collection, Margaret Herrick Library. See also Charles Casillo interview with Michael Selsman, July 21, 2015; also several anonymous sources.

197   "it was just too much": Donald Spoto interview with Patricia Newcomb,
       Donald Spoto Collection, Margaret Herrick Library.

197   gifted her with a mink coat: Donald Spoto interview with Lois Banner, Don-
       ald Spoto Collection, Margaret Herrick Library.

197   Sinatra had given her: George Masters, *The Master's Way to Beauty* (New York:
       E. P. Dutton, 1977).

197   "as a person": Spoto interview with Newcomb, Donald Spoto Collection,
       Margaret Herrick Library.

198   long time: Donald Spoto interview with Rupert Allan, Donald Spoto Col-
       lection, Margaret Herrick Library.

198   "worked with her": Charles Casillo interview with Michael Selsman, July 21,
       2015.

198   "caged animal": *Marilyn Monroe: The Final Days* (documentary), Prometheus
       Entertainment, 2001.

198   "something into it": Donald Spoto interview with Milt Ebbins, Donald Spoto
       Collection, Margaret Herrick Library.

198   lesbian relationship: Lois Banner notes on her interview with Patricia New-
       comb, Lois Banner Collection, Margaret Herrick Library.

198   "somewhat sexualized": Charles Casillo interview with Susan Strasberg,
       1998.

198   "sibling rivalry": Anthony Summers, *Goddess: The Secret Lives of Marilyn Mon-
       roe* (New York: Macmillan, 1985).

199   "anything homosexual": Dr. Ralph Greenson letter to a colleague shortly
       after Marilyn's death. In private hands.

199   "could be quite mean": Spoto interview with Newcomb, Donald Spoto Col-
       lection, Margaret Herrick Library.

200   "screaming at her": Spoto interview with Ebbins, Donald Spoto Collection,
       Margaret Herrick Library.

200   "when she lost control": Susan Strasberg, *Marilyn and Me: Sisters, Rivals, Friends*
       (New York: Time Warner Paperbacks, 1992).

201   her bra cups: Whitey Snyder told this to Abbott, who was a mortician, as
       Marilyn's body was being prepared for the funeral. Charles Casillo inter-
       view with Allan Abbott, October 9, 2015.

201   "want to know about him": Marilyn Monroe audiotape interview with
       Richard Meryman for *Life*, August 1962. In private hands.

201   "floor most of us": Julian Scheer interview with Carl Sandburg for *Cavalier*,
       1963.

202   "who glowed": Charles Casillo interview with Nancy Sinatra, July 22,
       2016.

204   "get over it": J. Randy Taraborrelli, *The Secret Life of Marilyn Monroe* (New
       York: Grand Central Publishing, 2009).

204   "in the balcony": Spoto interview with Ebbins, Donald Spoto Collection, Margaret Herrick Library.

205   "so drunk": Eddie Fisher, *Eddie: My Life, My Loves* (New York: HarperCollins, 1984).

205   "the show": James Kaplan, *Sinatra: The Chairman* (New York: Doubleday, 2015).

205   "pissed him off": Taraborrelli, *The Secret Life of Marilyn Monroe*.

206   look for her: Milt Ebbins told this anecdote to J. Randy Taraborrelli, which is used in *The Secret Life of Marilyn Monroe*. Ebbins also told the same anecdote to James Spada (as told to Charles Casillo in an August 9, 2016, interview), and to Donald Spoto, Donald Spoto Collection, Margaret Herrick Library. Ebbins also told the story directly to Charles Casillo in 1998.

206   "Is it a fling? Or is it a thing?": *Photoplay*, September 1961.

24. Age Three Five

208   "didn't help it any": Marilyn Monroe audiotape interview with Richard Meryman for *Life* magazine, August 1962. In private hands.

209   "massaging her feet": *Marilyn Monroe: 10 Years On*, Documentary, 1972.

210   "gave off light": Charles Casillo interview with Hap Roberts, March 16, 2016. See also, Donald Spoto interview with Ralph Roberts, Donald Spoto Collection at The Martha Herrick Library.

210   "gave me a roar": Joan Greenson's unpublished memoir (in private hands).

212   "infatuated" with Marilyn: Taraborrelli, *The Secret Life of Marilyn Monroe*. Jeanne Martin told this author the same, as did Michael Selsman, July 21, 2015.

212   Marilyn's "best friend": Anthony Summers interview with Eunice Murray, Anthony Summers Collection, Margaret Herrick Library.

212   "They were friends of mine": In Newcomb's interviews with Donald Spoto and Anthony Summer. Both interviews are in their respective collections at The Margaret Herrick Library.

212   Newcomb or Peter Lawford: Roberts states this in interviews with Donald Spoto and Anthony Summers. Both interviews are in their respective collections at The Margaret Herrick Library.

212   "smitten": George Smathers, *The Many Loves of Marilyn Monroe*, E! True Hollywood Story documentary, 2001.

213   "like a lady": Ibid.

213   "anyone like my brother": Taraborrelli, *The Secret Life of Marilyn Monroe*.

213   "she was pretty close": Donald Spoto interview with Edwin Guthman, Donald Spoto Collection, Margaret Herrick Library.

213   very sweet and very sad: Barbara Leaming, *Marilyn Monroe* (New York: Three Rivers Press, 2000).

213   Prowse's name recognition: James Kaplan, *Sinatra: The Chairman* (New York: Doubleday, 2015).

214   "paranoid undertones to it": Dr. Ralph Greenson letter to Dr. Marianne Kris, August 20, 1962 (in private hands).

25. Doctor-Patient Relations

215   sick borderline paranoid addict, as well as an actress: A copy of this letter is in the Anna Freud Papers at the Library of Congress.

216   day-to-day basis: I consulted Dr. Ralph Greenson, "Errors in Technique: Detection, Source, and Management" (in private hands). Hildi Greenson confirmed it in interviews with Donald Spoto and Anthony Summers, in their respective collections at The Margaret Herrick Library.

216   "and she could be delightful": Dr. Ralph Greenson letter to Dr. Marianne Kris, August 20, 1962 (in private hands).

217   "you become especially attached to": Lois Banner notes on an interview with Dr. Richard Litman, Lois Banner Collection, Margaret Herrick Library.

217   "and put herself in his hands": Donald Spoto interview with Ralph Roberts, Donald Spoto Collection, Margaret Herrick Library.

218   "the right Ralph": Donald Spoto interview with Patricia Newcomb, Donald Spoto Collection, Margaret Herrick Library.

218   "Whatever will she do?": Spoto interview with Roberts, Donald Spoto Collection, Margaret Herrick Library.

218   "if not insights just kindness": Greenson letter to Kris, August 20, 1962 (in private hands).

218   "respect or trust me": This can be found in a draft of Dr. Ralph Greenson's essay "Special Problems in Psychiatry with the Rich and Famous." Hildi Greenson told the story to several journalists including Anthony Summers and Donald Spoto, in their respective collections at The Margaret Herrick Library.

219   "atheist Jew": Anthony Summers interview with Joan Greenson, in the Anthony Summers Collection, Margaret Herrick Library. See also Greenson's unpublished memoir (in private hands).

222   "She wasn't really prepared": Donald Spoto interview with Mickey Rudin, Donald Spoto Collection, Margaret Herrick Library.

26. Compartmentalization

228   "Talk about temptation": Milt Ebbins interview with J. Randy Taraborrelli for *The Secret Life of Marilyn Monroe* (New York: Grand Central Publishing, 2009). Ebbins said similar things to Donald Spoto, Donald Spoto Collection, Margaret Herrick Library, and also in an interview with this author in 1998.

229   "She was magic to watch": Les Harding, *They Knew Marilyn Monroe, Famous Persons in the Life of the Hollywood Icon* (Jefferson, NC: McFarland, 2012).

229   the food was ruined: This story was told, with little variation, to Donald Spoto, in the Donald Spoto Collection, Margaret Herrick Library. Also see Taraborrelli, *The Secret Life of Marilyn Monroe*. I used these sources as well as a conversation I had with Milt Ebbins, who told me the story in 1998.

230   "Somehow I'm always overdrawn": Radie Harris, "The Empty Crib in the Nursery," *Photoplay*, December 1958.

230   to attend a Stanislavsky Festival: Patricia Bosworth, *Jane Fonda: The Private Life of a Public Woman* (Wilmington, MA: Mariner Books, 2012).

231   fascinated with Marilyn for years: Larry Tye, *Bobby Kennedy: The Making of a Liberal Icon* (New York: Random House, 2016).

231   "innocent and wide-eyed but supersexy": George Masters, *The Master's Way to Beauty* (New York: E. P. Dutton, 1977).

232   "very political talk": Anthony Summers, *Goddess: The Secret Lives of Marilyn Monroe* (New York: Macmillan, 1985).

232   "Not just to the kids but to her": Tye, *Bobby Kennedy*.

232   "about Civil Rights": Carl Rollyson, *Marilyn Monroe Day by Day: A Timeline of People, Places, and Events* (New York: Rowman & Littlefield, 2014).

233   Marilyn seemed to enjoy the intrigue: Joan Greenson's unpublished memoir (in private hands).

27. "Negated Sex Symbol"
236   "home of PETER LAWFORD in Hollywood": Marilyn Monroe's FBI files can be found on the internet. Also see Tim Coates, *Marilyn Monroe: The FBI Files* (Tim Coates Books, 2003).

236   "all her curves showing": George Masters, *The Master's Way to Beauty* (New York: E. P. Dutton, 1977).

237   "helped out of her chair onto the stage": James Bacon syndicated column, August 5, 1962. My reference is *The Burlington Free Press*.

237   "naturally with her": Charles Casillo interview with Stefanie Powers, July 29, 2016.

238   "worth more than this": Susan Strasberg, *Marilyn and Me: Sisters, Rivals, Friends* (New York: Time Warner Paperbacks, 1992).

238   "probably just as well": Charlton Heston, *Charlton Heston: The Actor's Life: Journals, 1956–1976* (New York: E. P. Dutton, 1978).

238   "like an aura": Strasberg, *Marilyn and Me*.

240   "together for the night": J. Randy Taraborrelli, *The Secret Life of Marilyn Monroe* (New York: Grand Central Publishing, 2009).

241   "Who wants to know saints?": Donald Spoto interview with Patricia Newcomb, Donald Spoto Collection, Margaret Herrick Library.

242   "never told anybody everything": Gloria Steinem, *Marilyn* (New York: Fine Communications, 1997).

242   "knew everything": Donald Spoto interview with Patricia Newcomb, Donald Spoto Collection, Margaret Herrick Library.

243   "known and accepted": Charles Casillo interview with anonymous source.

243   "that you wouldn't cover": Charles Casillo interview with Murray Garrett, July 30, 2016.

243   John F. Kennedy and then with Bobby: Charles Casillo interview with Susan Strasberg, 1998.

28. Starting Something

247   "they affect each other": *Marilyn Monroe: The Final Days* (documentary), Prometheus Entertainment, 2001.

248   "if it was necessary": Dr. Ralph Greenson letter to Dr. Marianne Kris, August 20, 1962 (in private hands).

29. Mass Seduction

250   "and do a good job": Joan Greenson interview with Joel Siegel on *20/20*, 1999.

250   a talisman: Ibid.

250   "over and over again": Donald Spoto interview with Ralph Roberts, Donald Spoto Collection, Margaret Herrick Library. See also Charles Casillo interview with Hap Roberts March 16, 2016.

251   "lacquered onto the body": Diahann Carroll interview with Joel Siegel, *20/20*, 1999.

253   "Come sit on my lap, little girl": Susan Strasberg, *Marilyn and Me: Sisters, Rivals, Friends* (New York: Time Warner Paperbacks, 1992).

253   "be wholly engaged": Arthur M. Schlesinger, Jr., *Journals 1952–2000* (New York: Penguin, 2008).

253   "their rivalry": Charles Casillo interview with Lou Harris, April 13, 2016.

254   "attractive to everyone": Ibid.

254   "No grand farewells": Strasberg, *Marilyn and Me*.

254   "white spun gold": Anthony Summers, *Goddess: The Secret Lives of Marilyn Monroe* (New York: Macmillan, 1985).

254   "Oh go to hell, Marilyn": James Haspiel, *Marilyn: The Ultimate Look at the Legend* (New York: Henry Holt, 1991).

255   "just goes too fast and falls asleep": Sally Bedell Smith, *Grace and Power: The Private World of the Kennedy White House* (New York: Random House, 2005).

255   "the best 20 seconds of my life": Thomas Reeves, *A Question of Character: A Life of John F. Kennedy* (London: Arrow, 1992).

255 "the service lift": Sarah Bradford, *America's Queen: The Life of Jacqueline Kennedy Onassis* (New York: Penguin, 2001).

256 "the real thing could ever be": "Marilyn Poses Nude—Again," *Photoplay*, September 1962.

30. Is Marilyn Finished?

258 "accept that fact": Donald Spoto interview with Mickey Rudin, Donald Spoto Collection, Margaret Herrick Library.

259 "She was a beautiful shell": Bill Shaiken, "Hit by a Bombshell," *Los Angeles Times*, December 14, 1997. See also, Jim McConnell, "Pearson Definitely Stood Tall," *The San Bernardino Sun*, February 7, 2012.

261 "He used my credibility with people I knew": Richard Reeves, *President Kennedy: Profile of Power* (New York: Simon & Schuster, 1994).

261 "It's starting to get around too much": J. Randy Taraborrelli, *The Secret Life of Marilyn Monroe* (New York: Grand Central Publishing, 2009).

261 "worth living anymore": Christopher Turner, "Marilyn Monroe on the Couch," *The Telegraph*, June 23, 2010.

262 "Is she finished?": Barbara Leaming, *Marilyn Monroe* (New York: Three Rivers Press, 2000).

263 "She had to finish that shitty picture": Donald Spoto interview with Mickey Rudin, Donald Spoto Collection, Margaret Herrick Library.

31. Elizabeth and Marilyn

265 too much time and money invested in *Cleopatra* and Taylor: *Cleopatra: The Film That Changed Hollywood* (documentary), Prometheus Entertainment, 2001.

267 "I will send some money to you": Charles Casillo interview with Kimothy Crues, January 12, 2016.

268 "you do the same": Ibid.

32. Last Sittings

272 "take all her clothes off": Bert Stern, *The Last Sitting* (New York: William Morrow, 1982).

272 "if she wasn't naked": Charles Casillo interview with Bert Stern, 1998.

272 "What a nice thing to say": Stern, *The Last Sitting*.

273 "That's a good idea": "'I wouldn't have taken nudes of Marilyn if she didn't want to': Photographer Bert Stern opens up about Monroe's last sitting," March 20, 2013, credited to *Daily Mail* reporter.

273 "should be talked into it": Charles Casillo interview with Bert Stern, 1998.

273 "Divine," he said: *Bert Stern: Original Madman*, Magic Film Productions, 2011.

274 "millions of women": Casillo interview with Stern, 1998.

274 "smoothness of her skin": Stern, *The Last Sitting*.

274 "Divinity. God. Living. Passion.": *Bert Stern: Original Madman.*

274 "all those nudes": Donald Spoto interview with Patricia Newcomb, Donald Spoto Collection, Margaret Herrick Library.

275 "wild during that session": *Eve & Marilyn.* BBC, 1997. On June 17, 1991.

275 "it was a nasty scar": Charles Casillo interview with Denis Ferrara, January 27, 2016 (Stern told this to Ferrara during an interview).

276 champagne and hard-boiled eggs: George Masters, *The Master's Way to Beauty* (E. P. Dutton, 1977).

276 "a hairpin or something like that": *Eve & Marilyn.*

276 "project her image of herself": *Bert Stern: Original Madman.*

278 "You wanted to take a bite out of her": Audiotape conversation between Diana Vreeland and George Plimpton, Tape 4 Side B. Courtesy of the Diana Vreeland Estate.

279 "fast forward to 1964 or '65": Charles Casillo interview with David Wills, January 12, 2017.

279 "turned out to be vodka": *In Vogue: The Editors Eye* (HBO documentary), 2001.

280 "and he kept going": *Icon*, interview with Leif-Erik Nygårds. Undated.

33. Sleepwalking

282 "I haven't slept": Donald Spoto interview with Hidi Greenson, Donald Spoto Collection, Margaret Herrick Library.

282 "stumbling around": Charles Casillo interview with Bill Asher, 1998.

282 "Why can't I be as happy as you two": Patricia Seaton Lawford, *The Peter Lawford Story: Life with the Kennedys, Monroe, and the Rat Pack* (New York: Carroll & Graf, 1988). Also told to this author in an interview with James Spada, August 9, 2016.

282 "It was a bad period": Bill Asher interview with Donald Spoto, Donald Spoto Collection, Margaret Herrick Library. He said essentially the same thing to this author in an interview in 1999.

283 "the only hope": Mickey Rudin interview with Donald Spoto, Donald Spoto Collection, Margaret Herrick Library.

284 "so they could exchange pills": Ibid.

284 "they'd bring pills": Ibid.

284 "loading her up with": Donald Spoto interview with Patricia Newcomb, Donald Spoto Collection, Margaret Herrick Library.

286 "beautiful woman": William Langley, "Marilyn Monroe 50 Years On: The Mystery of Marilyn's Last Days," *The Telegraph*, July 29, 2012.

286 "I would call breakable": Charles Casillo interview with Buddy Greco, October 13, 2015.

287 "Mr. Sinatra had eaten that": J. Randy Taraborrelli, *Sinatra, The Man Behind the Myth* (Edinburgh: Mainstream Publishing, 1998).

287   "had smashed": Casillo interview with Buddy Greco, October 13, 2015.

287   "this woman was Marilyn Monroe": Cami Sebring interview with Lois Banner, in notes, Lois Banner Collection at Margaret Herrick Library.

288   "Where's the goddamn coffee?": Taraborrelli, *Sinatra, The Man Behind the Myth.*

288   "roll her over a barrel": Charles Casillo interview with Betsy Duncan Hammes, August 15, 2016.

288   "didn't push it": Casillo interview with Buddy Greco, October 13, 2015.

290   "clearly apparent": Manoah Bowman with Natasha Gregson Wagner, *Natalie Wood: Reflections on a Legendary Life* (Philadelphia: Running Press, 2016).

290   "the night before she died": Anthony Summers, *Goddess: The Secret Lives of Marilyn Monroe* (New York: Macmillan, 1985).

290   "I hadn't seen anything that beautiful": Sam Kashner, "Six Decades In, Warren Beatty Is Still Seducing Hollywood," *Vanity Fair*, November 2016.

291   "what to do about it anymore": Charles Casillo interview with Leslie Caron, January 14, 2016.

291   "feeling it intensely": Ibid.

292   "I want to shut this off": Spoto interview with Newcomb, Donald Spoto Collection, Margaret Herrick Library.

34. Anger and Despair

293   "She was furious": Donald Spoto interview with Patricia Newcomb, Donald Spoto Collection, Margaret Herrick Library.

294   "for the weekend": Ibid.

294   She was beside herself: Charles Casillo interview with an anonymous source.

295   "just before that": Spoto interview with Newcomb, Donald Spoto Collection, Margaret Herrick Library.

297   "lonely and afraid": *Marilyn Monroe: Her Last Untold Secrets* (interview with Dr. George Kupchik for this tribute magazine, 1962, publisher unidentified).

297   "full active day": John Bates in an interview for the documentary *Say Goodbye to the President*, British Broadcasting Corporation, 1985.

298   helicopter to see Marilyn: Frank Neill, a Fox publicist, says that the helicopter carrying Bobby landed on the Fox lot near Stage 7. David Marshall, *The DD Group: An Online Investigation into the Death of Marilyn Monroe* (iUniverse, Inc., March 16, 2005). See also Keith Badman, *Marilyn Monroe: The Final Years* (New York: Thomas Dunne Books, 2012); Lois Banner, *Marilyn: The Passion and the Paradox* (New York: Bloomsbury, 2012).

298   "I know it was Bobby": *Say Goodbye to the President.*

298   "told Bobby to break it off": J. Randy Taraborrelli, *The Secret Life of Marilyn Monroe* (New York: Grand Central Publishing, 2009). See also *Say Goodbye to the President.*

299   "somewhat drugged": Dr. Ralph Greenson letter to Dr. Marianne Kris, August 20, 1962 (in private hands).

300   "I cannot say to anyone here": Ibid.

300   "important men in her life": Donald H. Wolfe, *The Last Days of Marilyn Monroe* (New York: William Morrow, 1998).

300   "feeling rejected by some of the people she had been close to": Ibid.

302   "capable of suicide": Donald Spoto interview with Patricia Newcomb, Donald Spoto Collection, Margaret Herrick Library.

302   "Nembutal for Marilyn": Anthony Summers interview with Hildi and Joan Greenson, Anthony Summers Collection, Margaret Herrick Library. See also Hildi Greenson interview with Donald Spoto, Donald Spoto Collection, Margaret Herrick Library; Donald Spoto interview with Patricia Newcomb, Donald Spoto Collection, Margaret Herrick Library; Patricia Newcomb taped interview with Robert Slatzer (in private hands).

35. Miscommunications

304   "poor little girl that had died": Anthony Summers, *Goddess: The Secret Lives of Marilyn Monroe* (New York: Macmillan, 1985).

305   diatribe against Patricia Newcomb: Lois Banner, *Marilyn: The Passion and the Paradox* (New York: Bloomsbury USA, 2012).

306   "you're a nice guy": Donald Spoto interview with Milt Ebbins, Donald Spoto Collection, Margaret Herrick Library. See also Charles Casillo interview with Milt Ebbins, 1998.

307   "she drops the phone": Donald Spoto interview with Mickey Rudin, Donald Spoto Collection, Margaret Herrick Library.

307   "Tell Peter not to worry about it": Spoto interview with Ebbins, Donald Spoto Collection, Margaret Herrick Library.

308   "I wasn't even home": Donald Spoto interview with Patricia Newcomb, Donald Spoto Collection, Margaret Herrick Library.

309   a vacation in Maine: This information comes from a November 2015 interview this author had with author James Spada, who saw the White House logs while researching a book that he didn't complete.

36. "We've Lost Her"

311   "No one could help her": Anthony Summers interview with Eunice Murray, Anthony Summers Collection, Margaret Herrick Library.

312   "You're the first one who knows about it": Donald Spoto interview with Milt Ebbins, Donald Spoto, Margaret Herrick Library. Ebbins added, "This is the gospel truth." Also see J. Randy Taraborrelli, *The Secret Life of Marilyn Monroe* (New York: Grand Central Publishing, 2009).

312   "She's dead": Donald Spoto interview with Patricia Newcomb, Donald Spoto Collection, Margaret Herrick Library.

Epilogue: Lingering Radiance

317   "she didn't know it": *Ms.*, August 1972.

317   "I guess I'll settle for what I am": Marilyn Monroe audiotape interview with
       Richard Meryman for *Life*, August 1962. In private hands.

BIBLIOGRAPHY

Books

Arnold, Eve. *Marilyn Monroe: An Appreciation*. New York: Knopf, 1987.

Bacall, Lauren. *By Myself*. New York: Knopf, 1978.

Badman, Keith. *Marilyn Monroe: The Final Years*. New York: St. Martin's Press/ Thomas Dunne Books, 2012.

Banner, Lois. *Marilyn: The Passion and the Paradox*. New York: Bloomsbury USA, 2012.

——. *MM—Personal: From the Private Archive of Marilyn Monroe*. New York: Harry N. Abrams, 2011.

Barbas, Samantha. *The First Lady of Hollywood: A Biography of Louella Parsons*. Berkeley: University of California Press, 2007.

Barris, George. *Marilyn: Her Life in Her Own Words: Marilyn Monroe's Revealing Last Words and Photographs*. New York: Citadel Press, 2001.

Bawden, James, and Ron Miller. *Classic Film Stars: Interviews from Hollywood's Golden Era*. Lexington: University Press of Kentucky, 2016.

Belmont, Georges. *Silver Marilyn: Marilyn Monroe and the Camera*. New York: Schirmer/ Mosel, 2007.

Bernard, Susan. *Marilyn: Intimate Exposures*. Edison, NJ: Sterling Signature, 2011.

Bogdanovich, Peter. *Who the Hell's in It: Portraits and Conversations*. New York: Knopf, 2004.

Bosworth, Patricia. *Jane Fonda: The Private Life of a Public Woman*. Wilmington, MA: Mariner Books, 2012.

——. *Montgomery Clift: A Biography*. Harcourt Brace Jovanovich, 1978.

Bowman, Manoah, with Natasha Gregson Wagner. *Natalie Wood: Reflections on a Legendary Life*. Philadelphia: Running Press, 2016.

Bowyer, Justin. *Conversations with Jack Cardiff, Art, Light and Direction in Cinema*. London: Batsford, 2014.

Braden, Joan. *Just Enough Rope*. New York: Villard, 1989.

Bradford, Sarah. *America's Queen: The Life of Jacqueline Kennedy Onassis*. New York: Penguin, 2001.

Burton, Richard. *The Richard Burton Diaries*. Edited by Chris Williams. New Haven, CT: Yale University Press, 2012.

Capote, Truman. *Music for Chameleons*. New York: Random House, 1979.

Cardiff, Jack. *Magic Hour: A Life in Movies*. London: Faber & Faber, 1997.

Carnicke, Sharon Marie. *Stanislavsky in Focus: An Acting Master for the Twenty-First Century. Routledge Theatre Classics*. Abingdon, UK: Routledge, 2008.

Carpozi, George Jr. *Marilyn Monroe: Her Own Story*. New York: Belmont, 1961.

Churchwell, Sarah. *The Many Lives of Marilyn Monroe*. London: Granta, 2004.

Clarke, Thurston. *Ask Not: The Inauguration of John F. Kennedy and the Speech That Changed America*. New York: Henry Holt, 2004.

Crowe, Cameron. *Conversations with Wilder*. New York: Knopf, 2001.

Cunningham, Ernest W. *The Ultimate Marilyn: All the Facts, Fantasies, and Scandals About the World's Best-Known Sex Symbol*. Folkestone, UK: Renaissance Books, 1998.

Curtis, Tony. *The Making of* Some Like It Hot: *My Memories of Marilyn Monroe and the Classic American Movie*. Hoboken, NJ: Wiley, 2009.

Dallek, Robert. *An Unfinished Life: John F. Kennedy*. New York: Back Bay Books, 2004.

de Dienes, Andre. *Marilyn, Mon Amour: The Private Album of Andre de Dienes, Her Preferred Photographer*. New York: St. Martin's Press, 1985.

Eiseman, Leatrice, and E. P. Cutler. *Pantone on Fashion: A Century of Color in Design*. San Francisco: Chronicle Books, 2014.

Field, Frederick Vanderbilt. *From Right to Left: An Autobiography*. Chicago: Lawrence Hill & Co., 1983.

Fisher, Eddie. *Eddie: My Life, My Loves*. New York: HarperCollins, 1984.

Flinn, Caryl. *Brass Diva: The Life and Legends of Ethel Merman*. Berkeley: University of California Press, 2007.

Gottfried, Martin. *Arthur Miller: His Life and Work*. Boston: Da Capo Press, 2004.

Grodin, Charles. *It Would Be So Nice If You Weren't Here: My Journey Through Show Business*. New York: Vintage, 1990.

Guiles, Fred Lawrence. *Joan Crawford: The Last Word*. New York: Birch Lane Press, 1995.

———. *Legend: The Life and Death of Marilyn Monroe*. New York Stein & Day, 1984.

———. *Norma Jeane: The Life of Marilyn Monroe*. Vadnais Heights, MN: Paragon House, 1993.

Hadleigh, Boze. *Marilyn Forever: Musings on an American Icon by the Stars of Yesterday and Today*. Lanham, MD: Taylor Trade Publishing, 2016.

Hansford, Andrew, and Karen Homer. *Dressing Marilyn: How a Hollywood Icon Was Styled by William Travilla*. London: Goodman, 2011.

Harding, Les. *They Knew Marilyn Monroe, Famous Persons in the Life of the Hollywood Icon*. Jefferson, NC: McFarland, 2012.

Harrison, Rex. *Rex: An Autobiography*. New York: William Morrow, 1974.

Haspiel, James. *Marilyn: The Ultimate Look at the Legend*. New York: Henry Holt, 1991.

Heston, Charlton. *Charlton Heston: The Actor's Life: Journals, 1956–1976*. New York: E. P. Dutton, 1978.

Kaplan, James. *Sinatra: The Chairman*. New York: Doubleday, 2015.

Kazan, Elia. *A Life*. New York: Knopf, 1988.

———. *The Selected Letters of Elia Kazan*. Edited by Albert J. Devlin. New York: Knopf, 2014.

Kidder, Clark. *Marilyn Monroe: Cover to Cover*. Iola, WI: Krause Publications, 2003.

Klein, Edward. *All Too Human: The Love Story of Jack and Jackie Kennedy*. New York: Pocket Books, 1996.

Kobal, John. *Marilyn Monroe—A Life on Film*. London: Hamlyn, 1974.

Kotsilibas-Davis, James. *Milton's Marilyn*. Edited by Joshua Greene. Munich: Schirmer/Mosel, 1994.

Langella, Frank. *Dropped Names*. New York: Harper Perennial, 2012.

Lawford, Patricia Seaton. *The Peter Lawford Story: Life with The Kennedys, Monroe, and the Rat Pack*. New York: Carroll & Graf, 1988.

Leaming, Barbara. *Marilyn Monroe*. New York Three Rivers Press, 2000.

Logan, Joshua. *Movie Stars, Real People, and Me*. New York: Delacorte Press, 1978.

McGilligan, Patrick. *Fritz Lang: The Nature of the Beast*. New York: St. Martins Press, 1997.

Mailer, Norman. *Marilyn: A Biography*. New York: Grosset & Dunlap, 1973.

Malone, Aubrey. *The Defiant One: A Biography of Tony Curtis*. Jefferson, NC: McFarland, 2013.

Marshall, David. *The DD Group: An Online Investigation into the Death of Marilyn Monroe*. iUniverse, Inc. March 16, 2005.

Marx, Groucho, and Richard Anobile. *The Marx Brothers Scrapbook*. New York: HarperCollins, 1989.

Masters, George. *The Master's Way to Beauty*. New York: E. P. Dutton, 1977.

Meyers, Jeffrey. *The Genius and the Goddess: Arthur Miller & Marilyn Monroe*. Champaign: University of Illinois Press, 2010.

Miller, Arthur. *After the Fall*. New York: Viking Press, 1967.

———. *Timebends: A Life*. New York: Grove Press, 1987.

———, and Serge Toubia. *The Misfits: Story of a Shoot*. New York: Phaidon, 2000.

Miracle, Berniece Baker, and Mona Rae Miracle. *My Sister Marilyn: A Memoir of Marilyn Monroe*. Chapel Hill, NC: Algonquin Books, 1994.

Monroe, Marilyn. *Fragments: Poems, Intimate Notes, Letters.* Edited by Stanley Buchthal and Bernard Comment. New York: Farrar, Straus and Giroux, 2010.

———, with Ben Hecht. *My Story.* Lanham, MD: Taylor Trade Publishing, 2006.

Montand, Yves, and Jeremy Leggatt. *You See, I Haven't Forgotten.* New York: Knopf, 1992.

Morgan, Michelle. *Marilyn Monroe: Private and Confidential.* New York: Skyhorse Publishing, 2012.

Reeves, Richard. *President Kennedy: Profile of Power.* New York: Simon & Schuster, 1994.

Reeves, Thomas. *A Question of Character: A Life of John F. Kennedy.* New York: Free Press, 1991.

Riese, Randall, and Neal Hitchens. *The Unabridged Marilyn: Her Life from A to Z.* New York: Random House Value Publishing, 1990.

Roberts, Ralph. *Mimosa.* Unpublished.

Rogers, Ariel. *Cinematic Appeals: The Experience of New Movie Technologies.* New York: Columbia University Press, 2013.

Rollyson, Carl E. *Marilyn Monroe: A Life of the Actress.* New English Library, 1990.

———. *Marilyn Monroe Day by Day: A Timeline of People, Places, and Events,* New York: Rowman & Littlefield, 2014.

Rooney, Mickey. *Life Is Too Short.* New York: Ballantine Books, 1992.

Rose, Frank. *The Agency: William Morris and the Hidden History of Show Business.* New York: HarperCollins, 1995.

Rosten, Norman. *Marilyn: The Untold Story.* New York: Signet, 1973.

Schiller, Lawrence. *Marilyn & Me: A Photographers Memories.* New York: Doubleday/ Nan A. Talese, 2012.

Schlesinger, Arthur M., Jr. *Journals 1952–2000.* New York: Penguin, 2008.

Schwarz, Ted. *Marilyn Revealed: The Ambitious Life of an American Icon.* New York: Taylor Trade Publishing, 2009.

Shaw, Sam, and Norman Rosten. *Marilyn: Among Friends.* New York: Henry Holt, 1988.

Shevey, Sandra. *The Marilyn Scandal: Her True Life Revealed by Those Who Knew Her.* New York: William Morrow, 1988.

Signoret, Simone. *Nostalgia Isn't What It Used to Be.* New York Harper & Row, 1978.

Smith, Sally Bedell. *Grace and Power: The Private World of the Kennedy White House.* New York: Random House, 2005.

Spada, James. *Monroe: Her Life in Pictures.* Charlotte, NC: Main Street Books, 1982.

———. *Peter Lawford: The Man Who Kept the Secrets.* New York: Bantam, 1991.

Spoto, Donald. *Marilyn Monroe: The Biography.* New York: HarperCollins, 1993.

Steinem, Gloria. *Marilyn.* New York: Fine Communications, 1997.

Stern, Bert. *The Last Sitting.* New York: William Morrow, 1982.

Strasberg, Susan. *Marilyn and Me: Sisters, Rivals, Friends.* New York: Time Warner Paperbacks, 1992.

Summers, Anthony. *Goddess: The Secret Lives of Marilyn Monroe*. New York: Macmillan, 1985.

Taraborrelli, J. Randy. *Jackie, Ethel, Joan: Women of Camelot*. New York: Grand Central Publishing, 2012.

———. *The Secret Life of Marilyn Monroe*. New York: Grand Central Publishing, 2010.

———. *Sinatra: The Man Behind the Myth*. Edinburgh: Mainstream Publishing, 1998.

Tye, Larry. *Bobby Kennedy: The Making of a Liberal Icon*. New York: Random House, 2016.

Victor, Adam. *The Marilyn Encyclopedia*. New York: Overlook Press, 1999.

Vogel, Michelle. *Marilyn Monroe: Her Films, Her Life*. Jefferson, NC: McFarland, 2014.

Wagner, Robert. *Pieces of My Heart: A Life*. New York: It Books, 2009.

Weatherby, W. J. *Conversations with Marilyn*. Vadnais Heights, MN: Paragon House, 1992.

Widener, Don. *Lemmon: A Biography*. New York: Macmillan, 1975.

Wills, David. *Marilyn: In the Flash*. New York: Dey Street Books, 2015.

———. *Marilyn Monroe: Metamorphosis*. New York: It Books, 2011.

Wilson, Earl. *The Show Business Nobody Knows*. New York: Bantam Books, 1973.

Wolfe, Donald H. *The Last Days of Marilyn Monroe*. New York: William Morrow, 1998.

Ziegler, Philip. *Olivier*. London: MacLehose Press, 2015.

Zolotow, Maurice. *Marilyn Monroe*. New York: Bantam Books, 1961.

Documentaries

Backstory: The Making of Bus Stop. AMC Productions, 2001.

Bert Stern: Original Madman. Magic Film Productions, 2011.

Cleopatra: The Film That Changed Hollywood. Prometheus Entertainment, 2001.

The Death of Marilyn Monroe. Unsolved History, TV Episode, Termite Art Productions, 2003.

Eve & Marilyn. BBC, 1997.

In Vogue: The Editors Eye. HBO Documentary, 2012.

Marilyn in Manhattan. Parco International, 1997.

Marilyn Monroe: The Final Days. Prometheus Entertainment, 2002.

Marilyn Monroe: Life After Death. United Artists Theatre Circuit, 1994.

Marilyn Monroe: The Mortal Goddess. A&E Home Video Documentary, 1999.

Marilyn Monroe: 10 Years On. Documentary, 1972.

Marilyn on Marilyn. British Broadcasting Corporation, 2001.

Marilyn: Something's Got to Give. Fox Entertainment, 1992.

Say Goodbye to the President. British Broadcasting Corporation, CTV Television Network, Landreth Associates, 1985.

The Making of Some Like It Hot. Sony, 2006.

The Many Loves of Marilyn Monroe. E! Entertainment Television, The E! True Hollywood Story, 2001.

Marilyn Monroe—Life After Death. United Artists Theatre Circuit, 1994.

Marilyn Monroe: Beyond the Legend—An A&E Biography, 1988.

Television Interviews

Cinéma Cinémas: Jack Lemmon—Hollywood Juillet 1987. Documentary directed by Claude Ventura.

The David Letterman Show. Yves Montand interview, 1987.

The Discovery of Marilyn Monroe. Documentary on YouTube, includes interviews with Robert Mitchum, Jane Russell, and Jim Dougherty.

Inside Edition. Jim Dougherty talks about Marilyn Monroe, 1990.

Larry King Live. Interview with Lauren Bacall, May 6, 2005.

Larry King Live. 35th Anniversary of Marilyn Monroe's Death, 1997.

Larry King Live. Marilyn Monroe 75th Birthday Special, June 1, 2001.

Sally Jesse Raphael Show. Special on 30th Anniversary of Marilyn Monroe's Death, 1992.

60 Minutes. Mike Wallace interviews Arthur Miller, 1999

INDEX